CW01594663

SWAMI ABHISHIKTANANDA

SWAMI ABHISHIKTANANDA

His life told through his letters

JAMES STUART

Foreword by
Dr DONALD NICHOLL

ISPCK
2000

SWĀMĪ ABHISHIKTĀNANDA: His life told through his letters—Published by the Indian Society for Promoting Christian Knowledge (ISPCK), Post Box 1585, Kashmere Gate, Delhi—110006.

First published 1989
Revised Edition 1995
Reprinted 2000

© Abhishiktananda Society, Delhi

The copyright of the letters quoted in this book belongs in each case to the original recipient. In particular, Canon J. Lemarié (Chartres) and Mme O. Baumer-Despeigne (Frauenfeld) have formally stated that no use may be made of letters addressed to them without their written permission.

Macintosh Laser typeset and Cover design by ISPCK, Post Box 1585, 1654, Madarsa Road, Kashmere Gate, Delhi—110006, Tel : 2913692, Fax : 011-2930045.

Printed at Academy Press, E-40, Sector III, Noida (U.P.).

Contents

Illustrations

between pages 182-3

Foreword

THE REQUEST to write a Foreword to the present book came as a surprise. After all, I never met Abhishiktananda in the flesh, as did so many people who have written about him. Moreover, I am a layperson, whereas he spent almost all his life as a monk and hermit amidst monks and hermits.

On reflection, however, I am less surprised by the request, because the time has now come to show that Abhishiktananda's message is a message for all human beings, not just for monks and nuns. Moreover we need to emphasize that in order to receive the message of a spiritual master it is not essential to have met him in the flesh. Indeed, as Abhishiktananda often points out, the disciples on the road to Emmaus did not recognize the presence even of Jesus until he had passed beyond the reach of their senses. It has also to be said that the trading of anecdotes about a spiritual master's habits and quirks by his disciples, whilst sometimes bringing him closer, may easily degenerate into gossip and pander to curiosity.

The very last motive that could make it worth while to read the present book is curiosity—curiosity, for instance, about Abhishiktananda's difficulties with Abbé Monchanin, and similar intriguing episodes. Nor would there be much reward in studying the book, if one's dominant motive were the desire to test his theology against the yard-stick of one's own theological formulations. Because, although Abhishiktananda was, in fact, a much better theologian than he generally made out, and though he did anticipate and wrestle with the major dilemmas that he raised, nevertheless he was passionately aware of the great harm that has been inflicted over the centuries by theologians who, quite literally, did not know what—or who—they were talking about. And without experience of the reality the formulations are of no more use than a shaky compass in an unknown land.

This is especially true when the reality in question is the age-old experience of the land and peoples of India. For India is more than a geographical location; it is a dimension of the spirit where all who enter in are changed, and where Western-drawn maps and Western compasses are of little avail.

So the way to approach this life of Abhishiktananda, I suspect, is to see in it the traces of the pilgrimage made by a spiritual adventurer who was unusually pure in heart, and upon whose very flesh was branded the truth of Jesus' admonition to Peter: "I tell you most solemnly, when you were young you put on your own belt and walked where you liked; but when you grow old you will stretch out your hands, and somebody else will put a belt around you and take where you would rather not go." As it turned out, the young Breton Henri Le Saux was to be led into places where he found himself torn apart. Had he foreseen what was in store for him, he would scarcely have been transformed into that Abhishiktananda (Joy of the Anointed) who has since become a sign of joy and illumination for many seekers throughout the earth.

Accordingly, for those of us who wish to accompany him on his earthly pilgrimage, and even beyond, the indispensable precondition is that we do so through the medium of the Spirit. And the only preparation for the coming of the Spirit—or, rather, our awakening to Him—is to empty our minds of all preconceptions, man-made decisions and reason-based desires. Because what we are faced with is a journey into "the deep things of God"—a favourite phrase of Abhishiktananda's taken from the letter in which Paul tells the Corinthians that God has prepared for those who love him things beyond what any human being can see or hear or imagine. Yet the Spirit permeates everything, even the deep things of God, even God's own nature, for only the Spirit of God knows what God is.

How to live out in one's everyday life this truth enunciated by St Paul was often illustrated by Abhishiktananda with the aid of a Sanskrit term, *ākāsha.* The term *ākāsha* means both the infinite "exterior" space and the infinite "interior" space which are really but one, both spheres being permeated by that same Spirit which fills not only the whole cosmos but equally the human heart. This is possible because the Spirit, being God, is beyond all forms, and so is able to make his presence felt in any form; and being beyond all times, he yet fills all moments of time and is present to every event of history. Thus he is at the core of the universe and of the heart of man. He *is* that core.

For Abhishiktananda the great awakening to the Spirit came when he met the Indian holy man Sri Ramana Maharshi. That moment was determinative for the rest of his life. At that moment he *knew*, beyond a shadow of doubt, that he was in the presence of a human being who had been drawn so deep into the cave of the heart (Sanskrit, *guhā*) as to have touched the heart of the cosmos. This holy man, in consequence, had been blessed by a peace that is beyond human comprehension. And he radiated that peace.

For Abhishiktananda that first-hand experience, that knowledge, was to prove both bliss and agony—bliss, because he *knew* that the pearl of great price is not an illusion; yet agony also, because it compelled him to acknowledge that the pearl of great price is not the exclusive property of the Roman Catholic Church, as he had previously assumed.

Later on, towards the end of his life, the agony somewhat abated. Abhishiktananda was able to describe how certain Christians are called to plunge into those very depths that had been plumbed over the centuries by Hindu holy men. He spoke of how such Christians, when they surface again, will find that their faith has been strengthened and enriched by a previously unknown depth of experience. A kind of osmosis will have taken place in their souls between the Hindu experience and the Christian experience of the depths of the Heart of Christ. Those Christians will then be able to instruct their brethren in the royal way of the interior life, teaching them how to place themselves entirely at the disposal of the Spirit.

However, for any seeker to imagine that Abhishiktananda provides him with a ready-made formula for such Hindu-Christian osmosis would not merely be an unfortunate mistake; it would be a betrayal of Abhishiktananda's intentions and his agony. For whilst no one else need now undergo the same excruciating agony as he did, yet all of us, with our intellects and compassion stretched to the utmost, are obliged to read very slowly his anguished cries (especially in the pages of his Diary), his ceaseless self-questioning as to whether he was any longer a Christian and whether he would have to abandon the Church which had mothered and shaped him. Only a very arrogant person would claim to skip lightly over such an abyss on to the safe ground at the other side.

In the end Abhishiktananda did not lose his balance. The fact that he did not do so can be traced—so far as human reason can discern—to his grasp upon two strands of his own tradition. The first ensured that he never ceased to celebrate the Eucharist, even at the most unlikely times and in the most unlikely places. The second made sure that his ardent devotion to the person of Jesus was never dimmed. In later years he came to see more vividly that in the Eucharist the entire cosmos is integrated, where both matter and human consciousness are brought together in union through the Spirit of God and the action of Jesus, who manifests God in his fullness.

And yet that statement could prove misleading if it were not accompanied with an explanation that the fullness spoken of cannot be identified exclusively with the image of Jesus coined by the culture first of the Mediterranean world and later of the European world. For the experience of Jesus was beyond all expression—even by Jesus himself—in the conceptual and verbal possibilities of his own culture or that of the European centuries. Fortunately for Abhishiktananda he found to hand a Hindu term, *pūrnam,* which not only proved far richer in connotation than the Western term "Fullness", but also provided him with a most valuable gift to share with the Church.

In the light of *pūrnam* Abhishiktananda was able to see how limited until now has been the human family's understanding of Jesus' experience of God. He came to see also that the Spirit, who alone can reveal to us the depth of Jesus' experience, had long been at work in the lives of Hindus and in their sacred scriptures. In Hinduism, therefore, are to be found potentialities of the human spirit which go far beyond what has so far been considered possible within the limits of Western culture. Hence the encounter with Hinduism is an occasion to liberate the spirit within Christians and thereby enable them to realize more fully the riches contained in the revealed words of their own scriptures and to share more intimately in the experience of Jesus as Son of the Father and yet one with him. Also the encounter with Hinduism—as well as with Buddhism, Islam and other great religious traditions of mankind—will usher in a radically new stage in the awareness and development of the Church. As a result, the Mediterranean-based form of Christianity, which is still predominant, will soon be seen as only one of the historical possibilities of living the Christian faith.

It is clear from the present book that by the last years of his life Abhishiktananda himself had largely passed beyond the limits of culturally-conditioned Christianity—or, indeed, beyond the bounds of culturally-conditioned Hinduism—and was behaving with a freedom which is only possible at the level of the spirit. Thus he felt free laughingly to disappoint the expectations of a Sister who was looking to him for some holy words: he told her that God is as much in the making of a good soup or the careful handling of a railway train as he is in our most beautiful meditations. Similarly, with a humorous eye upon himself, he remarks that there is as much true prayer when one's attention is concentrated on an ache, as there is in the marvellous silence when we think we are in ecstasy. In a like vein he tells a correspondent not to pay much attention to those who love the esoteric, who run around to ashrams and 'saints'. "The discovery of the mystery," he writes, "is so much simpler than that. It is right beside you, in the opening of a flower, the song of a bird, the smile of a child."

Admittedly his warning against the esoteric is likely to raise a smile in anyone who tries to accompany Abhishiktananda through the thickets of Hindu metaphysics. But even in those thickets he never lost sight of his goal, which was the same as that indicated by the far from esoteric Saint Seraphim of Sarov, who used to say, "The whole aim of Christian life is to acquire the Holy Spirit." And it is surely a sign of how faithful he remained to the call of the Holy Spirit that some words of his should chime in so perfectly with a remarkable statement of Seraphim, who said: "I tell you that when God visits us in his ineffable goodness we must be still even from prayer. In prayer the soul utters words of speech, but when the Holy Spirit has come you must be in complete silence." The corresponding statement by Abhishiktananda runs: "At the end there is no place for prayer, for praise, but the silence which is the origin and completion of all words, when all the manifestations of God have to be left behind, and with all his strength man must aim at the Silence in which alone God is in himself."

DONALD NICHOLL

Preface

A SIGN for our times—so Swami Abhishiktananda is regarded by many of those who knew him personally, or who have come across his writings.

The life of this French monk, who came to India in 1948 and remained there until his death in 1973, was certainly unusual. Its significance does not, however, depend on its exotic aspects—though these may be the first to strike the western reader.

His true significance lies in his Indian experience and in his response to it. When he awoke to the truth of *advaita* (non-duality), which lies at the heart of the Hindu Scriptures (especially the Upanishads) and is realized in the lives of Hindu saints, he sought to make himself wholly transparent to it. Yet he was and remained, as he put it, "viscerally" Christian, and had no illusions about the possibility of harmonizing Hindu and Christian experience at the level of mind. This involved accepting and living with a spiritual tension which at times tore him asunder. He knew well the insecurity and discomfort of one who tries to maintain a foothold on either side of a gulf.

He accepted this position primarily because he "could do no other". But it gave him a new outlook and important insights which he felt obliged to share with others. In his writings he endeavoured to awaken his fellow-Christians in the West to the treasures which the Spirit has prepared for them in the East, being convinced that the Church could not be truly Catholic, so long as it was restricted to its predominantly Mediterranean expression. At the same time he sought to alert theologians to the questions which are posed to the traditional formulations of Christian faith when it is confronted with the spiritual experience of the East. In our one world the meeting of East and West is inescapable, and he longed for theologians to take it seriously. But above all, he stressed the need to rediscover the contemplative dimension of faith, without which he did not see how the Church could respond to the problems of our time or to its meeting with other faiths.

Outside India Abhishiktananda is chiefly known through his books, of which most were written for western readers, though some (especially *Gnanananda* and *The Further Shore*) have also interested Hindus. Even sixteen years after his death they continue to be in demand, especially in English. His style of writing has been described as "very attractive—even intoxicating".[1] The reason for this is not merely its originality and often poetical quality, but because it is the expression of a lived experience. This is why it speaks directly to men and women in search of a deeper dimension in their lives. Those who read his books

1. R.H.S. Boyd, *Introduction to Indian Christian Theology* (revised edition), Madras 1975, p. 296.

want to know more about the man himself, already glimpsed behind his words—as is shown by letters which come to the publishers and the Abhishiktananda Society. The interest that he arouses is also indicated by the books and articles which have been written about him (Bibliography, Section D). In addition, several scholars have been or are engaged in researching aspects of his life and work.

The present biography enables us to follow the development of his experience in India and to understand the background from which he wrote. It also supplements his personal Diary which was published in French in 1986;[2] for this is essentially a sustained interior dialogue, and contains very few biographical details.

To a great extent it has been possible to tell the story of his life by linking together extracts from his correspondence. Abhishiktananda was a compulsive letter-writer, and his letters were such that his friends thought them worth preserving. This book draws on over fifteen such collections (others may still be found), and these enable his life in India to be followed almost from week to week. Their use enables him to "speak for himself", and to reveal himself as he was—deeply committed, yet always vulnerable, an acosmic who still remained very human. Like everyone else, he had his weaknesses—his reactions to other people were often hasty, his judgements sometimes harsh and one-sided, and he could be inconsistent, even "mixed-up", as a friend once said. It might be felt that to publish such material is an abuse of confidence, but those who knew him have no doubt that he would approve of such treatment, for he deplored any attempt to turn him into a "myth" and readily laughed at himself—"One clown is enough!", he said to the same friend, as an argument against others imitating his unusual life style.

The following pages seek only to convey a faithful picture of the Abhishiktananda that we knew. Apart from necessary explanations, there is no attempt to "interpret" him, still less to fit him into any category, as some have done on the insufficient basis of his writings alone. We simply follow as closely as possible his long pilgrimage, which is also that of Everyman, towards integration and simplicity.

* * *

The original intention in 1974 was to publish a Memoir of Abhishiktananda, based on his friends' recollections, together with some extracts from his letters. The editing of this volume was entrusted to Sister Sara Grant, RSCJ.

As she studied the letters, however, the idea came to the editor (with whom the present writer was associated from 1975) that they might be put together in such a way as to provide a vivid mosaic of Swamiji's life in India, told largely in his own words. A first draft was prepared, using the material which was available at that stage.

Then in 1976 one of Abhishiktananda's sisters contributed a complete series of his letters, covering the years from 1952 to 1973, which were used to make a

2. *La montée au fond du coeur: le journal intime du moine chrétien—sannyasi hindou*, ed. R. Panikkar, Paris 1986. An English translation is under preparation.

fuller draft. After this, Sister Sara, in view of other obligations, was constrained to pass on the responsibility of finalizing the book to her colleague. For several years the work hung fire, but the delay was in fact providential. Between 1982 and 1987 a number of other valuable collections of letters became available, which have greatly enriched the book in its final shape.

Acknowledgements

We are deeply grateful to all those who have supplied material for this book, or who have helped in other ways:

A. Those who contributed their recollections for the proposed Memoir in 1974:

Fr M. Amaladoss, SJ
Sr Shanti Fernandez, RSCJ
Fr Aroojis Gratian
Madame Renée Le Fur
Mr Hyacinthe Le Saux
Sr Marie-Thérèse Le Saux, OSB
Madame Louise Montagnon-Le Saux
Fr Shigeto Oshida, OP
Dr Raimundo Panikkar
Mrs Mary Rogers
Fr Murray Rogers
Shri Ramesh Srivastava (d. 1985)
Mrs Anne-Marie Stokes
Mother M. Théophane, SMA (d. 1982)
The Revd Y. D. Tiwari
Fr Chacko Valiaveetil, SJ

As this book evolved from a 'Memoir' to a biography, it was not possible to use these contributions in their original form, but a number of them have been drawn upon in the text, and they are preserved in the archives of the Society. Dr Panikkar's "Letter to Abhishiktananda" and Fr Murray Rogers' essay "Swamiji—the Friend" have been published elsewhere (see Bibliography). The notes by Fr Oshida and Mrs Mary Rogers appeared in the *Occasional Bulletin* (Nos 6 and 3).

More recently Canon J. Lemarié provided notes on Dom Le Saux's life in his Abbey, and Mr John Alter recorded his impression of Abhishiktananda at Rajpur in 1972.

B. Those who have made available, or permitted the use of, collections of Abhishiktananda's7 letters, or other documents:

Dr Bettina Bäumer: extracts of letters (1969-1972); dossier of bibliographical notes left by Abhishiktananda.

Madame O. Baumer-Despeigne: letters to herself (1966-1973); letters to Marc Chaduc (1969-1973), left in her keeping; letters to Mr & Mrs Miller (1970); numerous documents.

The Carmel of Lisieux: for permitting Madame Baumer to transcribe or photocopy two collections of letters—

(a) those to Mother Françoise-Thérèse (1959-1973), supplementing the extracts previously supplied by herself and those published in *Les yeux de lumière:*

(b) those to Sr Térèse de Jésus (1959-1973), supplementing her previous extracts.

Fr J. Dupuis, SJ: letter of 1971.

Mrs A. Fonseca: letters (1970-1973).

Dom J.-G. Gélineau, OSB: extracts of the letters to Fr E. Landry, OSB (1968-1973); letter to Fr R. Williamson, OSB (1950).

Sr Sara Grant, RSCJ: letters (1970-1972).

Canon J. Lemarié: letters (1948 and 1952-1973); letter to Fr J. Monchanin of 18.8.47.

Madame A.-L. Guguen-Le Saux: extracts of letters (1969-1972).

Sr Marie-Thérèse Le Saux, OSB: letters (1952-1973).

Dom P. Miquel, OSB, Abbot of Ligugé: copy of an essay in his possession.

Madame L. Montagnon-Le Saux: letters to Alfred Le Saux (1948-1954)), then to herself (1954-1973). Photocopies of the whole dossier kindly made by Mr Patrice Chagnard.

Madame M.-N. Soulaine: letters to her uncle, Fr R. Macé (1929-1969), and other documents.

Mother Marie-Gilbert, Carmel of St Pair: letters (1961-1972).

Dr Donald Nicholl: letter of 1971.

Dr R. Panikkar; extracts of letters made by Susri N. Shanta, and originals (1964-1973).

Fr Murray Rogers: letters of 1973; various documents.

Mrs A.-M. Stokes: extracts of letters (1959-1973).

Sister Superior of Roberts Nursing Home, Indore: for permitting Madame Baumer to transcribe or photocopy letters to Mother Théophane (1958-1968).

Fr Robert Vachon: letters and reminiscence of 1970.

A French hermit in Italy: extracts of letters (1965-1973).

Very special thanks are due to Madame Baumer, who not only took the trouble to search out and obtain permission for the use of several most important collections, but also undertook the immense labour copying many hundreds of letters.

C. Those who helped in the understanding of the nuances in Abhishiktananda's French, or made suggestions for the improvement of the manuscript: especially Dr B. Bäumer, Madame O. Baumer-Despeigne, Fr J. Dupuis, Fr John E. Sclater, Mr Maurice Salen, Susri N. Shanta, Fr Hal Weidner.

D. Those who provided, or permitted the use of, photographs for the illustrations:

Mme O. Baumer for her pictures—4,1; 8.2; and the portrait on the cover.

Mlle Yvonne Macé and Mme M.-N. Soulaine for copies of 2.1 and 2.

Sr Marie-Thérèse for postcard 1.2; and the copy of 2.3.

Mme L. Montagnon for copies of 5.1 and 2; 6.1, 2 and 3; 7.1 and 2.

Dr R. Panikkar for permitting the use of 6.1 and 2; 7.1.

Roberts Nursing Home for providing 8.3.

Swami Nityananda Giri for the portrait 4.3.

Sri Ramana Ashram for the portrait 4.2.

E. Those who helped to subsidize the cost of producing the original edition this book: the Trustees of the Teape Foundation, Cambridge; Fr Hal Weidner.

And finally, much gratitude to the Revd P.D. and Mrs Sham Rao for their hospitality at the Rajpur Centre during five periods of work in 1985-6.

J.S.

NOTE TO THE REVISED EDITION

Thanks are due to friends who kindly pointed out errors and slips in the original publication, all of which we hope have been corrected in the present edition.

Owing to the great increase in the cost of paper recently, the economic price (for India) of this new edition would have been Rs. 300/-. However the price has actually been fixed at Rs. 200/-, the publishers having been promised a subsidy towards the cost of production sufficient to offset their loss. It is hoped to raise the necessary sum with the help of the Abhishiktananda Society and other friends, who are now thanked in anticipation.

Abbreviations

Recipients of letter are indicated by initials before the date:

AF	Mrs Antonia Fonseca	MG	Mother Marie-Gilberte
ALG	Mme A.-L. Guguen-Le Saux	MR	Fr Murray Rogers
AMS	Mrs Anne-Marie Stokes	MT	Sr Marie-Thérèse Le Saux
F	Mr Alfred Le Saux/ Mme L. Montagnon-Le Saux	OB	Mme O. Baumer-Despeigne
		RM	Fr R. Macé
FT	Mother Françoise-Thérèse	RP	Dr R. Panikkar
JD	Fr J. Dupuis	RV	Fr R. Vachon
JS	J. Stuart	SG	Sr Sara Grant
L	Canon J. Lemarié	Th	Mother M. Théophane
M	Mr & Mrs Miller	TL	Sr Térèse de Jésus (Lemoine)
MC	Marc Chadue	X	Unknown

Other abbreviations:

CBCI	Catholic Bishops' Conference of India
CNI	Church of North India
CSI	Church of South India
Ermites	*Ermites du Saccidananda*
Eveil	*Éveil à soi—éveil à Dieu* (=*Prayer*)
IBA	*An Indian Benedictine Ashram*
ICI	*Informations catholiques internationales*
Initiation	*Initiation à la spiritualité des Upanishads* (=*The Further Shore*)
Intériorité	*Intériorité et révélation*
Meeting Point	*Hindu-Christian Meeting Point* (=*Rencontre*)
Quest	*In Quest of the Absolute*
Rencontre	*La rencontre de l'hindouisme et du christianisme*
Sagesse	*Sagesse hindoue mystique chrétienne* (=*Saccidananda*)
Secret	*The Secret of Arunachala* (=*Souvenirs*)
Siauve	*Mystique de l'Inde, mystère chrétien* (J. Monchanin)
Souvenirs	*Souvenirs d'Arunachala* (=*Secret*)
SPAA	*Swami Parama Arubi Anandam* (Memoir of Fr. J. Monchanin)
Une messe	*Une messe aux sources du Gange* (=*The Mountain of the Lord*)

1
Roots

> It seems only yesterday that we were ten, eleven years old—that wonderful age! And everything else seems to have overlaid it, like a cloak that you have put on for a long journey. (AMS, 3.8.71)

HENRI LE SAUX was born on 30 August 1910 at St Briac, a small town on the north coast of Brittany. He was the first child of Alfred Le Saux and Louise Sonnefraüd, who gave him the names Henri Briac Marie.

The Le Saux family

On his father's side Henri was descended from a long line of seafarers, but Alfred's mother, having seen her father, brother, two husbands and one of her sons lost at sea, understandably persuaded Alfred to remain on land. He therefore went into business at St Briac and established a provision store in which, after his marriage in 1905, he was assisted by his wife.

Louise's father was born in Alsace into a family which had originally come from Austria. As a young man during the Franco-Prussian war of 1870, he made his way through the enemy lines in order to join the French army. At end of the war he opted for France, stayed on in the army, and finally settled at St Briac, though the rest of the family remained in Alsace.

For seven years Henri was the only child, but eventually the Le Saux family increased until there were seven children, five girls and two boys. Henri was a lively and intelligent lad, and when at home took an active part in bringing up his younger brother and sisters, sharing their games, teaching them to swim and above all to sing. He had a harmonium in his room, round which the children often gathered. His first love was for the traditional songs of Brittany, to which was later added an equal enthusiasm for the splendours of Gregorian. This music remained dear to him to the end—a poignant memory which could stir him deeply.

It was a devoutly Catholic home, whose times and seasons were marked by the great festivals of the Church and by the missions which were periodically held in the parish church. Henri's father, despite the severe lameness caused by injuries received in the 1914-1918 war, was so frequently seen on his way to church that one small boy was moved to dub him 'the saint'. On the Feast of Corpus Christi it was the custom for children to take part in the procession, dressed up as one or other of the saints. As the family recalls, Henri, suitably clad in a sheepskin, used to take the part of John the Baptist—with unconscious appropriateness.

Vocation to the Priesthood

A sense of his calling to the priesthood seems to have shaped Henri's life from boyhood. His parents encouraged him in this and sent him in 1921[1] to the Minor Seminary at Châteaugiron, from which in 1926 he passed on to the Major Seminary at Rennes.

In 1924 his mother nearly died in giving birth to a sixth child (which did not survive). Next year, when another child was expected, Henri was in agony at the thought of losing his mother. To his prayers he added a vow that, if she were saved, he would go wherever he might be sent, "even to the most distant mission". He was doubtless thinking of his uncle Henri Sonnefraüd, a member of the Foreign Missionary Society of Paris, who had been sent to China in 1923.[2]

His studies for the priesthood proceeded quietly and uneventfully, punctuated by holidays at home when he relaxed with the family. Mornings were spent in helping his parents in their shop, and summer afternoons in playing with the younger members of the family on the beach at St Briac. His record as a student was outstanding, and one year he had the distinction of giving the address when the Cardinal Archbishop of Rennes visited the seminary. The authorities planned to send him to Rome for further studies, but he asked to be excused on the ground that this would prevent him from testing his vocation to the monastic life, to which by then he felt strongly drawn.

Monastic vocation

It appears that the seed of this vocation was sown by a fellow-seminarian, a close friend who confided to Henri his great desire to become a Benedictine. Henri, then aged sixteen, was far from sharing this enthusiasm; but when shortly afterwards this friend died, he became convinced that he had inherited his vocation to become a monk.

Among the family papers there survive the copies (or drafts) of a series of letters written by Henri between December 1928 and June 1929 to the novice-master of the Abbey of Sainte Anne de Kergonan (near Plouharnel, on the west coast of Brittany), which he had applied to enter. The first of these well expresses both the enthusiasm and the realism with which he regarded the possibility of becoming a monk:

> . . . What has drawn me from the beginning, and what still leads me on, is the hope of finding there the presence of God more immediately than anywhere else. I have a very ambitious spirit—and this is permissible, is it not? when it is a matter of seeking God—and I hope I shall not be disappointed.

1. The date given by Dom Le Saux's family is 1920, but two letters to them (F, 3.12.62; 9.5.64) establish the date as October 1921. In a message that he sent to a Reunion in 1968 he says that he entered the Major Seminary at Rennes in 1926.
2. This uncle was killed at Waichow in 1940.

> . . . However, while that is the theme of my prayers and thanksgivings, there are many times during the day when I feel downcast. The monastic life is splendid, but it is also very painful. Without counting the pangs of leaving home, there must be many days that are hard to bear. Poverty, for example, must at times be a heavy burden. I like to have things of my own, to have things which in some sense complete my "I", but in the monastery I have to feel that none of the things that I use belongs to me (. . .). And then to be condemned to avoid human society, to be for ever secluded within extremely narrow limits, to pass a lifetime of which every day is identical—all that is surely a grievous burden for human nature?
>
> . . . I feel an irresistible call, and yet I am afraid of being rash in binding myself for life. (. . .) Will you repeat for me your original judgment? I have need to be persuaded myself; however much I act as one who must soon follow the call of God, it seems to me so incredible that I should soon become a monk, that I dare not accept the idea. (4.12.28)

The would-be monk had not however reckoned with the possible obstacles that might come in his way, and when they came into view at the beginning of 1929 it looked as if his entry into the monastery might have to be deferred for several years. At the end of the Christmas vacation, when he broke the news to his parents, they surprised him with the vehemence of their opposition and their distress at the thought of thus 'losing' their eldest son. Apart from their natural sense of shock, they reminded him of the fact (which he had overlooked) that if anything should happen to them, the responsibility of supporting the other children would fall on him—the next oldest being then only aged eleven. Before entering the monastery could he not wait until she was grown up and could take his place? (Letter of 4.1.29)

In addition he learnt at the seminary that the Archbishop was not normally prepared to release any of his priests until they had given several years of service to the diocese. A further obstacle was that he still had to perform his military service, and the Abbot of Kergonan preferred that his monks should have done that before entering the monastery.

It was bitter disappointment, which was increased by his fear that a long delay might cause him to lose his vocation altogether. (Letter of 27.1.29)

After the Easter vacation, however, his hopes began to revive. He sensed that his parents' opposition was weakening, especially when he pointed out that during his first five years at the monastery, if the family had need of him, he could always revert to the secular priesthood. The Archbishop also showed signs of relaxing his ban. His next letter to the novice-master ends:

> . . . I hope, Father, that with the better weather God has enabled you to recover your health and to resume with your sons (among whom I trust that God will soon place me) the great work of guiding them towards holiness. For must not a monk at least be aiming at that? In becoming a monk I have a great ambition; and the way that God has used to bring me to this has been above all the sight of the mediocrity

> into which so many priests lapse after a few years in the ministry, and which at all costs I want to avoid. I hope that at least in the monastery I shall be able to love God as I should. (23.4.29)

A month later, after another visit home, he told the novice-master that he had been able to speak to his parents about his vocation:

> . . . Now it seems that my parents are pretty well resigned to my entering the religious life. The prospect of being separated is dreadful, but we feel that it is impossible to struggle against God any longer. So, as regards my family, the matter is almost settled. (27.5.29)

He also learnt from the Superior of the seminary that he could count on obtaining the Archbishop's permission to leave the diocese. Only the matter of military service remained to be settled with the Abbot, and he made a fervent appeal to be allowed to begin his monastic life without further delay.

The Abbot too was won over; and on receiving the news from the novice-master, Henri wrote:

> . . . After I got your letter I went to offer heartfelt thanks to our Lord, for it seemed to me that after twenty months of more or less clear and pressing calls, this was the definitive invitation to follow him which he is giving me through you.
>
> . . . And now that I review the course of my vocation, I marvel at the firm and gentle touch of Providence in detaching me little by little from all the natural attraction which the cloister might have for me, and allowing me to see in my entering the religious life nothing but the naked will of God. In all this I seem to be so much like a pawn, so to speak, and to be living in a kind of dream; I did not understand—and less than ever do I now understand—all the steps that I am taking. I can neither convince myself, nor can I even imagine, that I shall end this year in a monastery, and this idea seems to my natural mind both horrible and futile; but I feel myself driven by something which does not allow me to draw back or turn aside, and compels me, almost in spite of myself, to throw myself into the unknown which I see opening before me. (3.6.29)

Although Henri had made his decision, he still had to persuade himself and those who were nearest to him that he really would be leaving them in October. A glimpse of his inner struggle is given by one of his sisters: "Henri found it very hard to accept his monastic vocation. Once we were in his room by the harmonium, and I saw him clench his fists and say, My God, you can't possibly ask that of me!"

As the time of departure approached, his family and friends made no secret of their feelings. In one of a series of letters to a close friend at the seminary, Raymond Macé,[3] he wrote:

> Then it is true that I have caused you also to suffer so deeply. It is frightful to find oneself continually giving pain to those whom one

3. Raymond Macé (1908-1972), Canon of Rennes, continued to correspond with Dom Le Saux at least until 1969.

> loves. Believe me, that is the worst sorrow of those who go away: to abandon parents and friends, to give up an easy life, is hard and at times extremely painful, but even so the sacrifice is easy to make—it is enough to love a little to make oneself a holocaust to the Good Lord. Only, when it is a matter of offering up, making complete the sacrifice of those who are dear to us!—what can be worse than that? (RM, 17.7.29)

In this and other letters Henri did his best to console his friend, (and at the same time himself?), with edifying thoughts about submission to the will of God, the benefits of accepting the cross with courage and faith, and the truth of their abiding union in the Body of Christ, even when they were outwardly separated. But he admitted that the situation at home was what troubled him most:

> . . . For myself I dread having to speak again with my parents about my going away. I rarely have the chance of being alone with them for long enough to raise the matter. I wanted to talk to them on Sunday; only a totally unexpected thing happened which gave them quite enough worry and trouble for that day [this was an accidental fire in the shop which was fortunately discovered in time]. (. . .) So I am putting it off for the time being. I dread having to raise the subject, for whatever may come of it, it will be an ordeal for me. However I trust in the Lord. He will help me. (RM, 17.7.29)

In the end he succeeded in winning over his parents, and (according to another of his sisters) his mother accepted the decision because she realized that outside a monastery her son's great intelligence might tempt him to pride. But his last summer holiday at home, inevitably overshadowed by the constant thought of his departure, could not help being depressing (RM, 11.8.29), and it must have been a relief when at last October came.

Monk of Kergonan, 1929-1948

Henri Le Saux entered the monastery soon after his nineteenth birthday. After the customary few days as a guest he was admitted as a postulant. Thus began a stage of his life which was to last for another nineteen years. As the life of a monk is essentially hidden, it is not surprising that there are few details to record. However something can be learnt from the recollections of his family, from very occasional letters to his friend Raymond Macé, and from some notes contributed by a younger contemporary at Kergonan.[4] We also have an early fruit of his pen, in the form of a long manuscript, written at his mother's request in 1942.[5]

In a letter to his friend shortly before taking the habit he wrote at length about the monk's consecration to God being centred in a life of praise. In his Abbey

4. Joseph Lemarié, now Canon of Aquileia and of Chartres, corresponded with Dom Le Saux until the end.
5. A typed copy of this manuscript (109 pages) has been provided by his youngest sister. The Table of Contents indicates that there was to have been a fourth chapter on 'The Mother of God'

the Divine Office occupied at least fours hours daily, not to mention the time spent on preparing for it. Indeed every moment of a Benedictine's day, however commonplace, is treated as an offering to God:

> . . . A life perfectly suited to the pursuit of holiness; like anything else, of course, it needs guts to become a holy monk, but despite its difficulty I feel one is bound to aim high. A monk cannot accept mediocrity, only extremes are appropriate for him.
>
> The richness of monastic life I have only begun to glimpse now that I have entered it for good; and I still feel myself as if inundated, dazzled by it; it is too vast for one to be able to grasp it all at once.
>
> And God in his goodness has called me into this life. Why? A profound mystery of Providence. (. . .) This good fortune almost frightens me; but often the departure is easily made, so that you can be prepared for passing through some tunnels. . . (RM. 27.10.29)

Having completed his six months as a postulant, on 13 May 1930 Henri began the year as a novice which was to lead up his first profession in temporary vows. To describe his first months at Kergonan he said to Raymond:

> . . . I have given you the timetable and the daily programme; just multiply that by thirty and then by seven. . . . The only diversions are the liturgical feasts and the changes of [liturgical] seasons. We have said goodbye to everything except the True, the 'one thing needful', so . . .
>
> To say that one's nature does not complain from time to time—with you I can speak of these things—I would not dare. . . .

At Easter the family had come to see how he was getting on at the Abbey:

> . . . I was in high spirits and appeared very happy, but when I was alone, the tears flowed and I wished I could go home with them; but He did not will it, and so for his sake alone I remained, while the storm raged within. (. . .) The battle is sometimes fierce, but with Him one is always victorious. And now I am at peace, until such time as He ordains something different.

He also told his friend about the moving ceremony of his clothing as a novice and sent messages to his other friends at the seminary, explaining how they might visit him at Kergonan. (RM. 15.5.30)

A year later he made his first profession, and probably after that was called up for his military service. When this was over, he returned to the Abbey and continued his studies for the priesthood.

Shortly before making his final vows on Ascension Day (30 May) 1935, he wrote to urge Raymond to come to Kergonan for the Profession and to bring other old friends with him:

> . . . I am absolutely relying on you, for I have such a need at that moment to be surrounded with prayer, that the oblation may be pleasing to the Father.

He also asked him to use with his intention a prayer that he had chosen from the Missal:

> . . . You will pray it for me, won't you? so that the total religious life which I shall soon begin may be at the level of which I have always dreamed, that I may not be a commonplace monk—the Lord has no need of such—but a sacrifice *jugiter immolata* [continually offered]. (RM, 9.5.35)

His ordination as a priest took place in the same year on the Feast of St Thomas, Apostle of India (21 December). After his profession he was entrusted with several responsibilities in the community, especially as "Second Ceremoniary" (Assistant Master of Ceremonies) and Librarian. In the latter post he undertook the reorganization of the library, a heavy task which he later recalled with feeling. However, as Librarian, he had ample opportunity for wide reading, and was particularly drawn to the Greek Fathers and the Fathers of the Desert. When later he had to lecture to the younger monks, he loved to quote from Athanasius, Cyril of Alexandria and Gregory Palamas. He must also have begun his Indian studies for (as we shall see) his thoughts had been turned towards India since 1934.

In 1939 Dom Le Saux was recalled to the colours, but the disaster of 1940 terminated his military career. His unit was surrounded by enemy troops and had to surrender; but fortunately, before names were taken, he managed to escape and made his way back to the monastery. A year later he described his experiences to Fr Macé:

> . . . As you see, I am personally living peacefully at the monastery; this time last year, thank God, I was preserved from danger met at very close quarters and also from becoming a prisoner-of-war. After leaving Rennes, I spent some time at Quimper, then at Bordeaux, fought in Normandy and found myself one morning at Mayenne outflanked by German troops. As I had no desire to visit Germany, that evening I took the road to Fougères and the following night, thanks to a bicycle which was kindly lent to me, managed to reach St Briac dressed in a fantastic outfit. There for a month I acted dead, and when travelling became easier I returned here. (RM, 23.6.41)

The Abbey was requisitioned in 1942, and the monks had to migrate to Nétumières, near Vitry, until the end of the war.

The manuscript written for his mother in 1942 is called *Amour et Sagesse* (Love and Wisdom). It already displays characteristic features of his later writing. In the Foreword he calls it a "sketch of a book that will very likely never be written", and says that it was inspired by the sorrow of seeing "the noblest mystery of their faith (the Holy Trinity) . . . so little known, so little savoured, experienced, even by fervent Christians . . ." He regrets that theologians will not allow people "to accept in their literal sense the traditional formulas which affirm our being caught up into the Blessed Trinity". Of the three existing chapters, the first meditates at length on 'The Love of the Father', and the next two on 'The Gift of the Son' (on the Cross and in the Eucharist) He says that he avoids "theological speculations" and has not aimed at an exhaustive treatment of the subject. "These are simple, personal reflections on the marvellous aspects of the divine love and wisdom . . ." The underlying theology which he sought to express in simple terms is entirely traditional, but is lit up by personal devotion and is presented so as to kindle devotion. ". . . I have set down nothing here except what is my own; I have judged it unnecessary to reproduce what can be found everywhere—which explains the fragmentary nature of this essay" (TS, p.4). This principle was one which he followed in all his writing. There is also a familiar stress on God's transcendence, for example: "No word can express God, before him every thought falls short, every joy, every delight is nothing compared to the divine beatitude. Beyond, always beyond! It is not your gifts, Lord, that I desire, but yourself . . ."(TS, 108). "The Eucharist is already the source of that search for God in contemplation which withdraws monks and virgins from the company even of good people, and inspires them with a desire for a solitude that is ever more complete, in which to seek for the ineffable encounter" (TS, 109). Occasionally traces of his Indian reading also appear; he quotes Tagore's *Gitanjali* for God's loving condescension in accepting the devotion of his creatures (TS, 35-6), and notes the emphasis in Hinduism on divine love and the human response, including its "intuition of an incarnate God" (TS, 48-49).

At the end of the war the Bursar of the monastery needed the help of a practical and vigorous brother in repairing the Abbey buildings with a view to the return of the community, and selected Dom Le Saux for this task, which was completed a year later.

From 1946 to 1948 Dom Le Saux was once again the Librarian and now the "Senior Ceremoniary" at Kergonan. He was also given charge of the studies of the novices (three or four in number) in Canon Law and the history of the Church. His approach to the latter was less on the factual level than on that of the development of thought. He gave an excellent introduction to the writings of the Church Fathers by setting them in their historical context. He also shared with two special 'disciples' his notes on the Trinity and the Eucharist.

An abiding background

Dom Le Saux's mother died in 1944, while he was still in France. His father's death took place in November 1954, after he had been in India for some years. At the time of his funeral a parish mission was in progress, and the church was decorated with masses of flowers which surrounded the coffin. To the family this seemed a fitting valediction to one whose life had always breathed a serene faith. It was first through his parents and then through his monastery that Dom Le Saux's heart and mind were deeply rooted in the living tradition of the Catholic Church and in commitment to Christ. This, as he fully recognized, is what made possible the great boldness with which, as a lonely pioneer, he made himself open to the deepest spirituality of his adopted country, and was thereby enabled to make his unique contribution to the Church in India and beyond.[6]

After their mother's death, as his brother noted, Henri took her place as the one who chiefly held the family together. They knew that they could confide in him, and relied on his sensitive advice. By the time that he set out for India, four were already married, and a fifth wedding took place only two days after his

6. See *Hindu-Christian Meeting Point*, 104, for the "deep grounding in faith" which is "essential for any [Christian] who seeks to enter into close contact with Hindu thought"

ship sailed. His remaining sister, the youngest, a few years later (in 1952) "took her brother's place" at Kergonan and entered the sister-abbey of St Michel.

The strong family ties which were forged in the early years at St Briac were never broken. Throughout his twenty-five years in India their eldest brother faithfully maintained a regular correspondence with them, writing almost every month to the family as a whole and also to individuals, especially on their anniversaries. He took care to share with them as much as he could of the life he was leading, and in return constantly asked for news of their doings and of the progress of his nephews and nieces. His concern for their health and happiness was unfailing, and he followed it up with much good advice, both spiritual and practical. In the late 60s, when the younger members of the family were growing up and were faced with the problems of living in a world where so many of the old landmarks were disappearing, he well understood their dissatisfaction with conventional religion and their search for authenticity. He was greatly amused that they called him a 'hippy', and felt that they also understood him! The family often pressed him to come on a visit to France, but he steadfastly refused, and asked them instead to visit him in India. Eventually in 1972 one niece came overland with a friend to see this legendary uncle, which pleased him immensely.

The true *sannyāsī*,* which he sought to be, has indeed renounced everything—home, family, country—, but his renunciation would have been less real if he had totally forgotten his roots. What they meant to him is shown by a letter written in 1971 to a compatriot, originally from the west coast of Brittany, who had settled in New York:

> OM. At noon a letter from you from Brittany. I cannot resist writing to you there at once. You make me dream, relive those things which I usually push into the background in order to be able to live my life in peace. How aptly you said that after twenty years you slipped back at once like a snake into its old skin. It seems only yesterday that we were ten, eleven years old—that wonderful age! And everything else seems to have overlaid it, like a cloak that you have put on for a long journey. (. . .) Perhaps behind all the high-sounding reasons that I give for refusing and arguing against any possibility of returning there, is my fear of not being able to bear it emotionally, and the great difficulty I would have afterwards in taking up my 'role' again.
>
> I have found on the map of Finistère in my old 1924 Larousse (. . .) your village deep in a little cove . . . St Guénolé, Locquénolé, names which make me dream. I do not know Finistère; I am from St Malo and Cap Frehel, also deep in a cove (. . .). The Himalayas are splendid, and Arunachala is greater still; yet what can be compared to the sea of my Emerald Coast (not blue as a jay's wing, like yours)? All this belongs to the depth of my being. It is like those Tridentine Masses and the Gregorian chant of the monasteries, which I would doubtless put on again like a glove, even after having lived the marvellous experience of 'spontaneous' Masses or of those Masses in the Upanishadic tradition

* For Indian terms, please see the Glossary.

which I celebrate each morning and which help me to carry on (. . .). To pass from Manhattan to the moors of St Guénolé is probably as rude a shock as to pass from the Himalayas to a monastery on the moors of Carnac; and that is why I 'feel' so much all that your letter conveys. (. . .) Write again soon, I feel you so much closer in our Brittany. At least I can imagine it to some extent, despite the immense changes since the war; whereas for me New York and America are at a 'lunar' distance, and I guess that if I ever got there I should be *flattened* like some of the cosmonauts.

Before I send this off, a deep bow to the ocean for me, please! (AMS, 3.8.71)

* * *

Dom Le Saux left France on 26 July 1948, the feast of St Anne, patroness of Brittany and of his own monastery. On 15 August, the first anniversary of India's Independence and the feast of the Assumption, he disembarked at Colombo in Ceylon.

2
Call to India

I have had this dream for over thirteen years, and in recent years it has been continually in my thought and prayer.

(*Letter to Fr Monchanin*, 18.8.47)

THE CALL to India was heard by the young monk at Kergonan as early as 1934,[1] that is, within five years of his entering the monastery, and even before he had taken his final vows. As he told Fr Monchanin (p. 15, below), it took the form of an ardent desire to see and take part in the establishment of contemplative monastic life in the Indian Church; or, if that were not possible (as he had written to the Bishop of Tiruchi), then at least to lead a contemplative life in some hermitage in India.

The fundamental vow of the Benedictine is that of 'stability', whereby the monk binds himself to remain in his monastery until death. How was it that Dom Le Saux so soon and so strongly felt a call which would take him out of his monastery? There is no question of his deep attachment to the Rule of St Benedict or of his love for Kergonan, with which he maintained contact to the end of his life. He might have had reservations about certain aspects of his monastery, but he constantly acknowledged how much he owed to it (e.g., "Kergonan has been the background of all that I have been able to do here"; L, 22.9.73). The origin of any particular calling is in any case mysterious, and Dom Le Saux had an additional reason for remaining silent about his own—he did not wish to cause pain to his fellow-monks, since his departure might be taken as a criticism of the community that he left.

However, very occasionally in his Diary, and once in a letter to a close friend, he revealed that Kergonan, for all that it gave him, could not fully satisfy his deepest aspiration. This aspiration was foreshadowed even in his youthful letters to the novice-master, when he spoke of his great 'ambition' in seeking God. It is also focussed in the characteristic phrase, "Beyond, always beyond," in the book written for his mother in 1942. In a page of painful self-analysis in the Diary (5.2.56) he wrote about "this *inquietudo* [restlessness] (. . .) something psychologically much more deep in me (. . .) which is shown in a violent form in my distaste for the monastery and for my present situation. Compare my writing, my speech, my very thought, always running ahead of themselves, these constant plans for the future, for this or that, this opting for what is most total in the life

1. This date is supported by many references in letters and the Diary.

consecrated to God: mission, then monasticism, then total monasticism, [first] dreamed of, then realized. . ." (These three stages correspond with his boyhood thought of being a missionary, then his call to Kergonan, and finally the call to India.) It is thus clear that, when long afterwards he wrote to his friend, ". . . it was in my deep dissatisfaction that my desire to come to India was born" (L. 13.3.67), he referred to something much deeper than a reaction to the superficial irritations which are part and parcel of any community life.

The call was heard and accepted, but for long years there seemed to be no way in which it could be realized. Meanwhile Dom Le Saux prepared himself hopefully by the study of Indian Scriptures, so as to be ready when the time should come.

* * *

When the war ended in 1945, his Abbot gave him permission to approach various authorities who might be expected to look favourably on his project. Several times he received an initially encouraging response, but every attempt ended in disappointment, until he was on the point of giving up. He decided to make one last sounding, and in May 1947 wrote to the Bishop of Tiruchirappalli, asking his permission "to settle somewhere in the neighbourhood of Tiruchi so that, living in some hermitage, he might there lead the contemplative life, in the absolute simplicity of early Christian monasticism and at the same time in the closest possible conformity with the traditions of Indian *sannyāsa*" (15.5.47).[2]

As the letter was written in French, Bishop Mendonça passed it on for translation to a French priest who was working in his diocese and happened to be visiting him on that very day. This priest was Fr Jules Monchanin, who himself for several years had desired to adopt precisely this kind of life. To him Dom Le Saux's letter came as an 'answer from God', bringing news of a kindred spirit, in whose company his own dream might at last be realized.

Fr Jules Monchanin

Jules Monchanin[3] left France for India in 1939 at the age of 44. In his own country he had been exercising an extremely fruitful ministry, from which very naturally his bishop (Cardinal Gerlier of Lyon) at first hesitated to release him. He was widely known, not merely for his intellectual brilliance and the remarkable width of his interests, but equally for his profound spiritual gifts and his marvellous capacity for sympathy and friendship with people from the most varied backgrounds. All his contacts were marked by his faith and a wholly unselfconscious humility.[4] He was equally at home in the learned societies of Lyon and Paris, and in the daily life and struggle of a working-class parish.

His interest in India had been aroused at an early age by a book on Buddhism. Much later, when he was involved in counselling and training those who were preparing for missionary service, he began to realize that he himself might be

2. *Swami Parama Arubi Anandam* (Fr J. Monchanin): *A Memorial,* 16.
3. For Fr Monchanin, see Bibliography, Section I.
4. "It is in faith and humility inseparably conjoined . . . that we find the unifying centre of this complex personality" *(L'abbé Jules Monchanin, 29).*

called to give his life to the Church in India. This finally became clear to him at the time of a serious illness in March 1932, when "he promised the Lord that, if he survived, he would henceforth dedicate his life to the work that so strongly attracted him".[5]

His conception of this work is spelled out in some paragraphs of the Memorial[6] which Dom Le Saux wrote shortly after his companion's death in 1957:

> His temperament, intellect, education, and above all a special grace, had all prepared Fr Monchanin to enter easily into the spiritual and intellectual world of India, and to foresee the marvellous vocation that awaited her at the heart of the Church of the *parousia* [i.e. in its ultimate perfection]. One whose natural gift for contemplation was heightened by grace, having been nourished by the Greek Fathers, the mystics of the West, and above all the mediaeval Rhinelanders [Ruysbroeck, Tauler, Eckhart], he was fully prepared to penetrate that secret of contemplation which is at the source of all the most fundamental institutions of India, both philosophical and religious, the mystic centre of her being from which her whole civilization has sprung.
>
> Discovering with an ever-growing wonder the divine call hidden in the mystery of India, he also realized more and more clearly what it was that India was awaiting from the Church. He understood that India would never open herself completely to the Christian message, until she could recognize the Church—the bearer of the message—as essentially the Adorer of the mystery within, deeply recollected and one with her Spouse the Word, in the presence of the Father. (. . .)
>
> Little by little a dream took shape in the depth of his spirit. Why should he not himself go, as a Christian priest, to this holy land of India to take his part in the Church's task? What he envisaged was not the missionary life as it is commonly understood, but rather that he should be a witness to a life, rooted in the Church and at the same time in the midst of the world, which would be entirely consecrated to the contemplation of the Blessed Trinity. In his own words, his object was "to prepare for the awakening among Christians of the contemplative life in an integrally Indian form", and in spiritual partnership with others, Indians if possible, to attempt to develop in a Christian milieu the age-old contemplative urge of India. And, since this contemplative life was already expressed in India in a characteristic monastic institution [*sannyāsa*], it seemed clearly indicated that he should enter as far as possible into this tradition with a view to "crystallizing and trans-substantiating the spiritual quest of Hindu sannyasis".[7]

When Fr Monchanin came to India, in accordance with the spirit of the Society of Auxiliaries to the Missions (founded by Fr Vincent Lebbe) to which he belonged, he placed himself entirely at his Bishop's disposal—"I shall be content with the most modest post," he had written. The Bishop took him at his word, and as soon as he had acquired a modicum of Tamil he was sent to a

5. *Swami Parama Arubi Anandam (SPAA)*, 9.
6. *SPAA*.
7. *SPAA*, 7-9.

series of country parishes in the Tiruchi diocese. Here (except when incapacitated by asthma) he was constantly occupied in preaching, catechizing children, ministering to the sick and dying, visiting remote outstations by bullock-cart, and welcoming all who came to him for any kind of help. While devoting himself unstintingly to his pastoral work and living in heroic simplicity, he never ceased to dream of a life entirely given to solitude and contemplation. From time to time he was invited to rest at the Jesuit seminary at Shembaganūr in the Palni Hills or to give lectures in Pondicherry, which gave him a chance to share with others his reflections on the philosophical and theological trends of the day. He still kept abreast of the latest developments through his wide correspondence and through the books with which he was supplied by his friends.

On two occasions Fr Monchanin had worked in the parish of Kulittalai, a small town twenty miles up the Kavery from Tiruchirappalli, where a friend built him a modest presbytery, known as 'Bhakti Ashram'. In January 1948 he was appointed to Kulittalai for the third time and remained in charge of the parish until he and Dom Le Saux started their ashram in 1950.

On the day after reading Dom Le Saux's letter to the Bishop, Fr Monchanin wrote to a friend in Pondicherry:

> . . . I have a great hope (. . .) a Benedictine of Plouharnel (Morbihan) has written to the Bishop expressing his desire to come to India and to implant the contemplative life in a *completely* Indian form. Fearing that the traditions of the Order may prove an obstacle, he is asking for—and expects to obtain—an indult of exclaustration.[8] The Father Abbot will grant it . . . The Bishop agreed immediately, and the Superior of the Major Seminary was consulted . . . He is in favour of the experiment being made by me and the Benedictine from Brittany. I have written in the Bishop's name both to the Abbot (asking if he would agree to the *experiment* and promising my fraternal help), and to Fr Le Saux himself, telling him something of my own desire . . . I hope for *everything* from the Holy Spirit and from him *alone*. (8.8.47)[9]

To Dom Le Saux himself Fr Monchanin had written:

> Filled with the joy of the Holy Spirit, I write in the name of Mgr Mendonça who has just returned from Europe and America. (. . .) Your letter came to me as an answer from God. Since May 1939 I have been in the diocese of Trichinopoly. Mgr Mendonça in his great kindness welcomed me like a father. I have learnt English and Tamil. I am now serving in a small parish, where I am much more of a *hermit* than a parish priest . . .
>
> If you come, his Lordship is very willing for us to begin together a life of prayer, poverty and intellectual work. Learn as much English as you can. You will have no objection to a purely vegetarian diet (essential for the life of a *sannyāsī*). You will need unshakable courage (because you will have *disappointments*), complete detachment from the

8. i.e. formal permission for a monk to live outside his monastery for reasons deemed sufficient by the Roman authorities.

9. J. Monchanin, *Mystique de l'Inde, mystère chrétien*, ed. S. Siauve, 172-3; hereafter referred to as 'Siauve'.

things of the West, and a profound love for India. The Spirit will give you these three gifts. I am expecting you. India expects you. A priest friend, a Tamilian, will join us soon, I hope. Prepare yourself by prayer and the offering of yourself. In him you are my beloved brother. (7.8.47)[10]

Dom Le Saux introduces himself

In August Dom Le Saux replied to Fr Monchanin with a letter which is worth quoting at length, as it provides an excellent self-portrait and statement of his outlook, as he prepared to come to India:

Your letter was for me a great joy, and I too wonder if I should not look on it as an answer from heaven. For at last I can see that the enterprise which has been for so long the object of my most ardent desires, namely the establishment of monastic life in India, is about to take shape, and perhaps I shall have the happiness of being involved in it myself.

I have in fact had this dream for over thirteen years, and in recent years it has been continually in my thought and prayer. Two years ago I received my Father Abbot's permission to put out a certain number of feelers in this direction. I was given much encouragement, but as soon as the moment came for taking action, problems were raised or the offer of help was withdrawn. I began by contacting the Abbot of Bruges, and things were going well; but once I made it clear that my aim was an essentially contemplative life, and not one that was half contemplative and half apostolic, Dom N. answered that it would be better for each of us to follow his own line (. . .). At the same time I was in correspondence with the Bishops of Pondicherry and Salem. The latter's response was especially enthusiastic. The only difficulty was that his diocese was too new and too poor for him to be able to take the responsibility for such a foundation. So, after a few months of hope, every letter that came only brought a fresh disappointment. (However, in the midst of this I had one joy—a dearly loved brother of my own monastery offered of his own accord to come with me, and I know that with him I should have perfect communion in heart and mind.)

Then again, I approached Mgr Kierkels, the Apostolic Delegate. He answered me very kindly, but said that he could only attend to my business after his return from Europe (at the end of the year, I think)—always supposing that he could find some way of using my desire. This was all very uncertain, but I tried one last inquiry—I had quite decided to abandon the whole project if this brought no result, because I could not continue indefinitely in this state of uncertainty. I was aware of the flourishing state of Christianity in Madurai, and in *La Croix* of last November I had read the interview with Mgr Mendonça to which I referred the other day. So on the Feast of the Ascension I wrote this last letter and sent it off next day after placing in on the altar during the vigil which I keep every evening before the Tabernacle with the Brother

10. *In Quest of the Absolute*, 69-70; hereafter referred to as '*Quest*'.

already mentioned, when we repeat our '*Suscipe*'[11] in view of India. Since mid-June I was expecting an answer. I had begun to think that the Lord did not want me for India, and once more was about to abandon English, Tamil and the Upanishads, since I could not sacrifice more immediately useful occupations for these studies, which seemed less and less likely ever to be needed. And then your letter reached me two days ago.

It would have been really good if we could have met during your visit to France.[12] But why be sorry for what the Lord has not ordained? It would have been so simple for him to have put us in touch, because more than a year ago I had asked Father Abbot to let me find out your address, but he saw no point in it. However I did not know that you were thinking of establishing a Hindu monastic life, only that you were a French priest living in India and trying to penetrate by the light of Christ into the deep and beautiful truths hidden in Hindu thought. I had learnt this from an article by Fr Daniélou in *Études*[13] (a passing reference). Later on I found in an advertisement the title of your article in *Dieu vivant,*[14] but as a 'poor' monk, I was unable to buy it. I then had the joy of discovering this article in a pre-war issue of *Contemplation et apostolat* (almost identical, to judge from the Chronicle of *Revue thomiste*).[15] I say 'joy', because it really was a very great joy for me to find someone who loves India and enters with so much Christian sympathy into the very depths of Indian thought—something which for several years has been my own dearest occupation. You can imagine what it meant to discover someone whom the thought of the *ātman* leads to the contemplation of the divine Paraclete, and who behind the superficial pantheism discerns the extraordinary intuition of the Spirit reached by the great seers of the Upanishads . . . This will tell you the extent to which—even without knowing each other—we already share a deep communion in heart and mind with regard to our beloved India. Certainly I have not had either the time or the opportunity to pursue my initiation into things Indian beyond a very elementary level; but what surely is most deeply rooted in me is a profound love for India and a strong intellectual sympathy with its thought. It will tell you how happy I should be to join forces with you, if the project were to prove feasible.

You speak of probable disappointments. I expect them, and to make me better prepared, no doubt, the Lord has sent me a generous supply of them in recent years. I have looked a good number of them in the face, and a good number of obstacles too. I certainly know my weakness, but trust in the power of the Holy Spirit. However I would like you to reassure me especially on one point—the likelihood of the work that we envisage proving useful? Is there really a well-founded hope of

11. i.e., the formula of monastic profession.
12. Fr Monchanin had accompanied Bishop Mendonça on a visit to Europe in 1946-7.
13. Vol. 249 (1946), 21.
14. No. 3 (1945).
15. Vol. 46 (1946), 584

finding people capable of responding to the monastic ideal that we intend to put before them? Mgr Prunier [of Salem] assured me without hesitation that there is; and I have read as much, for example, in a number of periodicals. You are on the spot and are directly concerned with the question—what is your opinion? From here India, the land and its people, its heart and thought, are seen in a poetic haze; so on principle I am on my guard against mirage . . . And then another point—the existence of other experiments parallel to ours? Mgr Kierkels told me that there are at present two such, undertaken by religious who have long been in India, which have already been proposed to Rome (. . .)[16] I have heard mention of a possible Benedictine foundation in Travancore (but I think it would be run on European lines). Above all there are the Rosarians of Jaffna who recruit their novices mostly in Madurai, I think. So would there still be room for anything else that might be viable? I ask this because, while I deeply love 'holy India', while her call makes my heart ache, and while (in the event of our being unsuccessful) the life of a hermit in India would not be at all unwelcome, I am still bound to consider my present position as a member of a monastery in a rather difficult situation which my departure—especially if followed by a second—would further aggravate. (My Father Abbot makes no attempt to hide this from me, even though his faith leads him generously to give me permission to go.) I cannot sacrifice a present and very clear duty to a venture which offers no serious likelihood of success—whatever might be the future reserved for it by Providence.

I think it will now be good to put before you the basic principles for realizing our project to which my reading and reflection have led me. I certainly do not want to lay down anything *a priori*; for me a fundamental rule is adaptation to circumstances and submission to reality. I gave my ideas very briefly in my letter of 15 May. Here they are now, a little further elaborated. You must tell me what you think of them, and whether they fit in with yours.

Above all—and here I am sure we are in complete agreement—there must be total Indianization: however far your ideas about this may go, I am perfectly sure of being in agreement with you. But, in my opinion, our starting point should be the Rule itself, freed from the adaptations which have sometimes been imposed on it in recent centuries, with its original very flexible and universal spirit. I would like to offer to our dear Tamilians the Rule at the moment of its birth, as it were, so that little by little, with experience as the sole guide, specifically Hindu customs could be grafted onto it.

On this basis, like you, I envisage the tree of monasticism once more flourishing in all its variety, with hermits, solitaries and mendicants; we have to sanctify the whole contemplative thrust of India and christianize the monastic institutions through which she expresses the depth of her spirit. And around the monastery—the indispensable centre of all these

16. Sentences lost, owing to damage to the original.

varieties of monastic life, to which brothers called to a more special vocation would return for spiritual refreshment—I foresee the development of a very Hindu adaptation of Benedictine Oblates and Benedictine hospitality, in the form of an *āshram* where Hindus and Christians would come in search of nourishment for their spiritual life. I think the Rule of St Benedict is sufficiently flexible, in its depth and marvellous stability, to control all these forms of monastic living—in fact, it has already done so in the greatest periods of its history. I noticed this again quite recently, when preparing to give a course on ancient and mediaeval monastic history. Moreover you can easily understand that eighteen years of Benedictine life have made me deeply attached to the 'holy Rule', and that I dream of giving our blessed Father new children who will fashion a Christian India, as their elder brothers fashioned a Christian Europe. I have every hope that one day we shall discover together many interesting insights on all this; and I am sure that we shall find ourselves in agreement—your article once more convinces me of this.

I would most particularly like to preserve the non-clerical character of the primitive Rule. The clericalization of monastic life restricted its appeal to, or rather, its capacity to respond to the contemplative potentialities of the Christian spirit; the Middle Ages had to institute lay brothers who, in spite of the holiness attained by many of them, are only half-monks, lacking in particular the Office in choir which is at the very heart of Benedictine life, or more precisely, of all monastic life in community. If we give a clerical character to the monastery that we envisage, this will minimize its value (. . .).[16] I would like to throw wide open to Hindus the gates of a fully monastic life, to open them to all the many people in India who seem to be touched by the call of mysticism.

The conventual prayer would of course be in Tamil, for it should be the source and choice fruit of the private prayer which will fill the day. At the traditional canonical hours, dividing up the times of work (here again we would only have to apply the Holy Rule), we should have, not an exact replica of the monastic Office, but a wise adaptation of it, based on the Psalms, the scriptural Canticles, with readings from the Bible, the Fathers and the lives of the saints. And instead of our magnificent but untranslatable hymns, why not adopt specifically Hindu spiritual compositions? St Gregory the Great told Augustine of Canterbury to preserve for Christ the beautiful temples of idols; could we not preserve for him the beautiful tones inspired in Hindus poets by their deep love for God, even if this is externalized in invocations to Shiva or Kali?

You must be familiar with the experience in China of Père Lebbe, whom I often call the most authentic disciple of St Benedict in our day. His success, based on the very same principles which I am suggesting, has been remarkable; while other foundations in his neighbourhood, where they tried hard to reproduce the European way of life or twentieth-century Benedictinism, are stagnating.

Our life-style will certainly be very austere, much more so than is the case in our French monasteries. This will be no problem for me, quite the reverse. As you say—and as de Nobili, Britto, and those who followed their lead did in the past—we must live as sannyasis, and the life of *sannyāsa* is a Hindu institution which has its own traditional rules to which we should submit. Not indeed that we should set out to compete with Hindu ascetics—on the contrary, as Benedict did long ago, we will have to show the supreme importance of the interior life, and the subordinate place of externals; all the same, there is a minimum to which we must conform, and here again experience alone will be our guide. The Lord will give us the necessary strength. Thank God, I enjoy excellent health, even if the regular life of a monastery has not accustomed me to severe shocks, and my age is quite favourable (I am thirty-seven). . . but above all I trust in the Lord. Besides, I expect it will be possible to find a place with a healthy climate, not too extreme (. . .).

Monastic life cannot be healthy without serious work—"Idleness is the enemy of the soul," says St Benedict—and history shows that laziness is a risk faced by all monks, Christian, non-Christian, western or eastern. In my view work should be both intellectual and manual, according to the individual aptitudes of the monks. For my own part I much prefer intellectual work, but I think we should also bear in mind brothers who may have a more limited intelligence, but are none the less capable of a life of contemplation. In any case the need to support ourselves will probably leave us no option. Gandhi has asked Christian monks to give an example of manual labour. The bishops are asking us for a whole range of intellectual work (books, periodicals, publications, to start with!); and more generally, a rethinking of Christian dogma in Hindu terms, and a Christian reinterpretation of Hindu thought. And this last work attracts me strongly.

Still, whatever work we undertake, I am sure that in accordance with the most healthy monastic tradition it must be kept in its proper place, and not become an end in itself. We do not want to start an agricultural estate, or a centre for stock-breeding, or a publishing house, or a university; if the Lord grants this—and he surely will after two or three monastic generations, as he did in Europe—it will be splendid, but that will not be our aim. We are monks, seeking to enter even in this life into the kingdom of God. St Gregory in his *Life of St Benedict* (c.3) has a sentence which for me is the fundamental monastic motto: "Alone in the sight of the supreme Beholder he lived with himself." All the social usefulness of monasticism (economic, or religious and intellectual), if it is to be kept in its right place, must be a *fruit*, not an end in itself. And our exclusively contemplative aim must be all the more stubbornly defended, because the Bishops will need us and our participation will appear supremely useful. We shall have to protect ourselves in the same way as we are having to do just now in France.

Now—assuming that your verdict is favourable—there are a certain number of practical questions.

> My Father Abbot replied immediately (. . .) to Mgr Mendonça, asking for a declaration that he will accept me, so that he can apply for the indult of exclaustration which I need. He also raised the question of finance. The Monastery, which is in any case poor, is at present faced with repairs (war damage) of the order of several million francs, and can do absolutely nothing for me, either for my journey or for my support in India. And until now Father Abbot has not yet allowed me to take steps with a view to appealing for help.
>
> [Various questions follow, about the journey, expenses, clothing.]
>
> On all these questions I await your advice with an open mind, and also any other practical information that you can give me. This is of course for the transition period. However I, and the brother of whom I have spoken, dream of the day when we will be fully Tamilian, in our dress, in our life and customs, sitting in choir for the psalms in the lotus position—if indeed we ever manage to acquire it!—and taking our meals on banana leaves, seated on the ground . . .
>
> I shall have to send this letter—of necessity a long one—by seamail, as it would cost too much to send by air. I hope it will not take too long to reach you, and that without too much delay I shall know where I stand with regard to the decision which has to be taken, and then—if you still think you can call me—get myself ready for setting off. (. . .) (18.8.47)[17]

Fr Monchanin's reply to this letter is not available, but a few months later he wrote from Kulittalai:

> Is it too late—almost the last day of the month—to wish you a happy new year? It is a long time since I had any news of you. I have been quite ill myself (a very violent attack of ashtma). I have now more or less returned to my normal state. And here I am once more, through the kindness of my Bishop, appointed to Kulittalai. Now I am waiting for you to come—because you have really decided, haven't you, to respond to the call you heard fifteen years ago, to become an Indian in India? We shall start together. I will initiate you into Indian life—and you will initiate me into Benedictine life, because like you I firmly believe that the patriarch of the West must in the purpose of God become the patriarch of the East. His Rule, taken in its original form, is sufficiently flexible to be adapted to every kind of situation and spirituality. (. . .)

After dealing with a number of practical questions connected with Dom Le Saux's journey and arrival in India, he concluded:

> We shall have to begin very simply. . . but we must begin with great hope. (29.1.48)[18]

17. A copy of the original letter provided by Fr Lemarié, subsequently published in *Les yeux de lumière,* 10-19.

18. *Quest,* 71-71.

Arrival

Dom Le Saux's ship reached Colombo (which he may be excused for regarding as part of India) on 14 August 1948, and on the next day he wrote to his family:

> Yesterday evening we arrived off Colombo. Such joy and emotion! Immediately after supper (. . .) I went up on deck and began Vespers (. . .) my eyes fixed on the East. The sun had already set, and at the first psalm I saw a sudden gleam of light, the harbour lighthouse of Colombo. One by one other lights appeared beside it, and soon the horizon was twinkling with a myriad points of fire, a symbol of all those who are waiting and calling. At about 8 p.m. we dropped anchor in the harbour. I was glued to the ship's rail; people tried to talk to me, but I could only answer with difficulty. I had been waiting for this moment for fifteen years! The crescent moon was reflected in the black water, stars were few and the night was dark.
>
> The police came aboard and formalities began. These Sinhalese have perfect courtesy. To simplify matters I shall put myself in the hands of Cook's Travel Agency, who will see that I catch the train at 7.30 this evening. I slept on board last night, but got up very early today, as you can guess! Mass on board for the last time, but already we were in my India (. . .). Mass of the Assumption of our Lady—her entry into the heavenly places, my entry here—in thanksgiving and oblation.
>
> Now it is 9 a.m. Soon you will be getting up and thinking that I am here. I am just about to disembark. I am gathering up my rags of English—Tamil will only be needed tomorrow—and trying to find my way among rupees, shillings and pounds. (. . .) Fortunately (. . .) we shall be five priests taking the train for Madras.
>
> On Tuesday afternoon I shall be at Kulittalai. (. . .) From India with love. (F, 15.8.48)[19]

Next day Fr Monchanin reported to a friend:

> . . . The Benedictine Father has come! I can only praise God . . . in essentials—conception of our mission, understanding of Hinduism and the monastic life—he agrees, *more than I had ever hoped,* with what I—what we—have always desired. (16.8.48)[20]

A few days later he added:

> . . . As the days pass in his company, I wonder more and more at the almost incredible *convergence* of the Father's ideas and my own aspirations. And this is all the more *striking*, because at the human level . . . we are very different. (10,9.48)[21]

With this view Dom Le Saux was in full agreement, as he told his family at the end of a long letter recording his first impressions of India and Kulittalai:

> . . . This correspondence in outlook and thought with the Abbé M. is extraordinary. A providential coming together. The direction of the work to be undertaken becomes clear quite spontaneously. (F, 21.8.48)[22]

19. *Les yeux*, 153-4.
20. Siauve, 184.
21. Siauve, 185.
22. *Les yeux*, 160

3

Dom Le Saux—Swami Abhishiktananda

INITIATION 1948-1950

I was delighted to sense the French atmosphere of Pondi, but how much I felt 'at home' in the rue Dupleix, the Indian quarter (. . .). I have two loves! (Diary, 22.2.49)

What pleased me there [at Tiruvannamalai] above all was to be able to live as an Indian, exactly like one of my brothers, freed from all the respect, and equally from all the restraints, which are imposed by my dress as a European priest. (F. 29.8.49)

[After a musical evening with European friends] It was odd (. . .). It was as if there were two men in the depth of me—one a Hindu, who finds his happiness in the Rig-Veda and the Bhagavad Gita and delights in the recitation of Sanskrit and in Tamil music, and then another 'being', another 'self', who bears in himself a whole experience, literary and social, from a western country. (F, 29.12.50)

DOM LE SAUX began his Indian initiation from his first day at Kulittalai, and set to work preparing himself for the ashram life which he and Fr Monchanin hoped to lead. While continuing the studies which he had begun in France, he made frequent expeditions to different parts of Tamilnadu, in order to discover at first hand India and its people. Despite a certain social diffidence—natural in one whose adult life had been led in such restricted surroundings—he soon learnt to be at home alike with uneducated villagers and with the sophisticated folk of Pondicherry and Bangalore, and with Hindus no less than with Christians. He immersed himself enthusiastically in the life and culture of those whom he began to call 'my people', and above all sought direct contact with them in their spiritual experience.

During these first months in India he wrote a number of long descriptive letters to his family, giving vivid accounts of his experiences. In view of the nature of the material, it has seemed best in this chapter to present it according to subject, rather than to keep to the chronological order as is done in the later chapters.

Learning Indian ways

Dom Le Saux wasted no time in adopting an Indian life-style, with a delight that frequently shows itself in his letters. Four days after arriving at 'Bhakti

Ashram' (Fr Monchanin's presbytery, which consisted of three small rooms with a verandah in front) he wrote:

> . . . If you knew how natural everything seems to me here! It is as if I had lived here since my childhood.
>
> . . . Here I am in an entirely Indian setting. (. . .) Nothing European to spoil it, apart from a few motorcars.
>
> My life here? I am not yet allowed to sleep on a simple mat on the ground; mine is spread on a wooden bedstead, but next week we must change that. I also have a table and armchair—for transitions have to be made gently. But I take my meals in Indian style.
>
> . . . I sleep a lot, even in the afternoon, and in short am waiting until I get used to the country before adopting an ascetic life. This is common sense, all the more because I have to put in heavy intellectual work. (F. 21.8.48)[1]

As European furniture was not normally used by Indians, especially in villages, Dom Le Saux disciplined himself to sleep and live like them as far as possible on the ground. A year later he wrote:

> . . . More and more I am giving up the use of a chair except for writing, and struggle to accustom myself to living on my mat. Would that I had begun this exercise at the age of six months! You must start teaching the lotus position to A. and M. In view of the day when they come here to visit their uncle's ashram. (F, 18.12.49)

He was careful to practise customs which were part of ordinary good manners in Tamilnadu—such as leaving his footwear outside when entering a house, or not touching a cup with his lips when drinking—customs which he noted were commonly disregarded by missionaries and even by Indian clergy.

The diet at Bhakti Ashram was extremely simple, being kept as close to the standard of their village neigbhours as the requirements of health allowed. Dom Le Saux was a vegetarian on principle, but as it was unheard of for a European not to eat meat, there were occasions when courtesy demanded that he should break his rule. So one Christmas in Bangalore he felt bound to accept a meal in which "from the rich soup to the pudding made with eggs there was literally nothing that a *sannyasi* could eat without sinning!" (F, 29.12.50). After some time however his peculiarity in this respect became known, and he was saved from further embarrassment.

His dress at first was a white cotton habit in Benedictine style, but he soon came to prefer the local dress of a simple *veshti* (or *dhotī*), a strip of cotton cloth round the waist, with another strip (*tundu*) over the shoulders in cold weather. In February 1949 (Diary, 23.2.49) he bought his first *kāvi* (saffron cloth)—the outward sign of a *sannyāsī*— and began wearing it on occasions when it seemed suitable. His bishop fully approved, as Fr Monchanin noted with some surprise (29.3.49).[2] Dom Le Saux also soon abandoned the use of the clerical hat and shoes, though he put on sandals when visiting a town like Trichinopoly. His

1. *Les yeux*, 158, 160.
2. Siauve, 187.

simplicity in dress was occasionally misunderstood, and the reaction of some kind-hearted village Christians on one occasion was disconcerting.

> . . . I do not know if I look too poverty-stricken when I go about with bare feet, wearing a kind of large Indian shawl in place of a monastic habit, but the other Sunday they brought thirty rupees to the parish priest (. . .) to have some cassocks made for me! It was useless to protest, there was nothing I could do. It is always a great matter of surprise to see me walking about with bare feet and without a hat or, if in a town I am wearing sandals, to see me removing them before entering a house. (F, 9.11.49)

Apart from his studies in Sanskrit and the Hindu Scriptures, Dom Le Saux gave much time to learning spoken Tamil and English, in which he was helped by a young man who was lodging at the presbytery. By Christmas 1948 he felt able to begin hearing confessions and preaching in Tamil. In the following July he spent a month in a village, concentrating on improving his colloquial Tamil:

> . . . It seems that Tamil is at last beginning to come to me—none too soon; I begin to regain a little hope in this connection. (F, 1.8.49)

Again at the end of August he went to Trichinopoly, intending to spend three months in language study (F, 29.8.49), but this proved less profitable than he had hoped, and he gave up after six weeks. He suffered from a slight impediment in his speech which always caused him difficulty in enunciating clearly, but he persevered in his efforts to master the intricacies of Tamil:

> . . . I continue to pass my days gossiping in Tamil, so as little by little to fix these sounds in my head. (F, 18.12.49)

Villages and village churches

During his first two years Dom Le Saux visited many parts of Tamilnadu, acquainting himself with the life of towns and villages. In several places he came to know the village Christians and their pastors, appreciating the hospitality with which he was received and recognizing the quality of their faith, but sad to find them so isolated from their Hindu neighbours.

His first Christmas was spent in a village near Kulittalai:

> . . . I am going to Sinnandipatti (. . .) for Christmas. I must serve my apprenticeship in hearing confessions in Tamil. (F, 21.12.48)
>
> . . . (on Christmas Eve) at 6 p.m. I went to the confessional, feeling slightly nervous. The confessional was a string bed set up on end in the verandah of the presbytery (. . .) and for two hours I listened and tried to understand. I must admit that it was rather hard work but, all the same, without it all those good people would not have received communion at midnight. (. . .) At 11 p.m. I said matins, not without melancholy recollections of the beautiful chanting at Kergonan. And at midnight I had the joy of intoning the *Gloria* (. . .) for it was a sung Mass that they wanted. (. . .) Then how could one fail to say a few words at this Mass? I had prepared myself for this with much trepidation, and was quite surprised at myself when after the Gospel I turned round at

> the altar and began to speak out in front of a full church, using this strange new language. I spoke of my joy and their joy, and of the joy of God himself at his coming among us. There was an excellent silence, which rarely happens in Indian churches. It seems that a good many of them understood at least the outline of the sermon, for naturally there were plenty of mistakes in pronunciation. (F, 15.1.49)

There was one particular village near Dindigul, called Kosavapatti, of which the parish priest (Fr Arokiam) was a close friend of Fr Monchanin. Several times in 1949 Dom Le Saux was his guest, the first occasion being in February. The bishop had sent him away to recuperate after an illness

> . . . with a Tamil priest whom I know, where I get rest, good milk and enough to eat. (. . .) He is a priest who is very interested in the monastic life (he knows French), and I have some hope that he may join us. (F, 13.2.49)

He returned in July, intending to stay for only three days, but gladly yielded to his host's insistence that he should remain for a month. This time he was surprised to find himself a centre of attraction to the boys of the village:

> . . . I am constantly surrounded by a crowd of boys. (. . .) I actually had to come to India to discover how much I can be at home with a gang of urchins. Some of them are very gentle, and come up so charmingly to take my hand, while others are always ready for a scrap, and yet with me become lambs—to the astonishment of the *frangi* [European] priest. (F, 1.8.49)

He describes outings with these young friends, who called for him after school and competed for the privilege of taking him off to the fields, where they would climb the coconut palms and regale him with coconut milk. A European priest who went about barefoot and with head uncovered, sat on the ground like every one else, and also had a smattering of Tamil, was indeed a rarity. No wonder it was difficult to keep the number of his followers within bounds; one day he set out alone and returned with a party of forty-six!

Now as later the poverty of the villagers made a deep impression on him, and he frequently referred to it.[3] Wages were so low that he could not conceive how they managed to live; on an average a man earned one rupee a day, a woman half of that. At Kulittalai his own simple diet cost almost one rupee daily; yet one of his friends had to house, clothe and feed a family of seven on a monthly salary of Rs. 75.

> . . . How do you expect Communism not to prevail here? Yesterday evening I delighted one of my urchins by giving him a vest and shorts. The poor lad did not even have a single extra pair of shorts to change into when he did his washing. This same boy on Sunday had to be satisfied with a handful of rice in the morning to last him the whole day, and his case is far from unique. How do you suppose that one

3. Such poverty never ceased to move him and, as far as his means allowed, he quietly gave practical expression to his sympathy. For instance, he continued to send help to a family in Tamilnadu to the end of his life.

> could take one's meals with pleasure in the midst of this wretchedness, or fail to reduce one's personal expenditure to the minimum? (. . .) I am afraid to help anybody, because there are always ten or twenty more in the same plight. (F, 1.8.49)

During his stay in this village with its large Christian population the feast of St James was observed with a procession of cars which were dragged by hand to every part of the village, this being "an old Indian custom, shared by Hindus and Christians". The priests were woken at midnight by drums and fireworks, but apart from blessing the cars and the sandal-water had little else to do.

In November Dom Le Saux visited Kosavapatti again for the feast of the Departed:

> . . . Here All Saints is not a holiday, but the next day (Nov.2) is one of the greatest feasts of the year. There are as many communions as at Christmas. For my part I had to hear fifty confessions—naturally in Tamil—in the evening and next morning. People may say that it is the priests who invented confession; so far I have not been aware of this, but I must say that this sustained attention is very taxing. In the evening there is Benediction in the cemetery (. . .). On the graves they place lights and incense. During the prayers crackers are being continually exploded. Also on the graves heaps of other things—rice, maize, millet, fruit—which are later distributed to beggars. (F, 9.11.49).

Christian ashrams and religious houses

In view of the novelty of their ideas for the ashram the two founders could scarcely hope to find models among the existing religious communities in South India, as the great majority were thoroughly western in their life-style and laid more stress on active works than on contemplation. There were however two communities that interested them, being purely Indian foundations and also very austere; one was the community at Siluvaigiri, the other was the Rosarian house at Vadakankulam.

Siluvaigiri ('Hill of the Cross') is near Salem, about fifty miles to the north of Kulittalai. Dom Le Saux visited it first in November 1948 and again in January 1949. To reach there he and his guide had to cross the Kavery in a kind of coracle and then, after a four-hour bus journey, were setting out to walk the last three miles when they were benighted in a Christian village, whose priest insisted on their staying in his house.

> . . . Next morning we found a bus which deposited us at Siluvaigiri at 8.30. Imagine a vast amphitheatre of mountains with a river flowing down the middle, beside which the road runs. To reach the ashram you have to cross the river by the ford. A large building, very shabby, very poor, serves as the church; round it in lean-tos are the refectory, hall of studies, dormitories, cells. I have already told you about this attempt at a monastic life with a view to missionary work in the undeveloped

> dioceses in North India. There are two Malayali priests with about twenty young men whom they are preparing for the priesthood and for monastic life. I was so kindly received there last November that I have been in a hurry to return. I spent three very happy days there. (F, 15.1.49).

At the end of June Dom Le Saux accompanied Fr Monchanin to some centres in the south of Tamilnadu—Tuticorin (associated with St Francis Xavier) and Tirunelveli. At Vadakankulam they stayed with the Rosarians, a kind of Indian Trappists, who observed almost total silence in their simple laborious life. Dom Le Saux had a long talk with their Superior, 'a real saint':

> . . . He was keen to meet an authentic European monk and to learn how western monks live. Once more I have realized the advantage of having lived for twenty years in a monastery before undertaking anything here. In the monastic tradition there is a balance and an experience which is difficult to acquire by oneself. (F, 18.7.49)[4]

Dom Le Saux next went on alone to Manapār (south of Tuticorin), where he said Mass in a cave on the seashore in which Xavier had often stayed. Then he turned north to the Jesuit seminary (for S. Indian scholastics) at Shembaganur near Kodaikkanal. Here he received a warm welcome and was immediately requested to give some talks. He tried in vain to excuse himself on the ground of his poor English, but soon found himself having to address large groups of students on Gregorian chant and on the projected ashram.

> . . . There is nothing like being thrown in at the deep end, that is to say, finding oneself suddenly compelled to speak without any preparation in a language that one does not know! But that at least shows you that here too my welcome has been extremely friendly. At the end of two days they truly regarded me as one of themselves. There is among them a ferment of love for India together with a desire for life in Indian style, which the (. . .) do not really understand, but which thrills a certain number of (*words missing in photostat*). They no longer feel that they are on their own, and for my part I sense that my enterprise is supported by parallel longings. But I also feel how great is my responsibility here. It is not only that the monastery has to be launched, but this monastery must crystallize around itself a mass of latent desires. That which a Jesuit, having to carry with him his whole Order, would have difficulty in starting, I am able to do, as I am on my own. Then from this beginning which I have to establish, if it succeeds, various analogous movements will spring up which should give this South Indian mission—more or less stagnating at present—a new impulse. The fact is that now we must boldly live in an Indian fashion, think and pray in an Indian fashion, otherwise we shall always be regarded as foreigners, and no one will have any wish for Christ. (. . .) It was a joy at Shembaganur to work out common projects for the future. I was so well received there that I am invited to return in December to give

4. Fr Monchanin described their trip in a letter of 25/26.6.49; Siauve, 190-191.

> some lessons on Gregorian chant, and we are full of plans for that occasion. (F, 18.7.49)[5]

First contacts with Hindu ashrams

The two priests well understood that, if their ashram was to be authentic, they needed to gain experience of the life of Hindu ashrams. A few weeks after Dom Le Saux arrived, Fr Monchanin took him one day to see the neighbouring Ramakrishna Tapovanam (ashram):

> . . . This morning the monk of St Benedict went on pilgrimage to see the monks of Ramakrishna, a celebrated Hindu mystic who died fifty years ago. Such visits interest me enormously, but are not to be advertised either in France or in India, for no one would understand. It is ten miles from here. A very kind reception and a warm invitation to return. A place of marvellous peace, a wood on the banks of the Kavery. (. . .) But alas, how far these people are from us; they speak of Christ with admiration and read the Bible; but for them Christ is only one of the many manifestations of God on earth—Krishna, Buddha, Christ, Ramakrishna . . . They cannot understand that it is obligatory to have a definite faith, a fixed creed, and to belong to the Church. The nearer I come to these Hindus, the more I feel them at the same time close to me in their loyal search for God, and far from me in their psychological inability to admit that Christianity is the only authentic means of coming to God. (F, 16.9.48)

Fr Monchanin, commenting on the same visit, noted:

> . . . (Dom Le Saux) senses, quite independently of me, the human *impossibility* of the conversion of a Hindu who is truly Hindu (. . .): the more spiritual a Hindu becomes, the further in a sense he distances himself from Christianity. (17.9.48)[6]

Dom Le Saux clearly recognized that, at least at the intellectual level, Hinduism and Christianity are not compatible, and had no interest in superficial attempts to harmonize the two faiths. But the perceived gulf between Hindus and Christians came to him as a challenge, a barrier that had to be crossed. He felt an urge to discover for himself the truth in Hindu experience, which could only be done by coming to know spiritual Hindus on their own ground.

Before long he had the opportunity of meeting one of the greatest sages of modern India, Śrī Ramana Maharshi, in his ashram at Tiruvannāmalai. This meeting was to have a profound influence on the whole future course of his life, although its effect did not show itself immediately.

5. The surprising omission of reference to Fr Monchanin in this letter probably reflects Dom Le Saux's realization that in preparing for their foundation he could expect very little practical help from his companion. The latter's age (54), poor health and profoundly unworldly disposition made this inevitable, as soon became clear: "My companion is magnificently learned and is capable of marvellous intuitions, even though I fear it may be extremely difficult for him to express them in an orderly and coherent way (he is a man of intuition, not of execution—infer from this my work in the coming foundation)". (L, 22.11.48)
6. Siauve, 185.

The name of Sri Ramana had long been known to him. While in France he had read all the available literature, and hoped one day to have his *darshan.* Fr Monchanin had already visited the ashram once or twice, and, despite his reservations, freely acknowledged that he was deeply impressed:

> We often speak of the Maharshi . . . A truly human being, there is not an *atom* of Christianity in that serene and beautiful spirit. Such examples indicate better than anything else the gulf which I perceive ever more clearly between the *summits* of Christianity and of Hinduism. (31.10.48)[7]

Then, to their surprise, the Bishop himself proposed that they should not merely visit the ashram, but actually stay there. Fr Monchanin called this "a psychological quasi-miracle":

> . . . he is allowing—and even urging—us to study the life of a Hindu ashram *on the spot*. . . . We may stay at Tiruvannamalai (. . .) (22.11.48)[8]

Accordingly, at the end of January 1949, they arranged to spend a week together at the ashram, which lies on the outskirts of the town at the foot of the sacred mountain, Arunāchala. A full account of this visit is given in *The Secret of Arunāchala* (ch.1), which the author based on his first impressions recorded at the time in his Diary (24.1.49).

He arrived in a spirit of expectancy:

> I consider this stay at Tiruvannamalai as a real retreat and at the same time as an initiation into Hindu monastic life. I want to (. . .) enter into the great silence and peace which, as I have read and also been told, is to be found at the ashram. (Diary, 24.1.49)

And, as they sat among the crowd of devotees during the public *darshan,*

> . . . I concentrated on looking with deep attention at this man of whom I had read and heard so much. This visit could not fail to be a high point in my life. (. . .) This man had a message for me, a message which, if not conveyed in human words, would at least be spiritually communicated. (*Secret,* 4)

His first impression of the Maharshi was however somewhat disconcerting. He was irked by the extremely reverential atmosphere of the proceedings and by the constant use of the word '*Bhagavān*' ('Lord') in addressing or referring to Sri Ramana. (Later he came to understand it in its context.) He was also disappointed that Sri Ramana "seemed so natural, so 'ordinary', a kindly grandfather, shrewd and serene, very like my own (. . .) I did not know what to make of him. (. . .) The halo? In vain I strained my eyes trying to see it; all my efforts were useless" (*Secret,* 5,6). But soon afterwards, when Fr Monchanin introduced him

7. Siauve, 291; the following letters on pp. 291-294 throw an interesting light on Fr Monchanin's attitude to Sri Ramana.
8. Siauve, 185; The Bishop's proposal, even if now it no longer appears startling, was certainly bold at that date. He also suggested that they should wear *kavi* and build the ashram chapel in 'Hindu' style (letter of Fr Monchanin of 29.3.49; Siauve, 187). Without the approval and encouragement of their diocesan bishop the ashram could never have been launched, and he continued to support them later, when they were much criticized and misunderstood.

during the midday meal, he noted that "the Maharshi responded with (. . .) a smile that was filled with an unforgettable kindness" (Diary).

During the first day what most impressed him was the profound concentration of some of the devotees, and above all, the 'spell-binding' Vedic chants, sung morning and evening, by which "I simply allowed myself to be held and carried along."

Next morning Dom Le Saux woke with a fever, but all the same went to the *darshan* and continued to contemplate the Maharshi. In the afternoon Fr Monchanin took him to meet Ethel Merstone, a perceptive member of the ashram circle. When he expressed his disappointment, she bluntly told him: "You are not receptive; you must be receptive, open, before Bhagavān" (Diary). And during the evening *darshan,* whether as a result of his fever or because of Miss Merstone's advice, he found that something seemed to release in him "zones of para-consciousness":

> . . . Even before my mind was able to recognize the fact, and still less to express it, the invisible halo of this Sage had been perceived by something in me deeper than any words. (. . .) In the contemporary Sage of Arunachala it was the unique Sage of the eternal India that appeared to me (. . .) It was a call which pierced through everything, rent it in pieces and opened a mighty abyss. (*Secret,* 8-9)

The fever forced him to return to Kulittalai, where he remained in bed for three days. In the Diary he noted that his "dreams were all about Ramana", which he later spelled out in his book:

> . . . My dreams also included attempts—always vain—to incorporate in my previous mental structures without shattering them, these powerful new experiences which my contact with the Maharshi had brought to birth; new as they were, their hold on me was already too strong for it ever to be possible for me to disown them (*Secret,* 9).

(These 'structures' must be the traditional understanding and expression of the Christian faith in which he had been brought up and had hitherto accepted without question. If the Church was where he expected to find the Spirit at work, what was he to make of Sri Ramana?).

In writing to his family about this visit, he merely said:

> . . . Pilgrimage to a Hindu 'saint' who is regarded by Hindus as God himself. Extremely thought-provoking. It is one of the things that I would like to tell you about at length—when I have the time. (F, 13.2.49).

A second visit to Tiruvannamalai

Several months later, after the first anniversary of his arrival in India (15 August), he went to Trichinopoly to renew his residence permit and then for ten days to Tiruvannamalai, this time alone. Meanwhile, unknown to him, Sri Ramana had developed the tumour in his arm which led to his death in the following year. An operation had just taken place, and the ashram authorities were turning visitors away; however, thanks to Miss Merstone's intercession, Dom Le Saux was eventually allowed to stay. When the periods of *darshan* recommenced, they were naturally brief, and he used the extra time for getting to know some of those who could best help him to enter into the Maharshi's teaching, as he explains in *Secret,* 12-14.[9] The account of his experiences which he soon afterwards sent to his family shows how clearly he had begun to perceive the direction in which he was being drawn:

> I must now tell you a story which I shall not write about to K., and even here will only tell to friends who are absolutely trustworthy. I told you in February about my two-day visit to a Hindu ashram where they venerate a kind of living saint. I was always looking out for a chance to return. I spent the whole of last week there. No one knew about it, except my companion at Kulittalai. You can imagine how I enjoyed being able to live entirely as an Indian. I presented myself dressed in white, but from the next morning I put on (*words missing in photostat*). Picture two strips of cloth, of a kind of orange colour (*words missing*), about 1.10 by 1.80 m. One of them is wrapped round the waist and the other is thrown as you please over the shoulders; and that's all. Were my skin not so white, I should be content like most people with the first strip. You can't imagine how comfortable I felt. And everyone seemed to find it so natural. People addressed me as '*Sāmī*'; and '*Sāmī*' is the title given [in Tamilnadu] by Christians to their priests and by Hindus to brahmins and sannyasis. Foreign visitors asked me how many years I had lived in retirement at Ramana's ashram. I took my meals at the ashram—purely Indian, of course—but lived outside. They had chosen for me a small separate room, 3m. by 2m., a kind of outhouse behind a bungalow. In it there was absolutely nothing (in the ashram too, tables, benches and chairs are unknown). For reading and writing I sat on the ground in the opening of the doorway; very often I sat in the posture of meditation, facing the marvellous mountain of Arunachala (or Tiruvannamalai). I only abandoned my silence in case of necessity, or for spiritual conversations with some of the more mystically inclined disciples of Sri Ramana (. . .). How instructive it was to hear these people speaking to me about their spiritual life. They of course knew who I was; it was only the passing visitors to the ashram who took the white *sannyāsī* for a genuine convert to Hinduism.
>
> I often withdrew to the mountain close by, hiding myself in some crevice in the rocks which sheltered me from the sun, and there I meditated in the Indian way. Once I went to look at the hermits on the mountain. There are several caves on the side of the hill, more or less fitted up, where sadhus have lived and still live. At first I did not venture to disturb these venerable ascetics whom I saw motionless at the back of their caves. But one of them, seeing me going away, summoned me by clapping his hands, and so I squatted on a flat stone beside him. We shared some handfuls of peanuts which he had received as alms (for he went down daily to beg his food in the town). He

9. Also referred to in Fr Monchanin's letter of Sept. 1949 (Siauve, 292).

showed me the tomb of a Hindu saint who had lived there several centuries ago. Some fifty years ago Ramana himself passed several years in this cave in total silence. With what joy I meditated a long while, all alone inside this cave. Here I found being lived the same kind of life as that of the old Christian monks of Palestine and Egypt, who lived in mountain caves fifteen centuries before our time. I asked him if by any chance there was some unoccupied cave which I might have. He showed me one, but it was somewhat difficult of access; it was shaped like a dolmen, and one could not stand upright inside it. It would be quite tempting, were it not for the problem of food. Cooking my rice does not appeal to me much. To go and beg for my daily food would certainly be interesting, but for that I would have to abandon my blessed solitude each day. (. . .) One thing I have learnt in these Hindu surroundings is that one cannot be a real *sannyasi* if one keeps anything in reserve for the morrow, be it only two annas or a handful of rice. A '*samiar*" should entrust himself totally to Providence.

I said Mass all alone each morning in my little hut, on a box which I had fixed up for that purpose. And as in any case I am determined to say my Mass, I need a cave where I can stand upright, with a door that can be locked to prevent the profanation of the sacred vessels. Apart from that, I have been strongly advised to return after a few months, to pass the daytime on the mountain, coming down to the town to beg for my food (. . .) and in the evening to lie down and sleep in the porch of some temple (. . .). I now know that in India such an experience is valuable, indeed essential. Only, to try it (in a form that would have to be looked into more closely) would need courage—and permission!

What pleased me there above all was to be able to live as an Indian, exactly like one of my brothers, freed from all the respect, and equally from all the constraints, which are imposed by my dress as a European priest. I passed a week in marvellous peace, and have penetrated far deeper than ever before into the spirit of my Hindus, and so have understood better what India expects of me.

. . . What a profound joy to be totally one of my people, and what a profound joy to be so easily all alone before God. Only, if the Archbishop of Pondicherry (under whom this place comes) had learnt of it, what a scolding I should have had! My heart is now divided between the sacred river (Kavery) and the sacred mountain (Arunachala). (F, 29.8.49).

Hindu temples

In addition to ashrams Dom Le Saux also visited a number of the great temples in South India, familiarizing himself with their architecture and iconography, and above all seeking to appreciate the worship that was offered in them. Sympathetic as he was, he was still feeling his way in a totally new spiritual world. His background, and the natural fear of causing scandal to other Christians, made him uncertain how he should behave when asked to participate beyond a certain point. His bold approaches led him sometimes into embarrassing situations. For example, during his trip to the south of Tamilnadu in June 1949 he stopped at Tiruchendūr and was allowed to enter the sanctuary, even though they could see that he was not a Hindu. But he found that he was expected to apply to his forehead the sacred ash of Shiva; and though he realized that it was in principle like taking holy water at the door of a church,

> . . . I am afraid that to do that would have been a bit too much. However my brahmin himself placed the ash in my hand and explained how I should rub it on my forehead . . . This was just like what happened on another day, when I had been allowed to enter the innermost place of worship just at the moment when the celebrant turned round to distribute to the faithful the flowers and fruit with the ashes of what had been burnt in the offering. I was discreetly withdrawing (when he said): "Come in! Come in!" But that I could not do, and he was quite upset! (F, 18.7.49).

In October Dom Le Saux persuaded his slightly unwilling companion to join him on an expedition to the great temples of Chidambaram, Kumbakkonam and Tanjore, which in the event was enjoyed by both of them.[10]

> . . . [At Chidambaram] they were very liberal and showed us everything. They even wanted to give us rice and cakes presented to the images. You can understand that all the same our devotion could not go as far as that! (F, 9.11.49).

He found himself in an even more difficult situation in the following February when, clad in *kāvi*, he followed a group of children into the inner sanctuary of the temple at Srīrangam (carefully averting his eyes from the notice which prohibits the entry of all non-Hindus). After the children left,

> . . . I was pushed into the corridor; I resisted, they insisted, and the priest took up a tray containing camphor (. . .), set it alight, recounted the glories of Sri Rangam Nādar [i.e., Vishnu], and began to offer a *pūjā* in my honour. . . I have never had such good treatment but, all the same, it was nothing doing, for I should have had to make the *anjali*, prostrate, spread my hands over the flame and bring them to my eyes, put the ashes on my forehead, etc . . . I protested—horror, indignation! "But you never asked me . . . I have often entered temples!" Finally I excused myself as well as I could in Tamil and English, made any number of *namaskāram*—and my confession of faith did not rate a martyr's crown . . . Even so, it is rare for one of the 'barbarians' to have approached so close to the Lord Sri Ranga. (F, 26.2.50).

After some time Dom Le Saux came to terms with his inhibitions, at least in connection with the austere symbolism of Saiva worship. But he never seems to have felt at home with luxuriant externals of Vaishnavism.[11]

10. Fr Monchanin refers to the tour in letters of 16.10.49, 1.11.49 (Siauve, 194, 195).
11. See *Guru and Disciple*, 33; new edition (1990), 16.

The launching of the ashram

As he travelled about, Dom Le Saux constantly discussed their plans for the ashram with anyone who was interested, and was on the look out for possible recruits, especially among the diocesan clergy. One of these was his host at Kosavapatti, Fr Monchanin's friend Fr Arokiam, of whom there was some hope that he might join them (F, 13.2.49). Another who showed interest was a converted Parsi, a rich businessman who, though he did not join them, helped them in various ways.

On a visit to Pondicherry in February 1949 (Diary, 20.2.49) Dom Le Saux had a long talk with the Archbishop, Mgr Colas, about their plan. The Archbishop would have liked to see a regular Benedictine foundation started with six European monks. But Dom Le Saux explained that in the circumstances there was no hope of obtaining so many monks, and persuaded him that it would be more practical to aim at something simpler and more experimental, an ashram of three members, one of them (if possible) an Indian.

Yet even one Indian member proved difficult to find, as Fr Monchanin lamented:

> . . . If only God would send us one day the Indian companion, without whom nothing can be built! *Two* Europeans is more than enough, but *not one* Indian! (29.3.49)[12]

On his travels round the diocese of Trichinopoly Dom Le Saux was also searching for a suitable site for the ashram, and inspected several that were proposed. The most promising of these was an old mango grove beside the Kavery, only one and a half miles from Kulittalai, separated from the village of Tannirpalli by the main road to Trichinopoly. This had been offered by one of Fr Monchanin's parishioners, and as early as January 1949 Dom Le Saux mentioned that he had his eye on it (F, 15.1.49).

By the end of 1949 they felt that the time had come to launch out, even though much remained uncertain. As Fr Monchanin said:

> . . . The Father and I have decided to start in the spring—even if there are only two of us—the modest beginning of an ashram. It will be at Tannīrpalli (. . .) on the bank of the Kavery; two cells, a chapel of mud and thatch. *Within the ashram* we shall wear *kāvi.* Two priests — one from Trichi, already tested (but not very strong), another (very young) from Kumbakonam—*seem* to want this kind of life. Will they come? The Father hopes so. Less sure myself. Even if alone, we shall make a start. We have the priceless advantage of a Bishop who, without fully understanding us, leaves us free to launch out. (Dec. 1949)[13]

One uncertain factor was finance, and Dom Le Saux was specially concerned about how the ashram was to be supported:

> . . . In my next letter I will give you news about my first steps towards getting installed at Tannirpalli. But from now on the problem

12. Siauve, 187.
13. Siauve, 196.

> of money is going to raise its head again, as it did two years ago in connection with my coming to India. America is slow in replying [i.e., to inquiries about arranging for mass-stipends], and I do not know if my Parsi friend will be able to help . . . The Lord will attend to that, I am not worried. (F, 28.1.50)

A month later the construction of the huts had begun, but was proceeding very slowly:

> . . . I cannot yet send Papa any photos of my hermitage. In the last three weeks I have only got two days of work. The framework of three huts has been completed; there is nothing left to do except to make their roofs and walls of bamboo. Given two days of work, all would be finished—but in India everything goes so slowly. (F, 26.2.50).

But Dom Le Saux had to restrain his natural impatience, because the construction was being paid for by their proprietor, who was also rumoured to be intending to make a gift to the ashram of the mango grove itself.

The huts were eventually completed, and 21 March, the feast of St Benedict, was fixed for the inauguration of the ashram. Dom Le Saux's letter in which he described this to his family is missing, but Fr Monchanin wrote of it:

> . . . Yesterday was moving. I slept in the wood for the first time (fewer mosquitoes than in the presbytery at Kulittalai!) and nearly all our parishioners came to celebrate the inauguration. After the *Veni Creator* [hymn to the Holy Spirit], the Father's Mass (rustic altar in the open, set against the side of one of the huts, decorated with greenery and *kavi* material). I preached at it, saying goodbye to the people—not without a pang—and explaining our aim. Atmosphere of spiritual sympathy. Then my Mass—and the singing of the *Te Deum* [hymn to the Trinity]. I put on the orange robe (. . .) and that did not seem to shock anyone. (23.3.50)[14]

The official name of the ashram was "Saccidānanda Āshram" or "Eremus Sanctissimae Trinitatis" (Hermitage of the Most Holy Trinity);[15] but this was less commonly used than "Shāntivanam" (Grove of Peace), the name which they gave to the mango grove.

As their emblem they adopted the cross of St Benedict with the "OM" at the centre, and round the edge in Sanskrit: "Peace—Glory to Saccidānanda".

Further, in accordance with Indian tradition, they took new names for themselves. Fr Monchanin's name was "*Parama Arūbi Ānanda*" ("Bliss of the Supreme Formless One"), a sign of his special devotion to the Holy Spirit. Dom Le Saux became "*Abhishikteshvarānanda*" ("Bliss of the Anointed One, the Lord").[16] Such names symbolized their intention to live their faith close to the heart of

14. Siauve, 197.
15. *Saccidānanda—i.e., Sat* (being), *cit* (awareness), *ananda* (bliss); one of the deepest Hindu insights concerning God, with trinitarian overtones which are drawn out in Abhishiktananda's book of the same name.
16. *Abhiṣikteśvarānanda*— composed of *abhiṣikta* (anointed, i.e., Christ); *īśvara* (Lord); *ananda* (bliss). Sannyasis frequently have names ending with '*ānanda*'.

India in the style of Indian monks. Fr Monchanin does not seem to have made much use of his new name, but Dom Le Saux was increasingly known by his Indian name, later shortened to "Abhishiktānanda", which will therefore be used in the following pages.

4
Shantivanam—Arunachala

(1950-1957)

> We are really living a hermit's life here. I would never have thought that my dreams of 1934 would be so completely realized. (F, 24.9.50; after the first six months at Shantivanam)
>
> This Arunachala is strange . . . Never in my life have I felt so much at peace, so joyful, so near to God, or rather one with God, as on this mountain. (F, 21.8.52; after living for several months in a cave)

Shantivanam Ashram

THE ASHRAM in which the two swamis began to live in March 1950 was designed to be of the utmost simplicity. As Abhishiktananda described it in his Memoir of Fr Monchanin:

> The material structures were of the most primitive kind. The hermits each enjoyed a separate hut screened with bamboo and roofed with coconut leaves. One of the huts had a penthouse for the celebration of Mass. Naturally the cells were bare of furniture. On the sandy floor a few bricks had been laid against the damp, on which they sat and slept. The first rains did not fail to bring a number of disenchantments . . . (*SPAA*, 18)

It is therefore somewhat surprising to find Fr Monchanin referring to their cells as "too spacious and almost luxurious" (23.3.50) and "too luxurious . . . so comfortable" (1.4.50).[1] Both he and Abhishiktananda were determined not to live on a higher standard than that of their village neighbours; but for the sake of their health and in order to make it possible for others to share their life, the latter soon found it necessary to provide the ashram with a minimum of conveniences. Fr Monchanin was a genuinely unworldly man—"permanently lost in the higher spheres", as his friend once said (F, 21.1.51)—and with all his great gifts was quite incapable of being practical. The task of first building and then maintaining the ashram, as well as of managing its scanty resources, inevitably fell to Abhishiktananda, who occasionally grumbled about it to his family:

> . . . Do you realize how complicated a matter it is to prepare a place where one need no longer occupy oneself with worldly matters? One tries in vain to be small, simple, poor. How complicated it is, especially

1. Siauve, 198.

> when you generally have to act through intermediaries. During the five or six weeks that I have been here, I have constantly been occupied with some trifle. Our hovels begin to have a palatial air. So my floor of earth and sand and my bed of bricks laid side by side on the ground have been transformed into luxurious cement. The reason is that on a day of heavy rain—the first that I have experienced in my forest life—my cell became the refuge of all sorts of poor creatures that the rain had expelled from their burrows, in particular, two enormous scorpions (. . .) which chose to settle between the bricks, one at my head, the other at my feet! Now they have to enter by the door, and there are no more crevices where they can hide. (. . .) A sumptuous bathroom has been built for the days when there is no time to go and bathe in the sacred river. (. . .) The bathroom in fact is in the open air, simply surrounded by palm leaves. Over the well we have fixed a pulley, as that seems more convenient. And so on. (. . .)
>
> But we do not possess a rake, a shovel or a wheelbarrow, and I must admit that just now I long for these instruments of European civilization. It would be so simple to clear up the leaves in our wood. (. . .)
>
> We do not yet have a chapel, we always say Mass on a verandah. (F, 2.6.50)

Before long they had to replace with solid walls the bamboo screens of their huts, which were eaten up by white ants (termites) and gave ready access to snakes; and also to tile the roof of their kitchen to protect their stores from the monkeys "who considered themselves the permanent guests of the new inhabitants of their wood" (*SPAA*, 19). By June the move from Bhakti Ashram in Kulittalai was completed with the installation of the library in a temporary wooden structure.

The ideal of the Ashram

The two founders of the ashram had a clear perception of the aim of their undertaking—it was simply to *be* in the presence of God, without any further object at all. They saw this to be in line with the central tradition, alike of Christian monasticism and of Hindu *sannyāsa.* As Abhishiktananda said in the Memoir:

> More than anything else indeed the Christian *sannyāsī* ought to be *contemplative.* Contemplative life does not in the first place mean piety (*bhakti*), or the endless recitation of prayers, even liturgical ones. In this respect, though the Benedictine Rule may usefully provide for the organization and development of the life of Christian ashrams, it is further (cp. *Rule*, ch. 73) towards the contemplative ideal of the Desert Fathers that the Christian *sannyāsī* ought to tend, as it is embodied in the life and precepts of St Antony, Arsenius, John Climacus (. . .) The *sannyasi* is one who has been fascinated by the mystery of God (. . .) and remains simply *gazing* at it. (*SPAA,* 35)

Thus they drew inspiration from the Desert Fathers and also from St Benedict himself, when in his cave at Subiaco "alone in the sight of the Supreme Witness, he lived with himself" (often recalled words from the *Life* by Gregory the Great). At the same time they heard equally clearly the call that came to them through India's own agelong quest, embodied above all in "a monastic form which expressed with a realism rarely equalled the absoluteness and the transcendence of the Divine Mystery" (*SPAA*, 32). Accordingly the purpose of Shantivanam

> . . . could not consist in a more or less forced 'adaptation' of western Christian monasticism to the Indian context, but was nothing less than the assumption into the Church of the age-old Indian *sannyāsa* itself. (*SPAA*, 33)

It was natural that they should desire to keep the ashram as simple as possible, and to practise a poverty that was more radical than the formal 'poverty' of western monasticism. In this they were responding to the call of Brahmabandhav Upadhyaya[2] to the Church in India to be truly Indian and to abandon its western 'clothing'. Their poverty was to be an expression of the ideal of *sannyasa,* and at the same time of their identification with India's poor in their present condition. Fr Monchanin held that monks cannot live on a higher standard than that of their neighbours without surrendering any claim to be men of self-denial and asceticism; and that, if postulants were allowed to live more comfortably in their monasteries than they had done in their own homes, this could be a great impediment to sincerity and honesty in their vocations (*SPAA*, 22). Simplicity of life, however, should never be envisaged as a 'mortification', but rather as the unselfconscious consequence of their contemplation, the outward expression of inner freedom.

Daily life in the ashram

The Benedictine Rule divides the monk's day into three roughly equal parts. The principal part is that given to liturgical worship (the 'Divine Office', which is offered at the traditionally fixed times and sets a rhythm to the day) and to private prayer. The other two parts of the day are allotted to manual labour and to study, especially 'spiritual reading' (*lectio divina*).[3]

It seems that Abhishiktananda was at first in favour of following a detailed timetable in the ashram, but was dissuaded by Fr Monchanin, chiefly on the ground that this would not be in keeping with their aim of adapting the Rule to Indian conditions (cp. *Indian Ben. Ashram*, 44). So, for example, in a letter of 15.5.50 Fr Monchanin wrote about silence in the ashram that it " should proceed not from a rule but from an inner necessity". However certain hours of prayer were regularly observed in the ashram, especially at the three '*Sandhyā*' (at the meeting points of day and night and at midday, consecrated for worship by Indian and Christian tradition alike). On these occasions their devotions were enriched with Sanskrit and Tamil texts and songs, and followed an Indian style

2. Brahmabandhav Upadhyaya (1861-1907) was a gifted Bengali thinker and nationalist, who came to Christianity through the Brahmo Samaj. He aimed at "a Christianization of India which would not only respect but integrate all the traditional values of Hindustan", and hoped to see the Indian Church freed from its "hard coating of Europeanism". See *SPAA*, xvii-xix, 23-24; *The Blade* by Animananda (Calcutta, no date); forthcoming books by G. Gispert-Sauch and J.J. Lipner.
3. For *lectio divina,* see *Prayer,* ch. 8.

with regard to posture, greetings, etc. (These experiments prepared the way for later developments in Indianizing the Church's worship which became possible after Vatican II.) The latin Offices, which as priests they were obliged to say, were recited privately (cp. *Indian Ben. Ashram*, 74). Mass was celebrated daily after Lauds, when the faithful from Tannirpalli often came to assist. Early morning and evening also were special times for meditation, either in the ashram or beside the Kavery.

Manual work was virtually impossible for Fr Monchanin owing to his chronic tendency to asthma, and therefore fell mainly to his colleague.

Much time was given to study, theological and indological. Fr Monchanin already had a good library, and continued to receive important new publications as well as periodicals. These they often studied together, and Abhishiktananda no doubt profited greatly from his older colleague's learning and experience.

Their simple vegetarian meals were prepared by a cook (their only employee)—a main meal in the middle of the day, and lighter ones for breakfast and supper. Times of fasting (Lent and before certain Feasts) were observed according to the custom of Indian Christians.

For the greater part of the day they remained in silence, apart from times when they met after the main meal or after tea (*I.B.A.*, 58-60). At these times they spoke with visitors and discussed their reading or the affairs of the day. The deep peace (*shānti*) of the ashram particularly impressed those who came to it.

As normally there were only two members of the ashram, when one of them was away (Fr Monchanin at Pondicherry or Abhishiktananda at Arunachala, for example), the other would necessarily live in solitude—a state of affairs with which they were perfectly content. Only for one period, during 1955-1956, did the ashram have a full community life.

Visitors

Visitors soon began coming to Shantivanam. From the neighbouring village came Christians and Hindus, the latter chiefly for the silent *darshan* of the swamis, especially of Fr Monchanin. There were parties from convents and parishes in the diocese, and friends from Pondicherry and further afield. Later, as they became better known, they were sought out by Europeans who were passing through India, including 'seekers', often disillusioned with the Church as they knew it, who hoped to find something to satisfy their spiritual hunger. Some visitors were merely curious, others were critical, but most appreciated the peace and contemplative atmosphere of the ashram (*SPAA*, 40-41). Few however showed any inclination to share their life permanently.

Some Hindus also came to see what was happening at Shantivanam, having heard of this unusual new venture. To their great surprise, only a few weeks after the opening they even had an application for admission from one of their brahmin visitors:

> . . . I do not know what the Bishop (. . .) would say if he heard. A real Hindu monk, a brahmin wearing *kāvi.* He has been captivated. However he finds our life too austere, we are beyond the level even of holy people. The other day he told us very seriously that we shall

> certainly never have to be reborn (. . .). In Hindu terms he could not have put it more strongly. (F, 29.4.50)

The prospect of welcoming Swami Kaivalyananda Saraswati as a guest of the ashram delighted them, as his presence would provide an opportunity of close contact with living Hindu tradition. His first visit was in July:

> . . . For the past week we have had a companion. Certainly for a limited time, as our Christians would never understand. He is a genuine Hindu *sannyāsī* who is delighted with our hermitage, sharing our meals and our silence. His company is extremely instructive; it is one thing to read books, and quite another to converse with a Hindu who is truly seeking the Lord, though by ways very different from ours. One feels what a gulf there is. Yet this man is happy with us. To be able to live with us, he has to make sacrifices which for a Hindu are considerable; for he is a brahmin and is eating with non-brahmins and eating food prepared by a non-brahmin. As a rule they prefer to fast rather than defile themselves in this way. (F, 19.7.50).

The swami spent several other periods at the ashram, but is not heard of again after November, when Fr Monchanin said:

> . . . Our friend K. returned to us, simple and good as always. But his visit was cut short; he caught cold, finds our wood too damp, our life too austere (though it is hardly that!), and our food *sāttvik* [i.e., pure; perhaps too plain, unspiced?]. (20.11.50)[4]

The two hermits made light of their austerity, and could not understand why their visitors regarded them as such great ascetics. Abhishiktananda assured his family that "we live in luxury compared with the general standard of living", and referred to some snapshots of the ashram which he had sent them: "You will at least take note that I do not give the impression of being in bad health." (F, 19.7.50).

Making the ashram known—July to September 1950

Despite the support of their bishop, the aims and way of life of the two hermits were misunderstood in many Christian circles, from some of which came "bitter criticisms of the infant ashram" (*SPAA*, 27).

> . . . So long as our ideas were mere projects, there was almost universal sympathy. But when people saw them set out in black and white, and above all when they saw us living in a manner so contrary to the accepted conventions (among Christians), what would result? We could very well exist almost unnoticed for two months. But the day would come when we would have to show ourselves. In May I had a talk with the Bishop which somewhat disturbed me . . . So we had prepared a memorandum for the Bishop, in which in thirty long pages we told him our object, with our reasons for it, and submitted the

4. Siauve, 204.

details of our daily life. What would come of it? Above all, what would be said by those whose advice he sought?

However, at the end of July he came to Kulittalai for confirmations. He returned our memorandum without the slightest criticism; or rather, he told us the criticisms of various Jesuit Fathers whom he had consulted: "Standard of life too low", had said these good fathers. "They don't understand a thing," said the Bishop; "you are quite right to act in this way." He was delighted with our *kavi* dress, and even (most amazing) with the rosary that we wear round our necks, which exactly resembles those worn by Shivaite ascetics. He took my *tundu,* put it over his shoulders, put the rosary round his neck, and would not be satisfied until a photographer came and took us all three. His idea is to send an article with the photo to Catholic journals in India.[5] He went out for a walk with us in Kulittaiai—we with bare feet and wearing *kavi*—and received the *sandippu* with us on either side; that is to say, in the evening after the Confirmation the parishioners came to greet him and garlanded him (and us) with flowers (. . .). So from now on he is totally 'committed' to us. He makes our work his own, and worries himself very little over the criticisms which could be made against *him* in our connection, even by other bishops.

So after this, when it is appropriate, we are to go round the diocese in *kavi*; as regards other dioceses, that will depend on the local bishop. A week later we had to go to Trichy (till now we were disguising ourselves in white when we went there). First stop, the big Jesuit college. Some people were in the know—stupefaction, enthusiasm, politeness, reserve . . . depending on who it was. The Rector asked us to take our meal separately (actually we are launching out on a path—of total indianization—in which many young Jesuits see the salvation of a mission that is stagnating; and these young Jesuits meet plenty of trouble). So you can imagine the 'Boom' caused in these extremely conformist surroundings by the arrival of two strange figures dressed exactly like two sannyasis (like two 'pagans', as people say holding their noses). Besides, our absence from the meal was far more conspicuous than our presence would have been, and you can guess how the students gazed at us . . .

At the Holy Cross convent (teaching sisters, mostly French, our good friends) an enthusiastic reception. (. . .) From there we went to buy Mass wafers at the Convent of St Anne, entirely Tamil sisters with limited education; they could not have been more appalled by seeing the Devil himself walking in! (. . .) At the Bishop's house the priests received us very kindly, and the Bishop was very happy at the small stir which we aroused in Trichy—that is, among the pious folk there (. . .). Our hopes are fulfilled, more than fulfilled. Next month we are going to have our memorandum (. . .) printed (at present someone is correcting the English), so as to make known our object and its implementation,

5. This photograph was published in *Satya Bodhini* and in SPAA. See Illustration 3.1.

and perhaps to awaken those few vocations which we need to make a start.

. . . As to our chapel, we have some fine plans, but we cannot start until we have in hand Rs. 1000 or 1500.

. . . The food problem is getting serious in India, at least in the south. We are getting—even in the middle of a rice-growing area—only enough for three meals a week. At present we are also getting wheat, which enables us to have chapātis for supper . . . But the people do not like wheat, they are not used to it. As far as we are concerned, we have no difficulty, because our proprietor will always supply us with rice at a cheap rate or even free (though we are taking care not to become dependent). But it is hard for poor people (. . .). (F, 21.8.50)

The memorandum was not however printed until over a year later, by which time it had become a booklet of 90 pages. In September Abhishiktananda wrote:

. . . Fr Monchanin went to Pondi last Tuesday. I have sent the cook to spend a week with his mother, and am enjoying complete solitude in my wood (. . .). My big job is our famous booklet. From the 10-20 pages which it must originally have contained, it has now grown to over sixty. It has the appearance of a manifesto.[6] But I fear it will go over the heads of three-quarters of its readers. Then this English! The first time that I have the chance of getting into print, it has to be in English! And I do not have the gift of tongues. Fortunately we have friends [to help] (. . .). But we have to argue over every phrase, so as to be quite sure that in changing the words (correcting the mistakes) they are not also changing the sense. Then again, whenever I recopy the text after correction, I add something new. Someone will have to tear it away from me. I plan to go to Trichy tomorrow to give it to the Bishop for censorship before having it printed. Then we have to find Rs. 200 for the printing. I told Fr M. not to come back from Pondi until he has collected enough money. The worries of founders, and now of authors!

We are really living a hermit's life here. I would never have thought that my dreams of 1934 would be so completely realized . . .

There was certainly a need for the memorandum to meet the criticisms that were made of the ashram—lack of realism, syncretism, failure to do anything useful, like cultivating the land, opening a dispensary, doing missionary work or conducting research. While some praised them uncritically,

. . . there are naturally differences of opinion about us. Some frankly condemn us; those who make Europeans their ideal naturally find this example of indianization somewhat shocking. The priest of the most backward village in the diocese says of us: "As if we were not living in the 20th century!" (. . .) One of his parishioners is very anxious about our fate (. . .): "These poor priests, how sad to see them becoming Hindus; someone must certainly have put a spell on them!" But on the whole people are now in our favour, starting with the Bishop. Besides,

6. An echo of Fr Monchanin; see his letter of 5.9.50 (Siauve, 202).

our life *seems* so austere (without being so), and that covers everything else. (F, 24.9.50)

More Hindu contacts—late 1950

. . . Got to know a Hindu swami on the other side of the river.[7] One Sunday I went to see him, the next Sunday he came to see me, and at once we were friends. I have spent a week with him. There at least I feel at ease. I do not have to be afraid of scandalizing our Christians by my Hindu ways. Tomorrow I shall go back there. In him I have at last found someone who has practised *yoga*, and I am taking lessons in it. It is extremely instructive. It begins with gymnastic exercises, quite different from those of Europe, as one keeps oneself in very curious postures. The control of breathing, concentration of thought while fixing attention on the space between the eyes, etc. He is teaching me how they sing what for them correspond to our Psalms, etc. It is marvellous to be able to share the life of Hindus in this way. Most valuable experience for trying to discover by what path they will come from their Hinduism, from Shiva and Krishna, to Christ. One 'devotee' who was there in retreat absolutely insisted that I tell him the best way of practising his Hinduism and honouring Shiva and Krishna! You see, the crowning distinction is to become a director of conscience to devout Hindus! (. . .)

I plan next month, if possible, to go north (the Himalayas) to have a direct experience of the life of Hindu monks in one of those towns where three-quarters of the inhabitants are monks, like the Egyptian deserts of long ago.[8] The journey is relatively cheap (Rs. 50 for almost 4000 kms) (. . .) I hear that in those places sadhus are given their food free.

. . . The Bishop is always our best 'supporter'. "You are very bold," the Jesuit Provincial said to him the other day. "There's nothing wrong in that," he replied; "we ought to be bold." Thank the Lord with me (. . .). To think that he approves of my sojourns in Hindu ashrams. More than one bishop would suspend me for less. Yet it is necessary. How else can I obtain personal knowledge of the aspirations, possibilities and needs of my Hindu brothers? Most priests only know them in a quite external fashion; but they accept me so easily and simply, and treat me as one of themselves. I am startled to find myself more at my ease with them, among them, than anywhere else.

. . . I find that, thanks to these exercises, I have gained a remarkable degree of suppleness, and begin to be capable of reaching the so-called 'lotus' position. Soon I shall be able to remain in it. (F, 13.12.50)

7. At Tiruvangirimalai, on the north side of the Kavery.
8. Fr Monchanin did not encourage this plan: "I do not share my colleague's enthusiasm for Rishikesh; a place where sadhus, real or supposedly so (both kinds no doubt), devote themselves to delusive exercises, verging on a mirage." (20.12.50; Siauve, 202-3)

To Bangalore and Pondicherry—December 1950, January 1951

Shortly after this Abhishiktananda went to Bangalore to conduct a ten-day retreat for a recently founded Belgian-English community of sisters. Although he only had one week for preparation, his addresses (29 in all!) were well received. He marvelled at the sisters' ability to understand "my English, which consists of English words pronounced in French". In their convent he could maintain his vegetarian principles, but as the guest of the Bishop on Christmas Day, and later of European friends of Fr Monchanin, he had to admit ruefully that with them it was impossible. (F, 29.12.50).

At the end of the year he left Bangalore for Pondicherry, visiting Kānchīpūram (Conjeevaram) and Mahābalipūram on the way. Having been provided with a 2nd class berth for the night journey, "I slept like a pasha." Back at the ashram he sent his family an account of his trip:

> . . . spent Sunday at Conjeevaram, the ancient capital of S. India in the time of our Merovingians. Those kings have left some splendid temples. I have not so far seen such beautiful ones in India, with a simplicity, a purity of line, that since then has been forgotten. And with that, an extraordinary religious feeling which shines through the architecture itself. (. . .) A brahmin, an old priest, eighty years of age, took me off to his home, and at once I was friends with the gang of his small children. And when I left, he caught hold of my folded hands and brought them up to his forehead (. . .).

Mahabalipuram, "one of the wonders of the world", proved to be less impressive, because

> . . . unfortunately it has been secularized, like Mont St Michel, and people only go there as tourists. It is extraordinarily beautiful, like Conjeevaram, and more so, but the heart is not held by the sense of sacredness as at Conjeevaram.

At Pondicherry (where Sri Aurobindo had recently died) he made some interesting contacts, including a Colombian diplomat, who claimed to remember his previous incarnations and to be capable of travelling in his 'astral body' to Paris or Buenos Aires. (F, 21.1.51)

The Memorandum—January to August 1951

The manuscript of the enlarged memorandum was sent by the Bishop for censorship to a Jesuit. When it was returned in January, Fr Monchanin wrote:

> . . . The Shembaganur censor has examined our manuscript with great care and sympathy. He suggests a few modifications, asks for a revision of the English (complicated and heavy) and a supplementary chapter on the theological basis of the spirituality, in order to eliminate all danger of our position being confused with syncretism. (14.1.51)[9]

9. Siauve, 203.

This chapter, on 'Contemplation', was quickly written by Fr Monchanin and became chapter 1 of the booklet. He described it as "a sort of Christian and anti-pantheist 'profession of faith', so as to guard against the misunderstandings of hasty readers" (29.1.51)[10]

Further corrections and revisions continued for some time. The manuscript was typed in April, and by August was in the hands of the printer at Trichy.

The ashram chapel—January to October 1951

During most of 1951 Abishiktananda's letters to his family made frequent references to the building of the chapel. In January he wrote:

> . . . I think we are at last going to get down to building our temporary chapel. I discussed plans and funds during my journey [Bangalore and Pondicherry]. People have provided Rs. 1000, so we can start. Now it is a matter of collecting materials on the site of the work, and first, of making the bricks.[11] Oh, the anxieties of a 'contemplative'! (. . .) My journey to the Himalayas has been put off (. . .). (F, 21.1.51)

By March the bricks had been prepared and dried, but could not be fired for another month, as woodcutters were not available to cut the wood. Finance was another problem, as it was clear that at least a further Rs. 1000 would be needed. There was an additional uncertainty about the land. The Bishop refused to dedicate the chapel until their proprietor had confirmed his promise to donate the site of the ashram with a legal document, and this was not easily forthcoming.

> . . . How complicated the contemplative life is. I think it would be much easier for me to live as a real *sannyasi,* tramping the roads, or settling near some village, and receiving my daily food as alms. One day I think shall come to this. (F, 4.3.51)

At the end of March, as the bricks were still not ready, he took a fortnight off, spending ten days with the Rosarians, and going on to visit Cape Comorin (Kanyā Kumārī) at the extreme southern point of India. Here he inquired if he might enter the famous temple, and was told that he might, provided he took off his soutane and had bare shoulders. "But I am not a Hindu—look at my outrageously white skin. One can't be a Hindu without being born Hindu!" "White perhaps, but the heart is certainly Hindu!" was the answer in Tamil. However Abhishiktananda had to catch a train before the temple opened in the evening, and reflected that this was just as well, since there was a large Christian settlement close by, and "in India tongues travel faster than trains". (F, 8.4.51)

Building eventually began in May, and the main structure was completed in June.

> . . . Oh, a minute chapel, only nine feet square inside, just enough to hold the altar. In front it will be finished off with a *pāndal,* that is, a roof of palm leaves supported on bamboo poles. Small as it is, my Rs. 1000 will not have been spent in vain. It is the first time in my life that I am

10. Siauve, 203.
11. "Thursday morning the Father returns from Trichy (. . .) to begin the manufacture in our wood of 50, 000 bricks!" Monchanin, 29.1.51 (Siauve, 203).

> really anxious about money. You make plans, calculations, you trust the experts, and finally the cost exceeds your most pessimistic forecasts. It is necessary to be constantly at hand, to prevent the workers from going to sleep, and then to check if they are doing what you asked for. (F, 3.6.51)

The same letter describes the work force which, along with two or three skilled men, included some fifteen to twenty women labourers, employed on fetching and carrying, mixing cement, etc., on a daily wage of 10 annas. Caste-divisions made the supply of drinking water a further complication. As regards finance,

> . . . to do all the work that is planned and is immediately needed (the construction of two more cells near the chapel, a kitchen and . . .), I would require Rs. 1500, which I do not have. In a fortnight I shall find myself with an absolutely empty cash box, and my journey to the Himalayas put off indefinitely . . . (F, 3.6.51)

At the end of August Abhishiktananda had an 'interesting experience'. Fr Monchanin had gone to Pondi ("He has a very definite mission (. . .) to bring back something to recoup our finances"), the cook was on holiday, and there was sickness in the family of their proprietor, so that

> . . . I did not dare to ask them for rice. So I set myself the task of doing my own cooking and was delighted with the result. I had not imagined that it was so simple. (. . .) I am capable of being a real hermit. (F, 24.8.51)

In September the work on the chapel was at last completed, and the deed granting two acres of land to the ashram was handed over. They asked the Bishop to come to bless the chapel and to say the first Mass in it; but

> . . . there is an old trouble between the Bishop and our donor. (. . .) The Bishop is afraid to come. He wants us to have the inauguration unofficially as soon as possible, on some pretext. (F, 26.9.51)

The inauguration eventually took place on 11 October, but without the Bishop. Every effort was made to find a solution, but in vain, and they had to call six other priests for the ceremony.

> . . . "Those who were first invited were not worthy." In the end all went quite well. Besides, the Bishop has nothing at all against us; as far as one can see, he is more upset with himself for being so . . . cowardly. (F, Oct.51)

The chapel was modelled on the small square *mūlasthānam* (sanctuary) of the ancient Chola temple of Magadipettu in Pondicherry, in whose restoration Fr Monchanin had been interested (*SPAA*, 46). Abhishiktananda described their chapel as

> . . . dark and bare, save for an altar and tabernacle of roughly hewn granite and a few oil lamps. Despite the very limited means available, in its simplicity and bareness something had been caught of the sacredness and mystery, the 'numinous' quality which characterizes the sanc-

tuary of a Hindu temple—yet at the same time it was no slavish copy. (*SPAA*, 47)

Publication of the Memorandum—October 1951

The booklet, entitled *An Indian Benedictine Ashram*, was also released on the day of the inauguration of the chapel. Only 500 copies were printed, and nearly 300 were immediately posted to addresses in India and in eighteen other countries outside. The remainder were for sale, "which will help us a little to pay for the printing" (F, Oct. 51). In a letter accompanying one copy, Fr Monchanin wrote:

> . . . I am sending you a little booklet which I have produced with a companion, Fr Le Saux (a Benedictine). It will tell you about our form of life and our deep aspirations. (26.10.51)[12]

It was indeed their common work, even though (apart from the first chapter) almost all the actual writing had been done by Abhishiktananda,[13] who later remarked sadly on the difficulty he had in persuading his brilliant colleague to commit his thoughts to paper (*SPAA*, 43).

Reactions soon began to come in, very favourable on the whole, especially a long review by Fr Bayart, SJ, who "approved (of it) and praised (it) without reserve" (Monchanin, 26.6.52).[14] Encouraged by this, Abhishiktananda began to think of a fuller edition in French, in which he could express himself more freely.

Arrival of two Belgian monks—October, November 1951

In September the community at Siluvaigiri had sent for Abhishiktananda to plan for the reception of two monks who were being sent by the Abbey of St André de Bruges.

> They are afraid that they may find the poverty too great. I replied: "Then I will carry them off to Shantivanam, and on their return to you they will feel like being in a palace!" (F, 26.9.51).

The two monks[15] arrived at the end of October:

> . . . Last week I went again to Siluvaigiri to meet the two Belgian Benedictines who have come to form into a Benedictine community a group of about thirty young Malayalis who have been preparing for the priesthood there for four to five years. I was very happy to find my

12. Siauve, 205.
13. Some bibliographical notes by Abhishiktananda written about 1970 (part of a dossier on publications which he gave to Dr B. Bäumer) confirm that Fr Monchanin's share in the book consisted of the following (all reprinted in *SPAA*):
    Chapter 1 on Contemplation (*SPAA*, 159-170); a note on the "Indian Eschatological Church", p. 31-2 (*SPAA*, 80-82); the page on "Saccidananda", p. 76-77 (*SPAA*, 17-18); the Epilogue, p. 90-91 (*SPAA*, 38-39).
14. Siauve, 206. Fr Bayart's view was in *Clergy Monthly, India Missionary Bulletin*, 1952, 76-81. The book soon went out of print, but in 1964 was republished as *A Benedictine Ashram* by the Times Press, Douglas, Isle of Man (U.K.). Abhishiktananda only learnt of this in time to make a few corrections and add a Preface.
15. Fr Emmanuel de Meester and Fr Dominique van Rollenghen.

> brothers in St Benedict. We got on very well together, and have decided to work in close contact but without merging. For me it is in every way a great 'safeguard". And my future in India is assured in case some difficulty arises from elsewhere. Siluvaigiri is also very poor, but not so completely Indian as we are. They were very anxious at Siluvaigiri about the arrival of the two Europeans. They feared that they (. . .) would want to change everything to European style, and begged me to come myself to receive them and defend the poverty of Siluvaigiri. The two Belgian monks said that they were delighted with what they found, and after the first week began the practice of going barefoot and sitting on the ground. They are due to come to Shantivanam next week and will have the experience there of a totally Indian life-style without any admixture of Europeanism. Then I plan, if my funds are not too low at that point, to take them on a tour for a fortnight round the Hindu temples and monasteries of S. India (. . .). (F, Oct. 51).

In November the two guests came to Shantivanam, and after a week of learning to sleep on a mat, eat rice with their fingers and bathe in the Kavery, were taken by Abhishiktananda on a grand "pilgrimage to neighbouring Hindu sacred places which I know". His infectious enthusiasm shows through the following account of their tour which included Tiruvannamalai, and thus led to an important new development in his own life:

> . . . I introduced them to sadhus, Hindu schools and especially temples. I can't count the number of temples where they offered their respects (?!) to Shiva, Vishnu, Ganesh and their consorts. In between they also had to meet some bishops and priests (. . .). I very much fear their travel diary will contain a strange mixture. Take your map and see. . . Trichy, Srirangam, Tanjore, Kumbakkonam, Chidambaram, Villupuram, Tiruvannamalai, Gingee, Mahabalipuram, Kanchi . . . They have discovered wonderful forms of Indian art, the oldest being the most beautiful, of the 8th century (before Charlemagne!). They were in temples at the time of *puja*, and could realize the place that religion holds in the heart of Hindus, and what those images, which a European is so tempted to despise, mean for them. They will know a little about their new people—too many [*word missing*], alas, are absolutely ignorant of everything in Hinduism and despise it [. . .?]. It is extraordinary, the [. . .?] at which you can enter into contact with Hindus, as soon as you show the slightest sympathy. For instance, at Kanchipuram I had a warm and moving welcome from an old brahmin whom I got to know last December.
>
> At Tiruvannamalai I renewed my acquaintance with the ashram of Ramana Maharshi and the sadhus scattered in their caves around the mountain. Even women, one of whom lives alone and has kept complete silence for more than ten years . . . Also two men who seem to live in perfect silence. The best thing is that they have suggested most seriously that I myself should live in one of these caves. The proposal is certainly not displeasing to me. I should at least like to have there a time of completely silent and solitary retreat. For food they urge me to

live on milk and fruit—which however is too expensive for my very depleted purse—or else to come down each morning like the other sadhus to the gate of the temple, a coconut shell on my left arm, to receive as alms a few handfuls of rice. All of a sudden your big son and brother must seem to have gone completely off his head in the strong sun of the tropics!. . . Rest assured, the Archbishop of Pondicherry (. . .) to whose diocese this place belongs, would not look on the matter with a very kindly eye, and would quickly take away my desire to enter wholly into the game . . . And yet, it is in this world of Hindu monks that Christ should find his most faithful ones. And who will present him to them except authentic monks, living like them in poverty and also freed from all earthly cares? Whatever we may do, at Shantivanam we are aristocratic monks. One day some people will have to decide to play the game to the end . . .

This is what I shall certainly explain in the French edition of our booklet . . . Fortunately for you they are preparing a French translation at the Abbey of Pradines near Lyon.[16] I shall take the opportunity to stress my ideas on certain points. Pray the Lord that this booklet may bring a little water to our mill, I mean some rupees to our funds. We owe Rs. 200 to the printer, and do not have one anna to pay him.

. . . As regards the booklet, sent to every corner of the universe, we begin to get some comeback. Very few discordant notes. Alas that usually we are thought to be far more than we in fact are, and to be capable of far more than we will ever be able to do. (F, 2.12.51).

Shantivanam—Christmas 1951 to March 1952

. . . I have celebrated Christmas all alone in my wood (my companion went to Kulittalai to say his Masses, the parish priest being in another village), and for me nothing could be more pleasant—except, of course, the Office and chants of the monastery on this night.

. . . Christmas is kept as a holiday in India, a tradition coming from the English. But how agonizing it is on such a day to feel that my so greatly loved brothers are not sharing in the deep joy that I myself feel in the depth of my heart. So the joy of Christmas is for me terribly mixed with bitterness. (. . .) The further I go, the more I feel the gulf between my Hindu brothers and my Church. I am like someone who has one foot on one side of the gulf, and the other on the other side. I would like to throw a bridge across, but do not know where to fasten it, the walls are so smooth. The more I know my brothers, the more I think that Christ was referring to them, when he spoke of the camel passing through the eye of the needle.[17]

We are constantly getting good letters on the subject of our booklet. Replies are now beginning to come from Europe. I have had one very

16. This translation was not used, but instead one prepared by the Poor Clares of Rabat.
17. Abhishiktananda is here referring to the *spiritual* wealth of Hinduism as an obstacle to Hindus in hearing the Gospel.

encouraging letter from the Abbot of St André de Bruges, who at the same time told me of his joy and gratitude for the welcome given to the monks whom he sent to found Siluvaigiri. Will vocations come one day? I mean, real vocations; for if we had wished, we could have had a full dozen lads by now, coming for their rice (. . .). I can see nothing whatever of the future. The Lord gives light only for what is immediately before us. (F, 26.12.51).[18]

For the next three months Abhishiktananda remained in solitude at Shantivanam, while Fr Monchanin was away on a long tour in the north.[19] Letters to his family reveal the financial straits of the ashram since the building of the chapel. He could not emulate the detachment of his companion, for whom "money, when there is any, is for using or giving away, and when it runs out, he waits peacefully until it falls from high heaven" (F, 26.12.51). In December they had to instruct their cook to reduce his monthly expenditure well below the normal level. His sister was alarmed when in January he wrote to ask her

. . . What is the present rate of mass-stipends in France? If at present it is 200 fr. [about Rs.$1^1/_2$], you might perhaps obtain some for me here and there (. . .). But if it is less than 200 fr., then don't bother. Right now I can no longer even add milk or soya (?) to my millet. (F, 10.1.52).

Meanwhile he was concerned about conditions in France, and especially its involvement in the war in Vietnam. In India a general election was about to take place. He wondered what meaning it could have, when 90% of the electorate were illiterate, for whom "the economic and national horizon does not extend beyond their village or at most the nearest market town". He continued,

. . . in this mess the Capuchins in their *Voice of Assisi* (. . .) dare to ask in every letter for the return of the English. I have sent them, as one says in English, "a piece of my mind". After that, the marvel is that the Church does not have more difficulties here! (F, 12.1.52)

Abhishiktananda's family soon took practical steps to improve the situation, as his next letter shows:

It is my turn to be sorry. Poor Papa is denying himself (. . .) as if I was on the point of dying of hunger. But be very sure that four-fifths of the people here would be glad to live like me. And the other day in Trichy the Bishop observed to me how well I was looking. (. . .) It is true that during Advent and even after Christmas we lived in Lenten style, but I have now discovered the reason. . . (F, 5.2.52)

Their cook had been systematically cheating them, as was obvious as soon as Abishiktananda inspected his accounts. Apparently neither he nor Fr Monchanin

18. After two years Fr Monchanin noted that "our ideal hardly seems to attract our Indian priests". He mentions some of the reasons for this: lack of interest in 'Indian adaptation'; "we appear to them 'archaic' "; fear of dangerous syncretism; "our life too austere". "In short, in spite of 'lip homage', we have not yet received any serious application, and foresee (without any regret!) the prolongation of our eremitical solitude." (26.6.52; Siauve, 206).
19. *Quest,* 83 ff.

had ever done this before, and the temptation had been too much for poor Visuvāsan ('Faithful') . . .

> . . . Please do not be afraid for me. As regards mass-stipends, when we have none, the Bishop gives us some; but very often he does not have them himself, and the honoraria which he gives us are simply drawn from the funds of the diocese. (. . .) Do not worry about me. My diet has become very reasonable, having in view the climate and my kind of life. (F, 5.2.52)

To buttress his point he quotes the actual wages of building workers, in comparison with whom he was living 'in luxury'. And in the following month, when thanking them for their welcome gift, he described a Christian hermit whom he had recently seen:

> . . . who from the start of Lent goes off all alone to a mountain, without eating, drinking nothing but water, and without speaking . . . When he is praying he is transfigured. I really felt ashamed before him. (F, 24.3.52)

While awaiting Fr Monchanin's return from the north, Abhishiktananda had ample opportunity to reflect on the future and on the new venture to which he felt called at Arunachala. Something of this is revealed in a letter to his friend Joseph Lemarié—the beginning of an uninterrupted correspondence which continued to the end of his life. Fr Lemarié was a younger contemporary at Kergonan, who had recently received permission to live in another monastery in Paris, and was one with whom Abhishiktananda could share his thoughts in perfect confidence.

With regard to Shantivanam he was in two minds. After two years of experience it clearly meant much to him; but at the same time he was disappointed to see so little hope of growth and development. ("The future of Shantivanam? . . . for the moment it is the cave of Subiaco. Will it ever be anything else?") He felt frustrated in his relation with Fr Monchanin. Much as they had in common, the two men were radically different in one respect. For Fr Monchanin, study, thought and prayer were everything, and he was content to leave the future entirely in the hands of God. If God willed, the ashram would develop; if not, he was perfectly happy to remain a hermit. This was certainly a valid understanding of the ideal of sannyasa with which they had entered the ashram, as Abhishiktananda recognized; but to his nature there was also an active side which could not be denied, inherited no doubt from his seafaring ancestors. Patience never came easily to him. He had to be on the move, whether it was writing, developing the ashram, or going out to share the experience of his Hindu brothers. Thus the deep gulf between Hinduism and Christianity, about which Fr Monchanin thought so profoundly, was for Abhishiktananda a challenge to be met. He must "throw a bridge across", somehow find a foothold on both sides of the gulf.

If Shantivanam seemed to have no future (though "there would be one, if my companion were not a pure thinker. The hermitage will only develop into an institution if the Lord sends another companion. Without Fr M. I can do nothing, with him alone I can do nothing")—then the opening at Arunachala attracted him all the more strongly.

He also spoke to his friend in Paris about his feeling for Hindus and Hindu religion:

> . . . Deep contacts with Hindu thought, books and people. Even before I came here, they had already made a mark on me. A hidden spiritual sympathy, this sense of the Unity, of the ONE, of God at the source of my being, of the fading out of this 'ego' as soon as you penetrate into the interior of yourself so as to reach the unique 'I'. But this would require too many nuances (. . .). I feel that it was by God's mercy that I came here. I would have suffocated more and more! Yet I am missing the Choir Office. I have a terrible longing for it. But it is precisely my long acquaintance with the Liturgy and the Early Fathers that saves me from Shankara's *advaita. Advaita* is so overpowering!—disappearance in the One! And so is Hindu worship, at least in its purest manifestation—the offering of flowers and milk to the bare stone (. . .) placed in the holy of holies, that small dark chamber deep in the heart of the temple, which one only reaches after passing through numerous courts and halls. When in certain (Shivaite) temples I am allowed to enter there, I cannot but feel close to them; their symbolic worship, adumbrations that are incomplete rather than false. (. . .) I prostrate before my stone tabernacle, just as my brothers do before the stone of their Tiru (holy) Linga, their oblation being consummated in mine. They say "Anbe Sivam" (Shiva is Love), as we say "Deus Caritas" [God is Love]. Here I feel Paul's agony (Romans 9-11). I am torn, rent in two, between Christ and my brothers (. . .). When I pray "through Christ", they cannot follow me. And I can no longer rejoice in our feasts as formerly, because my people is not with me; and I cannot unite myself to my people in their symbolic worship, because I am a priest of the true worship; and thus I fail to have communion with my people in what is highest and most divine in them. The husband who cannot kneel beside his spouse! And I endeavour to work back to Christ, taking as my starting point the thought and religious devotion of my people. (Suppose) the eternal Hindu *sannyasi* one day at a turning of the road has met with Christ—but alas, Christ speaks and understands a western language, is dressed in western clothes! In India Jesus would have been dressed like me—of that I am sure. I like that series of Protestant pictures, in which Christ is wearing a simple *veshti (dhoti)* round his waist and a *tundu* (cloth) over his shoulder. The picture of the Transfiguration is really a Krishna transformed into, transfigured into Christ.[20]
>
> . . . The terrible thing is that my people feel no need for Christ. (. . .) An Advent mysticism means nothing to a Hindu. I was shattered to find this a few months ago. The greatest of them say: "Am I to look for salvation outside myself?. . . Realize who you are." (. . .) Among my brothers there are souls whom God has abundantly blessed. My highest

20. Probably a reference to the picture by A.D. Thomas in *The Life of Christ by an Indian Artist* (S.P.G., Westminster, London, 1948), 47.

spiritual moments in India have been at Tiruvannamalai near Ramana Maharshi (. . .), and it is there that they are offering me a cave. (L, 10.2.52)

He wrote to his friend again in March, elaborating his ideas on various subjects, such as the following:

> . . . More and more I see the singleness of the monk's aim (. . .) My contact with the Hindu monastic ideal, and my reaction against the general failure here to understand a life purely devoted to contemplation, make me more sternly insistent on this point. My English booklet already puts it clearly, the French edition will be even clearer.
>
> . . . People have not yet succeeded in grasping that I am here much more for the sake of Hindus than for Christians. And that my ideal would be to have an ashram, Hindu in form, where Hindus and Christians, each in his cell, would hold silent communion in the quest of the Unique.
>
> . . . It is certain that if the Christian liturgy had been created in India it would have been very different. (There follows a description of types of Hindu cult and suggestions for developing Christian worship in Indian style, the use of *āratī*, etc).
>
> . . . Were I a Hindu, I should be very anti-Christian (. . .) at least against the Church of our days which deracinates people—or rather, it has always done so here. I sometimes think that a truly Indian Church would be born out of a movement towards Christ developing within Hinduism, passing through gnostic stages, and very gradually transforming into Christian values the traditional symbols and concepts of India. From Christ the *Sadguru* (the supreme Teacher) little by little people would come to the divine Christ, the unique Incarnation. (L, 18.3.52)

Arunachala, the cave of Vanatti—March, April 1952

Fr Monchanin returned to Shantivanam on 23 March.

> My companion came back yesterday evening from his long journey in the north. He has found much sympathy and encouragement (. . .). I must 'pump' him on all that he has seen and heard.
>
> . . . I left you this morning to go and 'pump' my companion. Just think of it, he has been to Banaras. It is something like a Christian going to Jerusalem. So all our Hindu friends are anxious to have his *darshan* . . . (F, 24.3.52)

A few days later Abhishiktananda in turn set off for Tiruvannamalai, and on 29 March took up residence in the Vanatti cave, where he spent ten days in complete silence. After this, as he was not permitted to celebrate Maundy Thursday alone, he went to join the community at Siluvaigiri, from which the following letter was written:

> You will surely wish for a brief word of love from your Hindu hermit in Easter Week. And so, in order that we can rejoice together in

the Alleluia, I join you for a moment on this Good Friday—which is the source of the Alleluia. I have come to Siluvaigiri for Holy Week (. . .).

I passed the last two weeks in a marvellous dream. I have lived almost totally as a Hindu monk, and no longer as a more or less dilettante *sannyasi,* as I have been so far. I have already told you of the invitation to come and occupy a cave among real sadhus at the holy mountain of Arunachala (. . .). On the side of the mountain overlooking the town (. . .) a spacious cave, at least as big as the shop,[21] in good order too, the holes plugged with bricks and clay. A well close by, which is a rare blessing at Arunachala. As I made it understood that I did not want to be constantly disturbed by indiscreet questions, they concluded that I wanted to be a '*munivār*', i.e., completely silent. So I was caught out at my own game. For ten days I have not opened my mouth—except, of course, to pray to the Lord (. . .).

People came to see me, but they respected my silence. Even the police asked for my papers in a written note and accepted my reply in writing. People came, prostrated, offered me all the signs of reverence that are customarily offered to idols in temples. They sat in meditation; meanwhile the Buddha remained sitting in the lotus position, motionless at the back of his cave . . .

Morning, evening and night I sat on a small terrace at the entrance of my cave to sing the Office, and it was truly moving to pray thus for my town.

At midday I took my meal at the home of a rich banker and magistrate of the town, who held it an honour to give alms in this way to the new sadhu, a magnificent Indian meal, such as I have rarely seen at Shantivanam apart from great festivals. In the morning I was brought a bowl of milk, in the evening some bananas made my supper. I can assure you that with such ambrosia and also with such a meal at midday, hunger never made itself felt.

To be completely genuine, I only lacked one thing more. Instead of receiving my dinner in this royal style of alms, I should have gone to beg from door to door the few handfuls of rice that I needed. Perhaps that will come one day.

I hope to be able to renew the experience at greater length. They would not understand it there [at Arunachala], if I did not return as soon as possible. It is truly the first time that I have been fully conformed to the ideal of a Hindu *sannyasi,* in solitude, silence, poverty. And I was thinking: Suppose I never leave this place, but remain here alone, in silence, without an anna in my pocket, then only would I be genuine; and above all, that is what my friends there, old and new (all Hindus), expect of me. I am not yet strong enough for this, alas, apart from the fact that I have to look after my Shantivanam. But still, if possible, I shall come back from time to time to my blessed cave. For

21. A reference St Briac.

> rarely have I found the Lord as in those happy and peaceful days. I felt myself truly the Christian successor of the sadhus who for centuries have followed each other in the crevices of this sacred mountain. It is scarcely a year since the death of the last inhabitant of my cave. (. . .)
>
> Then I have taken note (. . .). It is by means of Christian ascetics that Christianity should be known in these Hindu pilgrimage places (. . .).
>
> Truly extraordinary the ways of Providence (. . .). (F, 11.4.52)

Arunachala—18 May to 10 August 1952

After a few days at Siluvaigiri Abhishiktananda returned to Shantivanam for some necessary business. As a priest of the diocese of Trichinopoly, he was not entitled to live at Arunachala (which came under the diocese of Pondicherry) without ecclesiastical permission, and this took some weeks to obtain.

> . . . As I told you, I plan to return to my dear solitude this evening. The great thing is that this time I am going there with all the necessary permissions. It is incredible! The first time I had made mistakes, so that the Bishop spoke to me about it. He had been enthusiastic about the idea, but I ought to have informed the Archbishop of Pondi (. . .). And contrary to all expectation, I have obtained from him, not indeed a positive permission, but that "he will ignore" my presence—and that in itself is marvellous! I wanted above all to pass the days between Ascension and Pentecost there, with the Blessed Virgin and the Apostles in the Upper Room waiting on the Holy Spirit. Will everything go as well as it did the first time? I hope so with all my heart. There I really enjoy a peace that is impossible to find here. When I got back [to Shantivanam], I found everything run down, so had to get busy—change the cook who was useless, have the well cleaned, etc., etc. When the Lord sends me someone to look after material affairs, I shall be very happy. (F, 18.5.52)

On his return to Arunachala Abhishiktananda again took up residence in the cave of Vanatti, and for the first three weeks observed a total silence. In a letter to Paris he noted:

> . . . This new experience is most instructive; I am immersed in a real psychological bath of silence. Physically it is harder than the first time. I feel the fasting. (. . .) I am afraid I shall be compelled to reduce the rigour of my evening fast. (. . .) And yet underlying everything there is (. . .) a profound sense of peace and joy. (L, 11.6.52)

After this, during the rest of June and throughout July, he went down every afternoon to meet and make friends with sadhus, temple priests and members of the Sri Ramana Ashram. Some of these contacts are vividly recalled in chapter 2 of *The Secret of Arunachala.*

In April 1952 his youngest sister had entered the Benedictine Abbey of St Michel de Kergonan to test her vocation. From this time on Abhishiktananda wrote to her four or five times every year until the end of his life. In July he wrote—

> From my cave at Arunachala, where I shall remain for another month (. . .). You entered your enclosure on the very day that I entered my dear cave and began my three weeks of silence. Now I am speaking again, and no day passes without my visiting some ashram or some sadhu. It is marvellous how some of them—all Hindus, of course—love the Lord. Today I had a conversation with the banker Chettiar (at whose house I take my midday meal) such as I have very rarely had with lay Christians . . . Everyone here is so friendly. If I did not have Shantivanam, I think I should remain here (. . .) at the heart of the sacred mountain. (. . .)
>
> From now on, you know, you are to some extent in my place at Kergonan. And if you pray well, my work here will be useful. To be able to be a worthy witness to Christ in the midst of these Hindu monks, I ought to be better than any of them—and some of them are indeed first-class. I ought to be able to fast, to keep calm, to remain for long periods in prayer and meditation . . . without which no one will regard me as genuine. (. . .) Think of your holy patroness [Teresa of Avila], who 'ran away' to be a missionary. I am not a missionary, but a poor Christian monk in the midst of Hindu monks. (MT, 7.7.52)

Soon after this he sent a set of snapshots to St Briac ("The hermit greets you at the entrance of his cave", "The interior of the cave", "Looking towards the temple and the town", etc.), accompanied by an account of the people he was meeting. In addition, no doubt to reassure them, he described some of his culinary triumphs—yet "everyone takes me for a great ascetic!" (F, 9-10.7.52)

Towards the end of July an open-air cinema was set up at the foot of the mountain, which made the nights horrible with its loud speaker (F, 21.7.52). Abhishiktananda thought of leaving Arunachala, but providentially met a new friend who found him another cave in a quiet place beside Arutpāl Tīrtham ("the Spring of the Milk of Grace"). Here he stayed for the first ten days of August in complete silence, and then returned to Shantivanam. Writing from the ashram, he said:

> . . . This Arunachala is strange (. . .). Never in my life have I felt so much at peace, so joyful, so near to God, or rather, one with God, as on this mountain. I understand why the Hindus revere it. Another strange fact. After entering my new cave I remained for a week in deep silence. And when I came down again to pay my farewell visits, two different people remarked that my face was radiant, of which I was quite unaware . . . I left my mountain with a very heavy heart, and since then I believe that only my body has left! That cannot be explained, still less written about. (. . .) But I had to return. The Bishop began to feel that I had stayed there too long. (F, 21.8.52)

The weeks passed in solitude and silence were profoundly illuminating for Abhishiktananda. *Advaita*—so often discussed with Fr Monchanin—had so far been only an inspiring idea. Now he began to have glimpses of what it is in reality: the transcendence of the ego and a 'descent' into the ground of his being, which is 'not-other-than' the divine Self (Diary, 5.4.52: "Plunge into oneself, at one's own greatest depth. Forget my own *aham* [I], be lost in the *aham* of the divine *Atman* which is at the source of my being, of my awareness of being. And in this unique—or primordial—*Aham* feel all beings as myself"). He pondered diligently the teaching of Sri Ramana,[22] which continually called him to an awakening at the deepest level beyond images and thought, and also helped him to realize better the interiority of Christ, his '*Sadguru*'. He soon began to regard his own life as a *sannyasi,* no longer chiefly as a means of being able to give an effective Christian witness to Hindus, but as an end in itself, a total consecration to God with no ulterior motive whatever (cp. Diary, 31.3.52); this explains "I am not a missionary" in the letter to his sister (MT, 7.7.52).

These moments of blinding illumination *(éblouissements,* as he later called them; OB, 8.3.68), which he reflected on in the pages of his Diary, were later given shape in the essays of *Guhāntara.*[23] The first essay in this collection, called "The special Grace of India",[24] virtually sets out a programme which he was to elaborate in much of his later writing. India's special grace is its stress on inwardness, its relentless search for inner reality to which all else is ultimately subordinated. He considered that for the Church its importance lies in its challenge to Christians to penetrate beyond the merely intellectual and moral level of their faith, and to recover the sadly neglected mystical dimension of their tradition. Unless there is a response to this, he could see no future for the Church in India.

Shantivanam—August 1952 to February 1953

Back at the ashram Abhishiktananda was at once immersed in practical matters which needed attention:

> Here I have work to do—hedges blown down by the strong wind of the south-west monsoon (. . .). white ants [termites] in my room, the ground all covered with thorns and dry palm leaves. It only sharpens my regret at having to leave my beloved solitude. (. . .) There I could only very rarely speak of the Lord Jesus, but in the end a good many truly spiritual Hindus know that there is a place for sadhus (monks) also in the Christian Church; and that is a big thing. (. . .)
>
> The ॐ which you see at the beginning of my letters (. . .) is pronounced AUM, and is for Hindus and also for Buddhists the symbol of God regarded as the Absolute, God in himself. As it is one of the points where Christianity and Hinduism can profitably meet, we have adopted it, and I have had it carved on the cross of St Benedict which hangs at my neck. (MT, 22.8.52)

Abhishiktananda had hoped to be able to make an early return to Arunachala, but this proved impossible. However, in the latter part of 1952 he was able to

22. See *Saccidananda,* chapters 2 and 3, for Ramana and his teaching.
23. The notes written at different times between March 1952 and December 1953 were put into shape in 1953 and 1954.
24. This essay, somewhat revised by the author at a later date, was published posthumously in *Initiation* (1979), 41-47. The Diary (20.3.52) shows that it was actually drafted just before he went to Arunachala.

widen his experience in other directions. In September, on his way back from a visit to the Rosarians, he spent two days in an unusual Muslim-Hindu ashram, whose guru was a patriarchal Muslim with two wives. These followers of the 'True Way' (Meivazhi) were in constant expectation of the end of the world, of which they were preparing themselves to be the only survivors:

> . . . I have been to see a Hindu-Muslim ashram sixty kms from here. My reception extremely understanding and cordial as always. They informed me that the end of the world was imminent (the poor guru, alas, was grieved at my scepticism!). They don't sleep there [at night?], so as to be always ready. The night is spent in singing. It was enchanting, spell-binding, those Tamil lyrics sung without a break all night long (. . .) in the midst of the jungle. (. . .) I was telling the guru about the Communists, who would be quite capable of driving me out, if they came to India. He said: "Impossible! In such a case, come here quickly, and we will arrange things so that no one will trouble you." (MT, 2.10.52)

In October he went to the hill-station of Yercaud to stay with the Brothers of St Gabriel. He went primarily to improve his English, attending morning classes in the school, and in the evening being sternly tutored by a Mill Hill Father. He also admitted to needing a change of climate and a spell of better diet (non-vegetarian!). He found the European atmosphere a strain ("no one with whom I can share my love of India"); but even so met an understanding Malayali priest who proposed that Abhishiktananda should visit the nearby Hindu centre at Tiruchengodu, where he was the local missionary (L, 1.11.52; 4.12. 52).

> . . . All Saints today (. . .). I meditate on the Office; but this 'visualization' of heaven means little to the *advaitin* that I have become. Heaven is to be 'in' God. (L, 1.11.52)

He was still at Yercaud at the beginning of December, when Fr Lemarié's reply containing news of events in the French Church reached him:

> . . . I fear that if I was in France, I would suffocate beneath the integrism. I am more free to think as I like in my cave at Arunachala. You again reproach me for not writing. But how could people accept what I would write and my notes of ideas sometimes caught 'on the wing'? Then, who would be interested in publishing what I might write? Still, our booklet, much enlarged, will perhaps appear in Paris next year (. . .). (L, 4.12.52)

The same letter refers to his anxiety about his position in India, in view of the Government's policy of refusing visas to missionaries, and also about his ecclesiastical status, as his Abbot seemed to hint at his being secularized: "Quite apart from sentiment, this would ruin my work. I should lose all credibility, if I ceased to be a monk."

After returning to Shantivanam he went for Christmas to a village near Salem, and on his way home kept his promise to visit Tiruchengodu. When he took the bus, he was seen off by a mixed group of Hindus and local Christians. The latter were not at all disturbed by his *sannyasi* dress, and asked their parish priest to invite him again (F, 29.12.52).

Meanwhile a ray of hope for the ashram had appeared:

> . . . Two requests have just come to us from Europe, one after the other, and quite unexpectedly, from people who want to join us, one a Belgian Trappist,[25] and the other a Benedictine from the Rhineland. (. . .) Pray that these vocations may be just what we need here, and that these monks may be able to come to India, for at present the Indian Government is making it very difficult for missionaries to come here. (MT, 28.12.52)

As always, Abhishiktananda had his hands full with practical work at Shantivanam. A cyclone at the end of November had done much damage, and in addition the kitchen had to be given a stronger roof to protect it from the monkeys who constantly broke in, as well as from small boys who followed their example (MT, 14.1.53). His return to Arunachala had to be put off once more:

> . . . Fr Monchanin had a bad attack of asthma last month—that is what kept me here. I shall not be able to return to Arunachala before the beginning of Lent. He [Fr. M.] is certainly much too intellectual and idealistic to produce all he might, as all who know him complain. But that cannot take away from his very great intellectual and spiritual worth. He has an uncommon quality of humility, gentleness, peace and poverty of spirit. (L, 10.2.53)

Arunachala—March 1953

When eventually he was free to return to Arunachala, Abhishiktananda passed four weeks in the cave of Arutpal Tirtham which he had discovered in the previous August, and then went on to Siluvaigiri for the great days of Holy Week and Easter. On reaching his cave he wrote to his family:

> Here I am, again a hermit since this morning. Long have I dreamed of it. (. . .) I have come back to the same cave, my second one. The silent nun [Lakshmī Devī] has left after twelve years. Another has taken her place. Beside me another young Hindu monk. The greatest silence reigns here. You would never know that anyone was living behind these doors. A real Charterhouse. When will Arunachala be inhabited by Christian monks? (F, 4.3.53)

The mother of one of his French friends at the ashram (Sujātā, *Secret,* 41-2) was staying with her daughter and greatly missed receiving daily Communion. Abhishiktananda therefore came down each morning to their house to say Mass for her and after breakfast took back to his cave his food for midday. He only had to cook for himself in the evening, sweet potatoes and tea. "So my regime is going to be much less ascetic than last year," he added for the benefit of his family, who had commented unfavourably on the the pictures of "the hermit in his cave" which he had sent them. (F, 4.3.53)

25. This was Fr Francis Mahieu, monk of the Abbey of N-D. de Scourmont (Chimay), who eventually came to Shantivanam in 1955.

During these days he was much stirred by his meeting with one of the visitors to the Ramana Ashram, who deliberately sought him out in his cave. This 'Harilāl', as he is called in *Secret* (chap. 4), was a consistent and uncompromising *advaitin.* After taking Abhishiktananda's measure in some searching exchanges, he tried to persuade him to take the final plunge into pure *advaita* and abandon every kind of religious observance. This proposal could not be accepted, but the challenge left Abhishiktananda with the uncomfortable feeling that he was like a bather who feels the water with his toe, but puts off taking the plunge "which alone will give peace" (cp. Diary, 23.3.53). This contact ripened into a lasting friendship.

On his last Sunday (Palm Sunday), at the beginning of Mass he sang the Blessing of Palms and the processional hymn, feeling "a nostalgia for the past which is no longer mine . . ." Later in the morning, when walking through the Temple, he found that the underground shrine of the Pātāla Linga had for once been left open. This crypt has an important place in the 'legend' of Sri Ramana, who made it a hiding place when he first came to Tiruvannamalai. Abhishiktananda took the opportunity of meditating there for a long time, and afterwards said that it was his 'truest meeting' with the Maharshi (*Secret,* 112-114).

These four weeks were a time of great happiness and fulfilment. "Why, despite all the inconveniences of life, do I feel happy and at peace here as nowhere else?" (Diary, 7.3.53) "Why have the highest points of my whole life been experienced at Arunachala?" (Diary, 30.3.53) He found himself to be in a far more simple and 'natural' state than had been the case in the previous year (cp. Diary, 16.3.53). "Is it that last year I had more the *idea* of *advaita,* of *sanmātrā* [pure being]— and the idea more than the *res* [the thing itself]?" (Diary, 21.3.53) He also noted that his taste for outwardly expressed worship, whether Christian or Hindu, had decreased (cp. 21.3.53).

There was however one outward expression—writing—which he allowed himself in these days. He had been intending to expand the booklet, *An Indian Benedictine Ashram,* so as to make its ideas more explicit; and now, on the basis of a French translation of the booklet, he wrote the greater part of what subsequently appeared as *Ermites du Saccidānanda* (MT, 3.7.66). And that was not all. Looking back five years later (Diary, 16.5.58) he recalled that Lent 1953 was the time when "in the cave of Arutpal Tirtham I understood *advaita*, and the essential pages of *Guhantara* were written."[26]

A few weeks after his return to Shantivanam he wrote at length to his friend in Paris, who was eager to hear about his recent experiences at Arunachala.

> . . . You already know how much I have been marked by my first two stays [in 1952] at Arunachala. The latest has had an even deeper effect on me. Each time I think I have reached the depths; but the deeper I go, the more I discover even deeper spheres within the depth. And how can I describe them? First, I will admit in all humility (. . .) that I have the impression that until this Lent I never understood what

26. This probably refers to parts of chapters 3 and 4 of *Guhantara* ("Au dedans" and "Cheminements intérieurs"), published in *Initiation,* 57-64 and *Intériorité* (1982) 48-67.

monastic life essentially is. I used to laugh at Fr Abbot, Dom Marsille, when like St Benedict he referred us to the original source of monasticism—the desert—in which I saw nothing but eccentricity and utopia. Now I have understood that St Benedict could only create Cassino and the Rule because he had first passed three years in blessed solitude. (. . .) Only in solitude does anyone enter the heart of monastic life, because only there he enters 'within', and monastic life is essentially a life '*within*'. Never mind that I needed India and the contact with Hindu monks (. . .) in order to understand that! I think I understood it last year, and that it was in me in the form of a mental concept. Now dare I say that it has become a matter of experience? To sum up in a word my spiritual state after two weeks there: Suppose the Lord were to suggest to me that I should live my whole life alone in a cave at Arunachala or elsewhere, relying only on public charity for food and the rest, unknown, (. . .) reading no book apart from what is essential to collect my thoughts and lead them into the depth . . . I think I can sincerely state that nothing would suit me better . . .

He then reproduced part of his conversation with 'Harilal'. He had begun by showing off his knowledge of Hindu Scriptures, but Harilal replied:

. . . "You have read a great deal—naturally—so did I at one time, but now I read little (. . .). There is only one book, the 'living' book that is within you . . . Reading is only one step on the ladder. Instead of reading, think (i.e., meditate); instead of thinking, keep essential silence within, a silence beyond (. . .) both the thought and the non-thought that within you meet the Supreme." And that is true. The first two weeks I had read, I had done some Sanskrit, but afterwards that was no longer possible . . . And if it might still be possible sometimes to read and think about ordinary things—in fact, often it was not—, it became more difficult and tasteless to think about the things of God. For all that one says, reads, writes and thinks about God is far from God . . . idols (. . .). The simple man carves a piece of wood and bows down before it (. . .). The intelligent man forms a concept and does the same. He thinks he has 'arrived', because he has made himself a god on his own scale! (. . .)

You see where I am going? From long habit I am still extremely attached to the Liturgy (. . .) and yet the Liturgy no longer speaks to me. (. . .) If I had spent Holy Week in my solitude, without Office or Mass, it would have meant more to me than it did at Siluvaigiri. (. . .) I well understand all that you might say in opposition to my point of view. Is it just a passing mood? or permanent? I do not know, and it bothers me little. (. . .) Last year I liked to think of myself at Arunachala as the priest of my people, singing the *Gloria* and the Our Father . . . This year only one thing attracts me—the 'Within', beyond space and time (. . .), fullness and void . . . Some time back I wrote to you about plans for the Christian adoption of certain liturgical gestures used by Hindus . . . now I no longer feel capable of this, as I no longer feel a personal interest (while still recognizing their interest for others), and so anything I might work out would be artificial . . . Last year I wanted to enter the Hindu temple (. . .) but this year I have the impression that I have interiorly transcended Hinduism itself, like a true Hindu *sannyasi* who little by little would be set free from his need for externals. It is not because I am a Christian that I have lost interest in the outward aspect of Hinduism (. . .) but as being 'the guest of the Within', as having penetrated within. But here again, to leave behind is only healthy, if it has been preceded by appreciation, nostalgia, anguish . . .

One day while I was there, I had a letter from Fr Monchanin that was crammed with learned information (about India). I replied: "If you only knew how remote all that learning appears to me here!" (. . .) Learning is as 'useless' as making polish.[27] Reading hinders the intellectual from entering 'within', just as much as trade, gardening or whatever. (. . .)

So you see what Arunachala has done to me, gain or loss, gain for my loss, loss because gain. Outward things have lost their taste—be it study, chanting the psalms, or thought and meditation about things 'on high'. 'On high' is really 'within'. . . St John acquires a wonderful meaning here . . . (. . .)

Don't denounce me to the Holy Office! But your heart and your own 'wisdom' will understand what my poor and inexact words are trying to express. Then do you see how little interest the foundation of an Order has for me henceforth? (. . .)

You were wanting notes on Arunachala (. . .). Here you will at least have its essence. (. . .) The French translation (of the booklet) will certainly be ready soon. Many new pages will have been added to it; many of these will have been written at Arunachala . . . The title will perhaps be "Ermites du Saccidānanda"; subtitle—"an attempt at a Christian integration of the Hindu monastic tradition". (Details of the chapters follow, almost as eventually published, with an extra chapter which he hoped to add.)

His experience at Arunachala had not, however, entirely detached Abhishiktananda from his concern and hopes for Shantivanam. In the same letter he mentions four European monks (apart from the Belgian Trappist, Fr Mahieu) who might possibly be able to join them ("but on the other hand, not a single Tamil priest!"). But just before he had said:

. . . I hope you have met Fr Mahieu. I hope for his coming, and at the same time I 'fear' it; for if he comes we shall have to make a foundation; and 'to found' [*fonder*] is something external, despite the etymology [*fond,* depth].

Towards the end of the letter he came back to his recent experience:

I have said before how much one's outlook changes when far from France (. . .). Quite simply—and this may also be only a temporary and

27. An allusion to one of Fr Lemarié's activities at his monastery.

passing impression—all that matters in monastic life is the help it affords for entering within. All the rest (. . .) is simply *māyā*! And yet, so long as we are in this world and in this *māyā*-body, we have to play the game, I to plant banana trees, translate my booklet, prepare accommodation for those who will join us, you to make polish here, liturgies there . . . (. . .)

If you meet again (. . .) that dear Fr Arnaud,[28] you may share with him all that you think right of what I am able to write to you. Naturally I cannot write to them so freely there. The fact is that there they take in deadly earnest and as if they were scholastic definitions, what are no more than approximations, always imprecise, 'sightings', helps in aiming at the reality which cannot be described.

. . . At all events (. . .) it is passing strange that the dreams—to all appearance, utopian—of 1934, even before my solemn profession, should have been realized here, and above all at Arunachala, so exactly, even in details; and that a temperament so little fitted as mine for the life of a hermit, should have found there a fullness never, never experienced anywhere else. 'Fullness'—make no mistake—is not a matter of feeling. Do we feel the state of perfect health?—unless in contrast to a previous state of ill-health? When the spirit comes to its natural state (. . .) (cp. the return to Paradise of the Greek Fathers; cp. Tauler), how would it feel it? It is precisely the 'naturalness' of my life at Arunachala that has been my experience this year. Last year it was still something novel, more or less forced perhaps, conceptual. This year it has seemed to me so simple, so natural, so connatural (*saha-ja*) for me to be quite simply and for ever a Hindu-Christian *sannyasi* . . .

P.S. Am I deluding myself in all this? What does it matter after all? I am not attached either to today's or to yesterday's experience. The experience is everything, its conceptualization does not matter. All experience is surely outside time. If at the present moment it assists the leap into the Eternal, that is all that it is for. (L, 29.4.53)

Shantivanam—April to October 1953

After Easter at Siluvaigiri Abhishiktananda returned to Shantivanam and continued his work on the manuscript of *Ermites.* In the middle of June he took a fortnight's holiday with Fr Dominique, visiting many shrines in the south, especially Rāmeshwaram and St Francis Xavier's cave at Manapār. The future of the ashram was much in his mind.

. . . Fr Dominique returned even more enthusiastic about the ideal of Shantivanam. (. . .) Glad to hear that you have met Fr Mahieu. The other day the Bishop called me to ask what to write to him about getting his exclaustration. The big difficulty for him will be the visa. If only Delhi will grant the necessary visas, we will surely be four by Christmas. Two weeks ago I wrote to Fr Abbot of Bruges about our canonical position. I am proposing a monastic cell under his fatherly

28. Fr Louis Arnaud, monk of Kergonan, who from 1947 thought of coming to India.

> direction and patronage, but without his monastery having any [financial] obligation. Sent a draft of the constitution of the 'Hermits of Saccidananda'. No idea what will come of this.
>
> . . . As regards the book, I still need two weeks to finalize it. (. . .) Fr Monchanin does not think that the final chapter—"Au dedans' ["Within"], a series of essays on the soul of the *sannyasi*—should be published. It is too bold, he says. In my opinion it is quite essential . . . I will send it to you in strict confidence. You will please show it under the same condition to someone who could understand it, and tell me if it really is unwise to publish it, at least in part. (L, 24.6.53)

Abhishiktananda set very great store by this chapter, which sought to convey the essence of his experience at Arunachala. If, however, it could not appear as the conclusion of *Ermites*, he planned to combine it with other essays written at Arunachala in a second book, '*Guhantara*'. [29]

During July he was hard at work on the fair copy of *Ermites*, as he told his family:

> . . . I would have liked to write a brief word to each of you, but I am horribly busy with my book. I have to recopy the whole thing, 360 (?) pages large size. Working under pressure for three-four weeks. As soon as possible I have to go to Trichy and then Karūr to see about my permit and my naturalization [thus beginning a process which lasted eight years]. (. . .)
>
> Received a word from M.Th. [his youngest sister]. Always full of enthusiasm. I certainly never exulted like her in my dear Kergonan, and the result was that one fine day I wandered away to the banks of the Kavery and the caves of Arunachala. (F, 20.7.53)

Ermites was despatched to Paris early in August (though it still lacked the opening chapter which was to be written by Fr Monchanin). In the letter announcing this he revealed that his recent hopes of getting recruits for the ashram had faded. Once again a solitary life at Arunachala seemed to be the only solution for his problems, for "I am so weary of having to struggle constantly for the last three years with Fr M., or more precisely to drag him along (. . .). He will never come out of his dream." (L, 1.8.53)

In mid-August he was called to a village (five hours distant by bullock-cart) to give Extreme Unction to someone who died before he could arrive. However he stayed on to celebrate the feast of 15 August at the village, and saw the 'black misery' of the people, whose wells after five years of drought were dry, and who had no work. On his way back he met the news that the Kavery was in flood, and returned to find the ashram under water (F, 26.8.53). Another source of anxiety at this time was the uncertainty over the renewal of his indult of exclaustration, and he was distinctly upset at his Abbot's suggestion that he should go to Rome and apply for it in person—"as if I had 1000 dollars at my disposal!" (F, 2.10.53)

29. It eventually became ch. 3 of *Guhāntara;* two sections are in *Initiation*, 41-47, 57-64.

In October he was summoned to Siluvaigiri in connection with a crisis in the monastery, and only in November was he at last free to return to Arunachala. (L, 26.10.53)

Arunachala—4 November to 27 December 1953

> Arrived a week ago today. For three months I was looking forward to the moment when I should be free to come here (. . .) This time I am a Sybarite. My cave is hardly a cave, or rather, there is a minute cave where one can just about stand upright; but in front there is a small thatched hut in which I live. In the SE corner is a stone seat on which I am sitting to write to you (. . .). In the SW corner I have made my altar out of a packing case. The NE corner has four stones to make a hearth, and the last corner holds the precious dead wood which I gather thorn by thorn on my daily stroll. (. . .) I have decided this year to be my own cook. Those enormous meals swallowed last year at the home of my generous Chettiar, followed by a climb up a rocky path in the blazing sun, left me exhausted for the rest of the afternoon. Then I have discovered (. . .) a kind of wheat flour, also powdered milk, sugar, salt; with that in half an hour at midday I make myself a pot of gruel (. . .). Morning and evening I make a cup of tea with some bread. (. . .) All in all, for 8 to 10 annas daily, I live very well. (F, 11.11.53)

The cave-hut described in this letter had previously belonged to one of his women hermit friends (Rādhābāī; cp. *Secret,* 65f), and was close to his previous cave at Arutpal Tirtham, which was temporarily occupied. One of the highlights of his visit to Arunachala was the great festival of *Thībam* (Lights) in the middle of November, which he had not so far been able to witness.

> Last month I was present at the great annual festival of Tiruvannamalai, the festival of lights. Crowds of pilgrims from all round. Ten days, or rather, ten nights, of ceremonies in the Temple and of processions round the Temple with monumental cars of carved wood or else silver coaches. On the last evening, at the moment when the sun set and the full moon rose on the horizon, a huge flame shot up from the mountain and was greeted by the acclamations of the crowd which packed the Temple and had been singing for hours, as it awaited this marvellous moment. During the night, together with the pilgrims in the bright moonlight, I slowly and silently made the circuit of the mountain (12 kms!), from whose summit, like the flame of a lantern, arose the holy light. (MT, 18.12.53; cp. *Secret,* 129-136)

During the festival he and Fr Dominique, who had come to join him, met many visiting sadhus, including one remarkable old hermit who, on seeing his books, said: "What is the use of all that? You open them, and you close them. What is that, compared with the book of the heart?" (L, Nov. 53).

A few days after the festival his hut was broken into by a thief, after which he was advised by his friends to move back into his old cave at Arutpal Tirtham which was once again empty. The thief removed the small amount of money that he kept in his case, but considerately left untouched his papers and other belongings. His friend Arunachala Aiyar, a temple sadhu, to whom he confided his loss, told him to see this as a call to deeper simplicity, and counselled him to live henceforth on *bhiksha* (alms). Next day he went out to make the attempt . . . but courage failed him, when he found that he had to knock on closed doors! His comment in his Diary (27.11.53) was: "I was too comfortably 'lodged' in the little house of Vadalūr Ammal. That is why the 'Self' took the form of a thief to dislodge me and to call me to be more completely stripped. I should have totally missed the point, if I had simply arranged for a money order to be sent here to restore my previous situation." (But how he managed during the following month remains a mystery.)

He had an amusing story against himself to share with his family, of which a hilarious account is given in *Secret,* 62-65:

> Wednesday was a total fast for Hindus, and Thursday (yesterday) there was a great feast for everyone. [There follows an account of the embarrassing predicament in which he was caught as a result of his inexperience, when he had to absorb three enormous meals in the course of a single morning]. It goes without saying that since the third dinner, exactly twenty-four hours ago. I have been unable to touch another morsel of food, but have contented myself with taking tea two or three times to assist digestion. All the sins of gluttony during my past life were surely expiated yesterday morning! (MT, 18.12.53)

Before returning to Shantivanam he wrote to his family:

> There is just time for my Christmas wishes from the cave of Arunachala to reach you. This year I am going to celebrate Christmas in my blessed cave; don't you think that is marvellous? I have no need to make a cave of paper rocks, but my altar will be on a rock, and in truth the furniture of my cave will not be much more elaborate than it was in the cave at Bethlehem . . . (F, 19.12.53)

Two long letters to Fr Lemarié (8.12.53, 29.12.53) dealt mainly with matters connected with publication—the typing and correcting of manuscripts, sending out copies for assessment, submission to the censorship, etc.

Ermites. When this had been typed in Paris, Fr Lemarié returned it with his comments in December. Further comments were awaited from Abbé Duperray, Fr Daniélou and the Paris censorship, after which Abhishiktananda intended to prepare it for printing. He was assured by Fr Monchanin (L, 29.12.53) that he had already sent his revision of the first chapter to Abbé Duperray—though somewhat mysteriously it had to be written (again?) in great haste in 1955 (L, 16.5.55).

In advance of the publication Abhishiktananda made plans for portions of the book to appear in periodicals. Two extracts from his 'fundamental' chapter ("Au nom de l'Inde") were printed in 1955 in *Église vivante* [30]—but under the name

30. *Église vivante,* 1955, 30ff and 86ff. The mistaken attribution (by the editor, Fr Daniélou) to Fr Monchanin explains why Siauve (*op. cit.*, vi) says that Fr M. wrote "a large part" of ch.2 of *Ermites*. However, the bibliographical notes (see Note 13 above) make it clear that the writer was Abhishiktananda, and indeed that Fr M. "disagreed with ch. 2 as regards the place given to the cosmic religions in relation to that of Israel".

of J. Monchanin! He also proposed to write two other articles to prepare the ground for the book. One was to be an 'accurate' account of Shantivanam, to clarify some common misunderstandings about it. He also hoped that it might reassure his Father Abbot, by showing that the ashram was a valuable experiment, in which he himself had made a contribution (as "wherever people speak about Shantivanam, it is Fr Monchanin who gets the limelight"). Another idea was to produce an illustrated feature article on Arunachala. Neither of these proposals seems to have materialized.

Guhāntara. Some of the essays for this book were with Fr Lemarié, who arranged for them to be typed in Paris. Although Abhishiktananda was continually adding to them, he suggested that they might be submitted to the censor as a kind of supplement to *Ermites,* hoping that a single manuscript, presented as the joint work of Fr Monchanin and himself, if approved by the Paris censor, might more easily pass, or even escape, censorship at his Abbey. This, however, could not be done. More material for the book was written at Arunachala during November and December.[31] Two more items were promised in the near future—a Preface by Fr Monchanin[32] and a final essay to be added just before the conclusion.[33]

The relative importance in Abishiktananda's eyes of *Ermites* and *Guhantara* is shown by the following:

> . . . This message [of *Guhantara*] comes to me freshly every day, whether I read it in the Upanishads, in the Gītā, in Ramana, or in what I myself wrote, seated silently in caves at the heart of Arunachala. Each day I rediscover its meaning afresh, as if the words had poured forth even before I had become aware of them . . . So the message will have been passed on in essentials. The external message, the invitation to Christian monks to come and recollect themselves at the feet and in the very heart of Arunachala, thus taking their place in the great tradition of Hindu *sannyasa*, is the theme of *Ermites.* The deeper message is that which Arunachala whispers to him who is hidden within his (its) heart (. . .) in that mysterious depth from which the waters of grace gush forth upon his slopes (. . .). Who will understand this message, when he who has written it down hardly understands it and realizes every day that till then he has still not understood it? (L, 8.12.53)

31. This new material was

(a) An 'introductory note' on his almost untranslatable title for *Guhantara,* "Au sein du fond" ("At the heart of the depth"), which in fact is a poem, "Arunachala is a symbol . . ." He says that it "was sung to me by Arunachala one night before I went to sleep, and I relit my lamp several times to catch it. Perhaps it will convey some of the spell cast upon me by Arunachala (. . .)." Part of it is given in *Secret,* 51-54, and the full text is in chapter 1 of *Guhantara.*

(b) Some 'notes' (in fact, essays) on the Trinity seen in the light of *advaita,* "which seem to me indispensable, so that the book may adequately indicate the elements of a synthesis or a Christian reconstruction, to be attempted by whoever is one day given the grace for it" (L, Nov. 1953). These essays are chapters 5 and 6 of *Guhantara,* ("Dans le centre le plus profond" and "Ehieh asher ehieh"); see *Intériorité,* 68-102.

(c) Another 'pseudo-poem', "Au delà du fond", written at Christmas, which originally he thought of as a conclusion to the book. It has not been published, but forms the second half of chapter 1 of *Guhāntara.*

32. Fr Monchanin's Preface is printed in Siauve, 269-273.

33. This essay, "L'Épiphanie de Dieu", is chapter 7 of *Guhantara* ; see *Intériorité,* 103-126.

Abhishiktananda commented wryly on his involvement in all this 'business', to which even so he applied himself with his customary thoroughness:

> So there you have plenty of matters which are quite unsuitable for a hermit of Saccidananda, still less for one of Arunachala: books, journeys, money . . . Alas, the hermit's life is hardly possible except in the framework of a community which releases you from all these concerns for social relationships. The total freedom of the Hindu monk can only be a dream for a Christian monk or priest . . .
>
> I aspire to a greater degree of stripping, a greater freedom, a greater nakedness. Alas, neither body nor spirit are yet ready for it, but fortunately it is not impossible that one day Arunachala may complete his work in me. (L, 8.12.53)

Shantivanam—January to April 1954

The affairs of the ashram kept Abhishiktananda busy during most of the first four months of 1954. He had to repair hedges, irrigate the banana plantation, take measures to protect the library books from rats and white ants, follow up the application for Fr Mahieu's visa, raise money for the typing of his book:

> . . . Next week I may go to Pondi (. . .) I do not like Pondi. I have to disguise myself, to wear a white cassock, shoes and beret, eat meat and fish, drink wine, all things forbidden for a sannyasi like me! But it is the only way of seeing that my friend helps to finance my books. (F.12.1.54)

In February another Pondicherry friend, an Indian in the French judicial service, had to visit France. Abhishiktananda arranged for him to call on his family at St Briac and give them a firsthand account of Shantivanam, and in addition asked him to visit Fr Abbot at Kergonan, "to help him to understand how much people here are interested in the Shantivanam experiment" (F, 1.2.54).

Soon afterwards he escaped for three weeks to Shembaganur and stayed in the Jesuit seminary—"a good rest for body and mind. Recovered my strength to some extent, but once back here again I feel a lack of energy." While he was there he gave to two Little Sisters who were staying with the Carmelites "a very unconventional (*pas du tout formuliste*) retreat on Being and Not-being—*Guhantara* in short"; he also met a newly arrived French Carmelite and lent her his poem on Arunachala, of which "she at once completely got the point".[34] (L, 17.3.54)

For some months the renewal of his indult of exclaustration had been a cause of great anxiety. In April he was encouraged by the offer of the Abbot of Clervaux (Dom J. Winandy, who had been interested by the manuscript of *Ermites,* and afterwards contributed a Preface) to take up his case at Rome. His own Abbot, for whatever reason, was adopting an attitude of neutrality. This provoked Abhishiktananda to write a letter at Easter which, said Fr Abbot,

34. Sr Thérèse of Jesus, of the Shembaganur Carmel (not to be confused with the similarly named Sister of Lisieux, who came to India in 1965). See also Note 46.

surprised him "with its bitterness and despondency"—but "I was at the end of my tether" (L, 24.4.54; 17.6.54).

Abhishiktananda himself must have felt the incongruity between his agitation over the indult and the *advaitin* ideal to which he aspired. Perhaps that is why some weeks earlier, speaking of someone who "has not yet reached the depth of peace required to understand *Guhantara*", he added: "Have I, who dared to write it, understood it myself?" and as if to illustrate this, went on to speak of his chores at the ashram as "a distraction", done "without pleasure, though deliberately":

> . . . It distracts me from my 'advaitic' (. . .) life at Arunachala, with all that this gives of peace and depth, and at the same time of anguish for the Christian . . . If that life is real, a few weeks of living externally will not harm it. (L, 23.1.54)

He can hardly have forgotten that the true *advaitin* has passed beyond the *dvandvas* (opposing pairs) of being here or there, likes and dislikes, pleasure and pain. "Should ties and places count any more for him who has had the audacity to adopt the pseudonym of 'Guhantara' [i.e., the dweller in the cave]?"[35] (L, 17.3.54)

In March Abhishiktananda received a letter from Fr Paul Henry, SJ,[36] to whom the manuscript of *Guhantara* had been sent for his opinion:

> . . . Such a cordial and encouraging approval restores one's confidence. Into the bargain it has swept away the last hesitations of Fr Monchanin with regard to the publication of *Guhantara.* He is certainly no less 'gnostic' than I am, but not in the same way or on the same points. He was constantly bringing up the possible misinterpretations of my texts; however, little by little he has been won by the Trinitarian flights at the end and by the poem of Christmas time, etc. . . I have sent you the very fine Preface which he wrote for me two months back (. . .). I hope that *Guhantara* will be enriched by certain valuable notes by him (. . .). so, while each takes the responsibility for his own texts, *Guhantara* will not be simply my work,which will help with the censorship . . .
>
> Fr Henry only underlined certain special points. (. . .) There were in my view passages which could be questioned on quite other grounds. But Fr Henry has accepted 'with joy' the constant double register of the book and made no objection to its central purpose. (L, 2.4.54)

As in previous years he spent the last days of Holy Week at Siluvaigiri, and wrote from there to his family, sharing with them his hope that one of his books (*Ermites*) would soon be published and that it might be followed by a second one:

35. This shows that '*Guhantarah*' originated as a pseudonym, and was only used for the book as a convenient 'shorthand'. Not knowing this, Sanskritists hauled him over the coals for a supposed 'howler' in the *title* of the book. He refers to this in his note in the bibliographical dossier, Note 13 above.

36. Fr Paul Henry's letter of 10.3.54 is included in the dossier, Note 13 above.

> . . . The second book especially is very original. I am sure that nothing analogous [?] (of its kind) has been written on this subject. Also some people are very enthusiastic about it. But it will probably arouse some strong opposition. We shall see. (. . .) (F, 19.4.54)

After Easter he went on from Siluvaigiri to Arunachala, and stayed for a week[37] in the Skanda Ashram cave, where Sri Ramana himself had lived with his disciples for some years before the ashram was moved to its present site at the foot of the mountain. It was partly a business visit. He had a friend at the Ramana Ashram who knew Dr Katju, the Home Minister, and wanted to request him to intercede with Delhi for Fr Mahieu's visa. He was also making preparations for Fr Monchanin to come himself to Arunachala for an extended stay. (L, 24.4.54)

Letters to Fr Lemarié discussed a variety of topics, of which one or two examples may be given:

> . . . Hinduism has passed through the crisis of the 19th century, the crisis of Islam also; Buddhism flourished in India for 1200 years and more (. . .) and now there are not more than a few islands of Buddhism on the N-E frontier. *If I were a Hindu,* I should not be frightened by the progress of Christianity; I would consider that even if Christianity one day became the prevailing religion, in the end it would itself be assimilated. (. . .) It would probably be the same with Communism. (. . .) The Christian future of India is a pure matter of faith. (L, 23.1.54)
>
> [In connection with *Guhantara*] Fr Henry's suggestions about the Incarnate Word are very right. Here and there in *Guhantara* there are attempted flights on this subject, but (. . .). Sometimes perhaps I can glimpse a way in which, while being entirely true to *advaita,* I might try to penetrate to the divine mystery (the Trinity) in itself; I do not yet see how to penetrate to the mystery of the Embodied, to use the Gita's term. That will certainly come, for us or for others, and must come, as only so will Indian thought have integrated the mystery of the Incarnation and the associated mystery of creation. (. . .) We have to work out a Christian *advaita,* and you know now what that means; we shall not come to that by exploding *advaita* at the outset on the ground of its incompatibility. We have to strive to be faithful to *advaita* to the end. Only a heroic fidelity will make it possible, in God's own time, to transcend it (. . .). Not mutilation, but sublimation. (L, 2.4.54)
>
> . . . Easter is the great passing over to the pure reality of *advaita.* But how agonizing it is to be perched on the knife-edge between the opposite slopes of Hinduism and Christianity. (. . .) My presence at Arunachala seeks to be a sign, a "sacrament of the future" (. . .). Here the Mass, hidden and in humble, barely decent conditions; down below the great temple, with its marvellous liturgy! (L, 24.4.54)

37. The Diary and a letter (F, 25.5.54) shows that this stay was for one week only, not two weeks as he said in *Secret,* 69.

Arunachala—May to July 1954

After his week at Arunachala at the end of April Abhishiktananda returned to Shantivanam to meet Fr Voillaume (of the Little Brothers of Ch. de Foucauld) who was to visit the ashram on his way through India. However, as he told Fr Lemarié, he did not anticipate that they would have very much in common. He also had to organize Fr Monchanin's visit to Tiruvannamalai, which he hoped would at last enable his companion to realize something of the true significance of Arunachala.[38] They set out together in the middle of May. Letters to his family and to Fr Lemarié describe the visit.

> . . . After having celebrated Easter at Siluvaigiri, I spent a week here arranging for our present visit. Then, once some affairs were settled at Shantivanam, one evening two weeks ago we took the train for Tiruvannamalai—Fr Monchanin, our young cook and I. They have fixed us up in a very comfortable house (though unfurnished) a little outside the town. There we lived as 'sadhu-aesthetes'. I have shown things and people to Fr Monchanin, and he has at last understood the attraction that the holy mountain has for me. As always, a very cordial reception. What does it matter that we are Christians, since we are (they suppose) saintly people and real sadhus, and besides, we do not speak ill of Hinduism, but on the contrary give the impression of knowing it and thinking well of it.
>
> However this town life hardly suited me. Even though every evening I could contemplate the mass of Arunachala from the terrace, I felt that something was wrong. So I have come back to the mountain (without Fr Monchanin, who was confined to his room by an attack of asthma). I have discovered an empty cave which I had not previously known about.[39] A very great man, a *mahān* as they say, lived there for thirty years at the beginning of the century. Since then it has only been occupied at intervals (. . .). No one was holy enough to stay there. So yesterday evening I arrived. In the morning I come down to say Mass at the 'villa', and at noon they send me my meal. That means that, even living in a cave, I am once again only a fantasy-sadhu. (F, 27.5.54)
>
> . . . I have been here with Fr Monchanin since mid-May and will stay until about the middle of July. We have a house near to the Ramana Ashram, but I was soon taken with nostalgia for the mountain (. . .) Fr Monchanin has also been caught by the atmosphere of Tiruvannamalai. Now he understands *Guhantara* better. But I think he is too 'Greek' to go to the depths. India presses relentlessly beyond concepts, beyond the '*manas*' [mind]; how will the Greek, even if a follower of Plotinus, ever make the sacrifice of his '*nous*' [mind]? and yet, neither the Self, nor therefore India, will ever be reached through concepts.

38. Fr Monchanin's attitude is given in *Secret*, 49, where 'Purusha' means Fr M.:

> My friends had difficulty in understanding its (i.e., Arunachala's) attraction for me. "But the Maharshi is no longer there," objected Purusha; "and there are no longer even any real disciples about, with whom one could usefully discuss questions of philosophy and the spiritual life. And as for your caves, why give them such a mythical importance?"

39. The cave was that of Sadai Sami; cp. *Secret*, 69-70.

> The enthusiasm of the two women religious who read *Guhāntara.* One day I will send you what the Carmelite wrote to me.[40] These two discovered and recognized themselves in my poor pages. Only contemplatives will understand India and will be understood by India. (L, 17.6.54)

Fr Monchanin's account of the visit is quoted by Abbé Duperray:[41]

> We have spent six weeks in the exploration of Hinduism, seen at its best—pure *advaita,* in touch with and remembering the great saint and sage Ramana Maharshi. We both had the impression that we were living a 'Golden Legend' (where what is perceived and what is imagined are indistinguishable), and at times to be in direct contact with an experience, a transcendent apprehension which completely eludes all images, concepts and norms. A pure mysticism which, like the horizon, retires before the observer. The conceptual expression of it which is given by the most philosophical among them, is quite disappointing and contains obvious contradictions; the idea of *māyā* is an intellectual monstrosity.

It is hard to tell from this how far Fr Monchanin was really 'caught' by his experience of Arunachala. He returned to Shantivanam at the end of June, and was followed by Abhishiktananda a fortnight later.

During these two months Abhishiktananda had naturally had less opportunity to write than on previous visits, but even so

> . . . Other essays may result from my present stay here. I do not know if they will make a final chapter of *Guhantara,* or perhaps the first chapter of a second volume.[42] (L, 17.6.54)

In a letter to his sister at Kergonan he described some of his friends at Arunachala who appear in *Secret,* chapter 3, adding

> . . . None of these people are Christians, and all are so pious and religious that I fail to see from what angle I could possibly introduce them to the Gospel revelation. For their part my best friends would very much like me to become completely Hindu but, as they say, at least in my next birth I shall surely have the grace of being born again as a pure Hindu, thanks to the marvellous merits which I am accumulating in my present life! At bottom they are little troubled whether I am Hindu or Christian; they regard me as a holy man (I leave to them the responsibility for their judgment) (. . .).
>
> You will see in my books, when they appear, all that I have learnt here. To seek the Lord in your own heart, not outside, not in a memory but in reality, in your own greatest depth; why be anxious about your-

40. See note 46.
41. *Quest,* 91-92, where the visit is placed in 1953, by mistake for 1954. The 'Golden Legend' probably refers to the remarkable story of Sunderammāl, told in *Secret,* 95-100. Retelling it in *Vie Thérésienne,* No. 37, Jan. 1970, p.16, Abhishiktananda compared it to "un conte de légende dorée".
42. These essays eventually formed part of a volume, called sometimes 'Guhāja', and sometimes "Guhāntara 2". See note 53 below.

self, why talk to him about yourself, why ask him for this or that for yourself, even if it is for your own perfection? A simple gaze entirely fixed on him who is within (. . .). (MT, 28.6.54)

Shantivanam—July to December 1954

Abhishiktananda returned to the ashram in July. He was still awaiting news from Paris about his books and from Rome about the indult. Meanwhile he continued to write "new chapters for my second book (*Guhantara*). If they are not ready in time, they will provide the material for a later book" (F, 21.8.54). In his thought he was already reaching out beyond the position of *Guhantara:*

> As regards *Guhantara,* I am letting it be, while awaiting the decision from Paris. I should now leave it behind and find Christianity at the very heart of *advaita.* The intellect toils and turns and twists and is put out of joint. The heart smiles: How uselessly you give yourself trouble . . . The truth is altogether more simple! (L, 24.7.54)

On a visit to the Rosarian house at Manapparai (30 kms from Kulittalai), Abhishiktananda went to see the Superior,

> . . . aged 72, a holy Tamilian priest, the holiest (. . .) in all Tamilnad beyond a shadow of doubt. However, we were discussing the spiritual life, and I was speaking of centering the spiritual life on God, and on God as present in oneself. His reaction was: "In what form do you picture him?" (. . .) That says only too much about the preparation of Christian India for contemplative life, and its ability to catch up with the deep contemplative India. (L, 24.7.54)

In October he reported to his family with relief that his indult for another three years had at last been granted by Rome. During the month he was again engaged in building work:

> . . moved by a demon—unless it was a good angel—I decided to extend the chapel and replace the little shelter intended for the faithful with a *mandapam,* a kind of pillared hall in bricks, roofed for the time being with coconut leaves until such time as it can be tiled. (. . .) Very tiring (. . .). But still our ashram has to take shape, and the Lord will surely reward this act of faith. (F, 14.10.54)

News reached him in November of the sudden death of his father, Mr Alfred Le Saux. He told his friend in Paris how difficult he found it to speak words of consolation to his family

> . . . once you have even moistened your lips at the cup of *advaita.* Prayer, for example, can no longer have its psychological role of 'compensating' for the heart's pain, etc. I feel this so powerfully in these days of mourning; there is no more peace to be found in the anthropomorphism of 'enjoying' God, eternal life, etc . . . The encounter with *advaita* gives you a certain taste of Reality, which has the result that you no longer find anything else real or satisfying. But the deep peace of Hindu *advaita,* such as Ramana had, such as I feel almost within my own reach . . .—to that a Christian has no right to surrender himself. This

> is what wears me out more than all the difficulties and agonies that come from other directions. That is also what prevents me from knowing any more how to console the others after a separation like that which befell me today. I am very reluctant to use formulas about an anthropomorphic heaven that is so far from reality; but how to speak in accordance with the Real? (L, 10.11.54)

(Nevertheless Abhishiktananda did not fail to write letters to console his sisters at St Briac and Kergonan.)

A few days before this the censor's long-awaited report on *Guhantara* had arrived from Paris.[43] It was totally damning, attacking the book on every conceivable ground, and finding 'heresies' on every page. It was so totally negative as to be ludicrous:

> . . . The document—once we had got over the first moment of sheer astonishment—drew from Fr Monchanin and me a great roar of laughter, such as we rarely have occasion for. (. . .) One might have expected a severe criticism; at least it should have been intelligent, and by that very fact useful to the author himself. (. . .)
>
> But, to return to serious matters, it is unfortunately certain that we have there the opinion, or rather the inevitable reaction (. . .) of the average theologian and of the general missionary world. Among theology professors there are more like J.G. [the censor] than like P. Henry [whose appreciation was mentioned above] (. . .); and alas, there are in Holy Church a good number of large and small Ottaviani,[44] ready to lend an ear to this kind of denunciation. (. . .) So even if *Guhantara* appeared with an Imprimatur (. . .) it would very soon undergo attacks of this calibre in the press (reviews, etc.). And in our integrist days that could be serious. Not to mention Roman censures (. . .), there is the Internuncio who (. . .) has it against me that I am a monk outside my monastery. (. . .) and would only be too happy to have an excuse for sending me back there.
>
> As for a recasting of the book, that is pointless. (. . .) It is very clear that for the likes of J.G. it is the very aim of the book that is questionable. For him there is hardly a single page that does not stink of pantheism. (. . .)
>
> Practical conclusion. The publication of *Guhantara* seems to be put off indefinitely. If there were not the question of my vows of obedience and poverty, I might consider roneoing several hundred copies of the manuscript (. . .) so as to place it at the disposal of theologians capable of going further into the extremely serious problem which it poses (. . .).
>
> However a second volume of *Guhantara* is practically finished, over 200 pages. (. . .) It would be called "Vers l'unité sans mode" ("Towards full, unqualified, unity") . . .[45]

43. The report by Fr J. Guennou, MEP, is included in the bibliographical dossier; Note 13 above.
44. Cardinal Ottaviani was in charge of the 'Holy Office', now renamed 'The Congregation of the Doctrine of the Faith', the watchdog of orthodoxy in the Catholic Church.
45. i.e., Guhāja; see Note 53.

I shall send you (. . .) probably with this the reactions of a Carmelite, whom I have mentioned to you, to the reading of *Guhantara.*[46] (. . .) Tell Dom Jugler and Dom Miquel [47] how touched I am by their interest in *Guhantara* and the work of Shantivanam. A proof that Shantivanam and its thought have a value, in spite of being almost totally misunderstood (. . .).

. . . When shall I return to Arunachala? I had thought of spending the summer months here on the revision of *Guhantara.* In fact, instead of revising *Guhantara 1*, I had to put into shape *Guhantara 2.* Then planting trees, then the *mandapam.* I am eager to return there, to recover from these two months of 'distraction' (building). But first I need some physical rest—and physically Arunachala is tough. The body fears it as much as the heart calls for it. And it has to be privately admitted that the mind also fears it as much as the heart demands it. The Christian (the mind) is afraid of losing his footing . . . and yet Arunachala calls irresistibly . . . Is not *Guhantara* a kind of entreaty that both at the heart and at the summit of Arunachala, it should still be the Christ that I find: *adhuc tecum sum* [I am still with thee] . . .? At bottom the problem of *Guhantara* is the one that faces all those who have spiritual contacts with those whom the grace of Christ does not reach by the regular means (sacramental and others). The Spirit is [at work?] among Hindus, Buddhists, Muslims, Atheists, Marxists and non-Catholic Christians. The old ecclesiastical tradition hurled all these folk into hell without more ado. Whereas at this moment we have to admit that there are numerically very likely at least as many who worship the Father in spirit and truth outside the sacramental economy. So we have to integrate this mystery, while safeguarding the supreme value of the sacraments of the Church, and to free ourselves from the relics of the Judaistic mentality, so far at least as the human mind becomes capable of freeing itself, without collapsing into the stupid disintegration of religion in the form of theosophical syncretism . . . And that is why, since *Guhantara* poses the problem sharply, it should be known to Christian thinkers, in order to help them to go more deeply into the mystery; and the Church should be thought out in terms of the whole cosmic mystery and of the impenetrable mystery of God. The kingdom of Christ will surely spread not so much by way of subjection to the

46. Sr Thérèse of Jesus (Shembaganur) said in her note (also in the bibliographical dossier): "... What matters the thought in which it is clothed? something quite else is breathed by these pages—it is an 'experience' which sings through the medium of these lines . . . It is the breath of the Absolute, springing up like a flame . . . Whoever bears in his heart the ardent longing for this Absolute will hear the sound of the silence coming from the depth in which the soul is immersed." She also wrote these verses:

Ah que dire?/ non, tout taire / Ô mystère / Ô délire
Sur l' abîme / du silence / se balance / cette cîme
Tais-toi plume / silence âme / cette flamme / vous consume.
(July 1954, after reading *Guhantara*)

47. Dom Jugler was a theologian in Paris.
Dom Miquel was a monk in Paris, made Abbot of Ligugé in 1966. A letter to him of 19.6.56 is given in *Les yeux,* 175-6.

Christian 'Israel', as by a blossoming within the Church and within Christ of all that is already pregnant with the Church and with Christ.— Now I am going to say something which would make every missionary shudder. India's need at this moment is far less for 5000 zealous Christian apostles than for 5000 Hindu apostles inspired with the same zeal. What really and urgently matters in face of the rising tide of Marxism and rationalism is to re-awaken the religious sense of our Hindu brothers. (. . .) Which is most important? that individuals should be enrolled in the registers of the Church, or that they should live in a state of grace with God? All this is put too crudely and without the necessary qualifications (. . .) to state the problem . . . (L, 7.11.54)

Arunachala—Christmas 1954 to February 1955

Since 1952, whenever Abhishiktananda had stayed at Arunachala, he had lived in a cave. But when he returned just before Christmas 1954, he stayed in a cottage belonging to the Ramana Ashram at Mahāsthān at the foot of the mountain.

I have again celebrated Christmas all alone at Arunachala. It was right, wasn't it, that at least someone here should rejoice in the birth of the Lord Jesus, (. . .) And even though I was all alone, someone 'spoiled' me in a way that rarely happens to me. Yesterday morning an English woman of Jewish descent, Hindu by religion, whom I had met here six years ago and who has just come back, quietly left beside my door a plate containing preserved fruit, bananas, almonds, toffees . . . kind of her, wasn't it?[48]

This time I do not have a cave; there was not one available in which I could stand upright to say Mass.[49] And so they have given me a small cottage in a garden, from which I can contemplate at leisure the grandeur and the marvellous outline of my Arunachala. My meals give me very little trouble. In a nearby shop I can buy small cakes of rice-flour cooked in steam for breakfast and at midday; in the evening I make myself a little semolina with oil and flavoured with mustard seeds. Lighting the fire, cooking the meal and swallowing it takes less than half an hour. Besides, its digestion is not too complicated a matter. (. . .)

Oh yes, living beside me there is a family where every evening from 7 to 8 p.m. they sing their 'prayers'. If only you knew how beautiful it is! "Hare Rām, Hare Krishna, Arunāchala Siva." I look on from a stone seat a little way off. The whole of ancient India is brought back to me by their singing. (. . .)

From the mountain of Arunachala to the moors of Carnac, which you must be able to see from the roof of the attic. (MT, 26.12.54)

48. This was Miss Ethel Merstone; see chapter 3 above, and the letter L, 4.3.55 below.

49. So the rubrics ordained. Another example of Abhishiktananda's 'ortho-praxy' noted by Dr Panikkar in his "Letter to Abhishiktananda" (originally written for the 'Memoir' in 1975; later shortened for *Studies in Formative Spirituality* (Duquesne University, Pittsburg), Vol. III, No. 3, 429-451, in November 1982).

This letter to his sister at Kergonan was soon followed by another, written to greet her on the occasion of her first profession on 21st January (St Agnes). He asked for her prayers—"Here only one thing is necessary and is required of me by sincere Hindus: holiness"—and commended to her a life "in the cave of the heart" (MT, 15.1.55).

During these weeks at Arunachala Abishiktananda became friends with an Englishman, Harold Rose, who later came to live for a time at Shantivanam. Originally a Trappist novice, his long spiritual pilgrimage had led him to Tiruvannamalai, where he was the disciple of a Muslim sufi:

> . . .We often meet. When I go for my walk, I go and greet him and generally stay to dinner with him. I am not without hope that he may one day end his wanderings at Shantivanam. A very likable and gentle man. He comes to my Mass from time to time. (F, 22.1.55)

The manuscript of *Guhantara* was being circulated to various theologians and drew from them very varied reactions. In the previous summer Fr Monchanin, whose reservations about the book had not wholly been set at rest, recommended that it should be sent for an opinion to a learned Jesuit of Calcutta-Kurseong, Fr J. Bayart. His report was received at the beginning of 1955.[50] It was courteous and sympathetic, but finally no less devastating than that of the Paris censor. Abhishiktananda was deeply disappointed, and at the same time bewildered when another reputed theologian, Fr de Lubac, could give warm approval to his work:

> As regards *Guhantara* (. . .) Fr Bayart SJ, a theologian and one who knows Hinduism, a *friend*, has made considerable efforts to understand. Used a microscope as hard as he could, and naturally saw nothing, or at least nothing of what should have been seen. His friendship restrained the severity of his judgment, but did not hide it. A week later an excellent letter from Fr de Lubac, who asked for some clarifications, which however should not affect the basic idea. Said twice over how much he wants the work to appear, and that many people are reading and thinking about it. What am I to conclude? That only contemplatives will understand! (. . .)
>
> Lent *Guhantara* (. . .) to this lady[51] and my ex-Cistercian friend. Despite all their sympathy for me, they found it intolerably Christian and could not accept the claim that everything will finally be absorbed in Christianity, even if only at the end of the ages! Too Christian for Hindus, too Hindu for Christians . . . What does it matter? BE! (L, 4.3.55)

50. Fr Bayart's very detailed report is in the bibliographical dossier (see Note 13), along with some extracts from Fr Monchanin's letters about it to Abhishiktananda. Though he partly agreed with Fr Bayart, he sympathized with his colleague and did his best to comfort and encourage him. Fr Bayart had warmly commended *An Indian Benedictine Ashram* (Note 14 above), but was more reserved in his review of *Ermites* (Note 77). It is pleasant to record that in connection with Abhishiktananda's major work, *Sagesse hindoue, mystique chretienne* (E.T., *Saccidānanda*), published in 1965, he told the present writer that it had been the basis of the best retreat that he had ever made.

51 See Note 48.

Shantivanam—February to June 1955

In the year 1955, for the first time, there were solid grounds for hope that the long delayed take-off of the ashram might come to pass. To begin with, some young Indians were applying for admission as postulants. One was a local boy called Stephen, who had known Fr Monchanin since childhood, and joined the ashram in April. Another was Sachit Dhar, a Bengali, an ex-Marxist, whom Fr Monchanin had met two years before in Calcutta. He came to Shantivanam in July. Meanwhile Abhishiktananda, while on holiday with the Jesuits at Shembaganur, had met another lad "who has all the qualities and more that we dream of" (MT, 1.4.55). With regard to their postulants, however, letters reveal that between him and Fr Monchanin there was a very considerable difference of opinion about what they were aiming at:

> . . . Highest hopes for this 20-year-old met at Shembag, who seems to have the makings of a Christian Ramana. This year could be a year of take-off. But when Fr Monchanin returns from his latest trip to Pondi (. . .) I shall tell him frankly that I have definitely abandoned his idea of intellectuals. The temptation of being intellectual is as dangerous for the monk as the temptation of craftsmanship, industry or liturgy. (L, 28.3.55)
>
> . . . One day, when I get naturalized, I will come to see you. (. . .) But if on the other hand I begin to have disciples and to act as 'guru' (. . .) it will put an end to my travels (. . .). As for Arunachala, I shall certainly take my little ones there, and my dream would be to settle with them there. (F, 25.3.55)

Abhishiktananda's high hopes were soon deflated. As he told Fr Lemarié in June, "the postulant on whom I was counting as the 'cornerstone' of Shantivanam has been pinched from us by the Jesuits" (L, 20.6.55); as for the other one (Stephen), in the absence of this candidate, he doubted whether anything could be done with him.[52]

Then about the end of May they heard from Fr Mahieu that his visa had at last been granted, and that he would be reaching Bombay on 11 July. This news transformed the situation, and Abhishiktananda was sure that, if Fr Dominique could also obtain permission to join them, as he had long desired, there would be a solid nucleus on which to build.

> . . . The news of his visa was a happy surprise. So many hopes until now had been disappointed. He would like me to go and meet him at Bombay, and to take him on a short tour of North India. But the latest constructions in view of his arrival have swallowed up our savings at Shantivanam: a cell for him, a small parlour *(mandapam)* beside the front gate, two small cells for possible postulants (. . .). So I have told him that I shall go to Arunachala while waiting for him, and will come down to meet him at Trichy when we know his dates. I am rather 'nervous', as we say in English, in the face of the new responsibilities,

52. Stephen left the ashram in 1957.

> and all the same a little uneasy. Despite all the letters we have exchanged, will our understanding be complete? (. . .)
>
> Fr Dominique will perhaps come this evening for two days. I am very eager to see him, and to try to plan the future with him.—The true dweller in the depth, *'guhantara'*, plans nothing, worries about nothing, desires nothing, takes delight in nothing, is distressed about nothing. He lives in the essential joy . . . secure from everything 'outward'. How far I am from all that! (L, 20.6.55)

The same letter mentions another manuscript which was being taken to Paris by Miss S. Siauve. This was a further collection of eight essays, written during 1954, which he called sometimes "Guhantara 2" and sometimes "Guhāja" [53]. It was intended to be a sequel to *Guhantara*—"some attempts at solving the paradoxes of *Guhantara 1.*" He asked Fr Lemarié to show it to those who had been interested by the previous manuscript, and for some time hoped that it might be published. This however did not happen; and in Abhishiktananda's later judgment, about 1970, it was "more of a reflection, much less inspired" than *Guhantara.*[54]

Arrival of Fr Mahieu—July 1955

Abhishiktananda eventually yielded to Fr Mahieu's appeal to meet him in Bombay, and on the way first spent a few days at Arunachala in the Vīrupaksha cave.[55] This cave had sheltered Sri Ramana for several years before he moved with his disciples into the Skanda Ashram cave. Abhishiktananda had long waited for a chance to stay there, but it proved a disappointment, because the neighbourhood had become very noisy. This was the last time that he lived in a cave on the mountain.

On his way to Bombay he also stopped for a day in Bangalore to see another small Benedictine foundation (Nirmala Ashram), and there made the acquaintance of Dom Bede Griffiths—"a true monk, and capable of deep understanding of India". He reached Bombay in time to meet his new companion before he disembarked, and on board ship "felt again the emotions of 15.8.48" (when he had arrived in India). Three days later they began Fr Mahieu's Indian initiation with visits to ancient monastic centres:

> On Friday we saw an extraordinary Buddhist monastery, Kanheri, to the north of Bombay (2nd cent.), 109 caves carved out of the rock, a temple likewise and a meeting hall. Beautiful statues of the Buddha, so serene! In the jungle on a hillside, with the sea on the horizon (. . .). Extraordinary impression on Fr M. and myself. How we should like to

53. "*Guhaja: vers l'unité sans mode*" contains eight essays: Prière et silence; Le même et l'autre; Le Dieu vivant; Samedi-Saint; Création; Liberté; Vers l'Un; L'unité sans mode. None of it has been published.
54. Author's note in the bibliographical dossier.
55. The Virupaksha cave is described in Secret, 70-71. Although (by literary licence) this stay at Arunachala is placed before that in Mahasthan (Dec. 1954 to Jan. 1955; *Secret,* 71 ff), earlier drafts of the book prove that he left Virupaksha in order to go to Bombay, i.e., in July 1955 (cp. L, 18. 7. 55, 1st para).

> re-people it all. Yesterday evening we came here to Elephanta. Here Hindu temples cut out of the rock, only one well preserved. I was *thunderstruck!* I am more Hindu than Buddhist. You know the Shiva with three heads, incorrectly called *Trimūrti,* at least on our postage stamps—no picture can give an idea of it. When I saw it, I simply had to hold on to a pillar for support. The serenity and inner concentration of Shiva the creator, the central head. Late yesterday evening I stayed for a long time gazing at it, and in the ensuing darkness allowing myself to be bathed in its influence. This morning we said our Mass immediately in front of it. There is nothing *pagan* here. Tomorrow we leave for Ajanta, but I shall let the Father go on by himself towards Sanchi. (L, 18.7.55)[56]

We would have expected the meeting between the two monks to be a happy occasion, crowning their persevering efforts to obtain the visa and following on a sustained correspondence. Unfortunately things turned out very differently. Their relationship began unpromisingly and continued to be unhappy until Fr Mahieu left Shantivanam at the end of the following year. What went wrong? One thing is clear, that Abhishiktananda quickly gained the impression—or jumped to the conclusion—that the differences in character and outlook between himself and his new brother were so deep that it would be impossible for them to work together, even though he recognized Fr Mahieu's qualities. On the face of it, this was scarcely reasonable, and must surely be linked with the deep distress and uncertainty which afflicted him at this time, as the Diary reveals (see the next section).

> . . . I have had a little conversation with my new companion. He is . . . very Trappist (. . .). I sometimes find him a little too sensible—we have to be slightly mad here, don't we? But when he is keen on something, there is no holding him. (F, 16.7.55)

After eighteen years as a Cistercian, it hardly seems surprising that Fr Mahieu was 'very Trappist'! In addition, he had for several years served as novice-master in his Abbey, and had a strong and mature personality. As soon as he met Abhishiktananda, he probably sensed something of his underlying insecurity, shown in the way he talked, and unintentionally allowed his reaction to be felt. Abhishiktananda's acute sensitiveness is apparent in the following:

> . . . In my jungle I must have developed a very bad character and very poor discrimination, if I can judge from the reactions—and at the same time, from the silences—of my new brother. What does the future hold? The situation at Shantivanam is soon going to become more critical than ever. What does it matter to me personally? Provided I find a corner in India, where I should be free to be a poor hermit, I shall gladly leave it to others to run Shantivanam . . . (. . .) Fr M. will be at Shantivanam about the 15th. Then we shall see . . . What a pity, for this Father certainly has great intellectual and spiritual qualities. (L, 18.7.55)

56. *Lex yeux,* 163-4.

Before coming to India, Fr Mahieu had urged Abhishiktananda to accompany him on a tour of the North. In the event he changed his mind about this, and after they had visited Ajanta and Ellora, he went on his way alone, reaching Shantivanam only on 20 September. Abhishiktananda returned to Bombay and went to stay with a Parsee friend, Dr Dinshaw K. Mehta, who he thought might help him to resolve his problems.

A spiritual crisis—July and August 1955

On his return to Bombay, as he told Fr Lemarié,

> . . . Met a Parsi doctor, perfectly sound in mind, who receives mystical, but very *esoteric*, communications from Christ. They have deeply transformed him and crowned his own life and that of his circle, which is drawn from the highest society in India. An extremely interesting case. He receives me with great affection, and is inviting me to stay for several days with him. (L, 18.7.55)

Abhishiktananda's letters tell nothing of the significance of this meeting for his inner development, and only the Diary throws light on it. There he wrote (3.8.55): "These two weeks seem only too clearly to be the culminating point of a crisis which has gone on for two years or more." The origin of the crisis can be traced back to his first contact with Sri Ramana and Arunachala in 1949, when he strove vainly to "incorporate" the new experience "into his previous mental structures without shattering them"—in other words to reconcile it with the Christian faith, as he had so far understood it. From then began the tension between his deep rootedness in Christ and the Church on one side, and the progressive discovery of *advaita,* especially in the solitude of Arunachala and in his contacts with spiritual Hindus, on the other. He was determined to be loyal to both sides, and so the 'gulf' between the heights of Hinduism and Christianity which he ardently desired to bridge, was experienced in his own self, tearing him apart. It was to ease this tension that, in his reflections on the Christian revelation and Hindu experience, he sought to see how these apparently irreconcilable view-points might be integrated at their deepest levels. Insights that he was given were first noted in his Diary and later worked out in the essays of *Guhantara*; but above all in this writing he was voicing a heartfelt call to the Church to attend seriously to a problem which he was convinced was of crucial importance.

He always regarded *Guhantara* as his most creative work, but had to accept that it could not be published. He might laugh at its rejection by the Paris censorship, but it was even so a bitter disappointment. More wounding still were the criticisms of Fr Bayart, as his reaction in the Diary shows:

> Then I shall give up writing (. . .). Slaughtered by Fr Bayart. By regarding me as not being a Christian, they will end by making me so. Agony, agony. And deep down there is *advaita*, pure, total, complete. How it calls! Fascinating! (30.12.54 or probably Jan. 55)

In his distress he faced "the possibility (. . .) of having one day to sacrifice to my conscience my outward belonging to the Church" (29.7.55), and while staying with Dr Mehta found relief in not saying Mass for some days:

> . . . This week without Mass, and the Breviary recited in an hour at midday, has been a great relief. The Mass crystallizes my inner struggle, and the fact that materially I live by my Mass [i.e., from mass-stipends] makes it hateful for me to be saying my Mass perhaps in order to have something to eat today. (29.7.55)

Besides this major cause of inner tension, there was a further conflict in his mind concerning the ashram. Despite his grievous disappointment with Shantivanam, he still had a great desire to see it develop on the lines of his vision in *Ermites*; yet at the same time he felt insistently called to cut himself off from it, so as to follow wherever the Spirit might lead. Fr Mahieu's arrival only sharpened the conflict, once Abhishiktananda had persuaded himself (rightly or wrongly) that their incompatibility would make it impossible for them to collaborate. Should he remain there? Should he depart? In either case he anticipated formidable problems.

The meeting with Dr Mehta seemed to be providential, even though it was not possible for Abhishiktananda to accept his guidance in full. He was impressed with Dr Mehta's spiritual gifts, and took the opportunity of unburdening himself to a sympathetic hearer concerning the problems of his spiritual pilgrimage. This in itself must have given him relief after his years of solitary agony. Dr Mehta introduced him to his method of analysing the different levels of consciousness and to a technique of psychological introspection, which would help him to integrate his inner conflicts. In addition, he sought guidance concerning Abhishiktananda through his nightly meditations, in which he believed that he received prophetic communications from Christ. These were immediately committed to paper in the form of his 'scripts'. The tenor of these was that Abhishiktananda should abandon the Church and devote himself to 'interiorization', concentrated on the very personal but gnostic Christ of Dr Mehta's revelations. Abhishiktananda did not allow himself to be rushed off his feet, as he found this advice incompatible, not merely with his Christian faith, but also with the advaitic insight which allows no intermediary in the quest for the Absolute. On the other hand, the emphasis on total 'surrender' which Dr Mehta pressed on him, was truly enlightening and helped Abhishiktananda to understand himself more deeply and to find at least a measure of peace in the coming months.

During his time with Dr Mehta, early one Sunday morning, he made the disquieting discovery that the portable altar-stone in his box had somehow been broken. He was intending to fulfil his priestly obligation to celebrate Mass on Sunday, but according to Canon Law he could not celebrate without the altar-stone.[57] In deep dismay he asked himself the meaning of this 'sign'. Was it an invitation to renounce once for all the externals of the Church? Or was it a warning that he was treading a dangerous path? The sensible advice of the priest to whom he told his trouble—that he should get a substitute (an 'antemension') from the Bishop's house—was not quite the answer that he needed.

57. cp. Note 49.

One result of his contact with Dr Mehta is given in a paragraph of the Diary (2.8.55):

> I have been *stripped stark naked* in my soul in these days in Bombay-Poona. And my *pride* in having *realized* something has been swept away, and I have been made to understand that all that I had, not only through my intelligence and through my previous study and meditation, but also all that I thought I had learnt when hidden in the heart of Arunachala, was nothing, nothing at all, mere childish babble . . .
>
> Here I have to be just a disciple, and even to receive from this other person the message from him with whom I believed myself to be one. The great pride of being convinced that one has passed beyond *advaita,* when one has scarcely set foot on the path, begun the course.

After his return to Shantivanam (8 August) Abhishiktananda continued to reflect on his recent experiences. Though he was no nearer to a definitive solution of his problems, he had at least gained a better understanding of himself and heard the call to a deeper surrender.

> The answer to my ritual difficulties seems to me to be given in the Gita. If my *karma* is such that I am bound by sociological compulsions to celebrate Mass or to say the Office, for example, why seek to escape before liberation comes to me, from on high or from within? The important thing is to do nothing with attachment or in expectation of some result. (. . .) A day will come when it is no longer necessary, but it is not for man to decide when. I must not be attached to my Mass, and I must not desire to be set free from it. All attachment and all desire hinder the manifestation of the Spirit. (Diary, 18.9.55)
>
> I must *surrender* not only my impatience 'to plan', but still more my anxiety 'to know', to know 'intellectually' what all this means, and the solution of the mystery of the Church and the mystery of Christ, and also to know what is going to happen to me . . . Actually things will only happen 'according to' my going deeper into the heart, the within. (Diary, 16.11.55)

Shantivanam—August to December 1955

While awaiting Fr Mahieu's arrival, Abhishiktananda began writing a descriptive article on Indian monasticism, which was intended to draw attention to the book *Ermites* (still being printed), and also to be a supplement to it:

> I have set to work (. . .) courageously on the article on Indian monasticism, and think the fair copy will cover not less than thirty pages. You can extract from it whatever you like, and if you think it worth while, get it published by *La vie spirituelle* or *Église vivante* (. . .). But please don't let it be published under Fr Monchanin's name![58]

58. So far four pieces written by Abhishiktananda had been published under the name of 'J. Monchanin', and he felt that it was time for this to stop: *Église vivante*, 1952, p. 207, "Le monachisme et l'Inde" (translation of *I.B.A.*, ch.2); *Église vivante*, 1955, p. 30ff, 86ff. "L'heure de l'Inde" and "Le malentendu" (extracts from *Ermites*, ch. 2); *Bull. du Cercle St. J. Baptiste*, Dec. 1954, p. 14ff, "Tous noeuds détachés" (*Ermites*, ch.5).

> I shall probably not even read it to him, for he cannot be held responsible for my lucubrations. (L,13.9.55)

The first 30 pages of this lengthy article were sent off a few days later, with the promise of an additional 15 pages to follow.

> . . . My 'guru' in Bombay would give me a big scolding if he knew about it, for he wanted me for a long spell to put aside all commitments, all activities, even reading, so as to give myself completely to the practice of quasi-yogic concentration. (L, 18.9.55)

He had more time for this literary work, because

> . . . fortunately our postulant (with us since Easter) has a taste for gardening, which gives me a lot of freedom. (F, 25.8.55)

Once Fr Mahieu had arrived at the ashram (20 September), Abhishiktananda busied himself with initiating his new brother, introducing him to the local clergy, taking him to various places like Siluvaigiri (a week in October), and with him preparing their fellow-ashramites for the introduction of a fully sung liturgy. In the course of this Abhishiktananda overcame some of his earlier reservations and began to hope that he and Fr Mahieu would after all be able to work together. "He applies himself courageously to our life," he told his family (F, 27.10.55). "There is no comparison between his attitude in Bombay and his present attitude. There is once more a hope for something to emerge, with patience. (. . .) At the end of six weeks I have to admit that my apprehensions fall away more and more." (L, 8.11.55)

The singing of the liturgy was no doubt a sign of new hope for the ashram, and Abhishiktananda gave himself to it with enthusiasm:

> . . . So we have been singing Mass and the Office (Lauds to Compline, omitting Prime) since last Sunday in our mandapam, with prostrations, *anjali,* light and incense . . . And we begin our dinner with a psalm in Tamil and some Sanskrit texts . . . What will it all come to? Fr Mahieu was quite surprised to see me taking so much interest in the Office! In fact I am recovering the memory and the joys of the past . . . Am I right to allow myself to be caught up in this? Arunachala has dug depths in me which the Opus Dei [the Office] cannot touch . . . Perhaps it is a distraction, a falling back . . . However it is the way to lead our potential postulants to the heart of Arunachala (. . .).
>
> Despite the interest that I take in the present programme, I am still nostalgic for Arunachala. We have adopted the Benedictine Office with slight Cistercian adaptations and simplification of the musical tones. Siluvaigiri has lent us some books. (L, 8.11.55)

However, at the end of November Fr Mahieu departed to Tiruvannamalai, followed shortly afterwards by Abhishiktananda, and the singing came to an abrupt end. His account to his sister at Kergonan was:

> . . . For a whole month [November] we had the Office and Mass sung every day, but I very much prefer my solitary life as a hermit. I think I shall do all I can this year [i.e., 1956] so that I can withdraw on

my own, and leave the burden and hopes of Shantivanam to the Father. (MT, 29.12.55)

His frequent references to abandoning Shantivanam for Arunachala seem to have worried his sister:

> So it seems that you do not want your big brother to leave Shantivanam for a cave on Arunachala? At least that is what A. told me in her letter. All due respects to you, my lady Scholastica![59] But unfortunately I am not yet a St Benedict to do your bidding! I am too old and tired now to start a monastery.
>
> . . . My book [*Ermites*] is in the press, it seems. I expect the publisher will allow me enough copies so that I can send one to St Michel, and that you will be able to read it. (MT, 24.10.55)

Arunachala—December 1955

At the end of November Fr Mahieu went to Tiruvannamalai to witness the Thibam festival, taking with him the Tamilian postulant at the ashram, Stephen. Three days later they were joined by Abhishiktananda. He no doubt hoped that Fr Mahieu would feel something of the spell of the sacred mountain which meant so much to him. But the spell failed to work, and after a week Fr Mahieu departed for a tour of two months in Bangalore, Mysore and Travancore (L. 24.12.55; F, 20.12.55).

For the next two weeks Abhishiktananda took in hand the initiation of his 'novice', and was convinced that the had helped him to share in his own experience:

> . . . He at once felt at home at Arunachala, all his ancestral chords were touched, he was filled with a peace and a joy that he had never known in the heights of his Christian devotion. He could not understand the limits which I set to our 'participation' in Hindu worship. (L, 24.12.55)

This was surely one of the occasions (not infrequent) when Abhishiktananda's estimate of the character and capacities of those whom he hoped to train, was unduly optimistic. But he also sensed the possible risks involved in the sudden introduction of an immature youth to Hinduism, even after six months' training at Shantivanam:

> . . . He does not properly understand the danger to his faith, and yet, unless he stops short at a confused syncretism, he will surely also arrive at the the intoxicating wine of advaita. (L, 24.12.55)

The most important event during this stay at Arunachala was Abhishiktananda's meeting with another *sannyasi* who made a very deep impression on him—the sage Gnānānanda of Tirukoilūr:[60]

59. The sister of St Benedict; an allusion to the storm which came in answer to her prayer that on the occasion of their last meeting her brother should not leave her so soon.
60. The visit with Harold Rose is described in *Gnānānanda,* chapters 1 to 3 (E.T., *Guru and Disciple,* 17ff; new edition, 1990, 1 ff).

> . . . I have met in a place about 30 kms from Tiruvannamalai, through an unforeseen combination of circumstances, an old Hindu *sannyasi* (they say he is 120 years old; 70 or 150, what does it matter?), before whom, for the first time in my life, I could not resist making the great prostration of our Hindu tradition, and to whom I believe I might give myself over completely . . . I now know what India means by the term 'guru' . . . He is inviting me to make a long retreat with him in February in silence and pure meditation. Fr Dominique urges me to make the experiment wholeheartedly. The solution of the contradictions will be found at the end, in one direction or the other . . (L, 24.12.55)

This was the last time, apart from brief visits, that Abhishiktananda stayed at Arunachala, although he did not finally leave S. India until twelve years later. Some reasons for this surprising fact will be seen below.

Tensions come to a head—January 1956

In 1956 Abhishiktananda came to the painful conclusion that he would eventually have to leave Shantivanam. It will have been made even more painful by by his uncertainty about his canonical position, once he abandoned the work for which he had been given permission to leave his Abbey. There were several reasons for his decision. At Shantivanam he missed the peace and joy experienced at Arunachala, and in addition felt lonely and frustrated. His hope of being able to work harmoniously with Fr Mahieu had faded by the end of the year (L, 24.12.55), and at the same time there was little likelihood that Fr Dominique would be allowed to come to the ashram. But much more serious was the difference in outlook between Fr Monchanin and himself with regard to advaita.

Fr Monchanin had long been unhappy over the direction in which his younger colleague was moving, as is shown by an extract from a letter to E. Duperray:

> . . . I react in a contrary direction; never have I felt myself intellectually more *Christian* and also, I must say, more *Greek.* I experience a growing horror at the forms of muddled thinking in this 'beyond thought' which most often proves to be only a 'falling short of thought', in which everything gets drowned. (17.12.55)[61]

61. Siauve, 211-212. The editor noted that the leter also alluded to "the vertigo of advaita", a phrase sometimes used by Abhishiktananda. (See also, J. Monchanin, *Lettres à sa mère* (ed. Jacquin), 541, which identifies the recipient.)

To this period may also belong an undated note by Fr Monchanin (*Quest,* 119):

> It seems to me more and more doubtful that one could recover the essence of Christianity beyond *advaita* (Shankara's non-duality). *Advaita,* like *yoga,* and more so than it, is an abyss. He who immerses himself in it with a feeling that he has lost his balance (vertigo) cannot know what he will find at the bottom. I fear that it may be *himself* rather than the living trinitarian God.

Years later, in 1970, Abhishiktananda referred to Fr Monchanin's final view of *Advaita:*

> . . . J. Monchanin, in his last year, became more and more sceptical about the possibility of a harmony between Vedanta and Christianity and, fearing to see once more the disappearance of his faith in Greek rationalism which with difficulty he had recovered, preferred to give up Vedanta. (OB, 23.12.70)

It also seems likely that Abhishiktananda, tormented by his inner conflict, sometimes gave vent to outbursts like that in an already-quoted letter to Fr Lemarié:

> . . . another problem. Shantivanam, as I understand it, leads directly to a transcendence of Christianity in the very transcendence of Hinduism. I have felt this so strongly for the last three years; and now I have to recognize that the young Indians who will open themselves to me, and for whom I shall begin to open the way into their own spirit, will plunge into their own depths, to the very point where the light has shone before the eyes of our rishis. They will pay no attention to those artificial barriers which our Greco-Scholastic education has erected in our minds with its absolute ideas and 'essences'— those which are swept away by the mighty wind of the Spirit which carries India off to the very depths of Being. From now on there is not the slightest doubt that Shantivanam will soon come into conflict with the Church, not merely over questions of dress or of discipline, but over the fundamental questions. (L, 24.12.55)

Whether or not he uttered such radical thoughts at the ashram, the enthusiasm with which he spoke of his recent meeting with Gnanananda and of his intention to accept him as his guru will have been an added source of distress to Fr Monchanin, who did his best to dissuade him.

And yet Fr Monchanin himself felt the strong attraction of advaita, and admitted to being fascinated by Sri Ramana (see the letters in Siauve, 292-294). But he saw no way of crossing "the gulf which I perceive ever more clearly between the *heights* of Christianity and of Hinduism"—even if "in God alone there might be a convergence" (30.10.48; 20.5.49).[62] He had also at times dreamed of finding a Hindu guru ("essential if I am to know India otherwise than through books . . . Otherwise I shall never reach the *centre*—the intuition from which everything radiates . . .'; (11.8.39; cp. 12. 4. 50).[63] But of this dream he said: "I *know* it is impossible" (12.4.50). And this remained his position to the end.

Abhishiktananda, for his part, never questioned the existence of the gulf between Hinduism and Christianity at the level of concepts; indeed, he was only too painfully aware of it, through his efforts to live with it. But (as he had written in *Guhantara*)[64] he was convinced that it was precisely in reaching the summit (or penetrating to the depth) of their respective faiths that the spiritual Christian and the spiritual Hindu could and should meet. He longed for sympathetic understanding from Fr Monchanin, whom he regarded as largely responsible for the direction he had taken. But instead of this, there were only mutual reproaches:

> . . . The best thing is for him [Fr Mahieu] quietly to take my place (. . .); from now on I am going to work gently in this direction. Fr Monchanin will not see the problem, he lives in a world of his own, he accuses me of losing hope, of instability, of being carried away . . .

62. Siauve, 291.
63. Siauve, 149, 198.
64. In the essay "L'Épiphanie de Dieu", *Intériorité,* 118-119.

> He forgets that, if he himself had been willing to work for the realization of Shantivanam while there was still the opportunity, things might perhaps have taken another course. Discouraged by his inertia, I have been saved by Arunachala, and now I can never escape from it. (L. 24.12.55)

A month later he made it quite clear that he was indeed determined to leave Shantivanam:

> . . . Fr Monchanin, to whom finally I had to spell this out unambiguously, has taken it hard. (. . .) He accuses me of egoism, of betrayal . . . It is always the same. He lives in his dreams (. . .) and is knocked off his balance as soon as he is confronted with reality. (L, 20.1.56)

Notwithstanding these bitter exchanges, the two men still had a great deal in common, and their friendship stood the strain. A few days afterwards Fr Monchanin described an expedition to Nerūr:

> . . . We had yesterday—Swami Abhishiktananda and myself—a beautiful day: pilgrims at the *Samādhi* of Sadāshivabrahman! The temple pleased me greatly, and we remained seated for hours in silence and meditation (. . .). It is moving to see how India preserves the memory of her saints . . . Nerur is the place to find the eternal India. Sadashivabrahman reminds me of a saintly Carmelite nun, Acarie, whose motto was: "Anyone for whom God is not enough is too avaricious!" (26.1.56)[65]

With Gnanananda at Tapovanam—February, March 1956

"How mysterious that Christ can take for a Christian the form of a Shivaite guru!" (L, 20.1.56). Fr Monchanin made every effort to dissuade Abhishiktananda (Diary, 5.2.56), but he was determined to keep his appointment with Gnanananda, and eventually reached his ashram at the end of February. His high expectations were not disappointed:

> . . . I have just lived through 2-3 weeks which have been among the most unforgettable of my life in India. This time in a totally Hindu-Brahmin-Shivaite setting, not merely alongside them, but living with them as one of them . . . .
>
> I had arranged to meet my guru, Sri Gnāna-Ānanda (wisdom-bliss) on 26 February. When I arrived, he was not there. However I was taken in by the neighbouring brahmin village. Lodged in the Temple. People vied with each other to bring me food. All night alone with the Shiva *linga*. All this I will try to tell in a few pages which I will send you. Understood then the mystery hidden in Hinduism in Shivaite worship.[66]
>
> Here for a fortnight with my Guru. I have been totally 'caught'. (. . .) People prostrate before him with a veneration which fills their whole heart, and at his feet they feel close to him, enveloped in his fatherly

65. Siauve, 212.
66. Described in *Gnanananda*, chapters 4 to 6 (*Guru and Disciple*, 47ff; new edition, 1990, 29 ff.)

affection and animated towards him with childlike love and trust. (. . .) If that man were to ask me tomorrow to set out on the roads naked and silent like Sadāshiva Brahman, I would be unable to refuse. The mysterious ways of Providence! this meeting fulfilling at a higher level the meeting with my Parsi in Bombay! What will come of it all? In him I have felt the truth of *advaita* . . . He would like me to devote my whole time in future to meditation without thoughts, leaving aside not only all distractions and all useless conversation, but even all reading. He promises me that the experience will soon come if I act thus (. . .). But he has understood that I cannot abruptly break with Shantivanam. However my heart will be less than ever at Shantivanam. (. . .)

The attraction of this advaitin abyss, the abyss of Arunachala, is stronger than ever . . . What a conflict, when one has deeply lived the Christian *sacrament.* Here you are 'torn away' from signs. No reading, no prayer, no *puja* (. . .); only sustained *dhyāna* (meditation without thought) for those who are capable of it. Naturally no Mass here, and the breviary said entirely privately in an hour at midday. Once the *res* (the thing, reality) is attained, the sacrament recovers all its meaning; but when you are all alone in the undefined space between the sign and the *res,* irresistibly attracted by the one, and not feeling justified in abandoning the other . . .

The other Sunday, the 'night of Shiva' (Shivrātrī) was entirely spent in singing; nothing like those pseudo-vigils of Christmas or Easter, when we get up for two hours in the middle of the night. Songs, dances round the sacred flame. Hinduism has an extraordinary sense of God's 'play' in creation. Christianity on the other hand is tragic; it takes creation with deadly seriousness. The Hindu knows that creation does not exhaust God. The *advaitin* can worship Shiva and play his part in this world of mirage. Can he be a Christian? Christianity is perhaps too perfect. It has so wonderfully absorbed God into itself, that it is very difficult to find in it 'God in himself'.

How far I am here from Shantivanam and its future, from articles, etc. Shall I still be able to 'play the part' of writing about the ideal of Shantivanam? I should need months, perhaps years, of deep silence to find my bearings at this point which transcends the intellect. And how to explain to the Greeks—which is what Christians are—that God, the essential Mind, has nothing in common with anything that we can conceive of thought or intellect at the human, or even the angelic, level? You can guess the profound conflict of these two weeks. I shall try to write about it for the very limited circle of those who could understand it. But now it is a matter of penetrating beyond signs . . . (. . .)

Blessed Feast. Celebrate Easter through the signs, you who still can . . . (L, 14.3.56)[67]

67. *Les yeux,* 164-166; *Gnanananda,* ch. 7 foll.

On his return to Shantivanam he shared the happiness of these weeks with his family:

> . . . at Tirukoilur I spent three marvellous weeks. I met a man unlike any other that I have ever come across. Outwardly there is nothing extraordinary about him. He does not read your thoughts, does no miracles; but when he speaks to you, it is as if what he says was coming out of your own heart. For all that, it was mighty strange to see this Benedictine monk seated on a tiger skin beside the master, with bare shoulders, saluted with prostrations. (. . .)

Gnanananda (who knew only Tamil and Hindi) made much use of Abhishiktananda as a translator, because he felt that he understood "not merely the words but the depth of what he was saying."

> . . . Only he knew who I was. Most of those who passed through or who lived there were brahmins. I have never been in such close touch with them; but I had to be constantly on the watch not to make mistakes—the baths, the washing of feet, hands, mouth etc . . .

He was particularly touched by the children who sought him out to make their *namaskār* on their way to and from school.

> . . . How much I feel at my ease in that environment, rather than in parishes and bishops' houses (. . .). Here I live as if in a dream; I am not yet adjusted to Shantivanam. I must certainly make up my mind to write down all these experiences in a book. And this very month two periodicals have asked me for articles—at the very moment when the hermit has received from his guru the invitation to cut off all contact with the world! (F, 19.3. 56)

In lighter vein he wrote to his sister at Kergonan:

> . . . You see that I have become a real Hindu monk! My guru is the first man before whom I have been willing to prostrate. I now do it in fine style; a controlled fall to the ground, with arms extended, touching the ground first with the ears, than with the forehead; then half rising, you do it again, then you stand up and touch the master's feet with your hands, which are then brought up to the eyes . . . You see the drill you will have to perform, if one day your brother presents himself at the grill of St Michel! (MT, 25.3.56)

Various writings—March to May 1956

As soon as Abhishiktananda returned to Shantivanam in March, he took up several writing projects. This meant deferring the programme that Gnanananda had recommended, "a time free from everything, from all reading, all meditation on a given object." "I realize that this has to be done," he admitted to Fr Lemarié (L, 15.3.56); but for the time being the call to write and the affairs of the ashram kept him fully occupied until November.

The simultaneous requests for articles from two important periodicals will have been a great encouragement, as so far all that he had written had passed as the work of Fr Monchanin. The (incomplete) article on Indian monasticism (p.84-5 above) had caught the attention of Fr A.M. Henry OP, who said that he would be glad to publish it in *La vie spirituelle*. As soon as Abhishiktananda returned to Shantivanam he wrote the concluding section, which was an eloquent presentation of the ideal of the ashram. It very clearly reveals how much Shantivanam, despite all that he said about having lost interest in it, still meant to him.

The other request, for an article on Hinduism, was from *La vie intellectuelle*. He wrote this at great speed and despatched it in early April. It dealt with the vitality of contemporary Hinduism (L, 23.4.56).[68]

During his stay at Tirukoilur the idea had come to him of undertaking another kind of writing in the form of a narrative record of his experiences among Hindus. It was important to do this while they were still fresh in his mind, as few details of this type were recorded in his Diary.

> I am thinking seriously of noting down my impressions of this extraordinary week, perhaps in a rather novelistic form, and other stories could be added to it. To whet your appetite I will give you the chapter headings. The title might be: "At the 'heart' of India". It would include these chapters: The Brahmin village . . . Gnanananda's ashram . . .; to which I should add: Arunachala . . . its hermits . . . Ramana and his teaching . . . the story of his disciple Lakshmiamma[69] . . . that of Ram-Poonja (the extraordinary accounts of how they were brought to Ramana, which I heard from their own lips) . . . Will it ever be written? (L, 15.3.56)

A few weeks later he was at work on what he now called his 'souvenirs'. "Absolutely unpublishable!" he commented with unholy glee. "One day I will try to make two or three copies, and you will get one" (L, 23.4.56). These souvenirs are a record of his experiences among Hindus since 1952 and are filled with vivid evocations of people and places, spiced with humour (sometimes slightly malicious); they indeed convey an authentic impression of Hinduism at its best. After two revisions, the latest in 1968, they were eventually published—*Gnanananda* in 1970 (E.T. in *Guru and Disciple*), and *Souvenirs d'Arunachala* posthumously in 1975 (E.T. *The Secret of Arunachala*).

About the same time Abhishiktananda wrote an essay which throws light on his inner development and indicates the progress that he was making towards integration, as he came to terms with the tensions, both inward and outward, with which he had to live. It is called "Esseulement" (i.e., Total Isolation, Solitude),[70] and analyses his own condition of profound loneliness:

He who follows the *jñāna-mārga* [the path of 'knowledge', i.e. *advaita*] "is bound to find himself in a state of unbearable isolation." This arises from the systematic discrimination *(viveka)* between what is real and what is transitory, an undertaking which is far from being merely intellectual, but "involves the whole being". "This produces, as of necessity, an ever more complete disenchantment with all that is not the absolute . . . And this disenchantment cannot

68. For these two articles, see Note 77 below.
69. 'Lakshmiamma' seems to be a slip for 'Sunderammāl; see Note 41 above.
70. Notes in the Diary, 19.4. 56; essay in *Intériorité*, 127-136.

fail to impinge on matters of religion. Their relativity as regards time, space, mankind, etc., appears in such a bright light that the intelligence, thirsting for the true absolute, can no longer find satisfaction in them . . . The most essential articles of faith lose their flavour of truth . . . This loss has necessarily to be undergone, whether one one likes it or not . . . And to hear oneself accused of pride and lack of faith is no help—on the contrary, it plunges one deeper into this terrible isolation."

For Abhishiktananda the issue was not whether he should abandon one faith for another (Hinduism), for every faith is marked by relativity (though Hinduism has this strong point in its favour, that it fully recognizes its own relativity: "to fulfil the ultimate demands of his religion, the Hindu leaves behind all the rites and formulas of his religion"). In response to "the agonizing appeal of that mystery which transcends him", he felt bound to follow the quest for his true self, for the ultimate; and this path had to be trodden alone. "The agony is that everyone cries out to me to recover my footing at all costs, lest I should be lost—while in myself I no longer have any desire to do this." "No one from outside can help me . . . to discover *for myself* the secret of my origin and my destiny." So he concludes by comparing himself to the submarine captain who shuts the door of his conning-tower and descends into the depths, well knowing the risks—in his case of "taking *ersatz* [artificial] experiences for the real thing."

In April Abhishiktananda had the pleasing task of checking the final proofs of *Ermites,* which was finally published in August (L, 23.4.56; 22.8.56).

Fr A.M. Henry's interest in his article on Indian monasticism led Abhishiktananda to hope once more that perhaps part of his *Guhantara* writings, especially the less controversial second part *(Guhaja)* might after all be publishable. He asked Fr Lemarié (15.3.56) to supply copies to the Dominicans, and to sound them for their opinion. Meanwhile, hoping for a favourable response, he got ready once more to revise his manuscript. However, despite Fr Henry's sympathy, it received heavy criticism from their expert, Fr Régamey[71]—which was not surprising, in view of his reputation for extreme caution (L, 15.6.56). Fr Henry still persevered, and at the end of the year there was a possibility of its being accepted by Editions du Cerf, until once again their reader (Fr O. Cornelis) "slaughtered it" (L, 12.1.57). By now Abhishiktananda was resigned to the situation: "We must conclude that the Church is not ready—at least in the persons of those who have the say—to receive the message of India, the message inscribed by the Word for her in India . . ." (L, 12.1.57). Accordingly *Guhantara* remained unpublished during his lifetime; but it was some consolation that, apart from his small circle of personal friends, there were recognized theologians, notably Fr de Lubac, who discerned its importance.

Shantivanam—March to October 1956

On his return from Gnanananda, Abhishiktananda took the opportunity of having 'a very frank discussion" with Fr Mahieu about the ashram. The latter had been out during January and February, mainly in Travancore, and was now

71. This report is included in the bibliographical dossier.

back at Shantivanam, where he remained until the end of April. Fr Mahieu seems to have envisaged the ashram as a place where monks would live separately, as in an Oriental *laura,* apart from the one appointed to take full charge of any aspirants who might join them. In view of his experience as a novice-master, Fr Mahieu himself was the most obvious candidate for this post. But Abhishiktananda was upset by this proposal, called it utopian and unworkable, and said that it showed that no effective collaboration between them would be possible. In this he was perhaps influenced by having his own rather different ideas about the formation of possible aspirants, which he longed to be able to put into practice: "If one day the Lord should send a disciple, I should strive to help him to become quite simply a *sannyasi."* (L, 28.3.56)

This difference of opinion can hardly have encouraged Fr Mahieu to look upon Shantivanam as his permanent place. He had already given some indication of being drawn in the direction of Travancore, and in the same letter Abhishiktananda said, "I would much prefer him to find his way to Malabar. Fr Monchanin has begun to realize the seriousness of the situation." A few weeks later Fr Monchanin learnt indirectly that Fr Mahieu was already beginning to plan a new foundation in Travancore, and after Easter the three of them had a "very painful chapter (meeting)" (L, 23.4.56). In view of the very uncertain future of Shantivanam, Fr Monchanin took it badly. As for Abhishiktananda, he cannot have been wholly displeased: "I long increasingly to withdraw into solitude until the day when perhaps once again possibilities for Shantivanam will appear." Meanwhile his relations with Fr Monchanin continued to be unhappy: ". . . he cannot understand that I have little faith in his vague desires for an ordered life 'tomorrow', and (. . .) finds good Christian reasons to set against my trans-conceptual advaitism" (L, 23.4.56)

At the end of April Fr Mahieu left for two months of Sanskrit study in Travancore and Abhishiktananda went to talk things over with Fr Dominique at Siluvaigiri. On the way back

> . . . I passed near Salem and took the opportunity of going to see a Hindu village where my guru of Tirukoilur (. . .) had lived ten years ago. I meant to stay for a couple of hours. I found myself installed in his ashram (empty, but where his devotees come every evening for recollection and prayer), and had to stay three days. They even wanted me to remain there. All day long I had to give my *'darshan',* and to answer numerous questions on 'the way that leads to God'. Naturally there could be mention of Christ, but at least I gave them, without naming him, the Gospel's way of *love.* (MT, 24.6.56)

About the middle of 1956 the ashram community expanded, and for some months in the latter part of the year there were six regular members. The first to come was Harold Rose, whom Abhishiktananda had come to know at Arunachala; then came a Tamilian priest of the diocese, Fr Dharmanādhan, who spent three weeks with them in June and joined them at the end of August. Once again they began to sing the Office, abandoned since the previous November, apart from a few days in Holy Week. In addition to organizing the singing, Abhishiktananda was engaged on making the necessary extension to their buildings. In June, when he wrote to thank his sister at Kergonan for her felicitations on the silver jubilee of his monastic profession, he told her:

> . . . I am very busy these days. Imagine it, there are now six of us to sing the Office every day. Besides our Trappist and our Tamilian [Stephen], an Englishman has just arrived who, after passing through Buddhism, Islam and Hinduism has returned to the Church. I had seen a lot of him at Tiruvannamalai eighteen months ago, and often since then. He is altogether in his element here; we have built him a cell (. . .). He is a charming companion (. . .). Then there is a priest from Trichy, who has long been interested in our life, but had not felt himself called to it. He came for a few days and was thunderstruck. Let us see if the Bishop will release him. So we are quite a community. As a result we have had to build new cells, provide more room in the refectory, install a pump, etc. For a month I have had the awful job of being cellarer [i.e., storekeeper]; with that I have had to keep the Office going, as I am the only one that is familiar with it (our Trappist only returned from his travels a few days ago). We sing Lauds, Terce, Sext, None, Vespers and Compline, with Mass each morning after Lauds (Matins in private). We add hymns in Sanskrit and Tamil before and after the Office. We prostrate, give greetings in Indian style, offer the light just as I have seen it done in Hindu temples and ashrams [i.e., *āratī*]. All that is very interesting; but how much more interesting still is life in my cave at Arunachala or among my Hindus. How eager I am that others should take charge of Shantivanam, so that I may be able to return there. (MT, 24.6.56)

Although Abhishiktananda was constantly referring to his desire to leave Shantivanam and settle at Arunachala, it is reasonable to wonder how seriously it should be taken, as so many of his actions (and re-actions) point in a different direction. For instance, he disclaimed interest in the liturgical experiments which they were making in the ashram; but his account of them to Fr Lemarié was unmistakably that of an enthusiast (L, 15.6.56). (A few years later the importance of this pioneering work became evident, when the experience of Shantivanam was drawn upon by the Indian Church in the indigenization of its worship.) Even more significant were his continued efforts during this year to obtain recruits for the ashram from the West. "But Shantivanam must live!" he exclaimed to Fr Lemarié (L, 28.3.56), with reference to the final pages of his article on Indian monasticism, which were clearly written to invite vocations. A monk of St Wandrille (Dom A. Bescaud) had long wanted to join the ashram and, though at first Abhishiktananda had discouraged him, he now took active measures to help him to obtain a visa (L, 15.6.56). Through Fr Lemarié he kept in touch with a monk of Kergonan (Dom Louis A.); for him also he hoped for a visa, and "we will find the money for his passage". Nor had he lost hope that Fr Dominique might eventually come to them from Siluvaigiri.

There were two other important projects for the ashram which engaged his attention this year:

> . . . I must have told you about a project which we have in hand to enable priests to live by the spirit of Shantivanam in their ministry to non-Christians. It seems to be taking shape. Two priests seem to have decided to begin the work. We have written to the Bishop about it (. . .). One has been with us for the last three days for a long retreat [Fr Dharmanadhan, mentioned above]. He finds himself so naturally at home here, away from all the various constraints imposed on his Indian heart and soul by the western strait-jacket (. . .). If the Bishop accepts the plan, it could have important results and be the point of departure for an *absolutely necessary* transformation of the clergy . . . (L, 15.6.56)
>
> . . . Saw our Bishop last week. (. . .) He immediately agreed that Fr Dharmanadhan should join us as soon as he is ready. (. . .) This other 'scheme' which I should much like to see taking off is for 'Priests of Saccidananda', parallel to the Hermits of Saccidananda. The plan would be to entrust the parishes near Shantivanam to priests willing to live in the spirit of Shantivanam. Its influence would then begin to spread around. It will succeed *if* there is here a firm intention to make it work. We only need a serious effort on the part of Fr Monchanin. Shall we get the better of his inertia? He spoke out boldly to the Bishop for Fr Dharma. Shall we get him to follow it up? (. .) Fr M. could do more than anyone, *if only* he would. (L, 15.8.56)
>
> . . . Fr Dharmanadhan joined us on 31 August. I feel myself released from my obligations at the ashram. He certainly has the attitude needed at Shantivanam. He is dynamic, his presence will give a shock to the clergy, etc. . . . He will keep things moving with Fr Monchanin. (L, 18.9.56)

The other project about which Abhishiktananda often spoke in letters between August and October, was one in which he himself would have been much more deeply involved. This project was to found a second ashram near Trivandrum, in response to the invitation of the young and energetic Bishop of the Syro-Malankara rite, Mar Gregorios. When Abhishiktananda went to investigate, Fr Monchanin wrote:

> The prospects among the Syrians offer many advantages: an understanding archbishop, possibilities for a vernacular liturgy, very likely a better chance of recruits. They must be examined, but without making any commitment. I should prefer the formula of an ashram situated at the intersection of a Hindu and a Christian area: a kind of bridge between two spiritual worlds. So make a reconnaisance of the Malayali country.[72]

For Abhishiktananda personally, the scheme had several attractive features. He would be placed in an important centre of Hindu culture, and at the same time close to a Church in which (unlike that of Tamilnad) there would be every likelihood of vocations. His canonical position would be assured, once he was transferred to the Roman Congregation for Eastern churches. The problem of

72. *Quest*, 101.

learning Malayalam and Syriac, as well as of adopting a new rite, seemed not to be insuperable. He dreamed of being joined, not merely by the two monks mentioned above for whose visas he was negotiating, but also by his friend Fr Lemarié (whose expertise in Oriental liturgy would be invaluable) and even perhaps by Abbot Winandy (who had recently resigned from Clervaux). Fr Monchanin seemed to be favourable to the plan, though for some reason he would not allow Abhishiktananda to travel to Bombay in order to expedite the visas. (L, 22.8.56)

In September Abhishiktananda went to Trivandrum to give a retreat to some French sisters (Little Sisters of the Sacred Heart of Fr de Foucauld) and also to meet Mar Gregorios. On the way back he wrote to his sister from the train:

> . . . I am coming from Trivandrum. (. . .) I have been the guest of the archbishop of the diocese which was reunited with Rome. (. . .) I was received there, especially by the archbishop, with a kindness such as I have rarely met with before; and the people there are insisting that I should leave Shantivanam to others, and come to found a new Shantivanam at Trivandrum. Trivandrum is a strongly Hindu city, and they want me to settle right in the middle of the brahmin quarter. There would certainly be vocations among the Christians, and later on we could branch out in North India. It is very interesting and tempting, despite the business of learning Malayalam and Syriac. I wonder what they will say at Shantivanam when I tell them all this. (MT, 27.9.56)

Abhishiktananda was of course well aware that "Fr Mahieu has also been strongly tempted to work there", and was probably quoting him in saying that "Mar Gregorios had been very pressing with him [Fr.M.] when he passed that way" (L, 15.8.56). Even so Fr Mahieu had not yet told his colleagues how far advanced already were his plans for making a foundation (on Cistercian lines) in Travancore. Abhishiktananda learnt about this in September, and although Mar Gregorios was prepared to envisage *two* new foundations (L, 18.9.56), "I hesitated at first to make a start parallel to his, even though our two works would be as different as day from night.' (L, 13.10.56).

In the course of one of these letters he let slip a remark which helps to explain his ambivalence concerning Shantivanam and Arunachala:

> More and more I am moving towards attempting a new hermitage. Here [i.e., in Trivandrum] it would be a hermitage which would expand, while at Arunachala, or at Banaras, I should remain solitary to the end . . .
>
> Is this a dream without a future that I am sharing with you today? And shall I soon be caught again by the overwhelming attraction of the abyss of Hindu Arunachala? What do you think of all this? (L, 18.9.56)

The call to be a hermit at Arunachala which resounded in his heart could never be forgotten, and there is no question of his deep desire to respond to it. But the 'peace and joy' which he experienced in his caves were only bought at the cost of severe strain, both physical and spiritual. He was not ashamed to admit[73] that his attraction to Arunachala was accompanied by a very natural

73. For example, L, 7.11.54 (p. 76 above).

dread. Would his Christian faith be strong enough to stand the strain? And again, once he cut himself off from all Christian institutions, what chance would he have either of sharing his insights with disciples or of pursuing his wider aim of alerting the Church as a whole to the 'message of India'? One further reason for hesitating about Arunachala was that it was too close to Shantivanam (L, 21.1.57), and this proximity could be a cause of embarrassment in both directions. So, as he still needed a foothold and had not given up hope of realizing the ideal of Shantivanam, it can be well understood why he never took the final step.

Fr Mahieu's Departure—November 1956

In the latter part of 1956 Fr Mahieu's plans for the new ashram were taking shape. About that time also the Benedictine ashram (Nirmala Ashram) in Bangalore was closed, whereupon one of its members, Dom Bede Griffiths, offered himself as a partner in the new work. By November all was settled, and Fr Mahieu left Shantivanam to open the Kurisumāla Ashram (near Vagāmon in Kerala) in the following year.[74] Once he had left, Abhishiktananda's attitude towards him soon mellowed, and in the years to come they worked harmoniously together on several occasions.

Abhishiktananda's interest in the Trivandrum project will have been at least partly due to the continuing tension between himself and Fr Monchanin, for the difference in attitude between the one who was eager to make plans for practical action and the one who was content simply to wait on Providence could not be reconciled:

> . . . Here it is increasingly clear that the take-off can never come from Shantivanam as it is—the experience of the last six years and especially of the present year are conclusive. I would not judge Fr Monchanin as severely as you. He has no particular work 'of his own', nor does he have 'his own' plan; he lets things go on as they are. So in fact no collaboration with him is possible, since collaboration presupposes a 'plan'. Despite all his kindness, his gentleness, his learning, his goodness and his devotion—he is the best of companions, but the worst of partners (he cannot see this himself). Therefore it is best to accept things as they are, to leave him in charge at Shantivanam, and to make a start somewhere else. He will certainly not like the idea, but if Fr Mahieu does not go to Trivandrum, my present intention is definitely to go myself. I have lost interest in Shantivanam; I think it is high time for me to go and do the work of the Church elsewhere, otherwise I do not know if I could any longer resist the compelling appeal of genuine *sannyasa*. The biggest difficulty concerns Fr Dharmanadhan. It is clear that it is on me that he chiefly depends (. . .); I should certainly prefer him to work separately from me (we are four priests, each too well

74. For Kurisumala, see "Kurisumala Ashram: a Chronicle of the first twelve years" by Dom Francis M. Acharya (*Bulletin de l'A.I.M.,* English edition, No. 12 (1971), 40-65 and No. 13 (1972), 18-47); "*Kurisumala: a Symposium on Ashram Life*", edited by Francis Acharya, published by the Ashram, 1974.

> endowed and too independent to be able to make a 'team'), but he needs me for a certain time. (. . .) (L, 13.10.56)[75]

However, once it became clear that Fr Mahieu would be starting his ashram in Travancore (not Trivandrum), Abhishiktananda decided that he would have to abandon his own plans: "I can't settle as a hermit in the same diocese in which Fr Mahieu opens his Trappe." (L, 31.10.56)

A month of silence at Kumbakkonam—November, December 1956

At the end of this eventful year Abhishiktananda decided to follow the advice of Dr Mehta and Gnanananda by making a month-long retreat. Just before this he wrote to Fr Lemarié about the ultimate solution to their personal problems:

> . . . As to solutions, there are scarcely any. I think that to all our agonies there is only one real answer—that which is beyond concepts, in that mystery of the depth, which however only lights up for the one who has dared to penetrate into it by definitively passing beyond the whole level of sense and intellect, that is, the experience to which we are called by the *advaita* of our rishis. Alas, I have not yet had the courage to place myself in the conditions required for that experience . . . However, even its dawning is a blessing, and gives one a zest for life, whatever the turmoil on the surface. (L, 31.10.56)[76]

It must have been with a view to placing himself "in the conditions required for this experience" that Abhishiktananda arranged to spend a full month (5 Nov. to 8 Dec.) at 'Mauna Mandir' (the temple of silence) at Kumbakkonam (Tanjore District) in total seclusion and without books, apart from the New Testament and the Upanishads. His experience during these days is very fully recorded in the Diary. Even if the retreat did not lead him as far as he had hoped (he was still expecting a definitive 'experience'!), it was an important step in his pilgrimage and he saw some things more clearly, especially concerning the need to transcend his *ahamkāra*. "This *mauna mandir* takes its place beside my caves on Arunachala for the impression it made on me" (L, 11.12.56). In a letter to his sister he said:

> . . . I have just spent a month in total enclosure in a large room—a separate building in a garden—with bathroom attached, doors and windows shut, seeing no one, receiving my food through a revolving hatch like an enclosed nun. One of my Hindu friends spends 108 days there every year! I learnt of the place through him and spent the whole of November there, coming out on 8 December after my Mass (which I said alone in the room). I was choked with sobs when I had to open the door and speak. I had only one wish, which was to go back there in the evening . . . Now that I have to live at Shantivanam again, I am quite out of my element. (MT, 19.12.56)

In the same letter there is a paragraph about the joy of Christmas, one of many such that he wrote to her concerning the feasts of the Church:

75. *Les yeux*, 168-9 .
76. *Les yeux*, 169.

> . . . The joy of Christmas, you know, is not only the creche. The creche is just a sign. It is into the cave within the heart that we should go to hide ourselves, lose ourselves, forget ourselves; the true cave where Jesus is born in us, and being born in us makes us into himself. The cave is the bosom of the eternal Father, where the Word is born and comes to be from all eternity. Our joy at Christmas, joy in the family, joy in worship, etc., all that is so little beside the true joy, the joy of Jesus awaking to being that night in Bethlehem, the joy of the divine Word awaking to being in the bosom of the Father in eternity! Live in this cave in the depth of your heart, that mystery into which India has penetrated so deeply.
>
> I expect Lady Abbess has given you my book to read [*Ermites,* published in August]. There you will find about this cave, *guhā;* compare St Paul's "hidden with Christ in God". Also ask to read *La vie spirituelle, Supplément* for September, where there is a long article of mine ["Le monachisme chrétien aux Indes"], and also one in *La vie intellectuelle* for November ["L'hindouisme est-il toujours vivant?"][77]

Shantivanam—January, February 1957

At Christmas (in the absence of Fr Monchanin, who was away until 2 January) Abhishiktananda entertained guests at Shantivanam: a Rumanian—"a Ramakrishna nun, now at Gandhi's ashram at Wardha, profoundly Catholic"—and Dom Bede Griffiths, who was captivated by his first visit to the ashram.[78] This year Epiphany (6 January) was celebrated with High Mass followed by a dinner, at which a number of local Hindu friends and a *maulvī* were guests. In his Memoir of Fr Monchanin (*SPAA*, 45) Abhishiktananda spoke of the happiness which this gave to his companion. It was indeed a kind of anticipatory farewell, for in the following months Fr Monchanin's illness began which soon ended his life. To his sister Abhishiktananda described

> . . . the beautiful Feast of the Epiphany that we have had. At Christmas an English monk was here, and so we sang the whole Office and two Masses. And on Epiphany we invited some Hindu friends, as well as one Muslim. Then we all ate together in the same *mandapam,* after closing the doors of the sanctuary. They made splendid 'Wise Men of the East', don't you think? (MT, 7.2.57)

Soon afterwards, as he told his family.

> . . . Kulittalai was visited (. . .) by Gandhi's greatest disciple, Vinoba Bhave, who for the last six years has gone round India on foot (. . .) asking for the voluntary gift of land in village communities, with all

77. *Ermites du Saccidānanda* (Casterman), August 1956, reprinted 1957. Reviewed in *Clergy Monthly Supplement* (Vol. 3, June 1957, 244-246) by Fr J. Bayart, who praised the book highly, but noted an occasional lack (especially in ch. 2) of the sober restraint which had marked the English version *(I.B.A.)*.

    La vie sp., Supplément 38, Sept. 1956, 283-316; *La vie intellectuelle,* Nov. 1956, 2-40.

78. Dom Bede Griffiths was at Kurisumala from 1957-1968, since when he has been *acharya* at Shantivanam.

> that implies of devotion and unselfishness. I followed him on the next stage of the pilgrimage. He is very impressive. By his example he shows us what priests should be like, if they are to preach the Gospel of Christ effectively. (. . .) He received us most kindly: "With your *kavi* dress you look like brahmins of the North; what a pleasure to see you." And in the talk that followed, he referred to the two Christian sannyasis who have the OM on their cross. (F, 28.1.57)

At this time Abhishiktananda's thoughts were turned once more towards North India. For years he had hoped to go on a tour of exploration, but lack of money constantly made him put it off. But now the payment received for the articles published in the previous year at last made it possible. He also felt free to go, having dropped the Trivandrum project, especially now that Fr Dharmanadhan was at Shantivanam to keep things going and to look after Fr Monchanin. He himself badly needed a change, as he said to Fr Lemarié: "I do not know if my nerves will hold out much longer in this set-up." But at first Fr Monchanin was very unwilling to give him permission to go (L, 12.1.57).

A fortnight later he says he has made up his mind "at least so far as it depends on me; I have written about it to Fr Abbot [of Kergonan] to have, if not his permission, at least his No Objection":

> . . . Fr Monchanin is reluctantly resigned to it, but still does not really believe that this time I definitely intend to pursue my plan. This journey in the North is precisely with the object of finding where I can establish another ashram. I am very much drawn to the area round Hardwar (. . .). I plan to leave in mid-February. Fr Dominique (. . .) and others also strongly encourage me to go. Fr Monchanin, with extraordinary naivety, only accuses me of egotism. I do not know what will become of Shantivanam. I had dreamed of building up a monastery capable of perpetuating itself (. . .). Whatever the reason, this has failed. With Fr Dharmanadhan Shantivanam can work for priests, an excellent work, but one for which I do not feel myself fitted. As a single monk, I cannot maintain the monastic ideal here against secular priests (. . .)
>
> The business in Malabar had to be dropped for reasons already given (. . .). What will the ashram in the Himalayas produce? Above all, a place where I can 'sit' in peace (. . .). I could certainly have gone to settle at Arunachala, but it is too close to this place and I could not have dissociated myself from here as completely as I should . . . (L, 27.1.57)

In a postscript he refers to a review of *Ermites* which Fr Lemarié was writing for *Maison Dieu,* for which he had sent him information about the liturgical experiments at Shantivanam and also the recently printed texts which were sung; but asks him not to mention that they were using texts from the Upanishads, as this had been forbidden by the Council of Bangalore in 1950.[79]

79. The review (*Maison Dieu,* No. 52, 158-9) makes no reference to these details.

North Indian tour—March to September 1957

Abhishiktananda finally set off on 5 March:

> . . . Fr Monchanin was *very deeply* moved by my going. Yet for more than a month it has been in the air; but he only realized on the previous day that this journey was not merely an idea but a reality (. . .). Even so I really needed courage to depart. But I think it is necessary, and that it will be an excellent thing for all of us, whatever be the final results. (L, 6.3.57)

He pursued a roundabout route, including two days in Madras in order to follow up his application for Indian citizenship, and reached Bombay on the 23rd, where he was the guest of Dr Mehta. The latter ("so good, so affectionate") was not in favour of his going further north and had another plan for him. Abhishiktananda reflected on the differing advice given him by his three spiritual advisers:

> . . . with my two advaitins, Gnanananda (. . .) and Poonja [Harilal; both of these he had seen on his way to Bombay], it makes a very interesting trio of spiritual people. Each of them anxious to help me reach the goal, and each finding it hard to understand the incompatibilities with Christianity. (. . .) Dr Mehta trusts too much in my view to his 'experience'. I think he will one day come to the full advaitin realization which at present he regards as inferior to his own. I am giving him a new outlook on realization according to the Upanishads. (. . .) It has come to him [through his nightly 'messages' from Christ] that I ought not to go on to the north. He has proposed that I should go to a mountain twenty miles from Poona, where he has a bungalow in which I shall be able to give myself to solitary meditation for at least a month. I have agreed to this. We will see about the other things later. The future is completely obscure to me. It must not be thought that I have left Shantivanam for good. I am on the look out for another solution; we can decide later. Fr Monchanin is knocked off his balance by my leaving, and reproaches me bitterly, forgetting that he is chiefly responsible, through his 'wait and see' policy, for my nerves being at breaking point. (L, 30.3.57)

While at Bombay, he saw off a French visitor, Mme C. Drevet, a woman of wide experience who had spent a fortnight at the ashram. She was very fond of Fr Monchanin, but also disappointed by her meeting with him. Her advice to Abhishiktananda reassured him, for she urged him "not to give in to Fr Monchanin's distress" but to go his own separate way. Another encouragement was the discovery of a Bombay community (the Daughters of the Heart of Mary), who were "marvellously open", especially a Goan Sister whom he compared to his Carmelite friend at Shembaganur, one who would be equally ready for the plunge into *Guhantara*, "if I gave it to her", and the first Indian woman of that quality that he had met— "a great joy". (L, 30.3.57)

On his way to Dr Mehta's bungalow at Sinhgadh, Abhishiktananda spent several days in Poona at the Pontifical Athenaeum (philosophical and theological faculties, run by Jesuits), where he made "excellent contacts". Three or four of the neighbouring religious houses on the campus invited him for Holy Week, and in one of them (the Order of the Imitation of Christ) the young Malayali monks, whose mother-house he had visited in Trivandrum, demanded that he should give them an 8-day retreat in May ("Should I not sow the good seed wherever I can?") He also made the acquaintance of the Goan artist, Angelo da Fonseca, who shared his views on the regrettable westernization of the Catholic clergy, and introduced him to the Christa Prema Seva Sangh ashram[80] where he had his studio. Abhishiktananda appreciated the ashram for being "very simple, Franciscan, Indian", but commented: "Alas, celibacy does not thrive in Protestantism, and that is why several ashrams started here and there in India with great enthusiasm do not manage to survive. Now this ashram in Poona is little more than a memory." (L. 15.4.57)

He then went on to Sinhgadh, an old fort on the top of a hill overlooking Poona, from which he sent Easter greetings to his sister:

> . . . I am writing this morning from an old fort in the Maratha country, 1300 metres above sea-level and 600 metres above the surrounding plain. (. . .) There are barely six families living on the plateau (. . .) My dinner is prepared by an old Maratha who does not know a word of English. With the help of a word-list I make him understand the essentials. (. . .) At night, 20 kms away, we can see the lights of Poona (. . .). For several weeks I can enjoy this solitude which a friend in Bombay has arranged for me. (MT. 12.4.57)

Meanwhile he heard again from Fr Monchanin:

> . . . Fr M. is very angry that Madame Drevet has seen things so clearly, and practically accuses me of having put ideas into her head. Got a very unkind letter from him on Sunday. He is reproaching me harshly for 'running away' (. . .) What is the use of arguing with him? I go my own way quite peacefully (. . .), letting myself be guided by circumstances and Providence. (L, 15.4.57)

After only ten days at Sinhgadh he had to come down to Poona for Maundy Thursday and stayed on for three weeks, having decided not to return to his hilltop on account of the extreme austerity of the diet prescribed by Dr Mehta. The retreat which he gave to the seminarists at the end of his stay was a strain, as he had no notes with him and little time for preparation. The three addresses each day had to be hastily worked out as he went along. His chief problem was to express in Christian terms ideas "which I habitually think of in a vocabulary which is as much Upanishadic as Evangelical". However he thought his main points had gone home: first, that the contemplative life is "essential and requires the going beyond thought in the Father's presence at the deepest centre of oneself (and don't forget that these young men are accustomed to the Jesuit form of meditation)"; and second, a call for complete outward stripping—not penitential, but spontaneous—to accord with the simplicity of Indian life. (L, 27.5.57)

80. The C.P.S.S. Ashram was founded by Fr Jack Winslow, an Anglican missionary, in 1927. It chiefly flourished between 1927 and 1934.

While at Poona he also gave classes in Gregorian chant and conversed freely with numerous priests, professors and seminarists. He no doubt expressed his radical views about the Pontifical Seminary, so entirely western in its teaching and standard of living. "I would not shed a tear if, in some war, a bomb aimed at the aerodrome close by were to free the Indian Church from all that, and forced her to look at the formation of her clergy face to face with reality." His most significant meeting was with Raymond Panikkar, who had come from Banaras to take part in a summer camp for students. They discussed theology "on the road, in the sun, squeezed together in buses, in the restaurant, as well as sitting in a room. We continued our discussions (really serious) in Bombay in similar conditions. We shall renew them in Banaras after six weeks." (L, 27.5.57)

Leaving Poona he spent four days in Bombay, where he met the Anglican Bishop, W.Q. Lash, who had previously been the *āchārya* of the C.P.S.S. ashram in Poona. They found that they had much in common, including favourite Sanskrit verses which were dear to both of them; but, said Abhishiktananda,

> . . . how could I not feel sad to see how the Lord plays hide-and-seek with his Roman Catholic Church! Simplicity of life, spiritual values, understanding of the problem—that I should find them there, rather than at the cardinal's palace! (L, 27.5.57)

On 15 May Abhishiktananda reached Indore, which was to be his centre until August. Here he was warmly welcomed by the Bishop, Mgr Simons SVD, who invited him to settle in his diocese. After a day or two, during which he managed quick visits to Ujjain and Omkareshwar, he went on to fulfil an engagement to take part in a Study Week for priests in North India at Pachmarhi, attended by five bishops and forty priests. He was received with a sympathy which he had hardly expected, and felt that

> . . . this was a kind of semi-official recognition by the Church in North India. This comforts me for many things and restores my courage. It greatly pleased me—and I did not fail to tell my hearers this—to have been on Monday the guest of a Hindu ashram, and on Tuesday to be seated at a very distinguished clerical table! (. . .) I have the impression that most of these bishops would accept me with open arms.
>
> After all that, I look upon an installation in the North in the Hindi area as highly desirable. The sympathy so widely encountered would lead to possible 'disciples' being sent in my direction. But I have told them that I do not want lads who come to take a vow of 'security' in entering the noviciate. I need ones who are capable of a vow of 'insecurity' like their Hindu brothers. (. . .) I am wondering if the time of gestation (9 years) is not approaching an end. That sometimes frightens me, but it is also reinvigorating to feel myself 'accepted', just as I am, by the Church; it is so hard to feel suspected as a dangerous person. (L, 27-30.5.57)

On his return to Indore with the object of taking up the study of Hindi, Abhishiktananda came to know the French Sisters in charge of the Roberts Nursing Home, which became one of his most frequent ports of call in the coming years.[81] They gladly took him under their wing and, after nursing him through an attack of fever, helped him to get in touch with local Hindu society and to find a quiet room in which to stay. A month later he wrote to his sister about some of his experiences:

> . . . I came here to look round a little, and to study Hindi, which is essential in North India. This is where I met the French Sisters who have sent you the photos. One of them is from Pontivy; so one evening she brought me the songs of Th. Botrel,[82] and you can picture me with them singing all the songs of days gone by. It gave them great pleasure.
>
> Thanks to them I was immediately put in touch with some Hindus. Some days later these took me off in a car and installed me in a small room near a hall [Gita Bhavan], where every morning 200, 300, 400 people meet to sing devotional songs (to Radha and Krishna, of course) and to hear sermons. Next morning they planted me on a platform in the middle of three or four other sannyasis, and in no time I found myself firmly placed in front of the microphone. There was nothing for it but to consent. I spoke in English, and someone translated into Hindi, sentence by sentence. I spoke to them about the cave within the heart, and of the love which gives access to it. The result was that the next day I had to speak again, and after that continuously for three weeks. There was a slight stir after some time when the company learnt that I was a Christian[83] (I had made that quite clear to those who received me at the outset, but the information spread only gradually): but the great majority were on my side, and insisted that I should continue to speak. However, in the end I was allowed to hold my peace so as to avoid difficulties; but now every day people ask me: "Why are you not speaking any more? When are we going to hear you again?" I say to them: "But you already have two sermons every morning, isn't that enough?" "Yes," said a grandmother to me one day; "but you speak to us about the heart, while the others speak about externals."
>
> For the moment I am learning Hindi as hard as I can, as people would like me to speak directly in Hindi. Each Sunday I have to give two or three sermons. Next Sunday they are taking me to a place 50 kms form here [Dewas]. Naturally I do not mention Christ by name—that would ruin everything—but I preach to them about the presence of God, love, etc. These people attend to my slightest need—food, lodging, clothing. Here a sadhu does not have to spend anything, people vie with each other to look after him, far more than in Tamilnad. Everyone calls you *Mahārāj, Gurumahārāj, Mahātmaji.* In all my life I have never been such a celebrity! I do not know where it is all going to lead,

81. These Sisters belonged to the Franciscan Sisters of St Mary of the Angels. After 1957 Abhishiktananda corresponded regularly with Mother Théophane, who nursed him at Indore during his final illness in 1973.

82. A Breton song-writer .

83. Abhishiktananda had perhaps gone too far, "when I preached—discreetly, but without ambiguity—that it was not enough to repeat the name of Rama 10, 000 times a day, or to take three dips in the Ganges, in order to be purified . . ." (L, 28. 6. 57).

> but I must never show the slightest desire that anyone else should become a Christian, or I should be chased out at once. But even so, what I am doing seems to me very worth while. I am helping them to love more (and among my hearers there are some really fine people), and to listen to the inner voice. It is up to the Lord to lead on to the next stage.
>
> I say Mass every morning for the Sisters who wrote to you. They are always so kind to me. (. . .) Pray that the word which I sow may be fruitful, and that I may know how to proceed. From here I shall probably go to Banaras next month, and then return to the South. My intention is afterwards to come back to the North and go as far as the Himalayas, for that is the land of the sannyasis. Every *sannyasi* must have spent time in the Himalayas to be considered genuine. (MT, 3.7.57)

During this time in the North Abhishiktananda was discovering quite new aspects of what was expected of him as a *sannyasi,* as he was thrust into the role of a popular preacher. Apart from Gita Bhavan, he was in demand in other places too. At Dewas he found himself addressing a crowd of 1000. On another occasion he spoke for an hour in the Brahmo Samaj temple ("cold like a Protestant church") to a select group of 50-60 of these reformed Hindus (F, 27.7.57). Most surprising of all, he was one Sunday invited to preach to the Arya Samaj (strongly anti-Christian), and then asked to come again the following week. ("Our Bishop could not get over it, when I told him that!") But he had problems to face, one of which was

> . . . how to get myself accepted as a Christian *sannyasi?* The *sannyasi* is by definition free from every bond. Dependence on a Church, on a Superior, the obligation to perform religious rites, etc.—is that not incompatible with *sannyasa?* "Don't you yourself feel the contradiction involved in adding a qualification to *'sannyasi'?"* asked the Swamiji of Gita Bhavan. And the further north I go, the more tricky this will become. People ask me where I received *sannyasa?* who initiated me? who was my guru? (I can only say) "My guru is far away from here in Brittany . . ." [referring to the Abbot who received his profession]. All these problems are very new. I let myself be led by events; it is the Lord's business to steer the boat. (L, 28.6.57)

In July he had the news that "Fr Monchanin seems to be far from well. He has been taken to hospital in Pondi for a general examination" (L, 25.7.57). Since May relations between the two men had become easier: "Fr Monchanin's last letter made no reference to our difficulties. I think he is going to come round slowly to the idea" (L, 27-30.5.57). "Now we are no longer fighting in our letters. I simply tell him what is happening; but it will be a difficult moment when we meet again after three months" (L, 28.6.57). The difficulty was different and even worse than he expected, for as yet he had not realized the seriousness of Fr Monchanin's condition.

The last stage of Abhishiktananda's tour was at Banaras, where he spent the last half of August, staying with his friend R. Panikkar (then a Professor in the Kashi Hindu University) in the university quarter. His first impression of the city was disappointing, despite the beauty of the distant view across the Ganges, but he looked forward to a longer stay in the city itself at a later date. With his friend he had long discussions about the future, and took advantage of Dr Panikkar's forthcoming visit to Rome

> . . . to finalize a memorandum for Rome, in order to obtain a statute which would allow me to continue my work as a travelling monk. (F, 21.8.57)

Among many other interesting contacts at Banaras, he met a Rumanian Orthodox monk, an enthusiast for the Hesychian tradition of prayer,[84] with whom he "dreamed of a Hesychast monastery on the slopes of the Himalayas. This spirituality would in fact be much closer to India than anything Ignatian." (L, 28.8.57)

The death of Fr Monchanin—October 1957

When Abhishiktananda reached Madras, he found a telegram summoning him to Pondicherry. The doctors had eventually discovered that Fr Monchanin was suffering from a deep-seated tumour requiring immediate surgery. It was decided that this had best be done in Paris. For the journey a free air passage was offered by the French Foreign Office. A few days later Abhishiktananda accompanied him by air to Bombay and saw him onto the international flight.

> . . . This has just struck me like a thunderbolt on my arrival this morning at Pondi (. . .). Despite all that I may have thought or written, you know the place which he holds in my life. As he has been corresponding with you through me, a visit from you will certainly please him. (. . .). My impression is that the chances of his recovery are very slight. (L, 5.9.57)

A few weeks later (on 10 October) Fr Monchanin died in Paris, serene and lucid to the end. The news reached Shantivanam on the next day, the sixth anniversary of the blessing of the ashram chapel. Fr Monchanin's last letter to his Bishop before leaving India had ended with these words: "I offer my life to God on behalf of Shantivanam, and my death also, if it be his will." To which Abhishiktananda added: "The Lord had already made his choice. The seed had to fall into the ground and die, in order to germinate and bear fruit" (*SPAA*, 70).

The future of Shantivanam

Many people thought that the going of Fr Monchanin would mean the end of Shantivanam, and some even wrote to offer their condolences. Abhishiktananda's remaining colleague, Fr Dharmanadhan, feeling himself the rightful successor to Fr Monchanin, wanted to transfer the ashram to Trichinopoly, where he could more easily carry on the work he had begun. However he was eventually persuaded by Abhishiktananda, supported by Fr Dominique, to leave the ashram as it was, and instead to go there himself. In November he left the ashram, having accepted a pastoral charge (L, 19.10.57).

84. Hesychasm (from Gk, *hesuchia* silence); see *Prayer*, ch. 5. Note 9 .

Once again Abhishiktananda felt himself pulled in different directions. As a result of his visit to the North, several bishops (especially Gorakhpur and Nagpur) were inviting him to settle in their diocese and to give himself to activities which he doubted were compatible with his calling to be a monk. At first he had thought that, if Fr Dharmanadar stayed on at the ashram, he would be able to divide his time between work in the North and periods at Shantivanam. But when the whole responsibility for the ashram fell on him, he decided that for the time being it must be given the priority.

Even after nearly eight years of disappointment, he had by no means abandoned hope for the ashram. He was in touch with several western monks whose coming might still make it possible for it to develop. The ideal which in the previous year had been powerfully presented in his article on Christian monasticism in India, was again stressed in the memorial article written for *La vie spirituelle* in the weeks after Fr Monchanin's death:

> . . . It is quite an important article on Fr Monchanin, in which I very strongly emphasize the essentially contemplative ideal of Shantivanam. I am going to try to have it translated here into English and Tamil. (L, 29.10.57)

In fact, the hoped for take-off was never realized in his time. Again and again his hopes of finding the right colleagues, Indian or European, were raised only to be dashed. And even after establishing his hermitage at Uttar Kashi in 1961, he continued to travel to and fro between the Himalayas and Tamilnadu in his determination to keep Shantivanam going. When finally he steeled himself in 1968 to entrust it to other hands, it was only because the burden of maintaining a double establishment had become too great.

The contemplative Benedictine ashram of which Fr Monchanin and he had dreamed in 1948 remained only a dream; and when eventually after 1968 Shantivanam did develop, it was in a somewhat different direction, corresponding to the charisma of its new *acharya.* The lack of success of the original founders was due to a number of factors, some external, others personal, originating in the differing strengths and weaknesses of the two men who, as Fr Monchanin realized as soon as they met, "at the human level were very different". Yet, even if it failed as an institution, there is no doubt that Shantivanam succeeded in pointing to an ideal of abiding significance. At the end of his Memoir of Fr Monchanin, Abhishiktananda summed this up as follows:

> The Hermitage of Shantivanam will remain, God willing, what it has been and continues to be, a place of peace and solitary contemplation. Expansion in human terms, success, numbers, are of no importance. All that belongs to the realm of *māyā,* appearance, and the monk is only concerned with *nitya,* the real. In his solitude he is none the less a monk, and his witness is none the less essential. In any case, Fr Monchanin kept to the end the certainty of theological hope: whatever might be the immediate future of Shantivanam in Tannirpalli on the banks of the Kavery, a day will surely dawn when, in all the sacred places of India from the Himalayas to Cape Comorin, from Bengal to Maharashtra, Shantivanams will arise, dedicated solely to the adoration

> of Saccidananda, bearing witness before God in eternity to India's final glorious destiny, and bearing witness before India, while time lasts, to God and his Church. (*SPAA,* 71)

As to the meaning for himself of the outward failure of Shantivanam, his own final perception was expressed in words written to his sister a few months before his death:

> . . . fortunately I came [to India] alone, and Fr Monchanin was not a practical man, so that we could never organize anything; then, being 'unsuccessful'. I was brought by the Spirit to the true source of India's monastic life. (MT, 6.7.73)

But at the end of 1957, despite all his uncertainties about its future, Abhishiktananda decided that it was incumbent on him to persevere in his efforts to build up the ashram:

> . . . The last months have been full of anxieties and preoccupations. You will have heard of Fr Monchanin's death—hence letters, visits, etc. His departure has shown me more than ever the place that Shantivanam has in the thoughts of many, whether they like it or whether they do not—but it is liked, and I have received much encouragement. I 'keep things going', even though all alone.
>
> A monk of St Wandrille is to join me next year; at present he is engaged in making his application to come. There is another also, I think, and probably more Indian lay people will come to Shantivanam than in the past. Next month I am expecting a brahmin from Madras who is much drawn to Christianity. Pray that the Lord will grant a 'take-off' to our Shantivanam. I would prefer to remain in solitude, but I cannot of my own choice let the work drop.
>
> A Christmas of light, of joy, of peace. Advent is at once the expectation and the 'Parousia' [coming, Presence]. He *comes,* and he is already *there* in the cave in the depth of the heart. He comes, or rather, we go to him from the 'time' in which we are to the eternity in which he is.
>
> . . . I am expecting for Christmas (. . .) three or four friends for a kind of meeting or theological conference, and am in the process of doing up Shantivanam for their reception, because the white ants have done a fantastic amount of damage during my journey. That is why I am so rushed today. (MT, 19.12.57)

After the meeting he told Fr Lemarié:

> We have just had a grand week—Fr Dominique, Fr Bede, Fr Panikkar. Long and deep discussions on *advaita* and Christian mysticism. (L, 29.12.57)

5

Shantivanam—Uttarkashi

(1958-1968)

> The Himalayas have conquered me! It is is beside the Ganges that Shantivanam ought to be. I do not know if that will ever happen, but how splendid it would be! (MT, 16.7.59)

Shantivanam—January to June 1958

AT THE END of 1957 Abhishiktananda could write: "The worst moments have passed, and the future is no longer purely a matter of stubborn faith" (L. 29.12.57). There was in fact no question of Shantivanam being closed after the death of Fr Monchanin and the departure of Fr Dharmanadhan; but it now became what it was to remain for the following eleven years—a simple hermitage, where Abhishiktananda lived in solitude for the greater part of each year, apart from the coming and going of visitors and occasional would-be postulants. He was content that it should be so, while awaiting with mixed hope and dread for a sign from Providence that it should develop into a community of monks. Throughout 1958 he corresponded with several European monks, especially with Dom Bescaud of St Wandrille, who continued his efforts to obtain a visa, and still hoped that Fr Dominique might be allowed to join him. At the end of the year a young Indian came to test his vocation at the ashram.

The article on Fr Monchanin which Abhishiktananda wrote soon after his death was published in the January 1958 issue of *La vie spirituelle,*[1] and he was urgently requested to write another for *Église vivante*. However some reactions to the former article inhibited him from writing another:

> . . . we are still at the stage of panegyrics, and no reservations are allowed. Here are two characteristic responses: I. "No man is a hero to his own valet"(!!); 2. "You have emphasized the outward facts, and then put your own interpretation on them. You have not recognized that you had to deal with a 'saint', and that has prevented you from understanding anything." Then again, my journey in the North has been regarded, and widely condemned, as a *desertion* of Fr M. I should truly need to be a "saint', not to have my nerves set on edge by all that apart from everything else (L, 17.1.58)

1. "Le père Monchanin"; *La vie spirituelle,* no. 435 (Jan. 1958), 71-95.

It was a slight consolation that these criticisms came from admirers of Fr Monchanin in France, not from his friends in Pondicherry who knew him better (L, 17.2.58); but the second article was never written. Instead Abhishiktananda concentrated on preparing a longer Memoir in English, based on the French article.

Just before Christmas Fr Lemarié's book, *La manifestation du Seigneur,*[2] had arrived at Shantivanam. This study of the liturgy of Christmas, Epiphany and the Presentation impressed and pleased Abhishiktananda, even though he never tired of stressing that what is Manifested is only fulfilled in the Unmanifested (e.g., L, 27.5.57): "The manifested and the manifester are entirely relative to what cannot be manifested"). His friend asked him for some notes on the Epiphany, no doubt as seen from India, and these were sent at the beginning of February. The self-depreciatory title, "Ramblings of a Hindu gnostic on the Feast of the Epiphany" underlined his dissatisfaction with what he described as "a kind of rough introduction to what I should have given you " (L, 3.2.58). But the article, though never published, has some interesting suggestions, especially about the need to deepen the cosmic and eschatological dimension of Christian festivals.

In his next letter he commented on the relation of liturgy to advaita:

> . . . Liturgy and advaita are on two different planes. When occasion offers, I allow myself to come back to liturgy, witness last Christmas (. . .). But afterwards . . . You have seen in *Guhantara* what I said discreetly about it. Liturgy is on one particular plane, and on this plane it is marvellous (. . .). Advaita places you on another plane, and says that all the other planes are a game, *līlā, māyā.* And the advantage of Shivaism is that it very readily accepts that it is a game which has to be left behind ("When I was a child, I thought as a child . . ."); while in the Church the plane of sacraments, liturgy, Church, is treated as absolute in itself. And therein lies the agonizing tension. It is precisely the role of Shantivanam within the Church to live this tension and there discover the further mystery. (. . .) But the Church, snugly protected at its centre from draughts, like 19th century episcopal palaces, (. . .) *does not understand.* (L.17.2.58)

In January his sister at St Michel had taken her final vows, and this drew from him a series of affectionate and encouraging letters. In one written just before Easter he spoke of his uneventful life:

> . . . I am still living in my solitude, even though this month I have had quite a few visitors. In a few months I shall know if the Lord wants me to stay here alone, or if he will send me two companions. (. . .)
>
> On Monday I am going to the monastery of Siluvaigiri[3] for Holy Week because, being all alone here, I am unable to celebrate the Liturgy of the season. On the way I shall go to see a Protestant ashram whose founder I know, a fine Tamilian Christian[4] who puts us Catholics to

2. Published in the collection 'Lex Orandi' by Éd. du Cerf in 1957.
3. The Siluvaigiri community had moved to Kengeri, a suburb of Bangalore, in 1957. Since then it has been known as the Asirvanam Monastery.
4. Dr Jesudasen, founder of the Tirupattur Ashram, near Jolarpet.

shame. The other day I was visited by a brahmin, also a Protestant, who has remained unmarried and has a magnificent influence on all around him.[5] He is a senior member of the Railway Board in Delhi. He is very keen that I should move my ashram to North India, where the Lord Jesus is so little known. (MT, 29.3.58)

A few weeks later, when writing to his family, he mentioned his deep concern at the news from France, which in the months preceding de Gaulle's return to power seemed to be on the brink of civil war. He also feared that a government of the Right would continue "the abominable war in Algeria which, like the one in Indo-China, has brought the name of France into disrepute throughout the world."

> . . . It makes no difference that I am a monk, and an Indian monk at that, I have not yet learnt not to worry about what happens in France, even though it is now ten years since I came away. It is for the Lord to guide events, and for men to live as Christians, with love and understanding for others. In France, as here, there are so many Christians who think that Christianity means going to Mass on Sundays and perhaps on weekdays too, but in practice have no love for their brothers, their workers, etc. It makes one ashamed before non-Christians to be the representative of such a Christianity. (F, 30.5.58)

There was also some distressing news from the family, to which he responded:

> . . . You see, the good Lord must be served and loved for his own sake, and not for the blessings he gives us. And when anyone loves him, he loves all his brothers. So few Christians are Christian in more than name and outward practice. All that happens, joys and sorrows, is from his hand, and he must be thanked for all of it (. . .). He is equally to be thanked for the (apparent) failure of Shantivanam to be a success in men's eyes, for example. We must not mix up our egoism and our own desires with our faith. (F, 30.5.58)

The remark about Shantivanam seems to have caused someone to suggest that he might as well give up and come home:

> . . . It is just about ten years since I left Kergonan, St Briac and France. Certainly I have no regrets. The Lord be blessed for all that he gives me here. I do not understand the missionaries of the past who always felt home-sick for their own countries. (. . .) It is like a wife, with husband and children at her side, continuing to miss her birthplace. And nothing could ever repay what India gives to anyone who gives himself to her whole-heartedly. That does not often happen, alas, but so much the worse for those who cannot understand her! (F, 21.6.58)[6]

Early in June he wrote to Fr Lemarié:

> . . . The life of Shantivanam continues to be one of waiting. The solitude would be nothing, were it not for this kind of 'mission', at once

5. Shri C.T. Venugopal, with whom Abhishiktananda often stayed in Delhi during the next few years. For Venugopal's impression of him, see *Witness to Christ* (C.I.S.R.S.), 15, 34.
6. *Les yeux*, 160.

> monastic and intellectual (the integration of Indian mysticism), which gnaws at your heart, of which you are reminded in season and out of season, and which comes up against an almost total lack of understanding. So when will the Church be willing to emerge from the bonds (of every kind and on every side) of the Roman Empire (dead!) and to be Catholic in real earnest?

Then, after noting Massignon's argument in the periodical *Comprendre* that statistics give no indication of the small number of Christians who are Easter communicants, he asked if the rest of humanity is to be condemned to hell, or else

> . . . one fine day we shall have to admit that holiness (. . .) is found just as often outside [the Church] as within, and that our Christian communities (. . .) are far from being exemplary. India never ceases to bring up against us the fact that the horrible wars of the 20th century are the work of *Christian* nations. So (people ask) why are they no longer Christian, has the spiritual power of the early days been exhausted?
>
> What view of the Church will make a place for the world? (. . .), will make room for the millions of conscious beings who have lived and do live outside the sacramental Church, and yet are each endowed with an eternal destiny? will integrate the holiness and wisdom of non-Romans and non-Christians? Otherwise the title 'Catholic' is a deception. (. . .) (L, 5.6.58)

In his next letter he commented on an article by Hromadka in *Comprendre* (no. 17):

> . . . He has felt the problem still more profoundly than Barth or Daniélou (in the same number). It appears that you need to have been immersed in the Communist world (here, the Hindu) to look at the problem otherwise than in terms of a Christianity which is unable to get free from its mediaeval complexes. (L, 9.6.58)

The same letter makes a first reference to a contact with the Carmel of Lisieux, which assumed great significance for Abhishiktananda in the coming years:

> . . . Have I told you that *Ermites* has penetrated the sanctuary of Lisieux through the intermediacy of Mme Charnelet,[7] the mother of the present Prioress (M. Françoise-Thérèse)? and that now they are praying for Shantivanam there? No small matter!

At the end of June Abhishiktananda took a week's holiday in Bangalore, staying with Fr Monchanin's friends, the Ingles, and frankly enjoyed the luxury of a European home and the music played on their 'marvellous Hi-Fi'. He also visited the Bangalore Carmel, where Sr Thérèse (the one who had appreciated *Guhantara*) was also staying. The Prioress called him for a long interview

7. Mme L. Charnelet, mother of the Prioress of Lisieux, M. Françoise-Thérèse. She heard of Abhishiktananda through one of the Sisters at Indore, M. Marie Noellie. Letters to her are printed in *Les yeux*, 133, 135. She died in 1959.

(through the grill), and was so interested that he had to return on the two following days:

> . . . I had not previously realized how spiritually deprived these enclosed nuns are. I shall certainly come again. If only, in every Indian Carmel, there were (as here) at least a few true Carmelites, contemplative and not merely 'pious'! (. . .) More and more I feel that I ought to write another *Guhantara* in a popular style, which would not frighten people but might help them to find themselves. (L. 29.6.58)

Shantivanam—July 1958 to April 1959

During the second half of 1958 Abhishiktananda remained continuously at the ashram. He had his hands full with the preparation and publication of his Memoir of Fr Monchanin in English and Tamil. There were also visitors to be entertained, especially in December when a second Study Week was held, this time with seven taking part; and from October he had with him a postulant.

Early in July a Tamil priest (Fr Arokianadar) stayed for a week, checking the Tamil version of the Memoir. They had to work hard at finding ways to express in Tamil terms like 'the call of India', '*pleroma*' and '*parousia*', hitherto unknown in Tamil literature. But he hoped the result would be comprehensible "to anyone with a minimum of education who was prepared to make a small effort to understand" (L, 12.7.58). Shortly afterwards Harold Rose came to help with the English version. The work took longer than was expected, and the manuscript was only ready for printing at the end of October.

In August a professor of French (J. Laurencin) spent two weeks at the ashram, 'pumping' Abhishiktananda about India. In a letter to his family he told them about this visit, and about the complications of his work on the Memoir, which even so he hoped "will help our ideal to be understood":

> . . . Meanwhile I live in my hermitage, always happy, and I admit that I have less desire than ever that others should come and share my life. The monk is made to be alone. (F, 23.8.58)

As he said also to Fr Lemarié:

> . . . I no longer have any desire for a monastic institution; it is too heavy a responsibility. I must make Shantivanam simply a hermitage without plans for the future, which it ought to have been from the beginning; or else go somewhere else on my own. I await the decision of Providence as regards Fr Bescaud before making up my mind. (L, 1.9.58)

However, a month later, Providence seemed to be giving a different signal:

> . . . Just think of it, since the beginning of this month I am no longer alone. A young Malayali, aged 25, has just arrived, sent by Fr Bede for some weeks of quiet studies, and has discovered here more than he had ever dreamed of in his desire for an Indianized Church. The lad has admirable qualities. All my own dreams are exceeded. The future must be left in God's hands, for indeed he is not cut out for lifelong solitude. All the same I feel sure that my 'relief' has been sent. He has done

three years at the seminary (philosophy). He sets himself and me too many questions. (. . .) But now I know that there are Indians capable of taking over Shantivanam—he is the sign; and I hope from the bottom of my heart that he will be the seed, the *real* founder of Shantivanam. (L, 29.10.58)

Conversation with Mathew, his new disciple, showed Abhishiktananda the bitterness felt by some Indians towards westerners:

> . . . They want nothing to do with Europeans. The most excellent proposals will be rejected, if they come from Europeans. One may regret this, but it is a fact. (. . .) "When the Europeans have gone, we shall settle our problems of Indianization by ourselves." Mathew was immensely surprised to find here a European who is totally *given* to India. (L, 29.10.58)

However it became clear after a few weeks that Mathew's calling was not to Shantivanam. When he went on his way, Abhishiktananda reflected that

> . . . he will have been the providential instrument to make me understand that I should not any longer persist in waiting for Indians to come and take my place at Shantivanam . . . (L, 31.12.58)

During November and December Abhishiktananda, helped by Mathew and Harold Rose, was kept very busy with the printing of the Memoir, which involved frequent visits to Trichy. His sister at Kergonan had complained that he sent her so little news, and his reply contained the following:

> . . . I should have told you that I am in touch with Lisieux (. . .). The other day I received an excellent letter from the Mother Prioress, telling me that they are praying for me at the Carmel, and that my photo is placed under a relic! Two days ago there came for me a relic of St Thérèse with some pictures (real photos). See how, despite everything, the good Lord smiles on each of us from time to time. But, in fact, is not everything his smile? What seems harsh to us is no less his love than everything else. Later on we realize it. (. . .)
>
> Next month we shall have a Study Week like last year. We shall be six this time. (. . .)
>
> There, that is the outward news of Shantivanam. The real news—of what is within—that cannot be told. It is joy and it is peace. That is what I should like to convey to you, less by means of words than heart to heart. (MT, 21.11.58)

The Study Week took place in the middle of December, and was attended by Fr Dominique, Fr Bede Griffiths, Fr Panikkar, Fr M.P. Christanand,[8] Harold Rose and Mathew. Once again Abhishiktananda was glad of the opportunity to discuss with friends some of the theological and spiritual problems with which he had long been wrestling. From this small beginning there followed some remarkable developments in the coming years.[9]

8. Fr Christanand was parish priest at Solan (Simla Hills). He had invited Abhishiktanda to establish his ashram there.
9. Described in *Hindu-Christian Meeting Point.*

By the end of the year the printing of the Memoir was almost finished, as he told his sister with relief:

> . . . I am hard at work on printing this book of which I have told you. It is no small job; I have just stopped correcting proofs in order to write to you. I have to go to Trichy two or three times a week. I hope it will be over in another week. You should receive a copy towards the middle of January (. . .). For the last month an English friend has been with me here, helping me to finalize the book. (. . .)
>
> Next year what will happen here, no one knows. I am invited to go to the Himalayas. Shall I go? I will tell you in my next letter. (MT, 29.12.58)

The Memoir (*Swami Parama Arubi Anandam*) was published in the middle of January 1959. The first 94 pages were a much expanded version of the original article in *La vie spirituelle.* This was followed by a 'Garland of Memories', collected from some twenty of Fr Monchanin's friends in India and abroad, and then by a number of extracts from his writings. The book was generously embellished with illustrations, so far as the limitations of the available paper allowed, and was a worthy tribute to that great soul. The shorter Tamil version also appeared at the same time.

After an arduous month devoted to despatching copies of the Memoir far and wide—to all the bishops in India, to Rome, to his family and friends, and to all who showed interest in Shantivanam—, Abhishiktananda betook himself to Bangalore for a rest. He first stayed at the Asirvanam monastery, meeting many people, and in particular a young monk who thought of coming to the ashram. Then he took a seven hour bus journey to see his friend Harilal at a manganese mine, and then returned to stay with the Ingles and at the Bangalore Carmel. Back in Shantivanam he told his sister about his holiday and of his plan to travel again to the north:

> . . . Four days at the Bangalore Carmel. I gave an instruction and was kept busy with direction and confessions in the parlour. (. . .) Really it is not pleasant to speak without being able to see anyone or anything through the veil. In a conversation, at least they answer; but in an address there is no way of knowing if they are asleep or dreaming instead of listening. It is only afterwards that you learn what effect it has had. (. . .)
>
> For Holy Week I am going to Fr de Foucauld's Little Sisters of the Sacred Heart (Trivandrum). I go there almost every year; they want a little conversation, spiritual direction, etc. (. . .)
>
> Then perhaps I shall once more go North. I have a great desire to breathe a little of the mountain air and at last to get to know the holy Himalayas . . . But to do that I must first arrange for someone to keep an eye on Shantivanam, which otherwise will be looted.
>
> Tomorrow I am expecting two Frenchwomen, one of whom is at the Aurobindo Ashram at Pondicherry and wants to come back to Christianity. For the time being an English friend is staying with me, who has just returned to Christianity after many years of peregrination. (. . .)

I feel so little inclination to give out, to train (though a monk of Bangalore, Kengeri, is asking to join me). Westerners are always anxious to be *doing!* but we come to India, and there we learn simply *to be*; and being is the most intense form of action. No external movement in the physical world is so intense as the movement at the heart of the atom, through which indeed it exists. So it is with us; and that is our essential vocation as monks, nuns, contemplatives. (MT, 19.3.59)

For ten days at the end of March he was with the Little Sisters at Trivandrum, and on Holy Saturday wrote from there to the Prioress at Lisieux, thanking her for some books that she had sent, and mentioning others that would be useful, if ever there were postulants at Shantivanam:

... So far God's plan in this respect is not at all clear. There too it is still the 'waiting' of Holy Saturday. This waiting itself is the seed from which all will grow tomorrow (. . .). What does it matter that those who have sown the seed should also work at the harvest? The essential thing is to sow very, very deeply in oneself. Then that will bear fruit all round. (FT, 28.3.59)

Shortly afterwards an incident occurred at the ashram which delayed the start of his journey. One night thieves broke into the chapel in search of money, and finding none removed two chalices and some vestments. Abhishiktananda decided to call the police and also to offer a reward for their return, even while recognizing that

... It was to recall us to insecurity and detachment. We were gradually getting too comfortably established at Shantivanam, and that is hardly proper for sadhus. (. . .) A Hindu friend in Trichy as good as scolded me for having informed the police. It is the Lord who gives under the form of friends, and it is he who takes away under the form of thieves. Why make distinctions and only love him when he gives us cake? (MT, 2.5.59)

First visit to the Himalayas—May to October 1959

On 30 April Abhishiktananda set off from Kulittalai for the North. At last his ten-year-old desire to see the Himalayas was to be fulfilled. His first objective was Binsar, 20 kms beyond Almora in the Kumaon Hills, where he planned to stay with a Hindu to whom he had been given an introduction. On the way he spent a fortnight at Indore with the French sisters who two years previously had enabled him to make many interesting contacts. His next stop was the village of Kareli (near Bareilly, U.P.), where he made his first visit to the ecumenical ashram of Jyotiniketan, a meeting which had been recommended to him by his friend C.T. Venugopal. Here he found Murray and Mary Rogers, Heather Sandeman and John Cole—undoubtedly the most 'excellent' of the 'contacts with Protestants' of which he later told his sister. Murray Rogers thus describes his arrival:

It was a dark night, and the little group of us were in the chapel for our Night Prayers, Compline. At its conclusion we had as usual (. . .)

> our last corporate act of the day, the Kiss of Peace, passed from one to the other. Having received and given the Peace, we turned to face the open door, and the last one gave the Peace to our neighbours in the two near-by villages who, though not present in their bodies, were always there in our hearts. That night, as she took a step or two towards the door, we saw in the light of the kerosene lanterns a figure—it was our first glimpse of Swamiji. He had been for an hour or more wandering in the groves, quite unable to see the ashram buildings until the gathering of the lanterns for Compline gave him a hint of our whereabouts; and there he was—the saffron *khadi,* the old bag that became so familiar, at least a couple of other bags hanging from his neck, and the smile. [10]

On both sides there were initial hesitations—normal in those days before Vatican II—but reserve was quickly broken down, friendship blossomed, and a deep and fruitful association began between Abhishiktananda and the members of the ashram. At that point, however, as the same writer noted: "Little did we know what was in store for us!"

At Almora he had his first breath-taking views of he high peaks, then walked on by the mountain road to Binsar.

> . . . Alone here with a Panjabi Hindu, philosophy graduate, two years in London, businessman in Delhi, now spending his time in solitude and meditation.[11] (. . .) Long, frank, friendly and at the same time pungent conversations on Christianity and Hinduism. He is a lover of Christ, but . . . a Hindu cannot accept either the Roman administrative or the Greek mental structure of the Church. A Christ who would straightaway be understood and loved by India, who would respond to the subconscious expectation of many people here, who would take to himself all the drives towards this mysterious 'unknown' without subjecting them to the tyranny of Platonic or Cartesian thought forms (as does the West and its Church), and who finally, like all divine forms in India, would allow himself, in his quality as manifestation, to be transcended in the mystery of the Self, of Being. The Christ of the Ascension making his hidden ascent to the Father's bosom, which in truth he never left.
>
> (He is) a young man who has deeply reflected, deeply meditated, and has authentically realized that incredible experience of being (the 'I am' of John 8), which is at once the axis and the summit of Hindu mysticism. We understood each other immediately and felt each other strangely close, but at the same time so distant that tears came to our eyes. The Church's claim to be the only 'way' revolts him (. . .). Useless for me to explain to him the grand theory of the Church—cosmic, Jewish, Christian—, to point out that every morning Melchizedech (. . .) is recalled in the Christian Mass. That does not get over the plain fact: how can one who has realized that 'he is', once

10. "Swamiji—the Friend", by C. Murray Rogers, *Religion and Society,* Vol. 23.1 (1976), 76-87. Reprinted in Vandana, *Swami Abhishiktananda—the Man and his Message* (1986).
11. Shri Vivek Datta.

more feel himself bound? He put to me the most pressing, existential questions about my own experiences . . .

Once more, a proof that only a Christian saint, a contemplative, a mystic, can touch India. Our clergy (. . .) know nothing of the problem. You have to have gone to the heart of India, spiritually as much as literally it. A torment, a crucifixion (. . .). (L, 3.6.59)

Abhishiktananda had planned to go on from Binsar and join the pilgrimage to Kedarnath and Badrinath before the coming of the rains, but the necessary permit had not arrived. He therefore visited a Quaker architect and his doctor wife (Laurie and Kuni Baker), to whom his new friends at Jyotiniketan had given him an introduction. While spending a week with them at Pithoragarh (on the border of Nepal) he wrote to another new correspondent, Mrs Anne-Marie Stokes, a fellow-Breton living in New York, where she was associated with the work of Dorothy Day: [12]

. . . It was a great joy to learn from your allusion to a friend[13] that there still are priest workers in France. I cannot but feel a deep and special sympathy for a vocation so close to mine—not of course in its working out, but in its conception. (. . .)

. . . I have been moved by many people whom I have met on this trip—Anglicans, Quakers (I am at present the guest of English Quakers). What Pharisees we Catholics often are, and how the Lord sometimes delights in making us aware that Love (the essential thing) is sometimes found in greater measure outside the Church than within it. (. . .)

. . . The more I live in India, and the more I am in touch with Hindus, the more certain I am that only spiritual means will transmit the message of the Gospel. The Church was poor and a *pariah* under the Roman Empire during the first three centuries, but she was victorious. Here in four centuries, with money, good works, protection and (colonial) power, and a host of missionaries, we have barely scratched the surface of India. (AMS 17.6.59)

Leaving Pithoragarh, Abhishiktananda spent the last half of June travelling in the Kumaon Hills, mainly on foot, and finally followed the Pindari river down to its junction with the Alakananda (Ganges) at Karnaprayag. As he still had no permit to go further north, he took the bus down the Ganges valley to Rishikesh and Hardwar (F, 5.7.59). In Hardwar he stayed with a Bengali sannyasi, Niranjanānand, for the first of many times.

After a few days of enthusiastic exploration of these holy places thronged with pilgrims and sadhus, he went on to Solan, a hill town on the road up to Simla, where he had been invited by Fr M.P. Christanand (who had taken part in the second Study Week). From Solan he wrote to his sister;

. . . I have been making a marvellous journey during the last two and a half months. For many weeks I have been among the Himalayas,

12. In 1957 Abhishiktananda had sent a note to Dorothy Day (of the Catholic Workers movement in New York) to inform her of the death of Fr Monchanin. As it was in French, Mrs Stokes was asked to translate it, and this led to a regular correspondence.

13. Fr J. Pichavan. Abhishiktananda's letters to him are unfortunately not available.

though not yet the great peaks 6, 7, 8000 metres high. I have often seen them from far off when the weather was clear. One had to look so high up in the sky to see them, that they gave the impression of not belonging to the earth at all. Then I have travelled, sometimes by bus but more often on foot, once 40 kms, then 70 kms, then 50 kms, for in most places there are no buses or motorable roads. It is marvellous to travel on foot like that. You are free, instead of being jammed together in trains or buses. There are enchanting solitudes and wonderful times of silence. Think of it, no noise of engines, no motor-horns, no radios or loudspeakers, etc. The solitude of Shantivanam is nothing compared to it. You cross hills and valleys, climbing up and down. Sometimes you follow beside a river, one of the streams which join up to form the Ganges, along a narrow valley beside the swift torrent (. . .) sheer cliffs on either side, maybe 500-1000 metres high. Then with the Ganges you descend towards the plain. The Himalayas open up, hills are less high, the Ganges spreads out, divides up and enters the plain to make it fertile.

I stayed for several days at Hardwar, just at this meeting point. Here there is a ceaseless pilgrimage. Thousands of people coming from every direction to bathe in the sacred river and then to follow the Ganges up into the mountains. I can only compare it with Lourdes, the great crowds, the devotion. At Hardwar there are hosts of monks. Five kms above and below the town you find ashrams and hermitages. Here, as nowhere else, you meet sadhus in every kind of dress and in none at all, in every shade of orange and ochre—but not a single Christian! All this worship, all these offerings, all this devotion, must find its fulfilment in the Mass, in the definitive offering of Jesus. The Himalayas have conquered me! It is beside the Ganges that Shantivanam ought to be. I do not know if that will ever happen, but how splendid it would be!

I have also had excellent contacts with Protestants, such good Christians. Tomorrow, in fact, I am leaving for Delhi where I shall be the guest of a Protestant friend, a brahmin convert from Madras.[14]

Next month I shall go higher in the Himalayas. I have just received the necessary permit for this. Those are the great pilgrimages, involving journeys of 200 or 300 kms on foot. As the heavy rains have begun, I am going to wait for a few weeks. I do not expect to return to the South before October. (. . .)

I can now stammer a few words in Hindi, the language of North India. (. . .) (MT, 16.7.59)

The next ten days were spent in Delhi, where Abhishiktananda had many people to see. Apart from ecclesiastical and a diplomatic calls, he met a number of Hindu friends, in particular two young men to whom his host at Binsar had given an introduction:

. . . Valuable meeting in Delhi (. . .). have I told you about those young men who are militant members of a right-wing revolutionary

14. See note 5, page 112.

party (anti-communist on religious, not political grounds), one of whom was converted back from Communism to Hinduism? After two hours of fierce discussion (about Christianity), they asked me to have half an hour of silent meditation![15] The Labour Minister [G.L. Nanda], and I don't know who else besides, received me *as a sadhu* to assist in the spiritual uplift of India, parallel to the Five Year Plans which are meant to bring about its material uplift . . . (L, 18.8.59)

As he thought it best to defer the start of his pilgrimage, Abhishiktananda returned for a second visit to Almora, travelling from Delhi via Agra and the ashram at Kareli, and wrote from there to his sister and to Fr Lemarié:

. . . I spent ten days in New Delhi, a modern city prefabricated by the English, set down alongside the old city. Very pleasant, wide roads, houses surrounded with gardens, but where only those with large salaries can live, salaries fifty times higher than most Indians get. (. . .)

Then I saw Agra, the city of the Moghuls. What wonderful palaces and mosques they built. How much more beautiful than anything the English did in Delhi! When I compared them, I was not proud of being European. (. . .)

From there I went on to stay with an English friend in a village. We were three priests, one an English Anglican, the second an American Presbyterian, and the third myself! Very moving to be together, praying, aware of our divisions, feeling the pain of them profoundly, waiting on the Lord in hope that the unity already realized in our hearts and in Christ's love might one day be manifested openly. (. . .) (MT, 18.8.59)

Then once more Almora (. . .). My interest in Almora is the Russian painter (American citizen), whom I mentioned before. Began in the style of Dürer, now 'abstract' in his own manner by penetrating (psychologically, something like Jung's psycho-analysis) into the interior of beings and things. Once the key is discovered, his abstractions have a marvellous, sometimes overwhelming, truth. He was keen to work on me, and is doing so just now. There are already two portraits completed (. . .) These two portraits are shattering and profoundly true. Behind the mask (is) what I ought to be, showing through. One is the 'pure being', neither dead nor alive, neither (in?) time nor space . . . the other is in some fashion the resurrection, the return to the world, in a form that again is shattering. (. . .)

. . . Rudolf [Ray] has discovered these two aspects, the pure one resting in being, the other coming down again (a kind of ikon, extremely impressive). Which to choose? The Lord will have to show the answer (. . .) (L, 18.8.59)

Just as he was about to set off on the pilgrimage at the end of August, Abhishiktananda fell ill with an attack of herpes. Fortunately he could obtain

15. Shri Ram Swarup and Shri Sita Ram Goel became friends whom Abhishiktananda often visited in Delhi. For their impressions of him, see *Occasional Bulletin*, no. 7, of November 1983.

treatment from his friends in Pithoragarh, and after two weeks in hospital and a week of recuperation in Kareli (Jyotiniketan) he was finally able to set out in the middle of September. From the shrine at Kedarnath he wrote to Fr Lemarié:

> . . . Last month I had health problems (herpes and neuralgia) which changed my programme. I had to return for two weeks to my Quaker friends at Pithoragarh—Christians who have taken the Gospel at its face value (. . .). This year the Lord has willed to make me realize that the Spirit also works beyond the frontiers of Rome . . . A disturbing problem which is set to the Church by the presence of the Spirit outside Rome and even apart from the Christian faith. (. . .)
>
> I am writing to you at midday, muffled up in blankets. The pilgrimage shrine (is open) from 15 May to 15 October, the rest of the time it is under snow . . . I shall not have time to go on to Badrinath (the other mountain shrine, a hundred miles from here). (L, 20.9.59)

An account of this first experience of Himalayan pilgrimage is given in *The Mountain of the Lord* (section 5).[16] On his way back to Shantivanam, as he passed through Delhi, he was able to give his sister two important items of news:

> A very brief word from Delhi for your Feast. I am back from the mountains, from Kedarnath, a place of pilgrimage at an altitude of 3600 metres, which is reached after walking 60 kms through mountain ranges among forests and waterfalls. Then at Hardwar with a sadhu friend. Then in Delhi for a few days. (. . .)
>
> I have received permission from the Bishop of Meerut (. . .) to come next year to settle experimentally beside the Ganges among the mountains; and my Hindu friends are pressing me to come. I am going to come and at least try it out. (Then) I am going to get my Indian nationality without delay. For all this, bless the Lord with me. I continue to be in touch with Lisieux; there they are praying specially for me today, the anniversary of St Thérèse (MT. 30.9.59)

After Delhi Abhishiktananda broke his journey at Jaipur and wrote to Fr Lemarié:

> . . . My Indian citizenship has been granted, and all that I have to do to make it effective is to complete the formality of renouncing my French nationality. Once more very interesting contacts in Delhi which enable me to have a glimpse of the future. An ashram in the Himalayas to which Protestant and Hindu friends will come. (. . .) I am now going back to the South. The most important matter will be to find some means of preserving Shantivanam with a view to my own visits and perhaps to possible successors. (L, 7.10.59)

Shantivanam—October 1959 to January 1960

Abhishiktananda reached his ashram in mid-October after an absence of five and a half months, and remained there mostly in solitude for the next four

16. See Bibliography

months. He admitted to feeling tired, and may already have been suffering from the condition which required a hernia operation in the following February. The future of the ashram was constantly on his mind. Soon after his return he wrote at length to the Prioress of Lisieux, explaining his view of the relevance of Carmel to India and sharing his hopes for Shantivanam:

> . . . I have just returned to Shantivanam and, being caught once more by the charm of this solitude, I now find it difficult to cope with the appeals which come to me from the North, urgent as they are. Will the Lord at last hear all the prayers that are made with the intention that, both from France and from India, vocations may appear which answer to the ideal of Shantivanam? Needless to say, I am probably the one who prays least of all for that. Surely there is a part of the soul in which 'asking' no longer makes much sense; as a Quaker friend said to me the other day, Why spend time 'giving information' to the Lord? (. . .) However, I should be very happy if the Lord were to send my relief . . .
>
> Certainly this vocation is Carmelite; it is also Carthusian, Benedictine, Franciscan . . . It is men who make these distinctions. (. . .) Each one says, "My way is best." But in the end the only use of our ways is to lead us to the 'non-way'. (. . .) The world (. . .) needs Franciscans like those of the very first days, people who take St Francis—and so Jesus—literally, without playing at being able to understand the situation better than the Saints did, or at rewriting the Gospels and the primitive Rules; it is these wandering Christian sannyasis that India awaits. However, the Carmel—at least as it is idealized in my vision of it—is perhaps what comes closest in the Church to India's deepest aspirations: the acosmics of the Desert Fathers; the "Flee, be silent, remain at rest" of Arsenius; the '*nada*' [nothing] of St John of the Cross; above all, the going beyond, the "establishment of oneself beyond oneself" of Tauler and Eckhart. That is what the Christian monk should live out in company with his *advaitin* brother, if he wants truly to complete in Christ the intuition of Being contained in the Saccidananda of the India of the *rishis.* And the completion in Christ of the mystical intuition of *advaita* is the fundamental ontological condition for the building up (not in statistics, not in masonry, but in reality) of the Church in India. That is essentially the aim and the role of the monk of Saccidananda. This was probably not said so strongly in *Ermites* [*du Saccidananda*], of which the first draft was done in 1950/1 and the French adaptation in 1953. [17] In those days I saw things more within the traditional framework; whereas now I should rather look for a working out on the lines of Egypt and of India: the guru, the abbot, with just a few disciples whom he trains, and who in their turn hive off. More than ever I am frightened of institutionalization. However—and I said this plainly in *Ermites*—I envisaged the Benedictine framework—which, as I used

17. The 'first draft' was *An Indian Benedictine Ashram* (1951). *Ermites du Sacc.* was mostly written in 1953, but not published until 1956.

> it and also otherwise, is so flexible—as a point of departure and as a practical necessity for the central ashram where monks are trained, while leaving the door wide open for later offshoots.
>
> But what now? The Lord will show through events themselves what is to be done, if one day he wills that Shantivanam should grow. We do not put new wine in old bottles. Between the forms of the East and those of the West there are only analogies; Christian monasticism in India will also be something special. Present-day Western Christian forms should likewise be left behind. What we need are *Indian* versions, lived in the flesh and in the spirit—not renovated copies of the 'Little Way' [of St Thérèse of Lisieux], of St Teresa of Avila, of St John of the Cross. A daughter should resemble her mother, but should go beyond her, be herself and not her mother . . .
>
> You will tell all this to Sister Térèse de Jésus, the novice mistress. If she likes, I will write at greater length another time, by ordinary mail. (FT, 26.10.59)[18]

For some years Abhishiktananda had been in touch with a French Carmelite at Shembaganur, who was one of the very few with whom he could share his deepest insights. Now at Lisieux he found others to whom he could open his heart, especially the Mother Prioress and the novice-mistress, Sr Térèse (Lemoine), who was later herself to come to India. Many of his letters to them have been preserved and are some of the best examples of his writing on spiritual matters. The contact with Lisieux was maintained to the end of his life; and very soon Lisieux introduced him to other Carmels in South India to which he began regular visits in the following year.

> . . . Ever closer relations with Lisieux. The other day the novice-mistress sent me a magnificent letter, showing wonderful understanding both of the real meaning of contemplation—beyond even what is specially characteristic of Carmel—and of the real needs of India as regards Christian contemplation (. . .) Does that not show that in the Lord's eyes the value of Shantivanam lies in its very solitude, and not in various developments before the eyes of men? (L, 8.12.59)

By the end of the year his hopes of obtaining recruits from France had again faded. While in Delhi, he had made a final attempt to obtain a visa for Fr Bescaud, and when this failed, he decided "that it was better so", especially in view of further correspondence with the Father. He also gave up his efforts for two other candidates (Y.M. and L.A.). His hopes turned instead to a young Mauritian seminarist at Rome, Philippe Fanchette, who had reacted well to a reading of *Guhantara,* but nothing could be expected of him in the near future.

During these months of solitude, Abhishiktananda took up some projects of writing, as he told Fr Lemarié:

> . . . To meet the wishes of friends in New York (Catholic Worker, Christian anarchists and pacifists) who wanted something on the basic spirituality of Shantivanam, I have written a few pages. One day

18. *Les yeux,* 137-139

I will send you a carbon copy, in case it could be used in France. (L, 8.12.59)

The text seems to have been lost. At the same time he was turning over in his mind an essay on "the ministry *(diakonia)* of solitude", "a presentation of the theology and spirituality of the hermit life (. . .) but it does not emerge; I have got rusty and lazy." He was also preparing some "Notes on Arunachala"[19] which he thought might be acceptable to some French periodical. "Only part of it would be mine. And it would have appear under a pseudonym." (L, 28.12.59)

This year there was no Study Week, and Abhishiktananda kept a solitary Christmas, apart from the midday Mass when he was joined by a few neighbours. Sending a Christmas greeting to his sister, the said:

> . . . I am taking full advantage of my solitude, having very few visitors. As my cook delights to chatter during meals, I have resolved not to speak to him except during tea (for I take my tea about 3.30—what an ascetic! You see that I have caught some shockingly unmortified habits in India!). So life is uneventful. On my return I did some repairs, and in particular strengthened the door of the chapel, in view of last April's burglary. People say I should have a good dog (I have one; but yesterday evening, when reading Isaiah 56:10, I found an exact description of him) . . . You see, I read Isaiah too, and not only the Upanishads! (. . .)
>
> My Christmas wish for my little sister is what I read at Mass this morning: "Rejoice, again I say, rejoice." For the Lord is not only near, he is here already! and in reality, there is only Him. (MT, 17.12.59)

When, however, he wrote to Fr Lemarié, his tone was rather less buoyant:

> . . . We are now in the middle of advent, that time which is so dear to you. I admit to being a little weary of these liturgical years coming again and again, which promise so much and leave you apparently where you were before. So the Jewish prophets, who always foretold wrath for tomorrow, used to paint the day following in shades of eschatological triumph. As age increases, I get tired of waiting for that to come. The John of the Gospel is no longer the John of Patmos [i.e., of the Revelation]: everything happens within (John 14), and as our sages here say: It is already here; just realize it!" (L, 8. 12. 59)

He returned to the subject after Christmas, reflecting sadly on the lack of 'response' to the messianic hopes with which the liturgy is filled:

> . . . And the response? the world become so terribly empty of love and of bread. (. . .) The prophets are always so topical in their reproaches. The new Jerusalem is so difficult to distinguish from the old, alike in its faithful, its scribes and its priests . . . The Day of the Lord is always for 'tomorrow' (. . .) Then what is God doing in his heaven, and what answer can be given to unbelievers? They would gladly enter

19. Later references (see p. 127) make it clear that these "Notes on Arunachala" were a collection of poems, some his own, and some renderings of Sri Ramana's. (L, 1.3.60; 9.3.60)

> a Church in which the Lord reigned, was loved (. . .). But we can only offer them a 'tomorrow'. (. . .)
>
> I ought to have written to you for Epiphany in the style of Second Isaiah, but this letter is more like Ecclesiastes! Perhaps I am tired this morning, as for the last two days I have been racking my brains to find a practical way of stabilizing Shantivanam without being tied here myself as a caretaker. (L, 28.12.59)

During January 1960, Abhishiktananda was visited by John Cole from the Jyotiniketan ashram, whom he had met in the previous year:

> . . . Last month I had a visit from an American Protestant missionary from the North, very agreeable, very simple. He spent a week with me here, then I took him off to Tiruvannamalai to see my mountain, my caves, and my Hindu friends over there. He was keen to know all about it. (F, 6.2.60)
>
> . . . A man desirous of solitude and prayer, but finding no help towards this in his own Church. Yet with no doubts about the position of his own 'Confession' [Church]. He would like an ashram life in the North. These ecumenical contacts of last year could be fruitful—not in external 'conversions', but in conversions to greater interiority, and in a spiritual influence within the separated Confessions, while awaiting the hour of the Lord. (L, 19.2.60)

Shantivanam and new contacts—February to December 1960

During the whole of this year Abhishiktananda remained at the ashram, except for visits to convents in South India, and resisted the appeals which came from the North (Indore, Jyotiniketan). At the end of February he had to have an operation for double hernia at Pondicherry, from which his recovery was slow; as late as September he reported to Mother Théophane at Indore that he still felt weak and tired. In August he reached his fiftieth birthday, a significant milestone for him; for "when you put a 5 at the beginning of your age, you really have only one foot in this world" (F, 8.11.60).

Outwardly the year was marked by developments in two directions. The most important was the deepening and widening of his Carmelite contacts; but at the same time he was extending his contacts with Christians belonging to other Churches, for like others before him he saw clearly that a divided Christendom makes no sense in India.

At Lisieux it was felt that Abhishiktananda's insights could help in the formation of their novices. They were already sending copies of his books (*Ermites* and the Memoir of Fr Monchanin) to the noviciates of other French Carmels. "It seems that the books have quite stolen their hearts," he told Mother Théophane (5.1.60); and wondered, "Is the Lord preparing among them future hermits for Kedarnath and Hardwar?" Meanwhile the novice-mistress at Lisieux was bombarding him with searching questions, to which he felt he must give of his best in answer (TL, 20.3.60). In the course of the year he sent to Lisieux several 'papers' through Fr Lemarié, whom he also asked to look into the possibility of their being published. In these he was no doubt seeking to express in a more popular and less startling form the fundamental insights of *Guhantara,* as he had already envisaged during his first contact with the Carmel of Bangalore (L, 29.6.58). But even in their new form they were sufficiently 'startling', and it is hardly surprising that they were not published in his lifetime.

The first 'paper' to be sent was a translation of some of Sri Ramana's poems, which had been specially typed in Pondi:

> . . . I sent off on Monday by seamail 60 typed pages (. . .). Most of the texts of Ramana have been translated by someone else, with some corrections by me.[20] Do you think that in French they might have some 'appeal' for those who do not know the Tamil and Hindu context? (. . .) I would like your opinion of the value *in themselves* of the texts. Only this evening I was discussing with a local Tamilian the problem of making the message of India comprehensible to Europeans (Tamil is even more difficult to translate than Sanskrit). (L, 1.3.60)
>
> . . . You may pass on to Lisieux the MSS sent in December.[21] (. . .). Please first read yourself the pieces on Arunachala. I must have told you long ago that I should have liked to insert these extracts from Ramana in a book on Arunachala, but it seems that there would be trouble over the rights (. . .).[22] (L, 9.3.60)

Lisieux also requested Abhishiktananda's help for some of their related Carmels in India, particularly those of Kumbakkonam and Pondicherry:

> . . . As regards Kumbakkonam, I will gladly help them, despite my very badly pronounced Tamil and the difficulty of not being able to see my audience, which totally prevents one from discovering whether one is understood or not. Only I must be very discreet. If Mother Prioress so wishes, let her send me a line; that will protect me from local susceptibilities. I had some sad experiences on that account at Sh. a few years back (. . .) (FT, 5.2.60)

Shortly afterwards, on his way to hospital, Abhishiktananda visited both of these Carmels, as he told his sister:

> . . . On the way to Pondi I stopped one afternoon at the Kumbakkonam Carmel, having been asked to do so by Lisieux. Just imagine, a parlour where the spikes on the grill are real spikes which prick, where in order to speak you have to remain standing and even to climb onto a narrow step! (. . .) On the other side was the Mother Prioress—a Belgian aged 72 who came last year. And we continued talking for nearly three hours. I told her that I would not come again until she had taken down the grill!

20. A copy of this MS, 60 pages neatly typed and in a smaller format than he normally used, is in a file 'Poems of Arunachala'. It contains renderings of poems by Sri Ramana (later published in *Sagesse,* appendix) and some of his own poems (extracts in *Souvenirs d'Arunachala,* ch. 3, and *Initiation*).
21. It is uncertain what these MSS were, but they may have included a copy of the article on "The Spirituality of Saccidananda', written for New York, of which Abhishiktananda promised Fr Lemarié a copy (L, 8.12.59).
22. The idea of publishing some of Sri Ramana's poems goes back to 1956 (L, 20.1.56), but the rights in French were held by someone in Paris who had already done a translation (very poor, in his view).

> The Carmel of Pondi which I went to see on the following day is fortunately less austere. It is the Carmel of Lisieux that puts me in touch like this with the Indian Carmels. They would like me to help them to become *very* contemplative. (MT, 5.3.60)

In the same letter he described appreciatively his experiences at the hospital, even though "I went down to the operating theatre with my heart full of the emotions and fears of a criminal about to be handed over to the executioner":

> . . . It was very efficiently done. I felt nothing, either before or after. (. . .) So for ten days I have been between two beautiful white sheets (to which I am quite unused). (. . .)
>
> It is an excellent discipline to have to stay in bed like this. (. . .) I sang, "Bless the Lord, you who are flat on your back; bless the Lord, you who run; bless him, you who eat, you who drink, you who cannot drink . . ." You know, when people came to me and said things like this: "Father, I have been praying so hard for you", I was tempted to reply: "Perhaps not hard enough, for if the Lord had heard you, he would have made me feel ill, sent a fever or a headache, so that I could share a little in his Passion, as St Benedict said." (MT, 5.3.60)

Before returning to Shantivanam, Abhishiktananda gave a talk in Tamil at the Pondicherry Carmel, which the Sisters at his hospital insisted on his repeating in French.

> . . . There are some people who are expectant. (. . .) It only needs a small spark to light the fire. (. . .) So with the spirit, once the spark is given . . .
>
> I was saying to the Sisters at the hospital, "Your life is only distracting, if you make your spiritual life and your contemplation something that is added to, superimposed on, reality. The divine life is in what happens this moment, the patient who has to be washed, the injection you have to give, etc. Once he is discovered in your Self and in the Self of each and every one, who or what can distract you from him?" One Sister asked (. . .), "What should I do, so as not to leave him?" I said: "How do you go about absenting yourself from him? He does not leave you, any more than the air which is all around you. Simply don't close your windpipe!" (Th, 23.3.60)

In the same letter to Mother Théophane, who had the care of the young Indian Sisters at Indore, he said:

> . . . make them understand little by little the secret of the 'Within'. I think Indians are generally open to it. And if priestly and religious life (in India) has not been too successful in that respect, it is probably due to the fact that the spirituality offered remains desperately external (virtues, little sacrifices, formal meditations, etc). A little fresh air from the ocean and the high mountain! (Th, 23.3.60)

He returned to Shantivanam in time for the Feast of St Benedict; and to commemorate the tenth anniversary of the foundation placed a stone cross on the site of the first Mass. (L, 16.3.60)

At Easter he went to Bangalore, first at the Asirvanam monastery (nothing more is heard of the monk who wanted to join him), and then for three intensive days of addresses and interviews at the Carmel.

At the ashram Abhishiktananda next prepared to host an ecumenical gathering organized by his Jyotiniketan friends. As he could not go to them, they came to him.

> . . . Tomorrow I am expecting the group of non-Catholics of whom I must have told you. There will be Anglicans, Lutherans, Presbyterians, a Jacobite, a Greek Orthodox, Church of South India . . . ten in all! Shantivanam will never have been so full. (MT, 29.4.60)

To Fr Lemarié he wrote:

> . . . We are in the middle of an ecumenical contemplative week. Eight taking part, ranging from a Congregationalist to an English Greek-Orthodox. Very soon we discovered our unity, no one felt left out. Our sessions are essentially directed towards contemplation. Our friend of the Orthodox Church contributed that fine Oriental spirituality in which he is soaked (. . .). This meeting is worth while much more for our *koinonia* [fellowship] than for the spoken exchanges. (L, 5.5.60)[23]

The same letter tells of the bequest of a useful sum of money from an old teacher of his, which was to be applied to his work in India. This not only relieved his anxiety about the unkeep of the ashram, but also enabled him to widen his reading in directions where he felt the need. Subsequent letters refer to some of the new books which he was able to order.[24] And, not least important, he took steps to relieve his friends from the problem of deciphering his handwriting by arranging for the purchase of a second-hand typewriter, which arrived few months later.

In June he learnt that at last,—nearly eight years after his original application for naturalization—"since last Saturday (. . .) I have all the rights and duties of an Indian citizen" (L, 16.6.60).

At Lisieux the translation of Sri Ramana's poems was very well received, and they were even compared to the poems of St John of the Cross (L, 3.6.60). In response to the Prioress Abhishiktananda wrote:

> . . . I truly did not think that these poems of Ramana could awaken such an echo in a Christian soul that had not been initiated into Indian thought. It confirmed what I had already discovered on several occasions, that a contemplative 'understands' India—the India that is far beyond externals and systems of thought—and that only contemplatives can reach the soul of India. (FT, 7.7.60)

The Prioress had queried a point in one of his handwritten 'notes'[25] and he agreed that it sounded most 'inhuman'. He had been too concise, and in order to

23. The meeting is described in *Meeting Point*, 9-11.
24. Cullmann, *Christ and Time*; Evkokimov, *Orthodoxy*; Meyendorff, *Palamas;* volumes of Fliche & Martin's *History of the Church*; etc.
25. From his reply it appears that he had questioned the value of petitionary prayer, which suggests that these 'notes' may have been a draft of his essay, "Il n'est qu'une Réalité", which was one of the papers sent to Lisieux, later published at the end of *Éveil à soi--éveil à Dieu.* (E.T. *In Spirit and Truth: an Essay on Prayer and Life*, 1989).

clear up the misunderstanding enclosed further notes with his reply. She had also been puzzled by something he had said about Christ being present in Hindu temples:

> The question of the dwelling of the Word in the Temple would also need a long article in explanation. I have roughed out a few pages on this—shall I get to the end? It is the whole problem of the particularity and the uniqueness of Catholicism. When you have had direct experience of the action of the Spirit among non-Catholics and non-Christians, you become keenly aware of this presence which you cannot deny and cannot easily explain. Please note that the pages which you question are not a theological statement. Their expression (hardly indeed logical!) sets out ideas about it in terms of overwhelming 'mysteries', which one scarcely knows how to express, an appeal to the Lord to grant the full light which will make understanding possible. Can there be differences of degree in the presence of God? (FT, 7.7.60)

In the following paragraphs he went on to speak of the divine presence in all things, but at the end admitted: "All that is terribly confused. I would like to write about it, but when I begin, it does not come."

However during the next three months he continued to work at it, and finally in October sent off a long typed article[26] which better expressed what he was trying to say. In this connection he said to Fr Lemarié:

> . . . I have just discovered how God could be present indivisibly everywhere and at the same time could be present differently in the temples of Shiva and in our churches. It was no doubt "Columbus' egg", but it has taken years to emerge from my subconscious. It came in response to the queries of Lisieux. The 'letter' already runs to sixty large pages, will probably go to eighty. When I have (. . .) had it typed, I will send it to you. (L, 29.9.60)

In August Abhishiktananda was again called by the Carmelites of Bangalore and Kumbakkonam to give them talks. "My ways of presenting the spiritual life, which had in them very little of 'unction' or tradition, seemed to go down well" (L, 12.8.60). A sample is given in a letter to his sister:

> . . . You know, when I go to the Bangalore Carmel (. . .) I do not spoil them, yet they constantly ask for more. (. . .) (I tell them,) We have renounced the joys of this world, and then look for substitutes in so-called spiritual joys. Only one thing is real, the present moment, in which I am face-to-face with God, begotten by the Father in Jesus the divine Word, in the communion of the Holy Spirit. All the rest [little pieties], how small they are, compared to this reality which is even now before me. We are like rich people with bags of gold, who waste their time over copper farthings. I only preach one thing: Realize what you

26. This was probably a first draft of an article, "Présence de Dieu—présence à Dieu", on which he commented in a letter to Sr Térèse (TL, 17.12.60). It was rewritten in 1961 at Uttarkashi (TS dated 25.10.61). Part of this was published in *Intériorité*, 139-151.

are, at this moment: see yourself in the bosom of the Trinity, where your baptism, your communion has placed you, and be faithful to yourselves, to what you are. (. . .) So long as you seek your own ends while pretending to seek God, you will never find God. (MT, 21.8.60)

On the way to Kumbakkonam Abhishiktananda visited a well known Tamil author, Karavelane, at Karaikkal:

. . . went at he end of August to Karaikkal (. . .). I spent my fiftieth birthday with a friend who had celebrated his sixtieth a few day before. His wife made us a delicious Tamilian dinner. (F, 19.9.60)

The tribute which Abhishiktananda wrote in his friend's honour on this occasion reveals an almost chauvinistic pride in Franco-Tamil culture! [27]

In the latter part of the year there were several ecumenical contacts. One of his visitors in September was the Orthodox monk (English by birth), Fr Lazarus Moore, who had attended the meeting in May and of whom he saw much in the coming years. In addition he welcomed at the ashram a young Sinhalese Anglican priest, John Cooray,[28] who stayed with him for a month:

. . . Last week I had here with Fr Dominique the Anglo-Russian monk who was here in May, and an Anglican priest from Ceylon (. . .). How marvellous it will be, when all the riches of the Church will be shared in common! *La vie spirituelle* has not exaggerated the value of Evdokimov's book [*Orthodoxy*]. I am reading and pondering it with joy. (L, 13.9.60)

. . . I still have with me the young priest from Ceylon who wants to found a kind of Shantivanam in Buddhist surroundings. Truly the Lord has the knack of making the influence of Shantivanam extend in directions of which one could never have dreamt. (L, 21.9.60)

. . . in any case the year here will have been under the sign of ecumenism. Next month on my way back from Trivandrum I may perhaps visit the seminary (ex-Anglican, now Church of South India) near Tirunelveli, as the guest of one of those who took part in the week in May. (L, 29.9.60)

Your letter awaited me here on my return from my travels: Poor Clares of Alwaye, Little Sisters of Trivandrum, Rosarians, Anglican Tamil seminary, a camp for Protestant students at Courtallam. The hermit is becoming a wanderer! But one cannot refuse to give contemplatives the true nourishment. And meetings with non-Catholics on their own ground are rare also. All that was the fruit of our ecumenical week last May, of which people want a repetition next year (. . .). It is highly instructive to enter into these circles from inside. They are

27. Printed in *Karavelane: volume commémoratif du soixantième anniversaire de naissance, 23 août, 1900-1960,* 12-21. Perhaps deliberately he did not include it in his list of publications and manuscripts.

28. The Revd John Cooray founded an ecumenical ashram in a Buddhist environment at Ibbegamuwa, near Kurunagala, in Sri Lanka, and took the name of Yohan Devananda. After some years it was converted into a cooperative farm.

> of course very far from *submitting* to Rome; but a return to communion with Rome is deeply desired (. . .). I had not expected them to pay so much attention to what comes from Rome.
>
> The professor who invited me has given the name 'Giovanni' [i.e., for Pope John XXIII] to his small son born in November 1958. (. . .). If only the Church was *spiritually radiant,* if it was not so firmly attached to the formulations of transient philosophies, if it did not obstruct the freedom of the Spirit (. . .) with such niggling regulations, it would not be long before we reached an understanding. (L, 24.10.60)
>
> . . . Just finished Cullmann's book (*Christ and Time*), after that of Evdokimov (*Orthodoxy*) and Meyendorff's (*Palamas*). Really there are treasures among our Brothers. The Pope must have felt that, when he embraced Dr Fisher [Archbishop of Canterbury]. (L, 26.12.60)

However, Abhishiktananda did not allow his ecumenical heart to run away with his head, as is shown by a comment to the Prioress of Lisieux about his programme in the coming year:

> . . . At Bareilly [Jyotiniketan] I shall have meetings with Protestants. That poses such difficult problems—(to have) great openness of heart and spirit, and at the same time to maintain the strict Catholic position without giving offence to 'the others'. The danger is always of either giving offence through intransigence or of giving the impression that 'everything goes'. It is for the Spirit to show the way. (FT, 17.12.60)

Questions continued to come from Lisieux, some of which Abhishiktananda answered in his letters, while others called for more extended treatment. In October he had sent off the long essay, referred to above, on the divine Presence:

> . . . A letter from Lisieux today speaks of the new papers sent to them. Once again it was a 'success'. Yet it was a stronger dose than the first set, while being in a different style from *Guhantara.* Your copy is at present in Rome; Philippe Fanchette will send it to you. Will all this be published one day? Here and there people are waiting for this food. But there are many others who reject it, not only for themselves but for others. (L, 19.11.60)

In answer to some points raised by the novice-mistress he wrote:

> . . . There are certainly some very bold statements in what I have sent you. It even gives me a start when you or Mother F-T repeat them back to me, such as that "Grace equals 'Nature' ". It all has to be understood in its context. I rely on you to find the missing links; but these dishes must not be served up too suddenly—our food is first of all milk, then baby-food, and only later bread and meat. (There follows his explanation of some points in the essay, which enable it to be identified; see Note 26.) (TL, 17.12.60)

At the end of 1960 Abhishiktananda was preparing for another visit to the North, to see his friends and make a trial of settling in the Himalayas. His last engagement in the South was once again at the Bangalore Carmel, where he had finally agreed to give an eight-day retreat after Christmas:

> . . . This frightens me no end. To speak three times a day for eight days, trying not to repeat myself too much, when all that is necessary is said in half an hour at the most. (. . .)
>
> From Bangalore I shall go (. . .) to Bombay, then to Indore (. . .). Of the three French Sisters (. . .) only Mother M. Théophane is left, a religious who (though busy with her patients from morning to night) is more contemplative than most of the 'contemplatives' whom I have met. (. . .) Then Delhi; at Bareilly a meeting with Protestants and Hindus; and I hope to go for Lent to the Himalayas.
>
> You must think that your brother makes light of enclosure. My enclosure now extends from the Himalayas to Cape Comorin, and from the Bay of Bengal to the Persian Gulf! (. . .)
>
> Does the wind blow fiercely at Carnac these days? Can you hear the breakers on the Côte Sauvage in the morning when you get up for the Office? (MT, 16.12.60)

To the Himalayas—January to April 1961

When Abhishiktananda left the ashram in January 1961, his goal was Uttarkāshī, a great centre for sadhus, deep in the Himalayas; but for various reasons he did not reach there until March. As usual he followed a circuitous route, having friends to see on the way—Harilal near Mysore, Dr Mehta in Bombay, his friends in Indore, Harilal's family at Lucknow and the Jyotiniketan ashram near Bareilly. In Delhi he found a new friend in the Swiss Ambassador, Dr. J-A. Cuttat, author of *The Encounter of Religions.* He fully shared Abhishiktananda's concern to introduce Christians to Indian spirituality, since he himself had returned from unbelief to faith at a deeper level after discovering in Hinduism the "sense of interiority" which he had not found in the Catholicism of his youth (TL, 2.2.61).

He wrote to his sister from Delhi:

> . . . I have seen a lot of people here: Catholics, Protestants, Quakers, Hindus. On Thursday I spent from midday to 6 p.m. in conversation with the Swiss Ambassador, a very good Catholic. I must confess to you how I was tempted, when I had lunch with him and some of his friends. They naturally served rice and vegetables to me, while a meat dish made the round of the table. That was nothing; but on the table there were two very attractive bottles of Burgundy, a Châteauneuf (. . .), and after the excellent coffee there was a bottle of Martell Three Star, something I had not seen for many years . . . I said firmly that I would content myself with looking at them . . . and enjoying them 'by proxy' only! (MT, 6.2.61)

A few days later, instead of going up to Hardwar and the Himalayas, he had to make a hasty return to the South. The Abbot of St André (Bruges) was coming to make a canonical visitation of the daughter-monastery of Asirvanam in Bangalore, and Abhishiktananda had been appointed as his interpreter.

He came back to Delhi at the beginning of March, but instead of going to the hills, was persuaded by his friends at Jyotiniketan to take part in an ecumenical discussion on Teilhard de Chardin's *Phenomenon of Man.* Then again he returned to Delhi, as he had important work to do with Dr Cuttat. There was a possibility of continuing the series of theological-spiritual discussions begun at Shantivanam in 1957 and 1958, and as Dr Cuttat offered himself as host, the meeting could be held on a more ambitious scale. A list of invitees was prepared, which on Abhishiktananda's insistence included some members of other Churches, so that their discussions might have an ecumenical dimension. The venue was to be after Easter in the Methodist holiday home at Almora, and the subject 'Vedantic and Christian experience' (F, 3(10).3.61).

Leaving further arrangements to be made by the Swiss Embassy, Abhishiktananda went to Hardwar and then up to Uttarkashi, which he reached on 13 March. His path was made smoother by a chance meeting in Delhi with a friend from Indore, Swami Premananda, who gave him an introduction to another Swami in Uttarkashi, thus solving the problem of accommodation (Th, 17.3.61). In several long letters he described his experience:

> . . . I am writing to you from a narrow valley in the Himalayas on the bank of the Ganges, here a fierce and noisy stream. I hear it rolling its boulders along only ten metres below. This is one of the holy places in the Himalayas, 160 kms from the plains, far from everywhere, with mountains all around. Nothing to distract you from the one essential. Buses have only reached here since last year by a road that makes you shudder. At every bend the bus grazes the edge of the abyss. A village of 2000 inhabitants, with 150-400 sadhus according to the season (for in winter it is cold, and there is snow). There is a charitable institution which provides their food, and each midday I go along with them to collect my chapatis and a ladleful of lentils. Morning and evening I supplement this with a cup of milk, and life is marvellous. The sadhus live either alone or or grouped in huts beside the Ganges. I celebrated Mass here for the first time on the day of the man born blind [Gospel for Wednesday after Lent IV]. (. . .) In this Mass I offered all the austerities, fasts, watchings, solitude, silence, prayers and meditations of the monks who for centuries have succeeded each other in this place. (. . .)
>
> How important it is that there should be a Christian monastic presence here. If I could arrange to have my own hut here, and spend at least a few months here each year. It is on the route of one of the three great pilgrimages to the sources of the Ganges, which people make with such fervour from May until October, when the road is blocked with snow.
>
> . . . I have so many friends now, all over the place, and I have to make excuses so as not to stay too long at Indore, Delhi, Bareilly, Hardwar. At Hardwar there is a Bengali sadhu with whom I always stay. (. . .) My Bengali friend would like me to settle there, but I prefer Uttarkashi. There I can better understand the mystery of India,

and can realize that it is by the way of asceticism and contemplation that India will hear the message of the Lord. (MT, 24.3.61)

. . . Here more than anywhere I am strongly tempted to pitch my tent! The Bishop of Meerut is very favourably disposed towards the plan—a Christian Eucharistic presence.

There are some strict ascetics here, like the one who at eighty, only last year, used to go about naked and spent several hours daily in midwinter standing in the Ganges. In general, they give me the impression of the monks of the Thebaid [Egypt, 4th century] or of the Middle Ages (. . .), simple, satisfied with a few ideas which they say or sing to themselves all day long. I have also met here a real 'celicole' [citizen of heaven] (. . .) with gentle and wonderfully peaceful eyes. He only knows Hindi, like everyone else here; and my Hindi is too poor for me to be able to speak with him on anything but the most general topics.

Yesterday I began five days of silence—I can't do more, as I have inquiries to make . . . I made the experiment yesterday of fasting on half a litre of milk and two cups of tea. I ought to be able to do that every Friday. (L, 18.3.61)

Abhishiktananda spent almost a month, which included Easter, at Uttarkashi and left for the meeting at Almora on 10 April. During this time he was granted a plot of land at Gyansu beside the Ganges on which he hoped to build a cell. He also wrote a long essay on "India and the Church", reflecting on a problem which was never far from his mind—the meaning of the Gospel in the Indian context.

. . . It was a marvellous month, and above all there was the Easter Vigil in deep solitude among all those brothers who, though risen in Jesus, are unable to accept the Easter message. (. . .)

At Uttarkashi they have given me a few hundred square metres *for life* on which to build a cell. It should be ready in July, and I am thinking of coming back in September. (. . .)

In those profoundly Hindu surroundings at Uttarkashi as well as in those which I frequent in Delhi, I have realized the extent to which the vast majority of Christians fail to see the problems. Only by the way of *interiority* will the Church be able to make contact with India, except at the superficial level. How to get this understood? Meetings like the one in Almora make it possible to open the eyes of a few, but we need many such. (L, 29.4.61)

This last paragraph gives the background to the essay on India and the Church which Abhishiktananda wrote at Uttarkashi.[29] In it he faces up to the powerful objections to Christianity with which his Hindu friends confronted him, and which indeed had long been painfully present in his own thinking. He also sympathizes with their sense of scandal that outsiders, knowing next to nothing of Hindu experience, should presume to question the sufficiency of India's

29. This essay, "L'Inde et l'Église", was also sent to Lisieux. A letter to Fr Lemarié (11.5.61) mentions his hope that it might be published, but this was never done.

sanātana dharma, the living and agelong tradition received from countless rishis and saints. If the Church were simply to present Christ's teaching, there would be no problem, for many Hindus accept it gladly. But the heart of the Gospel lies in the Church's faith that the death and resurrection of Christ have a universal and ultimate significance, of which the Church itself, despite the appalling disparity between its profession and its practice, is the 'Sacrament', the Body of Christ. The 'apologetic' which he goes on to offer does not attempt to deny the absoluteness of the experience of the *jñānī*, the one who like Sri Ramana is 'lost', 'vanished' in the mystery of Brahman, the One who alone is. But in the light of the Resurrection faith he suggests that God, by an act of unconditioned love, addresses a 'thou' (the same 'Thou' which is eternally addressed to the only Son) to the one who is lost in his not being and his sin, and thereby recalls him to being and to a *koinonia* (communion) which henceforth is not-other-than the inter-personal Being of God himself.

An important point is made at the end of the essay, after a long comparison of the experience of the Hindu and the Christian *jñani,* in which he says frankly that the former must be regarded as a very high degree of 'grace':

> The real problem is that man is not simply this ultimate point of awareness, which is perhaps inaccessible to his own consciousness incarnated in thoughts and sensations. Man is also this whole psychological and sensory world, the *śarīram* of Indian tradition, which Christianity saves from the Vedantin *māyā,* as in past days it saved it from Greek pneumatism and Gnostic angelism. For it is in the wholeness of his being that man's final perfection must be achieved.

In this essay, which was never published, Abhishiktananda struggled to express in words an experience which goes beyond words. However, many of his thoughts reappear in the book (*Sagesse*) which he wrote in the following year. During this solitary Easter at Uttarkashi he seems to have entered more deeply than before into the Paschal mystery, as a letter to Lisieux also indicates (FT, 23.3.61). The same letter also recognizes the insufficiency of a merely verbal apologetic:

> . . . The essential thing in India—how much I feel it here!—is not to preach, run schools, put up buildings, etc., but to radiate the deep experience of the Lord within.
>
> How *holy* one ought to be here, in the strongest sense of the word, in order to have the right to witness to the Lord. Prayer joined with fasting and watching, in the greatest possible poverty and, both beyond and at the heart of all that, the deep peace and joy of the inner experience which should shine through. That is truly what India expects of us as witnesses to Christ (. . .). (FT, 23.3.61)

It was probably on his way to or from Uttarkashi that the following incident took place:

> . . . Have I told you how the other day at Hardwar I had to give a totally impromptu sermon to a gathering of at least a thousand Hindus? It occurs to me now, because I was saying to them that everything here on earth is the gift of our heavenly Father and the sign of his love; our

trials are simply to see if we love him for himself, or only for his gifts.—But the best thing was the way in which I had to speak. A Hindu sannyasi friend had taken me along to visit some ashrams with him, and when we reached one of them (the Krishna Ashram), there was the crowd which I have just mentioned, and on the dais about fifty sadhus, one of whom was in the middle of an address in Hindi. Very soon I found myself seated near the microphone and was peacefully looking at the audience, when suddenly I heard the loud-speaker announce the arrival of a "French Mahatma" . . . called Abhishiktanandaji "who is going to speak to you in English for ten minutes; Swami Premanand-ji (my sannyasi friend) will translate into Hindi." Then and there the mike was placed in front of me, and my friend said, "Off you go!" (F, 10.5.61)

Meeting in Almora, April 1961

In anticipation of the meeting Abhishiktananda told Fr Lemarié what he was hoping for:

> . . . On 16 April we shall have the meeting on Vedantin experience and Christian experience, of which I have told you, arranged and financed by Dr J-A. Cuttat. (. . .) For anyone to be able to think or speak usefully about this problem, it should have been for him an existential and not merely a speculative problem. Those who have not met the real India—and they are legion—what do they know of this problem? They missionize like Don Quixote and fight with windmills, unaware of the fact that India at one and the same time awaits Christianity and guards itself against it. (L, 18.3.61)

Afterwards he gave an account of the week to his friend in New York:

> . . . . There was a wonderful meeting in Almora: Catholic priests, two "Anglican priests",[30] a Russian Orthodox monk (born in England), the Swiss Ambassador to India. (. . .) The theme was Christian religious experience and Hindu religious experience. Christians were gazing at Christ in the mystery of India, where Christ was appearing to them in his eschatological glory. They were days of wonderful fullness and communion of spirits. The presence of non-Catholics made this communion deeper still, each one aware of the divergent positions of others, and yet feeling himself in a very real unity with all, in the depth of the soul where the Lord dwells—the Church of the Fathers, the Church before the separations, as we said. I believe more and more in the very great value of these meetings held at the level of interiority, both between Christians and between Christians and Hindus. Each morning Mass was celebrated facing the great peaks of the Himalayas. (AMS, 12.5.61)

30. With some of his correspondents, though not with all, Abhishiktananda still felt bound to use these quotation marks.

It was indeed a wonderful happening. Abhishiktananda showed great skill as an animator, constantly encouraging the participants to share, not their ideas about spirituality, but their experience (examples of which are quoted in *Hindu-Christian Meeting Point,* ch. 2), and firmly bringing discussions back to the existential level when they became too rarified. It was not a conference that aimed at producing 'findings'; rather the concern was to take soundings and explore new attitudes, and to consider how these might be communicated to the wider Church. As the Vatican Council was then in preparation, there was was also some discussion how the message might be got through to the Council Fathers. Whether or not this actually happened, a new and positive attitude towards the adherents of other faiths was manifested in the Council documents, which was in line with the hopes expressed at Almora.

Shantivanam—May September 1961

From May until mid-September Abhishiktananda was at the ashram, except for five weeks when he was driven out by a disastrous flood. Much of his time will have been devoted to the 'postulant' referred to in this letter to his sister:

> . . . Recent months at Shantivanam have been quite eventful. At the beginning of July the Kavery suddenly rose and went on rising . . . Only our chapel remained above the level of the water. I had to be evacuated by boat. Next day I returned in a boat to salvage books etc. The Kavery has never played such tricks since 1924! and it lasted a long time. Finally I went off on a tour. Only last Monday I came back to Shantivanam. Our huts have stood up well, but everywhere it is mud, potholes and damp. I am writing to you perched on a bench, and it is on a bench that I live in my cell. And this morning the Kavery looks as if it wants to come back and begin all over again!
>
> Along with that I have had a postulant, an Indian sannyasi, who asked fervently for baptism. He was with me for two and a half months. A slightly difficult character, but I strove to be patient, so as not to discourage my neophyte. And then—he turned out to be a complete liar! He goes from priest to priest, from Catholics to Protestants, and to all the Protestant sects, pretending to be converted . . . Last week he used my name to get himself accepted in various houses in Bangalore. Finally he was exposed and handed over to the police . . . The Lord has his own ways of playing games with us! (MT, 18.8.61)

The 'postulant' was in fact a lunatic who had been in and out of asylums for years, but was very intelligent and able to play a part well enough to deceive not only Abhishiktananda but also the Bishop. It is sad to read the hopes that he aroused once again for the launching of the 'hermits of Saccidananda'. But at least he knew how to act the part of a '*śishya*' (disciple), and gave Abhishiktananda a first experience of what it is to be a 'guru'. "It is no small thing to be 'projected' without warning into this kind of fatherhood," he told one Sister (Th, 21.5.61); and to another, "I am learning my lesson with Atmaram, who knows his part as a (. . .) disciple much better than I know that of a guru" (TL, 27.5.61). When the truth came out, "it is probably a sign that all my desires for expansion are unacceptable to the Lord, and that all he asks of me is simply to remain for ever in solitude" (Th, 14.7.61).

When driven out by the flood Abhishiktananda visited several places in the South, including Kurisumala, the ashram in Kerala which Fr Mahieu had founded:

> . . . Spent four days with Fr Mahieu (. . .). A marvellous solitude, such as I have only met with in the Himalayas. But the climate—rain, wind, fog, cold . . . (I) soon had to run away. An austere life of silence and labour in Cistercian style, even though Fr M. changes steadily and becomes more and more 'oriental'. It is kept going thanks to his enthusiasm. If he can carry on long enough for that to penetrate his brethren, it will have a good future. In any case, it is the only monastic foundation here that is on its feet. (L, 18.9.61)

The experience of the Oriental rite followed at Kurisumala convinced Abhishiktananda that his earlier idea of developing a truly Indian rite on that basis was a mistake: "That will certainly not do to express the 'Christian' prayer of those who have been formed in the serenity and purity of the Upanishadic tradition." Further, the experience of an "Office . . . in an unknown tongue and an unknown script, where you never succeed in finding your place in the (book?) which they give you" would, he thought, be a good lesson for those who were holding out for the continued use of Latin in worship rather than the mother tongue.

During these months there was little chance for serious writing. In a letter of May (L, 11.5.61) he spoke of writing a supplement to one of his earlier papers[31] and of revising the new paper written at Uttarkashi, saying that he wished they could be published. He was still working on them in October however (TL, 21.10.61). He also began a new draft of the two narratives of his experiences with Gnanananda and at Arunachala.[32] Fr Lemarié had again suggested that they might be published, "but I don't want to make a display like . . ." (L, 15.7.61). His heart was not in it; "I don't see how to write this 'pilgrimage'. For a long time I have thought of presenting it by putting 'Arunachala' first. But it would have to be told in story form" (L, 18.9.61). He was always on his guard against seeming to project himself.

To the North twice more—September to December 1961

One of Abhishiktananda's stopping places on his way north in September 1961 was Manmad, where some of the Little Sisters of the Sacred Heart who had left the community in Trivandrum were in process of opening a new house. He then went on to Bareilly, where plans were being made at the Jyotiniketan ashram for taking part in the approaching Assembly of the World Council of Churches in New Delhi. He wrote about their life of great simplicity to the Prioress at Lisieux and said:

31. This was probably the article on "Présence" (note 26 above), not completed until October.
32. This was a revision of the two narratives originally written in 1956, which he usually referred to as "Pèlerinages". Part was sent with a view to possible publication to Fr Lemarié in March 1962 (L, 15.3.62), and the remainder at the end of 1963 (L, 12.12.63). As it was not accepted, he later wrote a final version, first of *Gnanananda* in 1968 (OB, 7.7.68), and then of *Souvenirs d'Arunachala* in 1970 (L, 6.10.70).

> . . . The problem of ecumenism looks quite different when you live in the midst of a group of deeply committed people, who are more so than Catholics. The longing for unity is very strong here. Why must the Catholic Church appear in the first instance so much as an 'organization', a legal system, much more than as a centre of life? From within you can find your feet in it, but how can you explain the real truth of the 'Roman' Church (as they call it) to those who can only judge it from outside? Here, as wherever he is asked to speak, my friend always leads people to what is essential, the interior life, silence and prayer. Just like Shantivanam, there are very few who understand him. (. . .) I shall come back here at the beginning of December to meet some of the delegates to the W.C.C. from Delhi. Some of them have already heard speak of Shantivanam; to all of them we would like to pass on India's appeal to the Church, beseeching her to be above all a praying Church. (FT, 9.10.61)

In mid-October Abhishiktananda went up to Uttarkashi to see how the building of his *kutiya* was progressing. He kept his friends informed about events:

> . . . I got here last Sunday (. . .). My friends were expecting me. Naturally my *kutiya* is not yet finished, but it is coming on well (. . .). This time I am the guest of a new sadhu, very kindly disposed towards the *angrezi* [English!] sadhu. (Th, 22.10.61)
>
> . . . I have had interesting conversations with some sadhus. There are some who certainly have an interior experience. Even if they express themselves in a way that disconcerts a European, there is something unmistakable in their look and their voice. (. . .) For the time being I can only take my place in their midst as discreetly as possible, not hiding the fact that I am a Christian, but only letting it be known where that is advisable. There has been and still is strong opposition on the part of one sadhu who anyhow has the reputation of being an awkward customer. (. . .)
>
> In December I will send you the notes of which you speak. I typed them out just before leaving Shantivanam, and now I am revising the text here and there. At present I am typing the 73-page paper, and may send all three papers to *La vie sp.*[33] These notes are only intended to awaken people. It is not a question of storing up ideas, but of finding the way to the source and of daring to accept "what you are". (TL, 21.10.61)
>
> . . . This place is really attractive. All the same, if it were not for Him, I should not be capable of staying here for a long time. (FT, 20.10.61)

Abhishiktananda had hoped to remain at Uttarkashi until it was time to return to Delhi for the W.C.C., Assembly. However, for the second time this year,

33. The "73-page paper" may have been the article on "Presence": (note 26 and L, 29.6.60); this and the other Lisieux 'papers' were shortly afterwards, during the W.C.C. Assembly at New Delhi, offered to a Dominican publisher from Paris, who raised unfulfilled hopes that they would be published.

his plans were upset by the arrival of a visitor from Europe. This time it was the Abbé Duperray, Fr Monchanin's friend, who came to India to see where he had lived. After only two weeks at Uttarkashi Abhishiktananda had to hasten back to Shantivanam to meet him, and again two weeks later took the train back to Delhi—for the fourth time in one year!

Despite the inconvenience of so much travelling, Abhishiktananda was glad to welcome the Abbé, with whom he had much to discuss, including his plan to divide his time between Shantivanam and Uttarkashi. This had met with much criticism in Pondicherry, but

> . . . the Abbé is much more reasonable on this question than the Pondi friends, for whom my leaving here will be a desertion; these ladies want someone to keep watch over the shrine (to which anyhow no one comes . . .) (L, 12.11.61)

They also discussed the question of publishing his book on Arunachala—"difficult, because my most interesting experiences have taken place within a stone's throw of the Fathers of the M.E. [Missions Étrangères de Paris]." who seemingly would not have approved!

Before returning to Delhi Abhishiktananda wrote to his sister:

> . . . I have just come from Uttarkashi and will return to Delhi next week. What a 'gyrovague' [vagrant monk] your brother is! When once you begin to travel about in India, it is quite normal to spend three or four days at a stretch in the train. All the more so, now that for long journeys in Third Class they provide compartments where berths are let down at night so that three people can sleep one above another. So like that it is not too tiring, at least when, as now, it is not too hot.
>
> I had to come back, because a great friend of Fr Monchanin—the one who was with him when he died—came to see the places where he lived. We had long talks together all this week, and visited various people. He left yesterday, and today I am resting and writing my mail.
>
> I spent two weeks again at Uttarkashi (. . .). What a beautiful place, as I have already told you. (. . .) Just at Uttarkashi the gorge widens a little, and there are a few fields and houses. There are sadhus everywhere, but especially in two localities. At Gyansu, where I am, there are about ten little houses for sadhus, right on the bank of the river. That is where they are building my '*kutiya*', as they call these little houses, built of stones and mud, and roofed with large untrimmed slates which are brought down from the mountainside on men's backs (. . .). I have found some very kind friends there who only speak Hindi (. . .), so every day I was making progress in Hindi. (. . .) My *kutiya* is coming up and by next Easter, if all goes well, I should be settled into it. In the mean time I was staying in a small lean-to, 2 metres by 1.60 in size. For an altar I had just a window recess, 50 cms wide. (. . .) Fortunately I know by heart all the Ordinary of the Mass and much of the Proper. (. . .) In this minute room, using a miniature petrol stove, I sometimes also did my own cooking, and at least made tea morning and evening. You can't imagine how delicious the Ganges water is.

> Before taking my bath in it, I used to wait until the sun had risen over the mountains and somewhat warmed the atmosphere. Then, summoning all my courage, I went to the river and at least splashed myself with water when it was too icy to take a plunge. But afterwards, what a marvellous feeling! Solitude. The noise of the river drowns every other sound. There the world is wholly forgotten, nothing distracts you from the one essential. How I long to return.
>
> Next week I am going back to Delhi and Bareilly for some ecumenical meetings. (MT, 12.11.61)

A few weeks previously Abhishiktananda had received a letter from another French Carmelite, Sr Marie-Gilberte of the Carmel of St Pair. She had been impressed by the reading of his *Ermites* and had apparently also been in contact with his Carmelite friend (Sr Thérèse) of Shembaganur who was in France for medical treatment. Fired by Abhishiktananda's vision of starting a very simple, austere and contemplative Carmel in India, she had written to offer herself. In his reply he pointed out the great difficulty of obtaining a visa, but said:

> . . . In any case, prepare yourself through an ever deepening contemplation. That is the essential preparation for any work of the Church here. That makes up for all the rest, while without it all the rest is but 'sounding brass' . . Sr Thérèse (of Shembag) will keep you informed about the situation and about the best way to bring into existence here a Carmel which would not have as its chief aim the construction of a copy of the convent at Avila (. . .). When the Rule of Blessed Albert has been absorbed in its admirable brevity, then externals corresponding to the real needs of India will develop of themselves; and I am sure St Teresa would love to stay in such Carmels . . . (MG, 16.11.61)

A week later he returned to Delhi for the Assembly of the W.C.C., which he followed with great interest, making many new contacts (Orthodox theologians, Taizé, etc):

> . . . A most impressive atmosphere. All nationalities, all kinds of dress. Lay attire predominates (and there are many women). (. ...) Five official Catholic observers and 10-20 unofficial (. . .). Relaxed, simple, fraternal atmosphere. (. . .) I wish some Roman cardinals were here incognito to take note of the atmosphere. (. . .) This evening a public meeting, at which an African woman (. . .) without using aggressive phrases or aiming at eloquence, but with a simplicity that was even more devastating, put in the dock the behaviour of the white man—and the white missionary—towards the blacks. How much that hour taught me about Africa and its 'feelings'.
>
> One might question the methods (a little too 'parliamentary' perhaps) used by all these groups in search of unity, but there is certainly a working of the Spirit (. . .), a real longing for unity. (TL, 23.11.61)

After the Assembly Abhishiktananda spent a further week at Jyotiniketan along with some of the delegates. Then he went south—Indore, Manmad and Bombay—and reached Shantivanam early in January 1962.

Shantivanam—January to March 1962

For the Feast of the Epiphany Abhishiktananda had a visitor, Ilse Friedeberg of the W.C.C. Institute at Bossey:

> . . . I have been visited by a German—Lutheran by origin, Orthodox in heart—whom I met in Delhi and who had long known of Shantivanam. Her vocation is to work for Christian unity above all by prayer and encounters in the Spirit. We sang together Lauds and Vespers, and in the evening, before the offering of the light accompanied by the *Trisagion,* we sang in Tamil, Russian and Greek, the *Phos Hilaron,* [Joyful Light]; you know, that beautiful hymn which the ancient Syrian Churches used to sing at sunset to Christ, the True Light.
>
> I expect to remain here until about the middle of March. I am awaiting the outcome of the letters between the Bishop here and the Bishop of Meerut. They do not want me to leave Shantivanam for good. Unfortunately I have no one sufficiently interested and committed to take charge of Shantivanam in my absence. (FT, 14.1.62)

One day in February a young man, who for six years had been the ashram's cook, came with his wife to show their newborn son to the Swami, who soon after told his family about their plight:

> . . . You can't imagine such poverty. He works in a sugar-mill and earns about 70 NF per month. Had I not been able to give him 30-50 F at the time of the birth, I do not know what he would have done. The mother is only seventeen; her family is so poor that she was married off at the first opportunity, so as to have one less mouth to feed. The other day I went to their house. Apart from what they have on their backs and a minimum of pots and pans, nothing. Yet they are happy with their baby son. But his salary does not allow him to provide the mother with the nourishment that she would need to give enough milk. (F, 7.3.62)

Not knowing what would be the best way of giving practical assistance, he sought the expert advice of Mother Théophane at Indore (Th, 15.2.62).

During these months at the ashram Abhishiktananda was unusually inactive. He called it 'laziness', but he probably needed a time of rest after the exertions of the previous year. He confessed to having a dread of travelling, "so exhausting", with its additional complication of the need for advance booking so as to ensure a berth. It was also obviously a relief that an engagement in Ceylon had to be cancelled, because his Indian passport had not arrived. He did not even read much (L, 15.3.62). His only literary activity seems to have been the revision of what he had written in 1956 about his experiences at Arunachala (still called 'Pèlerinages', 'Pilgrimages of Aruneya'), on which Fr Lemarié had encouraged him to persevere:

> . . . Have you received my papers? This week I will send you a continuation with a general outline. It will still lack two subordinate [*sous*?] chapters which I will write up later. On no account can it be published just as it is. There are, for example, some bitchy remarks

> about (. . .). I shall probably finish off the part which deals with Arunachala. As regards the rest, I shall only get down to it if it really has some chance of arousing interest. It will not be as difficult to read as *Guhantara* was. (L, 15.3.62)

Meanwhile he was preparing for a second meeting of what came to be known as the 'Cuttat group', which was to continue the discussion of Hindu and Christian spirituality begun at Almora in 1961. The meeting was arranged for the first week of April at the ecumenical Retreat and Study Centre in Rajpur near Dehra Dun. [34]

In the North—April to June 1962

At the meeting in Rajpur there was a wider representation of other Churches than had been the case at Almora.

> . . . These meetings become more and more pan-Christian, and all thank God for this; for it is a unique occasion when true Christians mutually discover each other. (AMS, 3.6.62)

In order to ensure that the discussions might be better focussed than they had been in 1961, Abhishiktananda arranged for papers to be read on the experience of certain great contemplatives in the Hindu and Christian traditions (summarized in *Hindu-Christian Meeting Point,* ch.2). He himself took the case of Sri Ramana Maharshi, and his paper became the starting point of the book which he soon afterwards began writing at Uttarkashi. His verdict on the meeting was:

> . . . Our conference this year was a little too philosophical. Last year I had ruled out invitations to 'philosophers'. This year they came. However, the idea that the Lord is speaking to us and calling us by means of the interiority of Hindu spirituality is making headway. (L, 13.4.62)

Eager though he was to return to Uttarkashi, Abhishiktananda first had to fulfil an important rendezvous at Bombay. His Carmelite friend, Sr Thérèse of Shembaganur, was due to arrive from France on 23 April, and "she very much wants to meet and discuss the possibilities of a Carmel which would truly respond to what India is expecting" (L, 13.4.62). At this point it did seem possible that she and two other like-minded Carmelites might be able to found a Carmel on the lines of Abhishiktananda's ideal.

After meeting the Sister he was at last free to take the road to Uttarkashi, which he reached on 2 May. Next day he wrote to his sister:

> . . . Found your letter yesterday when I arrived at Uttarkashi, where I am going to spend at least two months. (. . .)
>
> My little house is not yet finished. In my absence they naturally did nothing. Today they are going to put on the roof, and I hope to be able to occupy it in ten days' time. Meanwhile I have been provided with

34. The Rajpur Centre was opened in 1954 by the Revd James Alter and his wife. From 1962 onwards Abhishiktananda was a frequent visitor, and for a year in 1972-3 was given the use of two rooms.

a room. I shall see how these two months work out, and whether I can really hope to settle here for good, or at least for long periods. (. . .) Last year I told you about my life here. This time I am going to be a little more bourgeois and to do my own cooking, and so to fast rather less.

Today, Mother's anniversary. I said Mass on a window-ledge, using a nice little chalice that has just come from Lisieux. It is Easter time, death must be seen from the other side. Only the body passes away; the 'I' which I utter with Jesus—addressing the Father—never has an end. 'I' do not die! Whoever believes in Jesus has passed from death to life. (MT, 3.5.62)

Three weeks later he wrote to Fr Lemarié:

From the hermitage of Uttarkashi! I was at last able to enter my Carthusian cell last Monday (21 May). Before my entry the house had been ritually hallowed by a sacred Vedic fire. Only then was it handed over . . . The ground floor measures 2.70 by 2.40 metres. One half is covered by a loft where I can sit in peace and get a magnificent view over the Ganges through a little window. In the corner is an altar made out of boxes. Later, when it seems wise, I will make something better. Just now they are building a lean-to of planks and corrugated iron for my kitchen. I am still too taken up with worries about building and materials to enjoy it fully. The landlord's children are charming little brahmins (. . .). Their orthodox father busies himself with pilgrims on the way to Gangotri, directing their prayers and pujas and their sacred bath before they set off on the last stage of their pilgrimage.

There are few sadhus whose personal reputation is high. Most are accused of greed, seeking for money or position. I am quite happy to remain on the sidelines. (. . .) Very slowly and discreetly I am letting it be known to Jwala Prasad, my host, that I am a Christian, talking to him about Christian monks, and yesterday when a letter came from Lisieux, telling him about Carmels and my sermons to contemplatives. I have to go slowly, but he is taking it very well. (L, 24.5.62)

At the end of May Abhishiktananda was joined for a few days by John Cole from Jyotiniketan who came to Uttarkashi shortly before the authorities placed the area out of bounds on account of the threat from China. From then on censorship began, and letters were delayed or lost. When telling his sister not to think that she had been forgotten, if this happened, he added: "Each morning when I said Mass up there, there was a regular 'world tour' during my Memento." (MT, 16.7.62)

During May and June Abhishiktananda was hard at work on the first draft of a new book, and reported just before leaving for the South:

. . . I have written more than 100 large size pages at Uttarkashi on "The Experience of Saccidananda: Advaitin experience and its Trinitarian fulfilment". I am going to type it out and get it into shape at Shantivanam. It should be ready by the autumn, and I think it might be published. (TL, 26.6.62)

Three years later the book was published under the title *Sagesse hindoue mystique chrétienne*. It was Abhishiktananda's most ambitious writing, and succeeded in expressing in a form more easily understood by western readers something at least of what he had so far vainly tried to get published in his earlier writings. The book also gives the impression that for the time being the problem of holding together Advaitic experience and Christian faith had become less acute for him through the adoption of a 'theology of fulfilment'. (A few years later this solution no longer satisfied him, as is shown by his new Foreword in the English edition.)

Shantivanam—July 1962 to January 1963

At the end of June Abhishiktananda returned to the South, making only a brief stop in Delhi. Writing from Shantivanam he told his sister of his plan to go back to Uttarkashi later in the year:

> . . . Everything went very well during my two-months' stay there, and I have a good mind to return in October. Just now it is the rainy season in the North, and the mountain roads which are dangerous enough in ordinary weather become much more so. (. . .) In the rains everything disintegrates, so that buses can no longer run. Pedestrians do acrobatics in order to cross the rubble and to avoid if possible ending their pilgrimage in the waters of the Ganges down below. Besides, every year the Ganges levies a generous toll—an expiatory sacrifice for the violation of its valleys—of a good half-dozen buses with their human cargo, not to mention trucks. After all, what does it matter? a little sooner, or a little later, that is where you have to go; why make a fuss about it?
>
> This evening I leave for a week in Bangalore. A meeting of theologians, then some sermons to the Carmelites, always insatiably hungry for spiritual nourishment. (. . .)
>
> This time I have my typewriter, and so my correspondents will no longer have so much to put up with from my handwriting. I now have to type out some articles, or rather a book, which I wrote at Uttarkashi. How convenient it would be, if you were at hand to be my secretary! (MT, 16.7.62)

In a letter to Fr Lemarié he contrasted Shantivanam and Gyansu (Uttarkashi):

> . . . It has been a joy once more to breathe the air of Shantivanam. The mountains are beautiful, but in the plains there is a brightness of colour which opens you up and 'expands' you wonderfully. Mountains concentrate you, limit your horizons, but make you go deep. The ideal solution would certainly be to keep both ashrams. It is chiefly a question of finance that deters me from keeping Shantivanam. Travelling and the hut at Gyansu have made a big hole in my funds. And I shall probably be obliged to buy the land round my place at Gyansu to avoid having neighbours. (L, 15.7.62)

There was another very practical reason for retaining Shantivanam for the time being; he needed the ashram library for reference in his various writings, especially the latest one (Th, 21.9.62; and see MT, 29.9.64). The preparation of this manuscript kept him busy until October, and he told Fr Lemarié that until it was finished he would be unable to take up the two remaining chapters of his experiences at Arunachala: "I see that you take a favourable view of the publication of "Pèlerinages", of which personally I am quite scared" (L, 15.7.62). The same letter refers to his disappointment at hearing nothing from the Dominican publisher who had shown great interest in his Lisieux 'papers' when they met at the W.C.C. Assembly in the previous November. However, another W.C.C. contact, Fr Boris Bobrinski, had asked for permission to print one of them in the periodical *Contacts,* and this appeared in January 1963.

He continued to encourage the Carmelite of St Pair, Sr Marie-Gilberte, who was hoping to respond to his call to found a truly primitive Carmel in India. Some months previously he had given her suggestions for preparatory reading. Now he wrote:

> . . . You have had news of my meeting with Sr Thérèse at Bombay. I am convinced that the Lord is preparing something, but when and how is his secret. (. . .) The important thing is to hold yourself in readiness and to be, as I say, on the watch for the signs of the Spirit which are always so unobstrusive . . . There is not the slightest doubt that India needs a contemplative Christian foundation, very free, aiming at the essential, just as India itself from the beginning has been drawn by the Absolute. That is entirely in conformity with the primitive Carmel. The outward desert imaging the interior desert, which St John of the Cross so admirably understood and expressed. It is not a question of making a foundation with a view to getting novices etc. . . . but simply of coming and leading here a life of dedication to the 'essential' in obedience to a summons from the Lord (. . .). It is only in this total freedom that the Spirit can work as he pleases; and in my view, if the Lord prolongs so interminably the preparations for a work that nevertheless seems so urgent, it must be that, alas, we are not ready for it. Keep in touch with Shembaganur and Lisieux. The essential preparation is a truly contemplative spirit. (. . .) For only a truly contemplative spirit makes possible the inward assimilation of the 'hidden manna' in the depth of the words and traditions of India. (MG, 16.7.62)

He also impressed on the Sister the need to have a good knowledge of English before coming to India, and insisted that she should not delay her coming once the way was open; for "with age we become too 'reasonable', and the Spirit can no longer give us a shake."

During August the Kavery threatened to repeat its performance of the previous year, and Abhishiktananda was advised to leave the ashram until the danger had passed. He first stayed with friends in the local village who had sheltered him on the last occasion, and then decided to go to a hospital in Dindigul for a medical check-up. He had no particular symptoms apart from a continual feeling of weariness (Th, 21.9.62).

> . . . I went to Dindigul, three hours by bus, to have a check-up in a hospital run by Belgian sisters. I quite hoped they would tell me that

> there was something or other not working properly, and that I should need a small operation which would result in my being cossetted for a fortnight, as I was two years ago in Pondi. Or else, that I needed rest, etc. Alas, all the tests with various instruments, blood samples, etc., showed that everything was in excellent order, and that there was absolutely nothing wrong except 'old age'! (F, 22.8.62)

The manuscript of "The Experience of Saccidananda" was finally edited and typed to his satisfaction and could be posted to Paris at the beginning of October (MT, 2.10.62). But Abhishiktananda decided to put off his return to the North for another month, partly on account of the threatening political situation on the frontier, which might close the road to Uttarkashi. There were other reasons too:

> . . . Then there is this blessed laziness. Uttarkashi is a serious matter! not small beer like Shantivanam . . . Then too, there are friends here who are unhappy. Some of them fiercely reproach me for abandoning "Fr Monchanin's ashram". However I should have very much liked to spend the winter there. (Th, 21.9.62)

Then in October a request came from his old friend Fr R. Macé in Rennes that he should put up a visitor who planned to come to the ashram at Christmas and to stay until Epiphany. This was a priest, also from Rennes, who wrote novels under the pseudonym of 'Jean Sulivan'. Having been impressed by one of his novels, and in any case anticipating the pleasure of meeting a fellow-Breton, Abhishiktananda resolved to remain at Shantivanam until January.

Meanwhile he had been told of the resignation of the Father Abbot of Kergonan, and asked his sister to send him further news:

> . . . I have scarcely had any news from St Anne [Kergonan] since Father Abbot resigned. I do not know the new Superior. However, I have written to him, and he sent me a very kind reply, quite amazed to hear that there was a monk of Kergonan in India. When you write, please give me news of St Anne. (MT, 2.10.62)

He was also concerned to hear that one of his nephews was to be sent to his old school, the minor seminary at Châteaugiron:

> . . . I still have wretched memories of Châteaugiron. Even apart from being separated from St Briac, it was so old-fashioned. Not even a room for showers (whereas here, anyone who does not take a daily bath is simply disgusting!), such a narrow training (one year, the order came that our shorts should cover the knees!—our dear professors probably had bad thoughts from seeing our knees), etc. However, if I had not been there, should I have kept my vocation? But then, L. is so young; couldn't you keep him near you at least until he is twelve? (. . .) I expect Ch. has modernized itself; but the longer I live, the more opposed I am to this education in a 'ghetto' which has done such damage to the Church. (F, 31.10.62)

News of the Vatican Council was beginning to come, and Abhishiktananda rejoiced to hear of the strong reaction of the Council to Cardinal Ottaviani's text on Scripture. "The Pope (. . .) is a real miracle. Bea (. . .) has truly done a marvellous job in the lst two years. I now think with Panikkar that the 'brew' cannot fail to produce results." (L, 19.11.62)

He also shared with Fr Lemarié some encouraging news about his manuscripts:

> . . . R. Panikkar has written to me of his keen desire that Pèlerinages [i.e. *Souvenirs*] should be published. I must discuss it with my visitor at Christmas, and first finish writing a few more pages. Yet I must preserve my anonymity.
>
> Regarding "The Experience of Saccidananda", Fr A.M. Henry, OP, wrote immediately that it is 'fascinating', even though very difficult on certain pages. However he is afraid that Editions du Cerf may not find that it is the kind of thing that appeals to their clientèle. (. . .) In any case, his appreciation is a consolation.

The same letter mentions that his sense of weariness was still troubling him:

> . . . for several months I have been feeling abnormally tired. Everything is in order; I got myself examined by a Belgian doctor, and there was nothing wrong. Probably a little nervous depression. But one day things go less well, and then I pick up again. (. . .) However. It is wretched to live amid such a lack of understanding on the part of one's neighbours. I avoid dining at the Bishop's house, so as to escape stupid questions. (The Bishop himself is fortunately more sensible.) I avoid ecclesiastics whom I do not know to be specially sympathetic. How happy I am in purely Hindu surroundings (. . .) with no one to ask, How many 'conversions'? or How many postulants? (L, 19.11.62)

One possible explanation of his depression may be revealed in the following remarks to his sister:

> . . . I have any amount of mail already, and the cost of postage has gone up terribly. Imagine, half a rupee for this aerogramme, almost one rupee for an air-letter—yet I am only just able to afford one rupee daily for my food. (. . .) I have recently had to give up fruit and good vegetables in order to make ends meet, as all prices have increased with national development (. . .) and the Five Year Plans. That is why I restrict my correspondence to what is absolutely essential. (MT, 14.12.62)

Just before the arrival of the visitor from Rennes, another would-be postulant presented himself:

> . . . Meanwhile, on Christmas Eve heaven sent me a young Indian aged twenty-six, who seems to be indeed a 'pearl' and to have what is needed to become the foundation stone of Shantivanam. He has a job worth Rs. 800 per month (. . .). This shows he has courage. Even so I was hesitating about getting myself involved once again, but Fr Dominique told me to accept him. (. . .) If he comes, it will be at the end of June. (L, 6.1.63)

Immediately after Christmas 'Jean Sulivan' arrived at the ashram, and Abhishiktananda reported to his family:

> . . . I have now had my visitor from Rennes. Raymond Macé will probably bring him to see you one day. We had a very interesting week together, with talk such as I rarely have. He will tell you what he thinks of Shantivanam. As I could not provide the poor man with beef or even omelettes, Christmas week was for him a week of fasting! (F, 25.1.63)

Jean Sulivan later described his meeting with "Abhis" at length in a book of his experiences, *Le plus petit abîme.*[35] Their meeting led Abhishiktananda to make a surprising confession to Fr Lemarié:

> . . . a very interesting Christmas week beside the Kavery. (. . .) a profound need for truth and authenticity. I recommend his books—good for knowing the world, for 'modern' thought. I must admit, alas, that no less than Fr Monchanin I remain a European and impenitently Greek! (L, 27.2.63)

In the North—January to June 1963

Abhishiktananda set off for the North in mid-January, first spending two days in Madras with Anand Kumar, his new postulant, whose Hindu family gave him a heart-warming welcome (F, 25.1.63). Then, by way of Indore and Delhi (Dr Cuttat), he came to Jyotiniketan and was there for the Feast of the Presentation (2 Feb.). In letters to Lisieux and New York he wrote:

> A word before going up to Uttarkashi from the Anglican ashram near Bareilly where I often come. Very fervent communion in the love of the Lord Christ, and at the same time aching hearts at being unable to 'break bread' together. Yesterday, for the Feast of 2 February, they asked if they might be present at my Mass, and followed it with great devotion. (FT, 3.2.63)
>
> . . . To stay with non-Catholic Christians, as in this ashram, is a great grace, yet it is heart-rending. We feel ourselves to be one in the Lord. Not one of us can deny the claim of the others to be truly Christian, none can doubt that, if death found us together, the next instant we would indeed be together in the great Koinonia [communion] of the Lord. Why do we have to be divided by the 'sign', when we are one within the '*res*' [the thing itself, the reality]? How can we not 'break bread' together, when we are already together in faith, in the ultimate reality? (AMS, 3.2.63)

It was during this visit to Jyotiniketan, while thinking with his friends about future meetings of the 'Cuttat group', that a fruitful new idea emerged. At the Rajpur meeting in April 1962 some of the participants, especially the Presbyterians, had expressed the hope that in future their programme should include times of common study and meditation on passages from the Bible. The new idea was that in the same way, as part of the Christians' own 'return to the sources', a prayerful and ecclesial reading together of the Upanishads should be attempted, parallel to their study of the Bible. A brief statement[36] was drawn up,

35. Published by Éditions Gallimard in 1965. Abhishiktananda is referred to in pages 171-260.
36. Copies of this 'statement' are in the Abhishiktananda Society files.

explaining the method which should be followed, as a preparation for those who were invited to the next meeting at Nagpur after Christmas. In the mean time they thought it wise to call together a small group to make a trial of the new idea, and arranged to meet in Delhi at the end of April.

On the way up to Uttarkashi Abhishiktananda stopped at Rajpur, wanting to share the new idea with the Alters, his Presbyterian friends at the Centre. Such contacts, he observed to Mother Théophane, "would be enough to make the flesh creep of those who are outside the ecumenical movement; but it is all very good, all the more because it has simply 'happened', unsought" (Th, 6.2.63).

He reached Uttarkashi on 10 February and remained there until after Easter:

> . . . It was a little cold when I arrived, but now it is much better, except when it rains like yesterday. But I have become sensitive to cold. Up here I am still wearing a sweater and very often put something over my shoulders. (. . .) My hut was in good shape. (. . .) I settled into it immediately. Marvellous solitude, very few visitors, as I speak so little Hindi. That means that I pass whole days without speaking, or almost so (especially on Fridays, when I put a notice on my door: Silence). How that helps you to enter into yourself and to live quite alone with the Lord. (. . .) Each day at noon I do my cooking, and make short work of it: rice, lentils and vegetables, all cooked together. In the morning a bowl of coffee with milk, in the evening a cup of chocolate, and when I am hungry a little semolina. You need little when you are re-collected. I shall make up for it when I return to the plains in Eastertide. But my life is indeed luxurious, compared with that of the sadhus who live round about. (MT, 9.3.63)

Later on he had more company:

> Nowadays I am seeing more people (. . .) More and more sadhus are coming up from the plains to enjoy the coolness of the summer here (. . .). For the past three weeks a Tamilian sadhu, who has been here for a year, has been coming to see me regularly. I wonder how he could have endured the winter, all the more since he contents himself with the food given to the sadhus with nothing hot in the morning (until 10 a.m.). What an example of serious monastic life! He has set me heaps of questions. Finally he wanted a life of Christ, then the Gospel. He was greatly impressed. He himself will soon be going down to the South, and will surely come to see me at Shantivanam. (F, 21.4.63)

As usual he had plenty of work to do on his manuscripts and, in particular, made a thorough revision of "The Experience of Saccidananda" on the lines suggested by Fr Henry, who thought that people would find it too difficult. He now worked "on the assumption that the 'average reader' is totally ignorant of India, of latin and of scholasticism" (L, 27.2.63). So far no publisher had been found, though Le Cerf was considering it. He asked Fr Lemarié's advice about this, and also about finding a weighty theologian to write a Preface—someone "who would give confidence to the censor and would attract readers" (L, 20.3.63).

His reading at this time included the Homilies of Chromatius in the edition which Fr Lemarié had just published, and Lossky's book on Eckhart:

. . . I must tell you what struck me terribly in the first sermon. Like St Gregory and the others, Chromatius takes great delight in laying into the Jews. It is so easy to go searching for muck always "somewhere else", instead of searching for what the Bible means *for me*, for my day! It is just the same now. The more I read the prophets, the more I find them terribly contemporary; for, in the clash between Paul and James, in the end it was not Paul and the law of the Spirit that won, but the legalism of the Jerusalem Church, soon to be backed up by Greek intellectualism and Roman juridicism. Where Jesus says 'Jews' and 'Pharisees', we ought to understand 'us'—from top to bottom of the ecclesiastical scale.

I have just been reading that very difficult *Eckhart* by Lossky. Once again, all he looks for in the Bible is the illustration of his theses, like the whole of post-patristic theology. And really, how badly Eckhart's metaphysics confuse his marvellous mystical intuitions. It is the grace of the Upanishads that makes you see that everything is so simple! (L, 20.3.63)

Mother Théophane evidently felt that his fasting during Lent was excessive, and was not convinced by his saying that "his sadhu neighbours would think him a glutton, if they could see his kitchen" (Th, 20.3.63). He had to reassure her by describing the three meals a day which he began to take after Easter (Th, 24.4.63)

Before going down to Delhi towards the end of April for the experiment in contemplative reading of the Bible and the Upanishads (p. 150-1), he told his family of his hopes:

. . . I am going down to Delhi for a meeting from Friday to Sunday. This time we shall have a bishop. The Council has done good to the Bishops, they are beginning to be converted. After the Bishops will come the turn of the clergy, and finally I think the Christian laity will follow suit. So hope is reborn that one day India will become Christian. (F, 21.4.63)

The meeting was held at the Cambridge Brotherhood, the home of a small Anglican community ("very close to Catholics", he told Fr Lemarié), where in later years he normally stayed when passing through Delhi. With a few friends the experiment was tried out of taking passages from the Bible and the Upanishads in alternate sessions. Those who took part, including on one day the Archbishop of Delhi, found it illuminating and approved the intention of following the same method at Nagpur after Christmas.

He next went to meet his postulant Anand, who came from Madras to spend a month with him at Uttarkashi. After visiting Agra and Vrindāvan they reached Uttarkashi on 10 May, and before returning to the plains they made a pilgrimage to Gangotri, the source of the Bhāgīrathī branch of the Ganges.

. . . In my last week I went on pilgrimage to Gangotrī (. . .) 65 kms on foot by very bad tracks, climbing up and down the hills; unbelievable lodging-places at night, unbelievable the food also. What is marvellous is the faith of those pilgrims, who every day in their hundreds brave

> all the difficulties, including the cold in the later stages (. . .) to come and worship in this sacred place. I was able to say Mass every day, at least in the evening, and was particularly happy to celebrate it at Gangotri, in a small hut raised on piles at the edge of the river. (MT, 12.6.63)

In a letter to Fr Lemarié he recorded his first impressions of his postulant:

> . . . For the last two weeks I have had my dear Anand with me. He is truly a choice spirit. But there will certainly be difficult days, for he has a strong personality, and I myself am pretty stubborn. However, Shantivanam can only be founded with men who think, speak and act 'with personality'. It is such a great responsibility that I am really frightened, like the apprentice sculptor before his marvellous blocks of marble. I do not feel strong enough to say to him 'Come'; but still less do I have the right to say 'Don't come'—for the tragic fact is that in the Indian Church, apart from Shantivanam, there is no possible alternative way of developing the gifts that he has received.
>
> Keep in your prayers also the Tamilian sadhu whom I met, and who before long may also come to Shantivanam, at least for a time (. . .). Such a fine spirit, so sincere, so pure and free from all desire. It is a tragedy that the Indian Church is not 'ready' to provide such spirits with room for the spiritual growth to which the Spirit is calling them! (L, 25.5.63)

Shantivanam—June to December 1963

Less than three weeks after his return to Shantivanam Abhishiktananda had to travel back to Delhi to attend a wedding, and then to Bombay to meet two young men who arrived from Rome on 7 July. One was Philippe Fanchette, a Mauritian seminarist who, after completing his studies at Rome, was returning home. He had been in touch with Abhishiktananda for several years and had read many of his unpublished manuscripts. He had hoped to test his vocation at Shantivanam, for which he seemed eminently suited, but his bishop refused to release him. He could therefore only come for a brief visit. The other was E. Aguilar, a Spaniard from Barcelona, who was sent together with Philippe by Fr Panikkar. His faith had been upset by his meeting with Hindu spirituality, and it was thought that he might find help at Shantivanam.

In Bombay they were held up for some days, as no seats were available on the trains to Madras. When eventually they reached the ashram on 18 July, Abhishiktananda was exhausted by much travelling and talking. He told Mother Théophane that he did not intend to go out again before the meeting in Nagpur at the end of the year, and remarked sadly:

> . . . It may be egoism, it may be because I am a difficult person, or it may be weariness with the Lord's 'fun and games' (as you call it), but I feel myself less and less capable of living and working with mankind . . .

In the same letter (Th, 24.7.63) he hints at his uncertainty in connection with Anand, who was intending to join him in mid-August: "He has great qualities, but his formation will be difficult if there are only two of us. He would need a group of at least three. Otherwise I am very hesitant about accepting him, despite his entreaties." He hoped that Anand would decide not to come; but come he did, and his attitude to the ashram made it abundantly clear that it was not the place for him. Abhishiktananda felt bound to persuade him that his vocation lay elsewhere, perhaps with the Jesuits with whom he had previously been in contact. His last word on the subject was to Mother Théophane:

> . . . As regards Anand, you were right about him from the start. Once again (I have been) caught by a mirage. (. . .) It was fortunate that I had him with me for a month in the North, otherwise we were heading straight for a disaster. (Th, 25.9.63)

With these and other visitors to the ashram, Abhishiktananda's hands were more than full. One visitor was the Tamilian sadhu whom he had met at Uttarkashi, who

> . . . has come for ten days and would certainly have stayed longer, but I have no room; and really there are too many people for me to cope with, especially when there is such a variety of languages and mentality. (Th, 25.9.63)

In a letter to Lisieux he reflected on the experience of the recent months:

> . . . The Lord plays some strange tricks! Is it to show that his will for Shantivanam is not at all in what we imagine it to be, and that for every 'mission' all he wants is for us to be recollected in him? Without this recollection in him, the Indian Church will never be capable of transforming Hindu India into Christian India. The spiritual life of most Christians remains at the same level as that of most Hindus. Only the outward forms are changed, but there has not been a real interior conversion. It is heart-breaking! In a Church as 'superficial' as this, a true Hindu—I mean one who already had a real inner life—would feel terribly 'out of place' if the day were to come when, touched by the grace of the Lord, he sought admission to it. But of this fundamental inadequacy the Christian world, alas, is hardly aware. We do all we can to develop the externals of Christianity (schools, etc.—in a word, all the things that the others also do); but for what is essential, no one spares a thought. How often I have discussed this in recent months with my companion from Mauritius. What is to be done to awaken those who are in charge? Not to mention that the same problem certainly presents itself elsewhere. Admittedly the Council is splendid; there is a breath of the Spirit such as the Church has rarely known in the past. And yet who has anything to say about what is essential? Who recalls that the Church is above all called to adore, and even so who understands this call as deserving more than a hasty word in passing, or rather, an exhortation to make a daily meditation and an annual retreat? (. . .) The other day I had sent a word of congratulation to a German

> priest-friend for an excellent article that he had just published. In his reply he said, to tease me: "Glad to hear from you; only I thought you were a 'hermit', and that hermits *tacendo docent,* teach by their silence!" that was well said indeed. But again, who is ready to be a hermit solely for God, without being bothered whether or not anyone in the world outside is interested in him? (FT, 10.10.63)

On the same day he wrote to his sister at Kergonan:

> . . . I have been so busy with guests and visitors for the last three months that I am quite lost. But in fact it was very pleasant to talk theology instead of only discussing cows, bullocks and rice-fields with my cook. By the way, we have a little calf, very sweet, just eight days old. (Do you remember the time when you were looking after the sheep (. . .)?) However, my companions will be leaving me in a few days, and I shall recover my blessed solitude. (. . .)
>
> . . . It is a marvellous meditation just to watch the little calf frisking about. In that way you become simple; and only in hearts become simple and entirely open can the Holy Spirit act freely, without you knowing whence he comes or whither he will lead you. Men—and nuns even more, if I know my Carmelites—take themselves much too seriously, they are nowhere near being like little children. Free and without anxiety, like small children—that is the true "Little Way". (MT, 10.10.63)

Of all those who might have joined Abhishiktananda at Shantivanam, Philippe Fanchette was the one from whom most might have been expected, but he was not allowed to stay. His bishop recalled him to Mauritius, and one night in October Abhishiktananda saw him on to the train at Trichy. "His heart was heavy, and mine also. He so much wanted to stay here." (F, 24.10.63)

More visitors came to the ashram in November, this time two young girls, who had also been directed from Rome to Shantivanam by Fr Panikkar:

> . . . As usual I have company. For the last ten days, apart from my Spaniard, I have two young girls, one Italian, the other Austrian.[37] All speak French very well. I was wondering how they would adapt to our ways at Shantivanam, but they settled down at once to sitting on the ground, eating rice with their fingers and sleeping on a mat. (. . .) They are very upset at having to leave tomorrow evening. It is odd how Shantivanam draws all these people who had already heard it spoken of in Salzburg and Rome!
>
> Last Sunday there was another girl who arrived unannounced. "I am a Breton," she said, when introducing herself. I asked her if she knew 'O Breiz ma Bro'. She said No; "Then how can you call yourself a Breton?" (F, 30.11.63)

New contacts with like-minded people in other parts of the world continued to be made, and were a source of encouragement. For instance, there was a contemplative community of women at Éygalières (Bouches de Rhône) who earned

37. Marina Vesci and Bettina Bäumer. They were later working in Varanasi, where they met Abhishiktananda on many occasions.

their living by manual labour— "They seem to know what true contemplation is " (MT, 10.10.63). Another specially prized contact was with a Breton priest-worker, to whom he had been introduced by his friend in New York:

> . . . I have just written to Fr Pichavan. What a marvellous spirit! So dedicated! May the Lord grant us many such witnesses. I waited for months without *daring* to reply to him. I felt so small before him. You know, monastic life, either alone or in community, runs such a risk of becoming commonplace. We reduce our needs, and then are only more bitterly set on satisfying at least those of them which we have retained—not to mention our self-satisfaction in our vocation. So when you see people slaving away like him, and constantly in touch with a pleasure-seeking and corrupted world (. . .), who even so preserve such a depth in their life, you rejoice in the Lord, and also have to make a humble self-examination . . . (AMS, 13.12.63)

During the year Abhishiktananda continued to write to Sr Marie-Gilberte about her preparation for the proposed Carmelite foundation. He was specially concerned to find a suitable place for her initiation to India, always supposing she had permission to come. For various reasons he thought it would be best for her to spend some time in one of the existing Carmels in South India before launching the new venture. Of these the Pondicherry Carmel seemed the most likely to receive her sympathetically, but for the fact that its Prioress was apparently not at all willing to admit European Sisters into her Tamilian community. Even so, he offered to approach the Prioress on her behalf. However, before he could do this, the Prioress herself invited him to conduct a retreat for the Carmel in the coming February:

> . . . Normally I should have found all manner of good reasons for refusing. But it was difficult not to see in this invitation a sign from Providence. So it will be much simpler in those circumstances to speak quietly about this matter than to go there specially for that.
>
> . . . I am sure the Lord is weaving [?] something around us. I do not know what it is, or how he will complete the other side of the cloth. Let us simply act from day to day in total surrender and humility. (. . .) Works like that of which we dream are not ours but his. To the extent that we butt in, we spoil the work, despite our good intentions. Once all those whom he wants for the work are 'ready', then all of a sudden the scattered bits of the design will come together as by magic. The Self is strongest! (MG, 3.11.63)

During the second half of the year there were so many visitors at the ashram that Abhishiktananda had little time for new writing. But he completed a revision of the account of his experiences with Gnanananda and at Arunachala (originally composed in 1956), which he had been promising Fr Lemarié since the previous year. Apart from simplifying the text of "Pèlerinages", he tried to preserve his anonymity by telling the story as far as possible in the third person, which was not difficult in the case of Gnanananda, but did not at all suit Arunachala. He also feared that his very positive approach to Hinduism might be shocking to his readers, and therefore tacked on a more 'Christian' preface and conclusion.

(In the final revision several years later he dispensed with this artificial device.) When sending it to Fr Lemarié he said:

> . . . So do what you like. I am weary of typing and revising this manuscript. It certainly contains some original matter but, even if in India I have got used to taking my bath in public without embarrassment, I remain very shy about sharing my confidences with all and sundry. The only thing that would set me at ease would be a well-guarded anonymity. (L, 12.12.63)

There were now quite a number of his manuscripts in Paris hanging fire, which he hoped might be published. It was some encouragement that one of the four Lisieux 'papers', "Pour une intégration chrétienne de la tradition mystique de l'Inde", appeared in *Contacts* (L, 25.5.63).[38] This in fact was an extract from the first chapter of *Guhantara*, the only portion to appear in his lifetime, and even so its authorship was concealed under the pseudonym of "Macarios the Indian". The other three 'papers'[39] were in the hands of a Dominican friend who was frustratingly uncommunicative, apart from a hint that they might be published by Centurion, of which nothing came. His latest manuscript, a collection of Fr Monchanin's letters, which he had made a year or so previously, was with the Abbé Duperray, Fr Monchanin's friend. He thought a selection would be well worth publishing, but nothing was done, and he eventually handed them all over to S. Siauve to use in her edition of Monchanin.[40]

During this year a German translation of *Ermites du Saccidananda*[41] was published (L, 24.4.63), and a publisher in the Isle of Man made a reprint of *An (Indian) Benedictine Ashram.* Abhishiktananda learned of this too late to do more than make a few corrections and add a new Preface. Stimulated by the same publisher's offer to undertake other books by him, Abhishiktananda planned a revision of *Ermites,* "in which the Benedictinism will remain in the background" (L, 18.10.63)

Nagpur meeting—28 December 1963 to 4 January 1964

After Christmas Abhishiktananda set off for the meeting at Nagpur, which proved to be the climax of the series hosted by Dr Cuttat. In anticipation of it he had written to his friend in New York:

> . . . At Nagpur we shall have a meeting like we have every year (but a larger group this time), at which we shall read the Bible in the morning and the Upanishads in the evening, seeking to hear in them what God has to say to us at the present time in each one's situation. If only the Church could at last understand the summons which the Spirit sends her through India! Would that at least our Indian bishops could hear this summons and pass it on to their brethren at the Council! But alas,

38. *Contacts: revue française de l'Orthodoxie,* ler trimestre, 1963, 41-51.
39. Probably these were "Notes on Arunachala", "Présence de Dieu—Présence à Dieu" and "L'Inde et l'Église".
40. Jules Monchanin, *Mystique de l'Inde mystère chrétien,* Fayard, 1974.
41. The translator was Professor (later Fr) M. Vereno, who in 1985 translated also *The Secret of Arunachala.*

how could they hear it? In April we had invited the Bishop of Delhi to one of our meetings. After an hour he said to us that he had never imagined that there were such pearls in the religious literature of India. Yet they spend years studying Shakespeare and Vergil! (AMS,13.12.63)

As usual Abhishiktananda had made careful preparations. He himself undertook to give the introduction to most of the Upanishad readings, and asked two Anglican friends to introduce the Bible passages. For their encouragement he wrote to Murray Rogers:

> . . . Like you I feel a little nervous. Let us be good *advaitis,* and not mind what people may think of us, but go straight on our way seeing only the 'atman' in everything, and being so void of everything inside that the Spirit may use us at his own free will.

Despite the tensions which surfaced occasionally, he felt that on the whole the meeting was a success, and wrote about it in several letters, for example:

> . . . The Nagpur meeting was interesting, though hard going at times. How is one to help people understand that which has been hidden away in India for the Church's own sake? One day I quoted [adapted] to them Origen's remark in the preface of his *Contra Celsum:* Your faith must indeed be very stunted, if it is frightened of seeing the greatness of the Upanishads shown in a clear light; such a faith is useless lumber! The Archbishop of Nagpur (nominated to Bhopal)[42] took great interest in our work. Almost every day he came to one or other of our sessions. He would like our group to be given official recognition by the hierarchy. (. . .) The meeting was reported in the local papers, and even rated an editorial. On the last day I went with Mr Cuttat to a village of leprosy patients 100 kms from Nagpur, "Anandavana", the Grove of Joy.[43] An admirable work. The gospel without Christ's name. There too I was carried off to the mike to give my 'blessing', and that also was reported in next day's paper. (L, 9.1.64)
>
> . . . Every evening I had to present and explain a chapter of the Upanishads. They are indeed so fine, you know, and it is not surprising that our priests and bishops have so little success with the Hindus. The sauce with which they serve up the Gospel is so insipid. It is like inviting someone to a banquet, and then offering him nothing but boiled noodles! That is something like the impression that Christianity, as it is lived and preached here, gives to those who know the spiritual riches of Hinduism. India will only finally become interested in the Gospel when it is preached in the manner of St Francis of Assisi, in poverty, simplicity, humility and prayer. Of that I am more and more convinced, and also more and more distressed to note that people refuse to believe it, or else give lip-service to it while making no attempt to change. Indeed, without a regular hurricane of the Holy Spirit we

42. Archbishop Eugene D'Souza.
43. Anandavan Colony near Wardha (Maharashtra), conducted by Shri Baba Amte.

> cannot expect much from men. You, the cloistered ones of every clime, win for us truly zealous priests and bishops! (MT, 5.2.64)

A full account of the Nagpur meeting was given in a book which Abhishiktananda drafted at Uttarkashi soon afterwards and which was published two years later.[44] The chapter which contains his presentation of texts from the Upanishads, "the Intuitions of the Rishis", is an excellent example of his manner of introducing people to the treasures which they contain. And, even if Nagpur fell short of what he had hoped for, it at least helped him to realize that he was no longer a solitary voice crying in the wilderness. It was, however, the last meeting of this kind in which he took part, although the series was continued on a smaller scale in the two following years. This was partly because Dr Cuttat was soon afterwards disabled by a serious accident, but more because someone at the meeting passed a remark which cast doubt on his integrity, and this wounded him so deeply that he was unwilling to risk it happening again.[45]

Shantivanam—January and February 1964

During January he learned that his friend R. Panikkar, after an interval of four years, would shortly be returning to India. He had recently defended a doctoral thesis, later published as *The Unknown Christ of Hinduism,* of which Abhishiktananda said that "its boldness far exceeds my *Guhantara*" (L, 22.9.63). In him he knew he would have a powerful ally, and looked forward to meeting him in Delhi in March.

From the Isle of Man he received the reprint of *A Benedictine Ashram,* "magnificently produced", but anticipated that its high price would adversely affect its sale, as indeed it did (L, 8.2.64). Its lack of success made the publisher abandon his idea of producing an English edition of other writings by Abhishiktananda.

As he planned to make a long stay at Uttarkashi this year, he remained quietly for some weeks at the ashram, enjoying the parcel of new books sent from Paris (Küng, Congar, Mouroux, etc.). He tried to begin the article requested for the periodical *Carmel,* but nothing would come. It was the same with his preparation for the retreat which he had to give at the Pondicherry Carmel in February:

> . . . all these days I am wondering what I am going to offer the Carmelites of Pondy during their week's retreat. Nothing comes, and I shall have to depend on the inspiration of the moment. In addition, I have had the flu for the past fortnight. In the end we shall see what they will find for themselves. As I have several times said at Bangalore—, a retreat of the waterpot, not of the tap. With a tap, you only have to turn it on and stand beneath it; with the waterpot, you have to draw up the water yourself. So all will depend on how much they can draw up by their prayers and their interest. (MT, 5.2.64)

The retreat was well received, as far as he could judge, and in a joint letter to the Prioress of Lisieux and to Sr Marie-Gilberte he said:

44. English version, *Hindu-Christian Meeting Point*; see bibliography.
45. Recorded by Murray Rogers, "Swamiji—the Friend", see Note 10 above.

> . . . I got a response for which I had not dared to hope, although what I said, as you can guess, was not at all what they are accustomed to hear in sermons. (MG, 23.2.64)

But the further purpose of his visit to the Pondy Carmel was to discover if the Prioress would accept Sr Marie-Gilberte in the community for a preparatory period, if she came to India. The Prioress was sympathetic but non-committal, and elicited the fact that another French Sister might also come for the same purpose. This was Sr Térèse of the Lisieux Carmel, though at that point it was very uncertain if she would be free to come. Abhishiktananda came away feeling that Pondy would be the best option for Sr Marie-Gilberte, and advised his correspondents about further steps they might take to obtain the consent of the Prioress.

Uttarkashi—March to June 1964

On his way to Uttarkashi Abhishiktananda stopped in Jyotiniketan and Delhi, where he met Raymond Panikkar and made arrangements for their pilgrimage to Gangotri in June. Passing through Hardwar he stayed as usual in the ashram of his Bengali friend Niranjananand, and from there sent Easter greetings to his sister:

> . . . I am writing from the ashram of a friend, a Bengali sadhu. In the other corner of the room he is giving some good teaching to some devout women, who sing with all their heart, "Rama, Krishna, etc." When they pass me they make a pious prostration (as you will have to learn to do, when you come here!). (MT, 17.3.64)

A month later he wrote to Fr Lemarié:

> . . . So I have been here at Uttarkashi in blessed solitude for the past month. I see very few people, and for three days a week I put a notice on my door: Silence. That forms you (or, as the case may be, deforms you) psychologically. Only what is essential remains. But one should not play about with it.
>
> While here I have got down to that report on Nagpur for which you asked. It is almost complete (but my typewriter is misbehaving badly these days, and there is no one here to put it right). I am afraid it has grown into a book of 100-120 pages (. . .). This week I will send it to Lisieux, asking them to see that it is in your hands by 15 June. Meanwhile I am going to make a summary of 7-8 pages, which I will send to you before that date. (L, 19.4.64)

A copy of this summary was sent to *Informations catholiques internationales (ICI)*, and unlike all his other recent manuscripts was immediately accepted for publication.[46] Before long the full report also found a publisher.

A letter to Lisieux speaks of his experience and work at Uttarkashi:

> . . . a word from this dear mountain where (. . .) I have celebrated Easter in great solitude and great joy. Solitude—such experiences are hard to explain. You need to have remained in it for a long time (and

46. "Les chrétiens méditent-ils les Upanishads", *ICI*, no. 221-22 (August 1964), 11-17.

yet the solitude here is still relative, though incomparably greater than in the South). All inessentials disappear from the mind, all that remains is the one thing necessary. A certain spiritual depth opens up somehow, but every time it seems quite new. You can no longer play at living in your alibis, as we nearly always do in our life as Christians or religious. Facing what alone is real. Naturally this could be dangerous and could lead to solipsism. And then it is hard both physically and psychologically. However, my life is quite sybaritic, compared to the first year. Each year my hut becomes more comfortable and my food likewise! But my strength decreases as I grow older—I realize it each year. I plan to stay here for a good month more, and even till the beginning of August (. . .). I am so happy here.

A week ago I sent you a manuscript (. . .). I was asked (by Fr Lemarié) for an account of our meeting at Nagpur. The account has grown into a book. (. . .) It will interest you and Sr Térèse. Meanwhile I am sending a word to Casterman to ask if they would be interested in this book. (. . .) I have also sent a brief report to *ICI* (. . .). There is a message from India which must be passed on. More and more I am convinced of this. But it should be expressed in simple terms that are intelligible to Christians whose approach to the mystery is so terribly Greek. All this work and my thoughts up here should help me to complete the article for *Carmel.* You see, we must get this message across. But this message is not conveyed in words. Souls have to be opened up from within. Then a few words are enough, and they get the point. But for most people this door to what is within is firmly barricaded, like those secret doors of ancient castles in fairy stories which have been forgotten for generations.

My text on Nagpur speaks very clearly (at least in this first draft) of the tension that existed there. There are people for whom the advaitin experience is an existential matter, and others for whom it is speculative, and worse still, certain people identify it with the ideas of those who follow Guénon[47] and other esotericists. So they do not *understand* the real problem. They argue and then pass sentence in the name of the faith, without really noticing that this experience is precisely summoning the faith to a great purification. St John of the Cross in his Nights has shown us clearly the substitutes for faith which we mistake for faith, devotion and contemplation. The tension was all the greater because the young Spaniard (of whom I must have told you) had asked to come. (. . .) The zealots attacked him with their own theology—of the head rather than of experience. The boy hit back. They told him that he was young and should take the word of experienced people. They scolded me for not having myself impressed these 'truths' on him . . . (FT, 4.5.64)

A few days later he wrote a memorandum for the Archbishop of Bombay on the newly created Roman Secretariat for Non-Christians[48] (F, 9.5.64).

47. René Guénon, author of *Orient et occident,* etc.

48. "Le Secrétariat pour les religions et le kairos présent de l'Église", a text supplied to the archives by the Jyotiniketan community in Hong Kong.

Pilgrimage to Gangotri—June and July 1964

On 19 May Raymond Panikkar arrived from Varanasi to spend three weeks with Abhishiktananda in the Himalayas. In the first week of June they followed the pilgrim route to Gangotri, and one day climbed up to Gomukh, the point where the stream issues from the glacier, so that they might celebrate Mass at the very source of the sacred river. After coming back to Uttarkashi to see off his friend, Abhishiktananda took a week's rest and then returned to Gangotri to spend three weeks in total silence.[49] This time he brought no books with him, and in place of the breviary recited Psalms from memory. In the last week the heavy rains began, and his return journey was "penitential"—"100 kms in three days on rocky paths, slippery, muddy, carrying my bag of bedding on my shoulder, at night sleeping in a corner of a 'caravansarai' [*dharamsala*] amid filth and a terrible crush" (L, 12.7.64). During his retreat at Gangotri he wrote a long letter to his sister:

> Can you guess where I am writing this letter from? Not just from Uttarkashi, but from Gangotri, the actual source of the Ganges, or at least of the Bhagirathi, one of its chief tributaries. Altitude 3,300 metres, 100 kms from Uttarkashi, of which 60 kms are on foot (. . .), sleeping close-packed on verandahs of caravansarais, eating what one can and when one can. On the path crowds of pilgrims, climbing up and coming down. Children at the breast, old women bent over their staves, and everywhere, as people pass, they say: "Glory to Mother Ganga!" but the sadhu's reply is "OM". Troops of sadhus, ranging from those who are totally naked to those covered in unimaginable cast-offs as protection against the cold.
>
> Here I am staying in a wooden hut. Facing me, high peaks covered with snow. On either side, immense pine-clad cliffs. I came here first with a priest-friend; and one morning we together followed up the course of the torrent in order to say Mass as close as possible to the source, in a hollow among the rocks a few steps away from the stream, while the sound of the water rushing over the boulders provided a mighty organ accompaniment. It was the Eucharistic fulfilment of all the prayers, offerings and austerities which over the centuries have mounted up from here to heaven!
>
> Now I am alone, and am keeping total silence for three weeks, apart from signs when absolutely essential. I have not brought a single book with me. A complete fast of the mind, while praying inwardly together with my brother sadhus, slowly murmuring the OM which says everything. Not allowing myself to locate God anywhere outside me, but recognizing that within as well as without there is only He alone. For, if there were God plus an 'other', he would no longer be God, the

49. In the account which he subsequently wrote (see below), the order of his friend's visit and his own time of silence is reversed, so as to make the Mass at the source of the Ganges the climax of the story.

Absolute! Nothing is left but he who says: I AM! Then what does it matter where I 'myself' am? It is his business! But how to say 'Him'? 'Who' is there to speak of 'Him'? Nothing is left but He who says 'I' '*aham*', from eternity to eternity. OM is precisely the word of the one who in the presence of the mystery can do no more.

It was on the Feast of the Sacred Heart that my friend and I were there together, the Feast of the source from which issued the Church; the very Source whose origin is in the bosom of the Father: Source of divinity, Source of being, Source of all, Source in which you are lost, if ever you dare to enter it, for from it no one ever returns! In it you pass into eternity.

The symbolism of the Source. See those snow peaks pointing straight at the sky, to win from it the life-giving water; they hold it as snow on their flanks, and from those snows comes the river which will give life to the plains below. Symbol of the monastic life, unmoving, pointing heavenwards, in the bosom of the Father, so that through them—monks and nuns—grace may flow! Unmoving, they are firmly set in the sky. The river continues to flow while they, without looking down, never cease to gather and gather. That is why Gangotri is a place that is particularly dear to sadhus. There are even some who live here all the year round—and in winter there are four to five feet of snow!

Each morning I go along with them to receive *bhikshā* [alms] of food. I hold out a piece of cloth for the rice and chapati, and my pot for a ladleful of split peas. If you could see me, with a loincloth round my waist, a patched blanket over my shoulders, a towel round my head as a turban! Become one of them, seeking to learn from their silence (one of them has kept silence for fifty years), their solitude, their dispossession, and also to bring these to fulfilment in the Christ, and to give them that which answers all their yearning for God.

I shall stay here until the new moon (. . .).

. . . I wrote to Fr Prior [Kergonan] for his feast (today). I wonder if he has had my letter. Ask him, if you see him. Joy in the Lord always! (MT, 28.6.64)

This letter reveals the intensity with which Abhishiktananda lived in both of the 'worlds' to which he was committed. But it gives no hint of the painful tensions resulting from this double loyalty, although this often appears in his Diary and was sometimes admitted to his close friends. For instance, in the following letter to his recent fellow pilgrim:

. . . I have just received a letter from Shri Poonja,[50] which I am copying on the back of a telegram. Is not this the real advaita? And as for ours, whatever we do, is it not a *qualified, viśishta advaita?*— and the advaita is lost as soon as there is qualification. There is a world of difference between being fascinated by one's own 'mental construc-

50. This was 'Harilal', often mentioned above. A copy of the letter is in the archives.

> tions' and having the genuine experience. It is good to feel yourself recalled to the real thing. How dramatic it is to be there between the two camps, misunderstood and rejected by both alike. And yet this painful struggle is necessary, so that one day the two arms of the cross may be reunited by those who will have been strong enough to bring them together against all opposition, in their body, their soul, their lacerated heart. (RP, 11.6.64)

Before leaving Uttarkashi for the plains, Abhishiktananda wrote to Fr Lemarié about his various manuscripts, and about some new ideas which were in his head. One of these was to produce an illustrated article on his recent pilgrimage, "Une messe aux sources du Gange".[51] Another was to work out some thoughts jotted down during his time at Gangotri concerning the use of the Psalter in Christian worship:

> . . . the idea came to me for a very naughty (?) article with a provocative title; "Is the Psalter a Christian prayer?" It is frightening, as soon as you give a little thought to all the things that conflict with the Gospel which we say with a clear conscience, when we simply repeat what the old Jewish scribes wrote long ago . . . (L, 12.7.64)

To his friend Panikkar he said it could make "a *bomb* of an article (. . .), if any periodical were sufficiently bold. The Psalter is terribly Jewish (. . .) and bogs down the Christian subconscious at a pre-Christian, non-evangelical level" (RP, 24.6.64). A note in his list of articles says that it was sent to *Concilium,* but not published. It is a vigorous statement of one side of a perennial problem, first raised by Marcion in the second century, which remains acute, especially in the Indian context.

The letter to Fr Lemarié continues:

> . . . Had an immediate response from *ICI* about my piece on Nagpur. They are going to use it as the starting point for a forthcoming 'documentation'. As for those tiresome publishers, I shall have to stop inundating you with unpublishable manuscripts. There are at least half a dozen of them now. (. . .) As regards "Une messe aux sources du Gange", I shall only send it to you, once you have been relieved of the present MSS. (L, 12.7.64)

But the tide was about to turn; and on reaching Delhi he found "an excellent letter from Centurion" about "The Experience of Saccidananda". No matter that they asked for a very thorough revision of the text, "the main point is that the theological committee has accepted it" for publication (L, 28.7.64).

The progress of the Vatican Council, which he was following carefully, made him unusually hopeful about the Church in its new springtime:

> . . . The Church has to be multiform. It was providentially born in a Semitic environment, but is not bound to it. The child does not remain in the cradle indefinitely. Everything else has been prepared by God in view of the Church. Those Psalms, of which I spoke just now, need no

51. The title under which it was published in 1967 by Le Seuil.

less transformation to be turned into Christian prayer than would be needed by our Upanishads or the Gita. R. Panikkar (. . .) is far bolder than I am about all that.

The Council is only a point of departure, letting in the clutch, the setting up of the apparatus which launches the rocket. Plenty of people are still trying to delay the 'count down', but it will take off and go into orbit, or rather, will finally soar into the infinite space of the Spirit. And the contribution of the East, when eventually it is accepted, will be that explosive force which will free the Church from the 'gravity' of its bond to a particular time and place which prevent it from being itself. (L, 12.7.64)

On his way to Shantivanam, Abhishiktananda wrote from Indore to Sr Marie-Gilberte:

. . . I thank the Lord that the decisions have at last been taken. If the Lord wants you here, he will straighten out everything that does not depend on you. If he prefers that you should live the 'mystery' of India in France, he will make that clear. (. . .)

. . . The further I go, the more I believe that the essential task in India is not to bring the Gospel to the Hindus, but to convert the Christians to the *Gospel* and to 'catholicism' (in the true sense of the word—see the Pope's speech). Then only the proclamation of the Gospel will be able to make a serious impact on religious India. (MG, 11.8.64)

Shantivanam—August 1964 to May 1965

The nine months which followed Abhishiktananda's return to the South were spent quietly at Shantivanam. He rarely went outside and there were few visitors (and no postulants!). He was hard at work on books and articles, encouraged by the realization that what he was writing would at last reach the public with the 'message' from India that he longed to communicate. He wrote to his sister on the patronal festival of her monastery (Michaelmas Day):

. . . Today will be a high day for you at the monastery (. . .). Make the most of it, for the liturgy is going to become more and more bare and functional; no more grand ceremonies, but a sober celebration in which everyone has a part. What a joy that the Council has given us that! The Council is such a great blessing. It is the breath of the Spirit—and indeed it was high time for that. The present Pope, outwardly more discreet than John XXIII, will guide the Church unfailingly along the path opened up by the man who will soon be Saint John XXIII! And what a joy to see the French episcopate always in the vanguard. The Pope has recognized in several speeches all that the Church owes to initiatives from France. Only two days ago I received his splendid encyclical.[52] What a call to "launch out into the deep", when you know how to interpret it.

52. The Encyclical *Ecclesiam suam* 1964), which referred particularly to Dialogue.

> Here on the 15th I began the Mass in Tamil, at least that part which is dialogued with the people. We still lack the books to do more. (. . .) My people are enthusiastic. At last they can understand something, and the Mass is no longer the business of the priest alone. I have even installed a portable altar facing the people, so as to be able really to 'preside' over the gathering for the breaking of bread.
>
> I left my solitude (a very real one) at Gangotri on 9 July, and walked back to Uttarkashi in three days. The next week I came down from the mountains, and for a month travelled round in North India, but could only fulfil about half of the invitations I had received. This took me as far as Banaras;[53] but as we become 'old', travel becomes increasingly difficult. Here I have regained my solitude beside the Kavery; in fact, apart from my journeys to the Himalayas, I hardly budge from here. A simple transference from one hermitage to another. I very much hope to be able to excuse myself from going to the [Eucharistic] Congress at Bombay. I have already refused an invitation to give an address to French pilgrims, which they had already announced without telling me! (. . .)
>
> Have you seen my article in *ICI* (. . .) which I sent them from Uttarkashi?[54] (. . .)
>
> Here I have a lot of work to do, putting several books and articles into shape, because only here do I have my library and the reference books which I need for editing what I write at Uttarkashi. An itch to write? but even so they contain some new ideas which it is good to disseminate, especially since Cardinal Marella's establishment[55] has been set up. I have just sent him my *Ermites* and the English book [Memoir of Fr M.]. (MT, 29.9.64)

Years later Abhishiktananda admitted to Murray Rogers that he was still "very French". But his pride in the French Church, revealed in the above letter, did not blind him to its weaknesses. For instance, when writing to his family about a nephew who had entered the Minor Seminary in which he himself had studied forty years earlier, he said:

> . . . The trouble with these seminaries is that the future priests are terribly cut off from reality. The day when they go for military service or are sent to parishes, they are absolutely 'lost'. Fortunately, at least in France, there are long holidays with their families. (F, 29.9.64)

Or, as he said to Mother Françoise-Thérèse:

53. One of his special friends here was the late Shri P.Y. Deshpande, who wrote about their first meeting (possibly at Nagpur):

> I carry the happiest memory of my first encounter with Swamiji. It was so unexpected and accidental. We became friends instantaneously. (. . .) What a man! An authentic sannyasi in the orthodox Vedic sense, despite his Christian background!
>
> In our very first encounter we chanted together the Ishopanishad in the Sanskrit. What an event! (Letter of 9.5.78)

54. See Note 46 above.
55. Cardinal Marella headed the new Secretariat for Non-Christians at Rome.

> . . . How to bring people out of their narrow-mindedness? (. . .) They are incapable of escaping from their blinkers. (. . .) Who will set us free to centre ourselves solely on God? And then that atmosphere of "This little child", "These children" . . .; I fear it is not much help towards living in the childlike innocence of which St Paul speaks to the Corinthians (14:20) or in that of St Thérèse of the Child Jesus. Personally I needed years to free myself (if indeed I have done so even now) from the infantilism and the lack of a sense of personal responsibility, which was effectively instilled into me on the pretext of obedience. (FT, 15.12.64)

Although Abhishiktananda refrained from attending the Eucharistic Congress in Bombay ("too many crowds and too expensive"), he was concerned about the impression that it made on people in India:

> . . . Foolish statements had caused strong anti-missionary reactions on the eve of the Congress. It had been said that the Pope was coming as a missionary to convert people and to bring alms to this country as the neediest in the world. That made a very bad impression, and people talked of receiving the Pope with black flags. All due to the tactlessness of the Christians and Europeans. (F, 12.12.64)

On the subject of poverty and aid he had this to say:

> . . . India's poverty—a difficult subject, little understood. But it is not by handing out charity that the problem will be solved, but by all round aid given *without ulterior motives* (whether political or religious), accepting India as it is and its people as they are, and helping them to come up on their own, helping them to work out a 'true' development. Simple handouts have done a great deal of harm. If you know the abuses of so-called Catholic Relief of all kinds! (. . .) The Church of the poor ought to be, not a Church that *gives* to the poor, but one which lives its poverty. (FT, 15.12.64)

A letter to Sr Marie-Gilberte indicates that the way was now open for both her and Sr Térèse (Lisieux) to come to the Pondicherry Carmel, and he advised her to apply for a visa in good time for entry in the following July or August. But at the same time there was some doubt whether her health was sufficiently good for life in India, and he counselled her: "Let us receive everything from the Lord, without picking and choosing." (MG, 20.11.64)

By the end of 1964 Abhishiktananda had made good progress with the writing that he had in hand. The article for the Carmelite quarterly, entitled "L'Inde et le Carmel", had been despatched and was published in the following year.[56] It was supplemented with an appendix of extracts from Indian spiritual writers (Sri Ramana, etc.), which he had selected in collaboration with the editor. The manuscript of his report on the Nagpur meeting had been offered to Le Seuil and immediately accepted.[57] He had also completed his account of the pilgrimage to

56. *Carmel: revue trimestrielle de spiritualité*, 1965, I, 9-23; II, 109-124; reprinted in *Les yeux*, 67 ff.

57. Published as *La rencontre de l'hindouisme et du christianisme*.

Gangotri, "Une messe aux sources du Gange", and some friends in Lyon (M. and Mme Andrieu) proposed its publication under a pseudonym (in the end it was published by Le Seuil). As for the much more troublesome revision of "The Experience of Saccidananda", by December half of it had been done to the satisfaction of the publishers. (L, 28.10.64; 29.11.64; 30.12.64)

After all this he must have been happy to welcome the guests who came from Varanasi to share his Christmas at the ashram—Raymond Panikkar and three Italian girls whose studies he was guiding.[58] Shortly afterwards he had a rendezvous with his friend at Tiruvannamalai, when they climbed to the summit of Arunachala to celebrate Mass in the same spirit as they had done at Gangotri (Th, 5.1.65)[59]

There were other visitors in February:

> . . . last week the visit of a Frenchwoman from the Alps who came here between two Hindu ashrams (where she had already found a marvellous spiritual deepening on an earlier visit). Contrary to her expectation, Shantivanam delighted her (. . .). She will soon enter a hermitage in Umbria, which has extraordinary similarities to Shantivanam.[60]
>
> Yesterday it was a Hindu sadhu (. . .) who has been praying to Jesus for years. Very little acquaintance with Christians, slight knowledge of the Gospel, and has made his own mantra to Jesus on the model of mantras to Shiva: "OM , glory to Jesus!" This he recites ceaselessly on his Shivaite rosary, looking to Jesus and his Mother that they will provide his food at the hands of the people in the villages through which he passes. He attributes to his own sins, and not to the malice of others, the hard words that he sometimes has to hear, imitates the patience of Jesus, etc. Isn't that marvellous! (. . .) I don't know what the Lord had in his mind (!) in bringing about this meeting. (MG, 10.2.65)

In her last letter Sr Marie-Gilberte had broken the news that her health problem was such that, miracles apart, she would not be allowed to come to India:

> . . . So here is another trial. You have made your sacrifice—your community, your family, everything—and now an even greater sacrifice is asked of you. (. . .) As I wrote to Sr Térèse of Lisieux a few months ago, before her 'miracle', India is much more a spiritual dimension than a geographical continent. How many people come to India, live there for a quarter or half a century, and never discover it—people who are incapable of drawing upon its treasures for the Church. That is the genuine Indian vocation within the Church, whether the body is in India or not. The Lord has made you feel this mystery, and we should thank him. Be in India and of India through your own inner depth. I am not talking about imagination or longing. India is there

58. Marina Vesci (second visit), Mara Lilli and Caterina Conio.

59. Abhishiktananda described this event in *The Mountain of the Lord* (ISPCK, 1990), p. 54, using literary licence to anticipate what actually took place six months later. The picture in the French edition, *Une messe*, facing p. 81, is of Arunachala.

60. This Sister and Abhishiktananda continued to correspond until 1973.

where you find the Lord of the innermost depth, the Lord of the *Guha* [Cave]. And the cave is the deepest centre of your heart and the deepest centre of the Father's heart. Live there, whatever may be your circumstances. Then when the Lord gives you the chance to come, you will be perfectly prepared. (. . .) Nothing can stop the melody of the OM or of the Abba Father. (. . .) The mystery of this OM which issues from the ABBA and which leads into it, that is truly the great secret of India. Whoever lives by *that,* has reached the heart of India.

And in all charity be glad for those who will come here ahead of you. Sr Térèse and probably also Sr Praxedes (. . .). (MG, 10.2.65)

Sr Praxedes was a Benedictine of the Abbey of Ravensburg in Germany, who like others had felt the call of India through Abhishiktananda's book *Ermites.* After some months of correspondence he felt that her call was genuine and encouraged her to come. She and Sr Térèse arrived in the following September.

Abhishiktananda could never forget the poverty with which he was surrounded, and one motive for living as simply as possible was that it enabled him to give to others. In one of his frequent references to mass-stipends, he said:

. . . More and more I have scruples about saying Mass for an honorarium. But at present it helps me to help others; and if this money eventually goes to help the poor, my conscience is set at ease. (L, 30.12.64)

His chief 'luxury' was to order books and periodicals which he thought would be useful; but quite often he countermanded them on learning their price:

. . . Don't get *Irenikon.* Prices are going up so much that I no longer know how to cope. The help given to one or two families becomes a heavy burden owing to their illnesses (. . .) all due to undernourishment (as a friend said to me: People don't die of starvation, they just go on starving!). (L, 19.3.65)

And when Mother Théophane took him to task about his diet, he asked:

. . . What can I do? Is it possible for example, to buy the litre of milk that would be needed every day, under the very nose of people who can hardly afford 100 or 200 grammes for their children? The same with fruit, etc. . . . (Th, 12.2.65)

Abhishiktananda's spirituality, for all his emphasis on the Absolute, was firmly 'earthed'. and he had no sympathy for an 'a-cosmism' which could calmly ignore the appeal of a neighbour. The *koinonia* which his faith confessed as the heart of the divine mystery, has to be given practical expression, as he said in a letter to his sister:

. . . The Church is a life conformed to the Gospel. Christians are those who love their brothers and seek to transform a civilization based on profit and egoism, which therefore is contrary to the Gospel. Priests and religious are those who take seriously the instructions given by Jesus to the seventy-two disciples when sending them out on mission. That is how the Church ought to appear. When the Church, or rather, Christians as a whole, radiate the pure light of the Gospel—with

> no smoke to hide the flame—then the unity of Christians will come to pass and the non-Christians will ask for baptism. (MT, 13.4.65)

There is a characteristic note an earlier letter:

> . . . The people in India whom I have found to be taking the Sermon on the Mount most seriously are a Quaker family who do not even recognize the necessity of baptism, and another family—Hindus—in Maharashtra, which runs an extraordinary colony for lepers.[61] (MT, 17.12.64)

In April he had the surprise of seeing Shantivanam featured in an official Roman paper:

> . . . Can you believe it, the *Osservatore Romano* of 18 February carried an article on Shantivanam: "Shantivanam—la foresta della pace". They have just sent me a copy. It was written by an Italian girl who spent Christmas here.[62] You see, Shantivanam is not so unknown outside India; and you must have seen my article in *ICI* [on the Nagpur meeting] already quoted several times. If Christians could hear India's summons to the depth within, what wonders the Spirit would work in them! But there are hopeful signs here and there. (MT, 13.4.65)

He was also delighted to receive a new book on Fr Monchanin:

> . . . Two days ago I received the Abbé Duperray's little book on Fr M.[63] It is excellent, and the way he has put the letters together is perfect. If only he would give us more on Fr M. He brings out better than I could have done the anguish of those first ten years. Unimaginable loneliness! (L,12.4.65)

By May 1965 the laborious process of revising his books for the press was at last completed. In connection with "The Experience of Saccidananda" he later recalled:

> . . . I had eight months of correspondence with my publishers: style, technical terms, ideas, everything was gone over minutely, page by page. The notes are often simply my replies, justifying phrases which I could not allow to be changed. More than once I lost heart and thought of giving up. (RP, 18.5.66)

For the past ten years and more Abhishiktananda had felt that he had a 'mission' to communicate to the Church the fruit of the experiences which had impressed him so profoundly. He wrote powerfully and eloquently, but again and again his manuscripts were found to be unpublishable. This might well have continued to the end of his life, if it had not been for the vast changes of outlook brought about by the Vatican Council, in particular, the opening up of the Church vis-a-vis the world and the other great religious traditions. Almost overnight Abhishiktananda ceased to be a voice crying in the wilderness, as

61. See Note 43 above.
62. The writer was C. Conio, later organizer of the Centro Inter-religioso Henri Le Saux in Milan.
63. J. Monchanin, *Écrits spirituels*; see bibliography.

publishers realized that there was now a public which would appreciate his 'message'. No doubt he had also learnt from experience—and was helped by his publishers to discover—how to express his insights in a manner that western readers could understand and accept. He seems, however, to have regretted the necessity for this, and spoke dismissively of his books as

> . . . so elementary. Only milk, and that with plenty of water and sugar added! When will Christians be ready to launch out on the highways of God? Not for centuries. So God will continue to raise up Maharishis for us? The prayer 'for the heathen' ought to turn into a prayer that the Christians may at last gather in the spiritual riches of the Gentiles, so that God might finally have no more need to conserve them outside the Church, precisely in order to prevent these riches from being lost. (L, 12.4.65)

The first and most substantial of his books, so far called "The Experience of Saccidananda", was published by Centurion in October 1965 under the title, *Sagesse hindou mystique chrétienne: du Védanta à la Trinité.* It was followed in January 1966 by his report on the Nagpur meeting under the title, *La rencontre de l'hindouisme et du christianisme,* published by Le Seuil. A third book. *Une messe aux sources du Gange,* appeared in French only in 1967; but an English version, translated and introduced by members of the Jyotiniketan ashram, and entitled *The Mountain of the Lord: Pilgrimage to Gangotri,* was published in India in 1966.[64]

These books reveal much concerning Abhishiktananda as he was in this 'middle stage' of his pilgrimage, because he could not help putting himself into his books—not out of egotism, but simply because the essentials of what he had to communicate were matters of his own experience. This accounts for the freshness and authenticity of his writing, whose prophetic and often poetical quality conveyed the urgency of his concern. In these books much of what he had first poured out in the pages of his Diary and then in *Guhantara* and other essays, is presented in a calmer and less explosive form. It is as if the blazing insights, which earlier on had shattered him so deeply, had now—at least for the time being and to some extent—been integrated.

His chief concerns in these three books can be clearly seen. One was to share with others his understanding and appreciation of the spiritual values of Hinduism (especially *advaita* and *sannyasa,* drawing on Ramana Maharishi in *Sagesse* and on the Upanishadic tradition in *Rencontre;* and its *bhakti,* shown in the practice of pilgrimage in *Une messe*). Another concern was to awaken his fellow-Christians to their own need for a 'return to the Source' and for a rediscovery of the interior dimension of their faith. This alone, he held, would enable them to meet the contemporary crisis of faith, and also to enter into a fruitful dialogue between West and East. A third concern, especially in *Sagesse,* was to work towards a theological integration of Hindu experience and Christian faith (a concern which always mystified his Hindu friends). He certainly did not claim to have found a 'solution', but at the most hoped to

64. For English editions, see bibliography.

have discovered a few pointers towards a very distant goal, as he said in the introduction to *Sagesse.*[65] At this stage in his thinking he was frankly working on the lines of a "theology of fulfilment, that is, of assuming the convergence upon the historical Christ and the Church, of all the religious and spiritual experiences of mankind,"[66] as is shown by the subtitle of *Sagesse* ("from Vedanta to the Trinity"). A few years later , when he came to prepare the English edition of this book, he admitted to his friends that this way of thinking no longer satisfied him.

In the North—June to December 1965

At the end of May Abhishiktananda set off for the North, making many stops on the way. His return to Uttarkashi was delayed until July by the late arrival of the proofs of *Sagesse.* When they reached him, he was delighted to find that they contained a preface by an Orthodox lay theologian, O.Clément, who said that his book "would be a bridge between Latin and Orthodox spirituality" (Th, 10.7.65). At Rishikesh he stayed in the Sivananda Ashram, whose new Acharya was Swami Chidananda,"a truly spiritual man" whose friendship he greatly valued. One day, with two other guests of the ashram, he celebrated Mass in the crypt of a small temple beside the Ganges, "sitting cross-legged round the bread and wine after the order and rite of Melchizedech (. . .). In our days a prophetic sign" (AMS, 12.7.65).[67]

When he reached Uttarkashi on 18 July, he knew that he would have to descend in September in order to meet the two Sisters, Térèse and Praxedes,[68] who would be coming from Europe. For both of them Abhishiktananda had a special responsibility, since it was through him that they had heard the call of India, and they were coming to place themselves under his guidance. Whether he liked it or not (for he frequently grumbled about the 'burden'), he could no longer refuse to be a guru.

Meanwhile he made the most of his time at Uttarkashi:

> . . . It is always a great joy to be here. It is like another world, 'another birth', as we say in India. Here the Upanishads open up to ever greater depths. I realize that no cursory reading of the Up. (any more than of the Bible) can reveal their secret. We are so conditioned by our western mentality! It is easy to say that we must make our souls and our minds virginally empty. But to go on from that to actually doing so! It means quite a different angle of vision. And we have to attain this angle of vision, not conceptually, but existentially. How far my book still falls short of the target. However it is probably as much as Christians can take. (. . .)
>
> The Ganges is roaring quite close to me here. It sings a ground bass which sets the key for everything. And in its harmonics all that can be

65. *Sagesse,* 20-21. For E.T. of this introduction, see *Saccidananda* (revised edition, 1984), 223ff.
66. *Saccidananda* (revised edition), xv.
67. For Melchizedek, see *Meeting Point,* 35.
68. Sr Térèse de Jésus, Carmelite of Lisieux, to whom he had been writing since 1959. Sr Praxedes, Benedictine of Ravensburg in West Germany.

sung is sung. Above all the OM, which has hardly left me since my retreat at Gangotri last year. (L, 24.7.65)

There were times when Abhishiktananda thought that India had killed all his interest in liturgy. However, the liturgical reform begun by the Vatican Council, and the green light which it gave to the development of indigenous forms of worship, caused him to take up once more the project of an 'Indian Liturgy'. In May he had written to Fr Lemarié:

> . . . Liturgy, where are you going? (. . .) A 'modern' liturgy must spring out of a 'modern experience' of the deeps of God and of the Paschal mystery. Our age is too external. We have to stick close to antiquity, hug the coast. Our wings are not strong enough for interstellar flight. Otherwise we will make a purely functional liturgy like that, for example, of the Church of South India. What we need is not so much a poet like Claudel, as contemplative praying groups like Taizé. (L, 9.5.65)

Now in July and August, in his cell at Uttarkashi, he began trying to see the way in which an Indian liturgy with a Sanskrit base might evolve:

> . . . In the loft fitted up in my hut I offer Mass each morning, seated like a brahmin priest, with ceremonies of offering water, incense, fire. I read the gospel in Sanskrit and also sing the Our Father in Sanskrit (. . .). When I come down, I will work it out with some chosen friends. For here, as nowhere else in the Church, Christ reveals himself as a priest "after the order of Melchizedek". (L, 29.7.65)
>
> . . . My Upanishadic 'rite' takes shape day by day. [Details follow.] But all that is very 'Hindu', and could only be understood by a very restricted circle. (L, 28.8.65)

This was only the beginning of his experiments, which he elaborated in the coming years.

Before returning from Uttarkashi Abhishiktananda "was practically compelled to buy the land on which my hut stands", and to do so had to draw on what was left of the bequest received in 1960 (L, 29.7.65):

> . . . Every year I feel myself more at home here. The fact of shortly becoming the proprietor of my field seems to me a sign, like that of Abraham when he bought the cave of Machpelah.[69] My contacts here are few, because I actively discourage the curious; but some are splendid, especially a young man of 25, admirably given to the Lord. I should not be surprised if our meeting last week was the prelude to something very important. A Hindu, of course, who spends hours each day singing the name of Rama. (L, 28.8.65; the young man was Ramesh Srivastava, of whom more below).

In September, despite difficulties caused by the war with Pakistan, Abhishiktananda travelled to Bombay to meet the two Sisters, one of who came

69. The land was acquired in the name of Abhishiktananda and R. Panikkar jointly. After 1973 another sadhu 'took over' the kutiya, but all was swept away in the great flood of 1978.

by sea, the other by air. After a few days in Bombay, Sr Térèse went as arranged to the Carmel of Pondicherry, while Abhishiktananda took Sr Praxedes to the North, as she was to begin her Indian initiation at a Leprosy Centre in Dehra Dun.

Before he could return to Uttarkashi he developed an abcess in his foot, and was kept in bed by the Alters at Rajpur for a week. He then went to Jyotiniketan to recuperate. This gave him the chance to share in an ecumenical study group on Dr Panikkar's book, *The Unknown Christ of Hinduism:*

> . . . What a problem is raised by the presence of the Gentiles in the Church, of the priest Melchizedek, of the sages like Job . . . and of all those here! How remote and academic the discussions of the Council seem, when you are confronted with the Real as here. It is the same with ecumenism. All that week at Jyotiniketan (I was) with Anglicans, Methodists, Presbyterians, Jacobites. How artificial the prohibition of intercommunion appears. On Wednesday we had a 'prophetic' Mass, all seated in a circle on the floor of the chapel, the bread and wine on a brass tray, with incense and light offered in Indian style. Upanishadic and Sanskrit hymns, Gelineau Psalms for Introit and Gradual, etc. And a second chapati on another tray for distribution as (at least) 'blessed bread'[70] at the end of the Mass. (L, 24.10.65)

It was during this year that the collaboration between Abhishiktananda and his friends at Jyotiniketan took a literary direction. The first fruit of this was their translation of his book about Gangotri *(Une messe)*, which was sent to Bangalore for publication. In order to avoid the need for an Imprimatur, the author's name did not appear, and instead it was introduced by Murray Rogers.[71]

When he returned to Uttarkashi at the end of October, Abhishiktananda took up a suggestion that had been made during his last visit to Delhi. At the Anglican Brotherhood where he was staying he had spoken to one of the members about recollection, and was at once asked to write down his thoughts for the Indian S.P.C.K. to publish. A month or so later he sent back a small book, which he had boldly written directly in English. After it had been edited by his friends, it was published in 1967. This book, called *Prayer,* was a persuasive call to the contemplative life, as the true way of prayer for every man. It proved to be his most popular work, and has been published in several other languages.[72]

It seems that by now Abhishiktananda had ceased to hope that Shantivanam would ever 'take off'. Its upkeep was a heavy burden, and he longed to hand over its responsibility to someone else, so that he could follow his calling to live in the North. In connection with cutting down his subscriptions to periodicals, he wrote:

> . . . The cost of living in India has doubled in a few years. And the recent war is going to push it up even further. I am living on my capital. (. . .) It is very likely that I shall settle for good at Uttarkashi, contenting myself with a few weeks at Shantivanam each year. (. . .) I am

70. The "*pain béni*" in France, like the Orthodox "*antidoron*", is a relic of the primitive Agapé.
71. *The Mountain of the Lord: Pilgrimage to Gangotri.* See bibliography.
72. See bibliography, nos. 8 and 12.

> waiting till I have seen Fr Dominique before taking a final decision (L, 29.11.65)

At the beginning of December Abhishiktananda came down to Varanasi to try out his liturgical experiments with Raymond Panikkar and other sympathetic friends, and remained there until Christmas:

> . . . Exhausting work, living at high speed, but enriching experiences. Discreet and timid attempts at an Indian liturgy, starting from my solitary experiments at Uttarkashi, this time in a group and concelebrated. (. . .) A powerful atmosphere here beside the Ganges. Almost every morning I walk for fifteen minutes along the 'ghats' (banks and steps where the pilgrims take their bath) to go to the Little Sisters of Jesus (. . .). The Mass sometime 'polyglot'—in Latin, Greek, Hindi, English, and of course Sanskrit.
>
> You have mentioned that you are pleased with the new Mass, announced by *ICI* for 1966. I would be glad if you would send me a word about this, in view of my translation which I shall check with a Hindu friend in Pondy about 15 January. No point in translating things that are going to be withdrawn. We ought to have an ashram where experiments could be worked out. Gradually translations are likely to be dropped, like ripe fruits, leaving a liturgy based on Hindu Scriptures, culminating in the Gospel. But that cannot be done in isolation, it needs a group for mutual enrichment. (L, 22.12.65)

On Christmas Eve he wrote to his sister:

> . . . Banaras is very cosmopolitan. In one group to which I have been introduced they sing Christmas carols in a variety of languages, including French. (. . .) Philosophical and theological discussions too. When you live in the midst of non-Christians, you cannot close the windows, draw the curtains, and get into a huddle beside the fire, because the Christ is present among them also. The Father loves them, the Father saves them, the Spirit works through them. That calls for a complete renewal of the theology of the Church . . .
>
> . . . I think you must have received my book [*Sagesse*] at the monastery. You will find there wonderful texts from Ruysbroeck, Eckhart and others (Al-Hallaj, Upanishads) which I have quoted. Here, all that is reduced to singing the OM in the unity of the Spirit.
>
> This evening I shall not be alone for Christmas. At 9 p.m. we start singing, then at 11 p.m. we shall read Hindu texts, the Prophets and the Gospel. The Mass follows, and then we shall have some sweets together. (MT, 24.12.65)

On his return to Shantivanam he wrote to his host at Varanasi:

> India has a message for the whole Church. Only on the further side of speculation will the Church rediscover the essential truths freed from myth. We should not create new myths, at least, not if we can help it. Myth will probably always remain underlying the expression of experience. But man will make use of myth as its master, not allowing

> it to control him. In an atmosphere like that of Banaras, I once again experience the itch to think, to do liturgy. Is that a temptation?
>
> . . . It is from Sanskrit that the liturgy and the Christian theology of India should come to birth.
>
> . . . Exhausted by the journey from Banaras, and with a bad cold, I shall need some days to recover. (RP, 7.1.66)

Shantivanam—January to August 1966

For the first eight months of the year Abhishiktananda remained at Shantivanam, apart from necessary trips to Pondicherry and elsewhere. Visitors to the ashram were few, and he was able to work on various articles which had been requested.

At the beginning of the year Fr Dominique decided that he must respond to the call of Shantivanam, and applied for permission to leave his monastery in Bangalore:

> . . . This will mean that Shantivanam will no longer have to be closed for six months every year. But Shantivanam can never be the real starting point. We are too close to a horribly conservative Church! (. . .) After having tasted the joy of being in the vanguard as a freelance, I no longer have the heart for half-answers; it will all depend on Fr D. (L, 7.1.66)

In January he visited Pondicherry to work with a pandit on the Sanskrit translation of the Mass, and also visited Sr Térèse, now happily settled at the Carmel. To her he wrote:

> . . . I shall have to be 'reborn' once more to become the perfect 'citizen of heaven'! The other day I missed my train at Villupuram. We were ten minutes late. I went up in smoke, wrote a protest in the 'complaint book'. (Alas, I have not yet attained *Shanti!*)
>
> . . . I have no further light as regards the future, even in the short term. We must live in expectation, simply and trustingly. It is His affair! Externals are so unimportant. I realize this more and more, even if age makes it increasingly difficult to adapt myself to some externals. (TL, 29.1.66)

During January the first copy of his book *Rencontre* arrived. The brief summary of this book which had appeared in *ICI* in 1964 had been translated into English, and through the good offices of a friend in Indore was published in the *Examiner*, the Catholic weekly of Bombay, in February.[73] He was also at work on the revision of the manuscript of *Prayer* and soon after prepared for Le Seuil the manuscript of *Une messe*, of which the English version was already being printed in India.[74] Meanwhile reactions to his *Sagesse* began to reach him, as well as reviews, mostly very favourable. His friend in New York was one who wrote about it:

73. "Christians meditate on the Upanishads", *Examiner* (Bombay) on 5, 12, 19 February, 1966.
74. Le Seuil felt that *Une messe* was too short to make a book, and asked for something more to be added to it. All that Abhishiktananda could offer was some of his poetry, "L'autre rive" (later included in part in *Initiation,* 31ff), but this was not accepted by the publisher.

. . . Once more we find the theme which you discovered in my book, even though it was not expressed there as clearly as you have done—otherwise the book would never have been accepted. Also there are things which may be told by one person to another, but which it is forbidden to broadcast openly. Thus in ancient times the great secret of *advaita* was restricted to those disciples whom the guru judged to be ready for it. Its wide diffusion in these days is not beneficial. For, to receive the higher truths, people must be prepared—in the depth of the spirit. Otherwise they hear words, which they interpret wrongly, at the level of the mind. All is 'sign', so nothing is the Absolute, but the Absolute is in everything. Yet should there not be witnesses in the world and in the Church to show that God, and the Church itself in its ultimate mystery, is beyond sign? But then, how will these witnesses still remain in the Church? Is this the Church of the beyond? then the sannyasi—outside the Church—would be the highest Christian? This borders on aberration, despite the truth that is concealed in it.

What a turmoil there is in the Church! I myself sometimes feel giddy, and yet I am not exactly timorous. But people, Christians and priests alike, are not ready for the amount of freedom for which they ask. (AMS, 29.1.66)

During February he was visited by a German SVD Father and a French Sister[75] (in the course of a pilgrimage she had come to consult Abhishiktananda about the possibility of starting an Indian monastic community which would express the same intuitions as Shantivanam). They found him in a very critical mood, of which traces can be seen in the following letter:

. . . Here and there, there is a great deal of good will. Unfortunately so few in the Church understand. I often admire your optimism. You see and admire the good things, and this saves you from seeing what is not going well. After all it is probably better that way; for there are days when I feel terribly low in face of Christians, priests and bishops, who so rarely have 'felt' God, and speak of him as if they were advertising something at the door of a shop! I have just been reading the latest Council texts. They are fine—but still so far from us in India. It is always a matter of the God who is thought, so rarely of the God who is lived, the God who has burst into our life. (. . .) So I try to travel peacefully and hopefully on my little path, leaving to the good Lord the trouble of sorting things out, for truly not much can be expected of men. (. . .) Don't worry, I shall recover my optimism in a few days, but there are certain days when it is right to feel Christ's 'passion' in the Church. What is essential is not making adaptations, even spectacular ones, but that every priest and bishop should first of all and *above all* be a man of God. The rest will follow of itself. (Th, 17.2.66)

The last remarks evidently reflect thoughts which he was working out for an article in *Carmel* on "The priest whom India, whom the world awaits". The first version, however, was found by the editor to be "too blunt"! (L, 19.8.66)

75. Fr K. Klostermaier and Sr N. Shanta.

At the beginning of March he went to the Shembaganur Carmel to give a retreat and to see his friend, the other Sr Thérèse.

It was another time of drought in India, and his nieces had gained the impression that large numbers of people were dying of hunger along the roadsides. To correct their ideas, he sent them "quite a dissertation" (F, 24.3.66). Hunger is not the main problem; the problem is widespread malnutrition, and the vicious circle in which people are imprisoned—low wages, therefore inability to buy nourishing food, causing lack of energy and so low productivity, and therefore low wages. "People say that the Indian worker is unproductive; but, eating only rice and having been undernourished since his conception, what strength could he have?" The situation is not helped by occasional gifts, still less by intergovernmental loans, which are burdened with heavy debt charges. What is needed is a reordering of international trade, and a change of the present system which allows the Trusts of Europe and the U.S.A. to pay a wretched price for the products of Asia and S. America (raw materials) and then make huge profits on them.

The rise in prices naturally affected the ashram, as he told Fr Lemarié:

> . . . The cost of living is shooting up. I shall soon need at least 300 NF [monthly] to cover the heavy cost of maintaining Shantivanam, correspondence, chapel, etc. So until further notice I shall have to limit my requests [for books]. (L, 18.2.66)

Once again the ashram was visited by a thief. When writing to his sister at Kergonan before Easter, he told her that his hut had been broken into and two tin trunks containing his wardrobe had been removed:

> . . . I asked myself if the theft of all my clothes meant a call from heaven to become a *'nāgā'* sadhu, that is, a sadhu clothed like the serpents [*naga*; i.e. naked]. But as I was going to Pondy in two days' time, I thought the hour had not yet come for this supreme detachment, and so went to have another tunic made!
>
> I am just back from Pondy, where I had to finalize a translation (in Sanskrit) of the Order of the Mass with a brahmin whom I know well. By the way, I had to give three talks at the Carmel about the Conciliar Decree on Religious. You also must have had questionaires to fill up on the observance of the Rule, enclosure, veils, grill, "everything that is out of date", as the Council puts it. But you Religious in France are young, you don't have the weight of four centuries like the Carmelites, and I imagine that many things have already had their aggiornamento. The important thing is to become adult, and to be even more strict in your freedom than you were under laws and regulations. So my word to them was to be *true* and to be *free.*
>
> Before that I had to go to Shembaganur to give a retreat to some other Carmelites. Two addresses in choir (in English), and then in the afternoon a much freer one in Tamil for the novices and postulants. What a strain it is to have tc give a retreat! I am incapable of preparing anything in advance, and then there is the torment of asking myself what on earth I can say. I have to sense much more through the

> heart than through the eyes whether it is 'going over', otherwise I am lost.
>
> . . . I have just sent another small book [*Une messe*] to Le Seuil. (. . .) have I really told you that there were at times no interior souls in the West? In any case there are often far more people who are devout rather than truly contemplative. If you get the message that I should like to convey through all these books and articles, it is that I want to invite people to a dimension of 'depth' which is undoubtedly known to some in the West, but is not however sufficiently widespread. Besides, that is why Fr E. of Le Centurion accepted my book [*Sagesse*].
>
> At the end of your epistle you asked me so many questions (. . .). Yes, I did meet Ramana Maharshi, I saw him twice. The other one must surely be Gnanananda, who also belonged to South India. No one ever struck me like that man did. I have even written a book about him; but it will only be published when I am in Paradise,[76] for it would not be understood. Live long enough, and you will find out about him. (MT, 4.4.66)

Sr Marie-Gilberte had written to tell him of an operation, but it was not yet clear what effect it would have on her health:

> . . . After all, what does it matter? During these years the Lord has taught you by experience that signs count for little. Everything in this world is a sign—health, sickness, India, France. The only thing that matters is—to awake! And it is always beyond signs that you awake. For the Awakening is to the unique Reality, below, above, without, within, beyond every word and every thought. Grace has followed you, and will follow you. (MG, 6.4.66)

In the same letter he gave news of Sr Térèse at Pondicherry:

> . . . Despite her timidity, she is preparing herself with great confidence for the coming work. (. . .) It would indeed be better not to delay unnecessarily, for Pondy can only be a transition, not a direct preparation. If all goes well, we should envisage a beginning in the first months of 1967.

And of Sr Thérèse of Shembaganur:

> . . . Unfortunately her health is a great handicap. She needs a very special diet, which prohibits all dreams for the future. (MG, 6.4.66)

About this time Abhishiktananda received a copy of an article by his friend Dr Cuttat (now Swiss Ambassador in Athens), published in *La mystique et les mystiques,* which he discussed at length with Dr Panikkar (RP, 7.4.66; 19.4.66). It disturbed him deeply, because he found it dangerously misleading in its presentation of Hinduism, all the more since it was brilliantly written. Hinduism reduced to a system of Ideas was not at all the Hinduism that he knew, and when from start to finish Hinduism was judged in terms of Western and Christian thought, he could not see that it deserved to be called 'dialogue'. He feared it

76. The book on Gnanananda was the first part of his "Pèlerinages", and was published in 1970.

would "prevent the western reader (only too happy to find comfort and reassurance so easily) from seeing that the real problem has not been touched." He was asked by Prof. M. Vereno of Salzburg to respond to the article from the eastern point of view in the periodical *Kairos,* but declined: "I have no desire to cross swords with dear Dr Cuttat. There is already enough of that, discreetly put, in my book [*Rencontre,* ch. 7]" (L, 13.4.66). Besides, he felt that his last two books themselves provided the best answer, as in them "I have tried to make myself transparent to the experience of India" (RP, 19.4.66)

Responses to *Sagesse* continued to reach him. Cardinal Bea sent him in exchange a copy of his own book. *The Church and Mankind.* He was particularly pleased by a letter from an elderly monk of Kergonan, Fr Landry: "I would never have dared to hope that he would take so much interest in a problematic that for him is quite novel" (L, 13.4.66). In connection with the book he wrote to Dr Panikkar:

> . . . it is clear that our books [i.e., yours and mine] are not intended for Hindus. Our immediate role, whether or not we have sought it, is to sensitize Christian thought to the treasures that await it here, and to prepare Christians for dialogue. We have to be among Hindus, both physically and spiritually, so as to *gather* the honey for the Church and to pass it on, while awaiting the hour when Christians as a whole will be capable of gathering it for themselves. (RP, 18.5.66)

Permission had now been given for Fr Dominique to come to Shantivanam, although not until the following Christmas; but his health gave cause for anxiety, and it was not certain that his coming would solve the problems of the ashram:

> . . . Shantivanam is really difficult to keep going. And in order for Fr Dominique to be installed there, it is absolutely essential to find him a companion; for if the upkeep of buildings etc. is hard enough—even unbearable—for me, what will it be for him? (RP, 18.5.66)

For some months Abhishiktananda had been trying to make arrangements for Sr Térèse to continue her initiation in a place where she would have more leisure than was possible at Pondicherry. He finally found a place for her and another Sister from the convent in the small hill-station of Yercaud (near Salem), and in June gave them a week's course on the Upanishads. Then after a visit to Bangalore, he was persuaded to come back for three week's holiday, to which period the following letters belong:

> . . . The moment in history in which we are living calls us to a stern purification of all our means—institutional, intellectual, etc. To recognize the essential beyond all the forms in which it repeatedly embodies itself. (This was, in fact, the great lesson which the Upanishads impressed on us all this week.) But then, in allowing the forms to yield their place, not to lose anything of the essential. The motives for abandoning forms are so mixed—just as mixed as those for keeping them intact. Who will be willing always to want nothing but the Spirit? Once again, only the contemplative spirit (. . .) will allow the Church, and every institution in the Church, to cross the 'bar'. (X, 14.6.66)

. . . I am writing from Yercaud (. . .) a small hill-station (. . .) full of convents, noviciates, etc. I am here on holiday for another week with the Cluny Sisters. Only saying Mass for the aged Sisters and those on holiday, and dividing the rest of my time between an armchair and walks of 10-12 kms through the coffee plantations. The last fortnight has done me a lot of good.

. . . Many other people go to Europe, I know; but first of all, I have nothing behind me to provide me with 4000F for my passage, plus the cost of staying there. Then, if I had the money, everyone would be upset with me, because I could not spend more than a week in each house. Also it would be too exhausting, as I should have to run about France from north to south, as well as taking in Spain and Italy! In particular, Montserrat and a women's hermitage in Umbria, crowds of people in Lyon, a monastery in Provence, etc., without mentioning Lisieux, Taizé, etc., the family and Kergonan.

The work of a monk is interior; it is 'in solitude' that the hermit fulfils his diaconia (ministry) in the Church.[77]

Gnanananda wrote nothing, but he said, and always said, marvellous things. I have a whole book of memories of him, in manuscript. It will probably be published when I am in paradise, like another book of my memories of Arunachala.[78] There would be loud protests if they were published now. But it is very certain that without Arunachala and Gnanananda I would never have written my last two books [*Sagesse, Rencontre*]. Besides, *Ermites* was written at Arunachala in the cave of Arutpal Tirtham (the Spring of the milk of grace), the last two at Uttarkashi.

Before the start of any new foundation in India, I would first—if I was the Internuncio—make them pass an examination on the Gita and the Upanishads; indeed, before that, if I was the Pope, I would set this examination to whoever I sent as Internuncio to Delhi!

. . . So you love the Upanishads. Only the other week I was expounding the Upanishads to two Sisters here. They really are the heights of human intuition.

You have also read the Maharshi's poems to Arunachala. The last one, called Rhapsody,[79] was translated by a Carmelite who put her whole heart into it.

. . . I believe that so long as the Church has not entered into the mystery of India, it will continue to vegetate. All I am trying to do is to awaken, here and also in Europe, a few souls to the real contemplative life which India demands. (MT, 3.7.66)

When writing on the same day to Fr Lemarié, he reflected on his future:

77. About this time Abhishiktananda completed his article, "La diaconie de l'ermite" (see Note 80).
78. This was *Souvenirs d'Arunachala* (the second part of "Pèlerinages"), rewritten for the third time in 1970, and published posthumously.
79. Printed in *Sagesse*, 288ff; English translation in *Saccidananda* (revised edition 1984), 219ff. See Notes 19 and 20. The Carmelite was Sr Thérèse of Shembaganur.

> . . . I hope to be able to install him [Fr D.] at Shantivanam and so to have more time to give to the North. As age increases, the least responsibility seems like a mountain. And this life seated on two chairs is too uncomfortable. Less and less at my ease with the clergy who understand nothing—and unable to be completely at my ease with Hindus who fail to understand that I have not gone beyond Hinduism and Christianity at the same time! I need some time away from all 'thinking' to give my nerves a rest . . . (L, 3.7.66)

Some of his friends were also urging him to accept the call to solitude of which he so often spoke, for example:

> . . . Mrs Stokes writes that my vocation is to be permanently in solitude. The trouble is that in practical terms my age makes this more and more difficult. (L, 7.5.66)

Some very encouraging responses to *Sagesse* came to Abhishiktananda from contemplatives in the West, who found that it enabled them to understand their own experience:

> . . . My book *Sagesse* brought me several moving testimonies from contemplatives (Christians), who for the first time in their life have recognized their own experience in the experience of the Self which I described in the first chapters. At noon today I received another shattering letter on this subject. Even John of the Cross, said the writer, had not been able to explain so clearly the interior stripping [nudity] and the passage from the 'self' to the 'Self' (words used spontaneously by this person, despite the shock given to his rational mind). How clearly it spells out the universal—and so, Christian, *katholikos*—value of the advaitin experience. What is needed above all is to invite Christians to make this experience their own. Otherwise the theological conclusions that we draw from this experience will continue to seem to them unthinkable or blasphemous. It is therefore only in a deepening of contemplative awareness in the Church that there lies any hope of the ecumenical and 'pan-ecumenical' passing beyond that we need. That can never happen at today's ordinary level of awareness. Until then there is only the loneliness of the prophet (. . .) and the impossibility of being at one's ease anywhere except with those few people who have an intuition of this 'transcendent' level—like travelling faster than sound, or escaping from the earth's gravity, to use physical metaphors. (RP, 5.7.66)
>
> . . . You cannot be torn apart in the depth of your soul, as we are by this double summons (from advaitin India on one side, and from Revelation on the other), and by this double opposition (from India and the Church, in their ritualism, their formalism and their intellectualism), without being lacerated even physically.
>
> . . . Yet another letter from Europe strengthens my conviction that the advaitin experience underlies all true mysticism, Christian included. All these letters in short say this: "Your book has taught me nothing new, but for the first time in my life I have understood what was

1. St. Briac-sur-mer, on the north coast of Brittany, birthplace of Henri Le Saux.

2. The Abbey of St. Anne at Kergonan, which Henri Le Saux entered on 15 October 1929. A chapel has since been added at the left.

1. A group of seminarians at Rennes, including R. Macé and H. Le Saux (seated, first and sixth from left).

2. On a visit to Mont St. Michel from the seminary.

3. The young soldier.

1. The two swamis with Bishop Mendonca at Shantivanam in 1950

2. The chapel at Shantivanam.

1. Arunachala. The Sri Ramana Ashram lies at the foot of the hill. (*Photo: O. Baumer*)

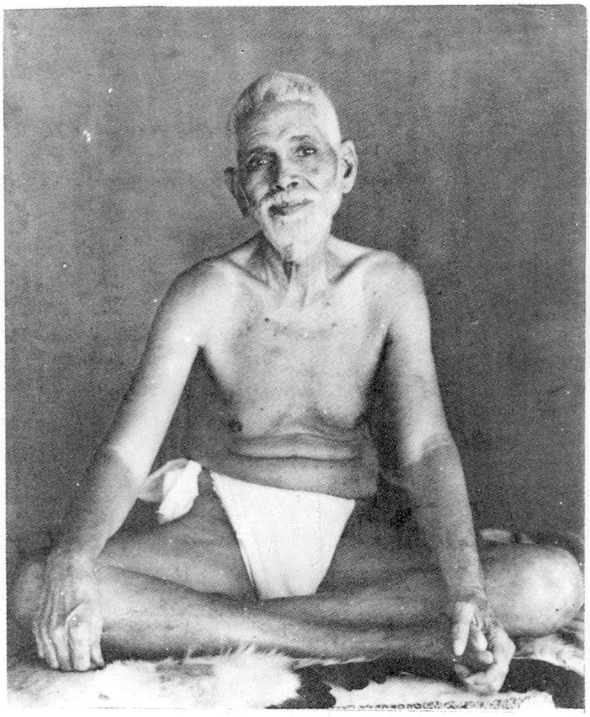

2. Sri Ramana Maharshi.

3. Sri Gnanananda Giri

1. At Jyotiniketan Ashram with Murray Rogers.

2. The Almora meeting of the 'Cuttat group', 1961. (*Photo: Li Gotami*)
(Back row: Fr Dominique, Fr Lazarus, J Stuart, Dr Cuttat, Abhishiktananda:
Front: Fr P. Fallon, Fr E. Zeitler, Fr Britto, Fr J. Deleury, Fr M. Rogers)

1. The *kutiya* at Gyansu, Uttarkashi, 1964. (*Photo: R. Panikkar*)

2. Celebrating Mass at Gangotri, 1964. (*Photo: R. Panikkar*)

3. On the suspension bridge at Laxman Jhula, Rishikesh, 1972. (*Photo: A. Le Saux*)

1. With Raimundo Panikkar at Banaras. (*Photo: Salvador Panikkar*)

2. An 'Indian' Mass celebrated at Andheri (Bombay), 1969

1. At the School of Prayer (Rajpur Centre, 1972) with P.K. Das, Marc and John Cole.

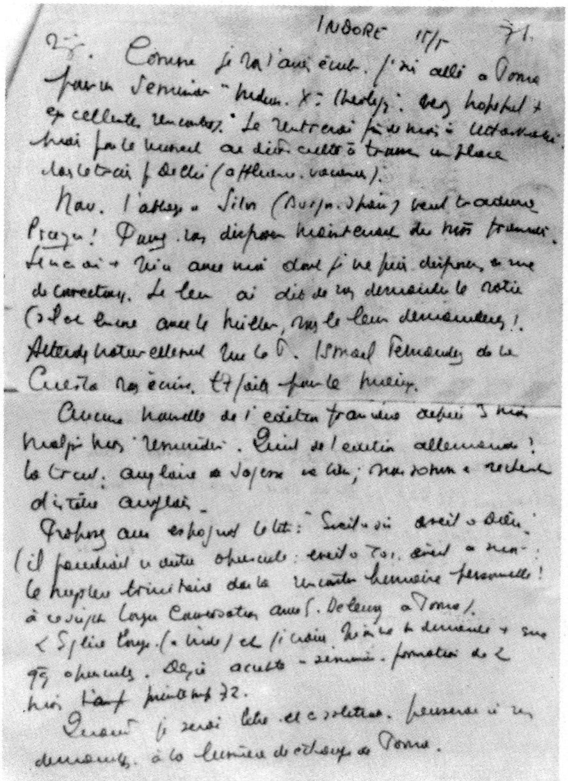

INDORE 17/5 71.

2. Specimen of Abhishiktananda's handwriting.

3. Mother M. Théophane.

> happening in my soul." That consoles one for many things, doesn't it? It is just one more proof that we are not heading in the wrong direction. (RP, 15.7.66)

On the same day he wrote to a new friend in Switzerland, with whom he frequently corresponded in the following years. Mrs O. Baumer had for long been deeply interested in Eastern spirituality. She was moved by reading *Sagesse* to share her problems with him:

> . . . The Church's meeting with India at this particular moment in history is designed to make Christians aware of their own treasures. India is predestined to bear witness to the non-dual dimension of the experience of God, just as Israel was to its prophetic dimension—the 'face to face' with God. All culminating in the Trinitarian revelation, the *Abba* of the Son, the OM of the Spirit.
>
> . . . The Church must first be sensitized to all that. Then the moment will come for drawing the obvious conclusions from certain revolutionary texts of the Council. But in faith it is all very simple. Naturally Hindus would see the problem differently, and not a few pages in my book would be shocking to them. That is because I have deliberately written for Christians, precisely in order to sensitize them to this whisper of the Spirit, to this OM which springs up in the depth of their heart.
>
> What we would like to have from Hindus is a full experience of Christianity (that of Ramakrishna was unfortunately very superficial), so as to lead eventually to real dialogue. (OB, 15.7.66)

Sr Marie-Gilberte had recovered from her operation, though it left her with a handicap. He wrote to her:

> . . . Your vocation is in the place where you are. Help the Carmel to penetrate on behalf of the Church into the depths which are her own heritage. Draw then from the mystery of India—learn above all to draw from the 'Self', which is not at all the monopoly of India. Study the soul of Jesus in this light (. . .)
>
> . . . To worry about not yet being wholly 'given' is likely to be a waste of time. Rather rejoice that you have been accepted, and still more that you have been called, 'established' in Being by an eternal love. That is solid prayer, the rock on which all is built. (MG, 15.8.66)

In August Abhishiktananda began to prepare for his return to North India. The following letter tells of his activities in recent months:

> . . . at present I am engaged in planting in preparation for the rainy season, and also in building a cell for Fr Dominique in January which will give sufficient protection from thieves. Where are the days when we used to live at Shantivanam in huts simply screened with bamboo?
>
> Also finished my articles, two for India, two for France, of which one is on the hermit's life for Ligugé (. . .) quite a short article, too brief.[80] I have also just revised an article requested by *Carmel* on "The

80. Published in *Lettre de Ligugé*, no. 121, 20-25.

> priest whom India, whom the world awaits"[81] of which the first draft was considered to be too blunt. The hermit is not attuned to the sensibilities of the world! I sent you in July (. . .) 'Gangotri' in English. I have just sent to Le Seuil the final corrections for the French edition [i.e., *Une messe*]. I have added some photos taken by Fr Panikkar. (L, 19.8.66)

The other two of the above-mentioned articles (for India) were written in English. One was "The Way of Dialogue", an essay contributed to *Inter-Religious Dialogue.*[82] In this Abhishiktananda discussed the need for dialogue and its difficulties, its pre-conditions. its true spirit and its ultimate aim, all in the light of his own experience. The second was a paper written in July for a consultation at the Lutheran Gurukul seminary in Madras, called "Baptism, Faith and Conversion", which as he said to Fr Lemarié, "usefully makes me clarify certain ideas" (L, 18.7.66). It was published in the following year in the *Indian Journal of Theology.*[83] While firmly based on orthodox tradition, the article manifests great openness to the real world in which the majority live and die without a chance of hearing the Gospel, though "God wills all men to be saved;" and it raises important questions for the Church.

In the North—September to December 1966

In the month between leaving Shantivanam and reaching Uttarkashi Abhishiktananda was mainly occupied in studying possible locations in which Sr Térèse might pursue her vocation once she was free to leave the Carmel at Pondicherry. He wrote to her three times during September, keeping her up to date with his inquiries and also discussing possible companions, since those who had been envisaged were disqualified by health. With Sr Théophane at Indore he thought about sites in the Indore and Bhopal dioceses, where she would have sympathetic bishops. He inspected Ujjain, an important religious centre off the beaten track, where the Sister would have little difficulty in earning her keep by embroidery work and teaching French. Even so, his preference was always for a place near the Ganges in the Hardwar-Rishikesh area. From Delhi he visited the Bishop of Meerut, and was encouraged by his acceptance of the idea, although such a location offered little hope of remunerative work.

Most of his time in Delhi was spent in revising the manuscript of his little book on Prayer, whose editor was still insisting on further improvements in the style and language. However he did not totally neglect his friends:

> . . . Have I told you about Delhi?—the strong contrasts [*douche écossaise*] which I so often experience? The other Saturday, lunch at noon with Hindu extremists (great friends!), who are anti-Christian, anti-Muslim, anti-West. The afternoon with a couple (American husband, French wife) who knew me through Sulivan's book.[84] And in the evening, dinner at the French Embassy in a Louis XIV decor (dinner by candle-

81. *Carmel,* 1966, IV, 270-284. Reprinted in *Les Yeux,* 103ff.
82. *Inter-Religious Dialogue,* ed, H. Jai Singh, C.I.S.R.S. Bangalore, 1967, 78-103.
83. *Indian Journal of Theology,* Vol. 16, no. 3, 189-203.
84. *Le plus petit abîme*; see Note 35.

light). They knew about my books, and as soon as they got wind of my presence, the phone rang! Then the following evening I was in a Hindu ashram at Hardwar. (L, 8.10.66)

He wrote to his sister from Hardwar, telling her about the past few weeks:

> . . . What contrasts! I do my best to be at ease everywhere, but there is an inevitable tension. But it is precisely this being torn apart between India and Europe, between Vedanta and Christianity, which enable me to live the fundamental *experience* and to express its mystery to some extent.
>
> . . . So I am going to Uttarkashi to meditate in peace. That will be good, but this will be a brief stay, as I have to be at Shantivanam for Christmas.
>
> . . . My head is spinning slightly this morning. Having come from Delhi to Hardwar, a day in a hot and crowded train, the previous evening at the Embassy until midnight, then up at 4.30 to say Mass and catch the train. Days are hot, but nights are good, and the Ganges this morning is ice-cold. It is 9 o'clock, and I am going to join the devout in taking my morning bath. The Ganges flows along beside the ashram where I am staying; there are stone steps down to the water and iron chains to hold, because it flows past at a fantastic speed. Yesterday evening at sunset I was sitting and admiring it. People here make leaf boats in which they put flowers and an earthenware oil lamp, and let them sail downstream . . . So all things slip away, but your *self* abides, firmly fixed at the centre. (MT, 25.9.66)

Before leaving Hardwar he visited Sr Praxedes at the leprosy home in Dehra Dun (TL, 28.9.66). Soon afterwards she began to follow her own path, which had little in common with Abhishiktananda. He then went up to Uttarkashi:

> . . . Reached Uttarkashi [2 October]. Recaptured by this mountain atmosphere, where all that is of the world is forgotten. (. . .) I need, at least from time to time, to be reimmersed in it. And the Church, in its leaders as in its active members, should also be plunged into it. (. . .) God found at the most subtle centre of the world, and so totally immanent in his transcendence. When shall we be freed from "God most high", "up there"? the Babylonian monarch! Vedanta is the answer to the questions posed by Robinson, Bonhoeffer, etc.[85] You know Robinson's latest? "The death of God" is a fact—the God of imagination and human conception. From his ashes the true God will arise.
>
> Two weeks ago at Hardwar, once more in a totally Hindu environment. In my element. But there you can assess the extent to which the Church has distanced itself from India—indeed, from everything (compare the experience of the Priest Workers). Its message cannot get across—its real message, I mean. The Bishop of Indore was telling me that the Hindu world is not ready for the Gospel; (for that, he said,

85. J.A.T. Robinson, *Honest to God*, etc.; D. Bonhoeffer, *Letters from Prison*.

we should have to wait until it collapses into western materialism). My view, on the other hand, is that the Church is not ready for India, alas! (. . .)[86]

At Dehra Dun last week a young brahmin, aged eighteen, begged me to take him with me. He has been dreaming of sannyasa for some years already. But I insisted that he should complete two more years of study. A momentary spark—or the start of a fire? Last year there was another who wanted to follow me, but he was not ready. As in the Gospel, he had first to go and bury his father . . . The day will come for him also, if I do not leave the world too soon.[87] (L, 8.10.66)

Thoughts about India and the Church appear in several letters from Uttarkashi:

. . . What a purification is needed of the Christian message and of Christian worship—both so stunted by being practised at the level of religion. Christians unfortunately live their Christianity as if it was one among other religions—merely better than the others, and so the true one. They have no faith in the transcendent character of Christianity. These days I am thinking of the harm that is done to the Gospel here, when it is preached by people who have behind them all the prestige, money, science and technology of the west. Must Christianity really be the religion of those who are rich in human wealth? Where are the Galilean fishermen, the Syrian shopkeepers and artisans? India could then receive the message, for it would be purely 'spiritual', and India, though tempted by materialism, would awaken at the call of a Buddha!

Let us plunge into the depth of India in the name of the Church, and there discover Christ the *Purusha*,[88] for he more truly pre-exists in the *Purusha* than in the Greek Logos and awaits his unveiling. I still believe what I once wrote: "The Indian Church will not come to birth until in the depth of a Hindu heart, the *Purusha* awakes as Christ!" that is to say, until in the depth of the advaitin experience there springs up the awakening to the Father. Let us prepare for that, even if no one understands. (. . .)

One evening a few years ago, seated here beside the Ganges, I was thinking about the Council, and was suddenly seized with uncontrollable laughter. Men hold discussions and make decisions about God. But before superimposing so-called 'divine' forms on the world, please first realize the overwhelming fullness of the Presence!

My wish for you is that you may lose yourself there, so as to find yourself as Him alone! (TL, 24.10.66)

. . . We are approaching a real nuclear explosion in the sphere of religion. The 'count down' was started by Pope John. A chain reaction will spread from Rome to the ends of the earth. All that is so-called

86. This conversation may have prompted Abhishiktaananda to write the article "Contemplative Life in India", "S.V. Swami", *Examiner* 13 and 20 Jan., 1967.

87. The two young men were Lalit Sharma and Ramesh Srivastava.

88. The *Purusha*, the archetypal, cosmic Man, e.g. in *Rig-Veda* 10.90.

'religious' consists of what is 'superimposed',[89] of a 'man-made' sacred intended to take the place of the truly Sacred, unperceived because of its translucidity (cp. the Ten Pictures of Zen[90]). Oxygen flasks inside a sealed cave, ignoring the fact that the air, *vāyu,* is everywhere. You have that terrible phrase on p. 63 [of *The Unknown Christ*] that Christianity is 'provisional', only of this world. True, but then . . .? It only has the consistence of *māyā* ??

We have to prepare the world for the inevitable break-up; to make the divine, *sat* [the Real], felt in its immanence and its transcendence, in its translucidity. *Apertis oculis attonitis auribus vacate et videte.*[91] Otherwise this explosion will be a disaster. Too soon. Atomic power in the hands of Neanderthal man, as Grousset said, I think.

How 'different' and 'clear' everything looks from the mountain top! How petty men's thoughts and deeds appear! It is more than ever the hour of the Upanishads. Both world and Church need them. (RP, 29.10.66)

At the end of November he told his family about the 'wonderful month' at Uttarkashi, despite the cold after 3 p.m., when the sun disappeared behind the mountains. However he had a magnificent overcoat, given some years previously by a 'Burmese Baptist', not to mention cups of tea and coffee to warm the interior. This year he had added to his kutiya a small guest room, roughly made out of planks of wood, and had put a barbed-wire fence round his garden which enabled him to grow flowers and even vegetables (F, 29.11.66)

News of some family problems drew from him these reflections:

> . . . All that you say is very natural, given the childish and mythical way in which most Christians present and live their religion. What is extraordinary is that even so people remain in the Church. It is the same here; people picture God as a sugar-daddy whose only job is to make life easy for us, and then they are astounded that he treats us like his own Son, with all that follows from that. It really makes one tremble to think of the responsibility of the clergy. They give children a routine to follow, tell them stories from the Old Testament, the Gospel and the legends of the saints, and then suppose that all that will survive once they begin to think for themselves.
>
> I have passed two blessed months among the mountains. (. . .) With me this week a young brahmin [Lalit, who came up for the Diwali holidays], who wants to join me. I met him two months ago in Dehra Dun, and without my saying anything to him directly, he was 'caught'. (. . .) Is it the real thing this time? Whatever the Lord wills. Also met here a wealthy Delhi merchant, who has left everything and now lives in solitude and silence in an ashram at Uttarkashi. Grace is at work among the Hindus!

89. In Indian thought all conceptualization about God or the Self is a "superimposition" (*adhyāropa*) upon the ultimate Reality which is beyond all concepts.
90. See, for example, *Zen Flesh, Zen Bones* (Pelican), 133-147.
91. A recollection apparently of *Rule of St Benedict,* Prologue 9.

> . . . This morning my small brahmin was present at my Mass. I got him to read the prayers in Hindi and 'imparted' to him (the *traditio*) the Our Father in Sanskrit. (MT, 27.11.66)

Before leaving Uttarkashi he wrote to Fr Lemarié:

> . . . Gyansu is marvellous. Only here do I feel myself to be fully alive. Why do I have to come down? But I have to be at Shantivanam before Christmas. (. . .) Fr Dominique will come soon after that, and several visitors are expected in January, including the French Ambassador!
>
> . . . As regards books, I think that this year again I must be content with renewing the subscriptions to *D.C.* and *Contacts*. The cost of living has gone up greatly since the devaluation, and the upkeep of Shantivanam is a bottomless pit. My small capital of few years ago is reduced every year to a disquieting extent, and it will be some time before Fr D. has any income of his own. The royalties on the two books will at best equal one year's expenses.

In connection with some monastic problems in Europe, he continued:

> . . . In all that what a need there is for the Vedantin air of the Himalayan heights. We need monasteries like Taizé and Solesmes, but still more there should also be in Europe *advaitin* ashrams to 'point' uncompromisingly towards the Beyond. During these two months of solitude my chief thought and grief was that the Church should be to such a small extent spiritually centred. At a time when its juridical and intellectual 'centering' is being shaken, it has no other hope (at the level of secondary causes) than this centering *at depth.* (. . .) Advaita relentlessly catapults you beyond all myth. This has to be said and written. But who listens? (L, 22.11.66)

During December Abhishiktananda toured North India, visiting his friends. He went to Dehra Dun (Lalit), Bareilly (Jyotiniketan), Banaras (R. Panikkar), Lucknow (Poonja), and finally to Delhi, for another session on his book *Prayer*, an "endless job".

It was probably on this visit to Jyotiniketan that he and Murray Rogers composed a letter "To our Christian brothers of the West who hope to serve the Church in India", which was published in *One in Christ* in 1967.[92] In this they suggested to the would-be missionary a much more humble and open approach to India than had so far been customary, and sought to offer a contribution to the rethinking of mission which was a feature of the time. However, the Indian Government shortly afterwards practically closed the door to the entry of new missionaries, and few have had the opportunity of following these admirable guidelines.

On his return to Shantivanam he wrote to his sister at Kergonan:

> . . . I came back here on the 23rd, after three and a half weeks of travelling, meeting Protestants, Hindus, even Catholic bishops! I am

92. See bibliography.

> alarmed at the number of different environments through which I have to pass. I would so much like to awaken the Indian Church to the problem, the 'challenge' posed to it by India, of which most people are terribly ignorant—greatly to the detriment of the Church's mission. If they could only know the Hindus whom I know and live among. (. . .) I came back very tired, but stayed at home for Christmas. Only tomorrow will I go to offer my greetings to the Bishop and buy various provisions, paper, etc. Besides, I had to listen to all the gossip and squabbles of the village. I am missing Uttarkashi, and perhaps next year I shall leave the South for good. (MT, 26.12.66)

Shantivanam—January to mid-August 1967

The pattern of 1967 was similar to that of 1966. Abhishiktananda remained at the ashram until August and rarely went out, apart from his customary visits to the Carmels of Shembaganur, Pondicherry and Bangalore. This was partly because Fr Dominique was now at Shantivanam and an unusual number of visitors came to the ashram.

"The months in the mountains were excellent from the point of view of health. (. . .) I am much better than I was six months ago," he assured Mother Théophane (5.1.67); but he admitted to Dr Panikkar (6.1.67) that "my rhythm of life gets slower with age." The labour of putting the ashram to rights after four months of absence weighed heavily on him, but he had to prepare for the visit of the French Ambassador and his wife (3 Jan.) and for the arrival of Fr Dominique soon afterwards:

> . . . This year I have found the return to Shantivanam too much of burden. Uttarkashi and the mountains have made too deep a mark on me. I mean that what I would like is either the genuine solitude that I have there, or else a chance of effective work in a receptive environment. But this half-way house, which Shantivanam has been since the beginning, is useless. (RP, 6.2.67)

In fact his life continued to alternate between periods of solitude at Gyansu and periods when he was called upon to communicate. Apart from his responsibility for those who increasingly sought his spiritual guidance, he began to have opportunities for effective work in the Indian Church, notably in connection with the National Seminar which took place in 1969. A first reference to the "aggiornamento of the Church in India" comes in a letter to his family of 26.1.67, with a view to which he had "to prepare some papers". In the previous October the Catholic Bishops' Conference of India (CBCI) had decided to set up a National Liturgical Centre at Bangalore under Fr D.S. Amalorpavadass, and to explore the possibility of developing Indian forms of liturgy and para-liturgy. It was natural that Abhishiktananda, as one who had experience in this sphere and who was now well known through his writings, should be consulted. This was probably the topic of an "unexpectedly interesting conversation" that he had with the co-adjutor Archbishop of Delhi in December 1966, which made him say: "Perhaps I have been wrong in sometimes holding back from meeting the 'pillars' [of the Church]" (L, 1.2.67).

His sense of being pulled in opposite directions was one of the contradictions that had to be accepted, as he said to Sr Térèse:

> . . . There is the call to remain in the cave, and there are the calls which come to you from outside, and the Spirit weaves its way [?] through both kinds. Formulas never solve problems, they merely keep up the appearances. There is as much latent egoism in the choice of solitude as in choosing to meet people. (TL, 16.2.67)

The deeper tension, involved in the attempt to live in different worlds at the same time, is referred to in a letter to New York:

> . . . There is always an element of aestheticism in the way we share the lot of the poor. There is always something that falls short of absolute truth. Take the case of the worker priest: if one day he has had enough, he can always ask his bishop for a parish or a chaplaincy. If he is on strike, there will always be some friend to give him food and shelter. (. . .) I know something about this myself, living as I do half with the established Church and half with those who possess nothing, half with Christians and half with Hindus—a very uncomfortable situation, believe me! It is here that I find your point about the 'bridge' very illuminating. It is precisely the fact of being a bridge that makes this uncomfortable situation worth while. The world, at every level, needs such bridges. If, to be a Hindu with Hindus, I had become a complete sannyasi, I would have been unable to communicate either the Hindu message to Christians or the Christian message to Hindus. And it is the same as between Europe and India. (. . .) We have to accept ourselves as the Lord has made us. I can neither have a brown skin nor speak an Indian mother-tongue. Instead of lamenting the fact, each has to infer from it where his own vocation lies. How complicated life is, more so than anything we can think up. However, the danger of this life as a 'bridge' is that we run the risk of not belonging finally to either side; whereas, however harrowing it may be, our duty is precisely to belong wholly to both sides. This is only possible in the mystery of God.
>
> . . . Why does the hermit not remain in his cave? Acosmism can in fact be egocentric (. . .). True acosmism coincides with total 'cosmism', as surely as true transcendence cannot in the end be distinguished from immanence. (AMS, 9.2.67)

Abhishiktananda's books continued to bring inquiries and requests for advice. There were some who wondered if they had a calling to come to India, others who were merely curious to meet this unusual person:

> . . . I have had to discourage quite a number of supposed vocations to India, some of them excellent in themselves—but, for example, when someone is aged 68?? (. . .) But yesterday an excellent letter from a Carmelite aged 28. I must follow it up, although so far, apart from T. of Lisieux, all have been disappointing, men and women alike. (L, 1.2.67)
>
> . . . It is a nuisance to be so well known. Here I try politely to avoid European visitors. I have put off two or three such in the last few

> weeks. (. . .) I am continually telling westerners to go and see Hindus, and not people of their own race—otherwise why make the journey? (L, 13.3.67)

News came of the death of a very old friend at Kergonan, Fr J. Lebreton, who had been specially kind to him during his noviciate and was one of the few who continued to write to him in India. He spoke of him in a letter to his sister, saying "He was humble and patient with me, and checked my impulsiveness." He also mentioned a young member of the family, who was passing through a difficult period:

> . . . Nowadays I have a good contact with . . . It seems to be much less a crisis of faith than one of growing up. However, it is rather your affair . . . When you think of it, I have not known any of my nephews and nieces except as small babies, so the poor children naturally wonder who is this strange bearded uncle, living so far away . . . (MT, 8.4.67)

A specially welcome visitor in May was his young Hindu friend, Lalit:

> . . . That lad from the North, about whom I have told you, came two weeks ago. He still has two more years of study to complete, but after that he is absolutely determined to join me. He is very likeable and possesses unusual qualities, in particular, a spontaneity and simplicity which are very rare here. (What an opening on the Hindu world is given by this close contact which I have with him. The Christian who lives 'happy' in his prefabricated world cannot imagine the *abyss* which from every point of view keeps him apart. Profoundly discouraged with the Church which is incapable of any real impact on the Hindu soul . . .) But I have become such an old buffer, an unsocial 'bear', that I no longer dare to accept any involvement. Is that wisdom, or is it egoism? Even so, I may have some rather demanding involvements in the future with these dear Carmelites. I would need to have a hard heart, which I don't have, to turn my back on all that (L, 15.5.67)

A month later Fr Francis Mahieu arrived to spend the first three months of a sabbatical year at the ashram, as a "return to the sources from which I had drawn so much inspiration in 1955, during my first year in India".[93] Fr Francis had in 1957 founded with Fr Bede Griffiths the Kurisumala ashram in Kerala, which by now was securely established. One of the objects of his sabbatical year was to prepare for his ashram to "set out positively for a monastic encounter with our Hindu brethren", and this was a "constant topic" in his talks with Abhishiktananda:

> . . . Fr Francis is strongly urging me to act, to arouse opinion, to prepare and put forward new formulas which would enable the Indian Church to come out of its coma. But as everyone else is holding back,

93. Fr Francis described his return to the ashram in a section, "Shantivanam Revisited" (pp. 56-59), of a "Twelve Years' Newsletter" about the Kurisumala Ashram, *Bulletin de l'A.I.M.* (English edition, Vanves), 1971, no. 12, 40-65 and 1972, no. 13, 18-47. He also wrote about Abhishiktananda in *Kurisumala: a symposium on Ashram Life* (ed. Francis Acharya), 1974, 68 and 71-74.

> I think that I also will go into hibernation—at Uttarkashi, for example. I no longer have the physical strength or vitality for such an enterprise. (RP, 14.8.67)

Both he and Fr Francis were also consultors to the new Liturgical Centre, and the latter urged his host to press on with his work on the 'Indian Liturgy' (L, 29.6.67). In those days the chapel at Shantivanam was a 'workshop' in which was tested out in their daily worship the possibility of using Indian Scriptures and ceremonial actions for Christian liturgy. He wrote about this in July to Fr Lemarié:

> . . . I am in process of completing the rebuilding of the roof and various other things in the chapel. I think that now things are going even better than before, and that we have a good solution to the problem of placing the altar for Mass facing the people. I am also making discreet preparations for something like they have in Shivaite temples, so as to say Mass seated. Once it is ready, we will see about using it . . . when the time comes (here, I mean—for privately in the North I do it all the time).
>
> People are now thinking very seriously about an Indian rite. The idea is excellent, but it would require a total transformation of the Church. I am in touch with the priest who is *de facto* in charge of the national Commission on Liturgy [Fr Amalorpavadass]. At present I am using flowers, incense and lights—all offered, and not merely placed above the altar as in Europe—at every Mass. But the heart of an Indian liturgy would be an Indian *anaphora.*[94] But Indian worship is *cosmic*, while the Eucharistic anaphora is of course the recapitulation of the history of salvation. I have some very fine Vedic texts to use as a Preface, but how to make a harmonious transition to the *Qui pridie*?[95] (L, 20.7.67)

The results of this time of experiment were gathered up by Abhishiktananda in an article, "A Study of Hindi Symbolism", which was completed in August (F, 5.8.67) and published in 1968 in *Word and Worship* [96]

The meeting of Fr Francis and Abhishiktananda was altogether happier than it had been in 1955-56, and led to an important decision about the future of the ashram. As Fr Francis put it: "We were both very much aware that our respective monastic charisms had taken us along different paths," but "I experienced in our meeting again after eleven years an unexpected and very deep joy, as I discovered how close we were at the deepest level."[97] Abhishiktananda expressed his own joy, rather characteristically, by saying: "Fr Mahieu has changed enormously, entirely for the good" (Was he aware how much he himself had

94. The *anaphora* (offering) is the central prayer of the Eucharist.
95. "Qui pridie . . ." ("Who on the night before he suffered . . .") begins the recital of the Institution of the Lord's Supper in the Eucharistic prayer.
96. *Word and Worship*, Vol. I, no. 8 (March 1968), 298-307; Vol. II, no. 2 (August 1968), 77-79. After the All-India Seminar of 1969, Abhishiktananda continued to work in close contact with the National Biblical and Catechetical Centre at Bangalore.
97. "Twelve Years' Newsletter" (Note 92 above), p.57.

mellowed over the years?). "He has now reached the point where we should have been able to start something excellent together in 1955!" (L, 10.8.67)

In this atmosphere of mutual confidence Abhishiktananda shared his anxieties about the ashram and the intolerable burden of maintaining it as well as the hermitage at Uttarkashi. He also felt his responsibility for Fr Dominique ("the perfect hermit"), who could not be expected to manage the ashram, but whose presence there was essential:

> . . . We are in process of studying a formula for 'salvaging' Shantivanam, as I can no longer continue there as caretaker, or even to look after Fr Dominique. (. . .) Fr Mahieu will take charge of Shantivanam. It will either be a new foundation of his in Tamilnad, or else a house of retreat/prayer, where he will send those of his monks who want a truly contemplative life, with an excellent Brother to be in charge of the estate (. . .). Fr Dominique could then provide the spiritual direction of Shantivanam from his hermitage at the bottom of the garden. If that works out, I shall vanish quietly in the Himalayas. (L, 10.8.67)

In September Fr Francis returned briefly to Kurisumala to place Abhishiktananda's offer before his community, which gladly accepted it. In handing over Shantivanam, Abhishiktananda's chief concern was that the ashram should continue "to follow the ancient Indian monastic traditions, so as to be a source of inspiration for Christians and non-Christians alike," as was stated in an agreement drawn up in August 1968 at the time of the transfer.[98] He also "insisted" that Fr Francis should personally take charge of the ashram, but in the event this was not possible.

Abhishiktananda left for the North in the middle of August. Fr Francis stayed on for several weeks, until a Spanish monk came to take his place as a companion to Fr Dominique. This monk, however, soon "had enough of Shantivanam", and Fr Dominique, left on his own, had little choice but to return to his monastery in Bangalore, when he was asked in November to take over as novice-master. (L, 7.12.67)

In the North—August to December 1967

On his way North Abhishiktananda stopped for three days at Bangalore to follow up his work on the Indian liturgy. Then he spent four days at Bombay, seeing among others Dr Klostermaier in connection with a proposal to set up a centre for Hindu studies in Varanasi. His host was his old friend, Dr D. Mehta:

> . . . Here I am in a circle which talks politics. This India is extraordinary! A mixture of humanist values, astrological beliefs, sincere search for God, and of course, plain egoism. Incredible how people in high places are attracted by everything that seems to them to come from the Beyond. I am staying with Dr Mehta (. . .). Every evening people come, prostrate, gathering up all that he says, recording it on tape. Talks which give good advice, but are crammed with cliches and without

98. *ibid.*, p.60. (Date confirmed in a private letter.)

> order . . . But it all comes from on high, and they listen open-mouthed.
>
> . . . Also went by chance to the pilgrimage basilica of Bandra. (. . .) These westernized Bombay Christians are basically more Hindu than our superstitious villagers. Your faith has to be well anchored, if it is to survive such visits! (l, 27.8.67)

From Bombay he went to Indore, where there was much concern about the new legislation which the Government, influenced by the swing to the Right in the recent elections, was introducing. All missionaries were required to obtain residence permits, and there were threats of large-scale expulsions. Then he went on to Delhi (where his book *Prayer* was at last being printed), to Rishikesh and to Bareilly. Here, as he told Mother Théophane.

> . . . my English Anglican friends have not had to get themselves 'registered' [for residence permits]. The CID [police] said to them: "I see that you are here only for spiritual purposes. Therefore you are not missionaries!" After that, is it surprising that India does not accept Christ? (Th, 11.9.67)

As Abhishiktananda was still unable to find a suitable place for Sr Térèse to continue her initiation, his friends at Jyotiniketan suggested that he should bring her there later in the year for a study-retreat on the Upanishads, in which they also would take part. He gladly accepted this invitation, provided the Sister also agreed.

From Bareilly he visited Lalit's home in Saharanpur, where he met his father, a Gandhian since 1922, a freedom-fighter, "often imprisoned and beaten by the British, just like the Vichy police treated the Resistance. A man of uncommon humility and selflessness." He went on to note

> . . . the fundamental problem which these meetings always raise: How on earth can one present the Church's formulas and institutions? In all these circles I am regarded as practically a Hindu. (L, 21.9.67)

His last call before setting out for Uttarkashi was at the Retreat and Study Centre in Rajpur to see the Alters:

> . . . American Presbyterians, such good friends, with whom I exchanged views on the crucial problems. The Church must get ready to see all its institutions (schools, hospitals, etc.) taken away, its financial support from overseas forbidden, visas refused and residence permits quietly not renewed. (. . .) Is the Church going to prepare itself for a new form of being present? All this is a blessing, and the indispensable stimulus to the aggiornamento. But those responsible must read the writing on the wall in good time.
>
> . . . This journey has been fascinating, enriching, with its constant changes of atmosphere, in every case so friendly. Being the *sākshī*, the 'witness' of Hindu tradition, moving about everywhere, given to all, happy in everything, free from everything. But I would like many more to share my experience. (L, 21.9.67)

This year his stay at Uttarkashi lasted barely five weeks (27 Sept. to 30 Oct.). It had been agreed that he and Sr Térèse should come to Jyotiniketan by the middle of November; but on his way through Rishikesh in September he had been invited by his friend Malou Lanvin to spend a week at the Sivananda Ashram with the Sister before going on to Bareilly. When passing on the invitation, he said:

> . . . This would be a very interesting initiation, even if naturally a little 'shocking' (but it would help you to free yourself from your legalistic mentality: What is/is not allowed! There is so little of 'you' in such questions: there is a whole 'mask' which raises questions, gets bothered . . .). And of course I also should have the opportunity of spending some days in this ashram, which I know well and which at present has an excellent 'president', kindly disposed to Christianity and very humble. (TL, 3.10.67)

It seems that the Sister hesitated to accept, and in his next letter he counselled her to trust in the Spirit and go forward boldly:

> . . . In a non-Catholic or non-Christian environment we should not check every step of our way by Canon Law—that would lead to terrible scruples. Canon Law is an aid—one should add, as with every law, that it applies in normal situations. For example, it is well known that the 'practice' of intercommunion goes much further than even the recent directives of Bea's Secretariat. But between what is done in practice (tacitly overlooked) and what is officially promulgated, there is always a gap. We should simply make as clear as possible our own deep and spiritual *Christian orientation,* and allow the Spirit to act in his own way through us. In the life you have chosen you will constantly find yourself facing borderline situations which call for very great freedom in the Spirit. That you are capable of doing that, I know well. And you know it even better—otherwise the Spirit would not have put into your heart such crazy desires! Take possession of your total freedom, not so much as regards external laws, habits or rules, but as regards that 'mask' which seeks to impose itself on you—and all too often succeeds in doing so—and in fact finds allies in very deep strata of your personality. Discover your real 'I' (. . .) This 'non-born' refers to what is beyond all time, all place, all circumstance; in it alone you have an insight, a 'glimpse', a certain experience already of the Absoluteness of God. We have to cut the bonds, 'the knots of the heart', as the Mundaka says, which bind us to the mask deep within us. It is a painful business.
>
> . . . It is with this freedom in the Spirit that you should approach your new life. Don't waste your time, either now or later, in comparing what you were (or thought you were) with present or future circumstances. (TL, 17.10.67)

During October his disciple Lalit joined him for a week:

> . . . That young brahmin Lalit spent his Dasserah holidays here with me. Very determined (as far as you can be at the age of 19) to join me. Much attached to me—the meaning of 'guru' that is so little known in the West, where the person is lost in the institution. I am very fond of

him, but remain free; I am so fond of my solitude, my 'independence'. But I also realize that with the advance of age, that will become physically more difficult.

. . . And now an unknown Englishman (who for the last six months has been sending me the *Herder Correspondence*) has deposited £50 in my name with Blackwells (of Oxford) for me to buy books! Truly Providence is good. (. . .) However, in these days I have so little desire to read, compared with the past! During the past month I have read nothing but the Upanishads, taking them slowly as *lectio divina* [spiritual reading]. Even this Sanskrit liturgy seems to me—in my solitude—so far from the goal. Here the OM is enough. How wearisome are the long series of Psalms! (L, 25.10.67)

A letter to his family refers again to the problems of young people:

. . . You should not worry too much about the children as they grow up. (. . .) The Church itself is in a serious crisis. We realize that too often we used to give the title of 'Christian life' to a certain kind of religious practice which had no influence on life, personal or social. On the other hand, sermons and religious classes were terribly lacking in substance, which explains why many young people reject religion as it is practised and presented. They want reality, a true commitment to God. It is the same problem here. I understand my nieces . . . so well. Naturally I do not say they are right in every respect. But really we too often forget that people grow up, and that the milk that suits a baby is not enough for an adult. From this mountain top all is so clear! But it is sad that so many Christians and priests still live fifty years behind the time. (F, 19.10.67)

Sr Térèse arrived safely from the South, and after a week in the Sivananda Ashram accompanied Abhishiktananda to Jyotiniketan:

. . . Here every morning we are reading the Upanishads, first a page at the morning Eucharist, and then a prayerful study in common for an hour in the morning or evening, on the lines of *Meeting Point.*[99] Very illuminating, when minds are 'attuned'. (OB, 9.12.67)

Odette Baumer had raised the question of "divine consciousness", to which he replied in two letters:

. . . I do not like the phrase "Divine Consciousness". It is terribly ambiguous. The word 'divine' stands for God in distinction from man, since it is not true that God and the creature are identical. The experience of Being is at a totally different level of awareness. There is always the danger of a false advaita, an advaita that is thought, not experienced (the congenital failing of works on advaita as a whole, whether Indian or European). Those who beguile themselves with a 'feeling of unity' are missing the mark. Advaita is a royal secret, only to be revealed at the last moment by the guru who knows—*tad-vid*—to the disciple who is near to, ready for, knowing it. (OB, 13.9.67)

99. i.e., in chapter 4, "The Intuitions of the Rishis".

. . . Yes, I have reservations about "Divine Consciousness". The word 'consciousness' is too debased and therefore misleading, just as much as the concept of 'person', when attributed to the Infinite, the Absolute. The divine consciousness has nothing to do with anything that we call 'consciousness'. God alone has consciousness of himself. All so-called awareness of God which man succeeds in recognizing in himself is mere projection. Awareness of God is something quite different. I am always afraid of the word 'divine'; it is so misunderstood, even though everyone thinks he understands it well. It is through a false understanding of "Divine Consciousness" that westerners rush to Rishikesh in search of 'experiences' and that Hindus besiege their gurus. (OB, 9.12.67)

While at Jyotiniketan he heard about Fr Dominique's return to Bangalore and about a delay in the transfer of Shantivanam:

. . . Certain internal problems and the state of Fr Bede's health prevent Fr Mahieu from maintaining his enthusiasm for taking over Shantivanam before Easter. I shall see him at the beginning of January. As things are, I have no choice but to drop Shantivanam. (. . .) It is a shame; but as, despite every effort, no help has come either personal or material, I shall not sacrifice myself for a place.

. . . Térèse has very well accustomed herself to her new life. The transition was a shock, but she reacted excellently. Now she is going by herself to Indore to learn English and Hindi in a much more conformist environment, which she already begins to dread. (L, 7.12.67)

After the month at Jyotiniketan he accompanied Sr Térèse as far as Bhopal, where she caught the train for Indore, while he continued South for his last Christmas at Shantivanam. At the end of the year he wrote to his sister at Kergonan:

. . . I have just got back here. (. . .) Plenty of work there in the North during these last months. Writing books and leading a life which here seems such a simple matter, turns you into a myth,[100] but at least the message goes over a little. Last week in Delhi I met Ch. B. who acknowledged with feeling that *Sagesse* had made it possible for him again to make the sign of the cross!

I certainly found the illustrations in my last book [*Une messe,* published in September] a trifle indiscreet, but what can I do, from so far away? Do you yet know a little English? At the beginning of the month I arranged for my 'latest-born' to be sent to you from Delhi, a small book in English on prayer, published by an Anglican publisher, but with the Imprimatur of the local Catholic Archbishop.[101] These ecumenical contacts are most enriching, they enable Christians to

100. As he wrote to his family (5.8.67): "That is all the news of the hermitage. It is amusing to see how people in Europe make a myth of it. More than one imagine that I constantly circulate from north to south of India on foot with a bag on my shoulder and begging my rice like a real sadhu. Alas, that would be far beyond my capacity at my age!"

101. *Prayer,* published by I.S.P.CK., Delhi.

> discover each other in depth, and that is the foundation for all further developments. (MT, 27.12.67)

Shantivanam—January to March 1968

Early in the year Abhishiktananda and Fr Francis made the final arrangements for the transfer of Shantivanam in the coming August or September.

During January he was visited by a young Parisian student who was preparing to enter a seminary and was one who "reconciles me to French youth—last year I had seen such awful specimens in the North" (F,30.1.68). They met again at Jyotiniketan after Easter.

In the last half of January he spent some days at Shembaganur, where "I have made preparations very quietly for a Carmelite foundation in the Ranchi district which, while being completely regular, will go a long way towards adaptation to its environment."[102] (L, 25.1. 68)

He also had an unusual request:

> . . . Would you believe it—the other day I had a letter from Cancale, a priest in my class (Châteaugiron/ Rennes) who invited me to take part in the annual reunion by sending a sermon for the occasion on a tape! As if I had tape-recorder or tapes! All the same, I was very touched by his remembering me.[103] (F, 30.1.68)

In February he was visited by Malou Lanvin, the friend who had invited Sr Térèse to Rishikesh, and who gave Abhishiktananda very practical help by maintaining an account for him in Lyon, into which his royalties could be paid.

During these last months he was busy preparing for his departure and packing all the papers and books that he would need in the North. He also began to prepare for the All-India Seminar and continued to work at the Sanskrit liturgy. He wrote about these and other matters to Odette Baumer:

> . . . I am glad you liked the little book (*Prayer*). Even though it is very elementary, to those who understand it conveys many things. Its essential aim was to help Christians to understand something of the Real in terms that they could grasp. I would have written it differently, if it had been addressed to Hindus. My Hindu friends have gently reproached me for having said on the first page that continual prayer is the calling and duty of Christians. "Surely, of everyone?" they said. As regards a possible version in French, I am awaiting the reaction of my publisher. If this is favourable, the translation would be slightly expanded.
>
> But first of all, I am busy rewriting in the third person what I used to call "Secrets of India" [Pèlerinages]. When it is ready, I will see about sending you a copy, at least of the first part, "Gnanananda". Then we can see about a possible publication (. . .).[104]

102. The Carmel of Soso, Gumla (Ranchi District), was opened in August 1968.
103. A copy of Abhishiktananda's address, dated 17.5.68, is in the Society's files.
104. This third and final version of *Gnanananda* was published in 1970.

> Your assessment of "Guhantara" is interesting. For me it is the direct expression of my first overwhelming experiences. Later I will look into the possibility of reworking it, but I feel little inclination to do so. What is the use of going on writing? It can all be said in a few lines. (. . .) At present I am engaged in working, semi-officially, on a liturgy in Sanskrit which would take up the themes and the texts of the great tradition. It is fascinating. (OB, 8.3.68)

Shortly before leaving Shantivanam, he wrote to his sister at Kergonan:

> . . . I am just on the point of departing. I shall celebrate the 21st [St Benedict; 18th anniversary of the ashram] here once more, and that evening I shall set off for Indore, Delhi, Bareilly, Hardwar and Uttarkashi. I shall probably come down again in August, and then I shall leave Shantivanam for good. On this trip I am already removing half of my belongings.
>
> Fr Landry wrote to me the other day, (. . .) told me about his heart-attack last autumn. At his age he is simply awaiting the Lord's call. When he goes, he will be the last person at the Abbey with whom I have continued to correspond.
>
> . . . Everything is changing so much, in the world and in the Church. Even here people are waking up. I have on my table a box (!) of papers from the Bishops' Conference in view of a seminar (. . .) which has to study the new form to be taken by the Indian Church. I have to respond under two heads: spirituality and dialogue.
>
> . . . Last week I went on pilgrimage to the place of martyrdom of John de Britto (canonized in 1948), who died in 1693, about 200 kms from here. All those early Jesuit missionaries lived in the style which we have revived at Shantivanam, the style of Indian monks. It was therefore high time for me to make the pilgrimage, too long deferred, before leaving Tamilnad perhaps for good. The old chapel is very attractive; but unfortunately, ten years ago they built in front of it a horror that resembles a cinema hall. How gladly I would pray, if I dared, that a thunderbolt should fall on this horrible building, and that eventually they should build a church in the beautiful traditional Indian style.
>
> As for my journeys in my astral body—so say those who know—it is up to you to establish communication when that happens . . . A young Hindu told me last year that when he wanted my presence I came to him in a green halo . . . Can't you do the same? (MT, 15.3.68)

In the North—March to July 1968

Abhishiktananda left Shantivanam on 21 March and went to Indore, where Sr Térèse was staying with Mother Théophane. He wrote to Fr Lemarié:

> . . . Glad to know what you think of *Prayer;* but have no fear, the French version is not even begun, and I am going to be fully occupied all this year, including the preparation for an important Seminar (. . .).

> . . . M. Duperray has written to me very kindly [about Shantivanam]. The issue is not my longing for the North, but the excessively heavy financial burden of Shantivanam. (. . .) And then, among the traditionally-minded Christians and clergy of the south I cannot do anything. There is a distinct possibility in 1969 of some young priests wanting to have some months of training with me, but that would be impossible at Shantivanam. (. . .) For that we should have to be at a respectful distance from the official Church and in a fully Hindu environment. (L, 31.3.68)

After a fortnight at Indore he went up to Rishikesh, where Fr Francis was staying at the Sivananda Ashram. He spent Holy Week at Jyotiniketan (7-14 April), and then returned to his American friends at Rajpur, "where I am going to leave part of my belongings. (. . .) It is better not to keep too many things at Gyansu" (F, 19.4.68). The battered cartons—originally containing US Aid dried milk—in which his books were stored when not in use became very familiar to some of his friends!

Before returning to his hermitage he had to fulfil other engagements, and remained in Rajpur and Rishikesh for two more weeks:

> . . . Next Monday I have to take part in a meeting of priests at Saharanpur. They want to know about the kind of life I lead. (F, 19.4.68)
>
> . . . Even at Gyansu I shall be pursued by two young Jesuits who have permission to spend a month of their holidays in a Hindu setting and are at present in Rishikesh. The years to come look like being less peaceful than past years. The tug-of-war between solitude and the calls of the Church. (. . .) Good meetings with diocesan priests of Meerut and Lucknow. The Spirit is at work. Should one not help people to become attentive to this whisper and to recognize it? (L, 18.4.68)
>
> . . . Since Palm Sunday I have been rushing about or extending my stays in order to please one set of people or another. And only yesterday I was unable to refuse Fr Francis Mahieu, who wants me in Delhi on Friday to see the Archbishop and the secretary of the CBCI about the famous Seminar.
>
> . . . The two Jesuit scholastics have collected a mass of information (. . .); extraordinarily keen, but incapable of making their own that 'very interior' level of the spirit in which alone the experience of the OM is comprehensible. The falsity and inadequacy of the whole training of clergy and Christians! This is what should be brought home, in season, out of season, to those in charge. (TL, 30.4.68)

In Rishikesh Abhishiktananda and Fr Francis had made great efforts to find a place in which Sr Térèse might lead a retired life, but without success. He continued to think that her best hope was to find somewhere under the wing of the Sivananda Ashram, and in subsequent letters from Uttarkashi urged her to take the plunge and make her own arrangements, without relying on him or anyone else. Only so would she overcome her hang-ups and the 'timidity' which held her back. Recognizing that her ultra-sheltered convent background was largely responsible for retarding her growth to maturity ("though you have extracted yourself from it much better than others"), he recommended Ramana's 'method' of finding liberation as preferable to any others, e.g. psychological methods. (TL, 1.6.68; 8.6.68). He concluded:

> . . . You will probably feel that I have been harsh today. But I believe that in the end you will have to raise yourself to that authentic level in which you are *yourself.* If you continue to put up with your hang-ups, you are going to be absolutely incapable of anything whatever, the moment you lose the support of L. (TL, 8.6.68)

This 'L.' was a friend, not a Christian, about whom in an earlier letter she had expressed her anxiety. Abhishiktananda's reply was forthright:[105]

> . . . Be very sure that L. is not on the way to perdition. Her sincerity, her givenness to God, are total. The privilege, or the duty, of going to God by the (. . .) way of the Church is only given *de facto* to a minority. This does not mean that we should give up proclaiming the message of Christ, or (still less) preparing ourselves to preach it by living it. (TL, 30.4.68)
>
> . . . The contact with L. will have been providential for you, for in her you have someone for whom the Absolute is real, whereas for most people this is only an idea or an escape. (TL, 8.6.68)

Abhishiktananda finally reached Uttarkashi about 5 May, but even then was not alone, as Lalit came to join him for three weeks. During this time he obtained an electric connection. This had become essential because of the difficulty of obtaining petrol; but its cost so far reduced his funds that he had to abandon his plan for another pilgrimage to Gangotri (F, 2.6.69)

In a letter to O. Baumer he referred to a review of *Sagesse* and *Rencontre:*

> . . . I was very hurt by the review in *Verbum Caro.*[106] I had not expected such a lack of understanding from Taizé. They have not seen that it was a matter of giving information to the Church, on the same lines as that which comes from people who are in contact with atheism, and not of taking a theological position. I can only conclude that Taizé probably remains more 'Calvinist' than I had realized. I thought for a moment of writing to Fr Max [Thurian] whom I know, but what is the use? (OB, 31.5.68)

He went on to express his disappointment with recent books by Fr Déchanet and Fr Lassalle, the former of which he found dangerously 'superficial', and concluded:

105. Another example of his attitude to 'seekers':

"Poor J. who makes me sad. Seeking everywhere . . . If only she could make up her mind once for all. Even for Buddhism, if she likes. She is really running after herself without realizing it, like so many of these western followers of Hinduism or Buddhism. Once she has made up her mind—but at bottom she certainly has no wish for this—she will find her peace in the Other, even if it is the Buddha. (. . .) If she wants to be a Hindu or a Buddhist, let her become one for good. Only that total sincerity, with the sacrifice which it will involve will bring her to God, and Christ will one day reward her sincerity with full faith." (Th, 1.5.66).

106. *Verbum Caro.* no. 80 (1966), 78-80. The review suggested that Abhishiktananda's theology was dangerously syncretistic.

> . . . As I am more and more persuaded, the salvation of the world and of the Church lies in realizing that fundamental experience of the human being, of which the best expression so far seems to have been given by the Upanishads. Any construction that seeks to be solid has to be built on this unbreakable block. (OB, 31.5.68)

During his two months at Uttarkashi Abhishiktananda wrote a long paper (afterwards published as a book *Towards the Renewal of the Church*) in which he set out in detail his proposals for the spiritual renewal of the Indian Church. It was written for presentation at a meeting in Andheri (Bombay) in July, which was part of the country-wide preparation for the all-India Seminar planned for May 1969. He told his family:

> . . . This autumn and winter there are going to be a whole series of meetings all over India (. . .) and we have to get ready for them. I have to take part in one of them in Bombay in mid-July, which should set the tone for those which will come later. So I have to prepare and type out articles etc. There are also the attempts at an Indian Liturgy, in Sanskrit etc. All this has given me much more work than usual here, and that is why I have brought my typewriter—for which you will certainly be thankful! (F, 2.6.68)

The meeting in Andheri, for which Abhishiktananda and Fr Francis were chiefly responsible, was held under the auspices of the Organizing Committee of the Seminar, and brought together teams from the first five workshops—Spirituality, Liturgy and Catechetics, Evangelism, Dialogue and Indian Culture. In June Abhishiktananda shared with R. Panikkar his hopes for the meeting:

> . . . I am happy that you are coming to Bombay. This meeting could be very important. It is a matter of deciding the main themes to be worked out in the Church—to prevent it becoming "the grave of God"![107] Above all I should like to see some structures coming out of it which would be able to guide the aggiornamento—a "brains-trust', a 'study group', an official commission, call it what you will, but something with authority (. . .). Still better—and this could happen—a group of priests, not just specialists, but men determined to apply the new principles in their personal life and ministry, and to do so now. The other day I had a long talk with Patrick [D'Souza].[108] He would be the man to lead it (. . .) Something on the lines of the Mission de France.
>
> . . . Here I am totally isolated from the world (. . .). age makes itself felt, strength and vitality diminish year by year. It is time to withdraw. The calls that now come to me are coming too late. (. . .) The time for enthusiasm has passed. (RP, 21.6.68)

In addition to his preparations for the Andheri meeting, Abhishiktananda finally completed the rewriting of an earlier book (the account of his experiences with Gnanananda). To protect his anonymity, it was written in the third person,

107. A reference to a book of that title by R. Adolfs, London, 1967.
108. Patrick D'Souza was Deputy Secretary of the Catholic Bishops' Conference of India and Secretary of the All-India Seminar. He is now Bishop of Varanasi.

and he was disguised as "Vanya". Despite his feeling that it was 'unpublishable', he sent it for consideration to Le Seuil, with a second copy to Mrs Baumer (OB, 7.7.68)

The meeting took place in the Jesuit house at Andheri in July. Abhishiktananda seems to have forgotten about feeling old, and together with Fr Francis clearly made a great contribution, as the following account shows:

> There were about twenty-five participants, including the Organizing Committee of the Seminar, a representative from Archbishop's House, and one or two specially invited experts, and the group was small enough to reflect together as one body, instead of breaking up into smaller units. The two swamis, perched in *sukhāsan* on their chairs (causing mild apprehension, as the vigour of their gestures increased with their growing enthusiasm), did much to maintain a free and charismatic atmosphere and encouraged the spontaneous and creative exchange of views. It was an exhilarating experience, and Abhishiktananda's background paper, later published as *Towards the Renewal of the Indian Church,*[109] opened vast new horizons to many of those present. The findings had an important repercussion in the subsequent Seminar.[110]

In Bombay and Poona Abhishiktananda took the opportunity of trying out his liturgical experiments, which were well received on the whole, though the 'Indian Mass' at Poona led to some heated letters in the *Examiner:*

> . . . Very interesting meetings in Bombay and Poona, young Jesuits. The Indians have taken over, and are going ahead—at least, some are—under full sail with Indianization. Masses 'underground', but very fervent. My articles have helped, and it is catching on. So on Monday at Andheri, there were twenty young Jesuits; on Tuesday, at the end of the Mass there were twice that number present; on Wednesday, I had two concelebrants . . . and a camera! We are in course of pressing the bishops to give the necessary permissions—otherwise there will be explosions, often without much meaning. (L, 15.9.68)

Farewell to the South—August, September 1968

At the beginning of August Abhishiktananda went to Shantivanam to prepare for handing it over to its new occupants. Fr Francis had wished to install them immediately, but Abhishiktananda pleaded for more time (L, 19.7.68), and the date was fixed for 27 August (F, 1.9.68). Shantivanam and the Kavery were too much a part of him to be abandoned light-heartedly, and the departure was "a severe strain, both physically and morally", as he told his sister (MT, 2.10.68); "it moved me more than I had anticipated" (AMS, 15.9.68)

On 28 August when the party from Kurisumala arrived to install Fr Bede Griffiths and his two companions, they found the ashram deserted! Abhishiktananda had quietly left for Madras. Afterwards he made excuses for his conduct—for instance, that he had got the impression that they wanted him

109. Published by Dharmaram College, Bangalore, 1969.
110. Sr Sara Grant, in an earlier draft of this book.

out of the way—but the true reason for his disappearance can easily be guessed.

Before returning to the North he remained in Madras for a month's holiday at Santhome, where he took part in the opening of Aikiya Alayam, a centre for Hindu-Christian dialogue, founded by a Jesuit friend, Fr Ignatius Hirudayam.

> . . . On the shore of the ocean. My garden gives straight on to the beach, making it possible for me to take long walks in the morning and evening, and to sit for long periods beside the breakers. And then to plunge into them with just that slight feeling of anxiety that a shark might be eyeing me from afar . . . Is that not something to give immense joy to a Breton, born beside the Channel? (AMS, 15.9.68)
>
> . . . Came to Madras, a new centre for research and inter-faith dialogue, started by a Tamilian Jesuit. He wanted me for the inauguration. On the 8th we had a ceremony with worship in Hindu style etc., which was well received by the Archbishops, etc. There is already a small very well disposed nucleus of Hindus and Christians. Yesterday evening, with a group of Madras notabilities (. . .) preparations for a 'parliament of religions' in Madras at the beginning of 1969. I have to prepare a paper this week, which might be very interesting. (. . .) Always caught between calls from outside and the demands of a solitary life. From various angles people ask me what is the meaning of all I have written about the solitary life.
>
> . . . The English translation of *Rencontre* is ready, and a publisher has been found, a joint Catholic-Protestant enterprise.[111]

After discussing the reactions to *Humanae vitae:*[112]

> . . . it is not by applying the brake that accidents are avoided. The Jesuit theologians (about to be ordained priests) raise the most difficult questions and are not satisfied with easy answers. I say to anyone who will listen that here one of the most urgent undertakings is a theology of the 'meeting of religions'. (L, 15.9.68)

During his stay at Madras Abhishiktananda began some notes for Fr Hirudayam which were published in 1975 under the title *Abhishiktananda on Aikiya Alayam.*[113] In this there are four sections: (a) the significance for the Church of a centre which combines research and dialogue; (b) a description of the worship at the inauguration, devised so that Hindus and Christians could wholeheartedly take part; (c) the symbolism of *'dīpapūjā'* (worship with lights), explaining its Christian significance; and (d) suggestions how Christians in India might celebrate *'dīpāvalī'* (the festival of lights) and other great Hindu festivals, as a joyful expression of their own faith and also as a means of coming closer to their Hindu neighbours.

At the end of September Abhishiktananda bade farewell to Tamilnadu and went straight up to Uttarkashi.

111. *Hindu-Christian Meeting Point,* translated by Sr Sara Grant. First edition published in Bombay by a Catholic publisher jointly with C.I.S.R.S., Bangalore. Reprinted by I.S.P.C.K., Delhi.
112. The Encyclical of Pope Paul VI on conjugal relations.
113. Obtainable from Fr I. Hirudayam, Aikiya Alayam, Madras.

6

Gyansu—1968-1973

> From now on I shall normally be living here. Many people tell me I ought not to stir from here; but others complain if I do not go and spend a few days or weeks with them, whenever they want to see me! (MT, 2.10.68)

ABHISHIKTANANDA now had the chance to "disappear in the Himalayas", as he had often spoken of doing. Far more than had been the case at Shantivanam, he would be free from visitors, as foreigners were scarcely ever allowed into the border area, and his *kutiya* at Gyansu (the name of a small hamlet a kilometre or so from Uttarkashi) had barely room for one guest. In the following three years (1969-71) he was able to spend six to eight months each year in solitude; but he was constantly asked for help in various projects and conferences, or pressed to come and meet his friends. Though he declined many invitations, he felt that some of them had to be accepted. However, during the last year and a half before his heart-attack in July 1973 he was only able to spend about four months altogether at Gyansu. This was partly because of the operation which kept him in the plains during the last half of 1972, but mainly because of the arrival of a young Frenchman with whom, as a totally committed disciple, he was able to share his deepest experience, and they could only meet outside the border area.

During the last years of his life Abhishiktananda realized as never before the 'truth' of *advaita* and constantly stressed its vital importance for the world and the Church. His reflections concerning the impact of this truth on Christian faith grew bolder, even though they remained tentative, and only to a very slight extent did he feel that he was approaching an 'answer' to this problem. At the same time his enthusiasm for *sannyasa* (renunciation) and the acosmic life as a privileged response to the advaitic experience grew deeper, even while he reminded himself that *sannyasa* itself is a 'myth', ultimately only a sign.

Gyansu—October 1968

On reaching Gyansu he wrote to O. Baumer:

> . . . To be living here as a rule is going to be a new experience. I can scarcely hope to be that acosmic being of whom I wrote in *Gangotri* [*Une messe*], but at least I might be able to be something of that sort.
>
> . . . I have told you about the hopes, and also the anxieties, which the new generation of theologians here arouse. The most important prob-

lem at present is that which is posed to all religions by the need for self-transcendence, for truth, for sincerity, which is characteristic of the contemporary world. Advaita is a marvellous thing in itself: too often, alas, people make of it a kind of new super-religion, which is as unsatisfactory as all the formulas which claim to transcend this advaita, and is also very often unconcerned about the real problems of mankind. I have been very struck by Garaudy's article in one of the latest issues of *Concilium.*[1] Advaita, which is the highest experience of the mind, cannot isolate people and produce esoteric groups. As man's supreme act, it cannot cut the umblical cord. It takes a man out of himself, in order to bring him to his fullness as man. Is that not the deep meaning of the Resurrection? Everything dies, but everything is reborn. Advaita should result in the total integration of the whole man, and in the integration of each man in the totality of mankind. Religion is a form of service, not an end in itself. (OB, 1.10.68)

His sister had asked him some questions about the new Roman liturgy:

. . . You mention the [new] Canons [of the Mass]. I have just received them. They really belong to a beautiful Mediterranean tradition. India is waiting for something else; but how can we reconcile the Patristic tradition, the Vedantic tradition, and the aspirations of the modern spirit? I am still at the stage of the archaeology of Vedanta. Taking off from that, we should now speak in a language that makes sense to the man of 1970—for India too has reached the 70s.

. . . What is it that you want from me about liturgical prayer? I must say that it has stood me in good stead, but that now very often the only prayer that goes to my heart is the OM, somewhat at least as I have explained it in English and in French! (MT, 2.10.68)

Discussing the current crisis in the Church with another correspondent he returned once again to the need for contemplation:

. . . There is plenty of froth in the present 'high tide'; but even so this tide is healthy in its essential approach. It is the moment for contemplatives. But what a vibrant presence they should have in the world, and in the depth of their silence! Not an escape, but a penetration to the very heart. That is what now I should like to understand and to make understood—and, first of all, to live. Respect for contemplative values in the Church and the world will not come because we preach about them, but because in our life of deep silence we are totally human! (X, 20.10.68)

Visits and meetings—November to mid-December 1968

In November Abhishiktananda went to the Jyotiniketan ashram for another long session on the Upanishads. Once again Sr Térèse took part, as did an Italian

1. *Concilium* 35 (May 1968), 27-45. A plea from a Marxist humanist for the Church to take a lead in building a true humanism.

research student from Varanasi, Maria Bidoli, whom he saw as a possible partner for Sr Térèse:

> . . . We have had an excellent time. Spiritual work in studying the Bible and the Upanishads, plenty of household work, long prayers, long conversations, and the time passed quickly. With us also a Swiss Sister from Grandchamp (the Women's branch of Taizé), on her way to Vietnam to work in a leprosarium of the Sisters of St Vincent de Paul. Really a splendid person. (. . .) Catholics have no monopoly in serving Christ. (. . .) Térèse has really become strong, after this year of living 'as a person'. She went with Maria to Allahabad and Banaras, and courageously made the return journey by herself. It is likely that they will be able to settle in Allahabad (. . .). (Th, 24.11.68)

At the ashram there were also experiments in spontaneous liturgy:

> . . . French periodicals enable me to keep in touch. In fact I follow things very closely—to the surprise of my European visitors—perhaps more closely than a sadhu should. However I think it is necessary and an essential basis for my reflection on Hindu-Christian meeting. Otherwise I should remain a pure antiquarian. For example, after many experiments with a Sanskrit liturgy. I am in process of discovering a free liturgy (or "Free Church", as Murray says with a smile), even with a Canon composed in the evening before going to sleep, for Mass the next morning. This immediately held the group's attention, and you could *hear its silence* during this almost extempore prayer in bad English. It really rang true! (AMS, 24.11.68)

> . . . Each morning the liturgical celebration with readings and chants from the Indian Scriptures, and a homily based on the Gospel. Each celebration focussed on the present circumstances—I mean, on a day of sowing, all the texts were chosen accordingly; another day, when our Hindu neighbours had a festival in the river (Ram-Ganga), we read a hymn to the Waters from the Rig-Veda, Isaiah 50 [? 55] and John 4. The day of the Saints of the Benedictine Order (13 Nov.), we remembered in thanksgiving and prayer all the holy monks of every rite, etc. (OB, 24.11.68)

> . . . Here, sitting on the ground around the oblations, the celebration one morning by an R.C. (me), the other by Murray, on the 11th (St Martin) I expanded the Preface of the Eucharistic Prayer to include *all* bishops and *all* priests, commemorating Rome, Constantinople, etc. (. . .) For the first part of the Canon, one day I took Ephesians 1 (. . .), the other John 1:1-14 and 13:1. Each Eucharist should express its own 'individuality'—nothing pre-fab., even of the highest quality! (L, 14.11.68)

At Jyotiniketan they also discussed the reactions to the recent Papal Encyclical, *Humanae vitae*. Abhishiktananda saw it as a "crisis of authority", which "only an explosion will resolve" (L, 14.11.68).

From Bareilly he prolonged his tour to Varanasi to discuss the Seminar with R. Panikkar, then to Patna to see "some very dear Hindu friends" (probably

Ramesh's family), back to Allahabad to see the house where Sr Térèse and Maria Bidoli had settled and also to make contact with the Seminary; and finally to Agra, where he took part in a regional seminar, held in preparation for the All-India one:

> . . . It was the Bishop of Banaras who, almost peremptorily, attached me to the group of his delegates. I was so taken by surprise that I did not even have a chance of refusing. Basically, it was very instructive. The participants were in general open and well disposed, but mostly unaware of the serious nature of the present crisis, and so unable to think of the revolutionary solutions which are essential in many areas. Only a few progressive leaders, but they might have been able to stir the assembly (. . .) if it had not been for the bishops—at least, two out of the four present—who saw it as their episcopal duty to hold the train very firmly to its ancient tracks. When I tried to explain to one of them (. . .) the frustration and the crisis among seminarists, etc., his answer was: "They are misguided!"—and that was that. He also produced this pearl for us: "If the bishop is satisfied, everyone should be satisfied!" The man who presented the theme of dialogue could easily point out to them that what they were rejecting in his text was precisely what they had voted for at the Council. (. . .) Even so, faith and hope. The Indian Church is stirring, even if dangerously. The chief organizer of the Seminar remains very confident, and sees a change in people's mentality coming about. The National Seminar could be very powerful, since all the experts will be brought together. (L, 17.12.68)

Gyansu—15 December 1968 to 6 March 1969

Writing to his family before Christmas, he described his preparations for resisting the cold, by making the *kutiya* draught-proof, covering the windows with plastic, and using his immersion-heater to make cups of Nescafé. After twenty years he was looking forward to the feel of snow in hands, (F, 17.12.68) He also wrote to his sister at Kergonan:

> . . . You mentioned the other day that you had liked *Prayer.* Here too it has been very well received. May it awaken people to real prayer, that of silence in the heart, repeating the name of Jesus, or the Abba, or else the OM of the silence of the Spirit. Life is so good, despite everything, when you are awakened in the depth of the heart. And as for the circumstances of our life, whatever they may be, they are only the outward manifestation of the unique Presence. I am just now engaged on writing an article about Hindu spirituality, a spirituality of the Presence, for an English periodical.[2] (MT, 17.12.68)

At the end of January he took the opportunity of entrusting some letters to a friend who was going down to the plains (he always avoided posting foreign mail in Uttarkashi, for fear of causing suspicion). In one he told his family

2. "An Approach to Hindu Spirituality", *Clergy Review* (London), March 1969.

about the snow, the charcoal stove which he lit on cold evenings, and the 'bore' of having fused the immersion-heater. He returned to a familiar theme, that it was quite natural for people in our day, in their thirst for sincerity, to revolt against a stunted, formal and sentimental Christianity:

> . . . I am not greatly worried, when someone out of sincerity refuses to make certain gestures which no longer mean anything to him. But what I do ask of each one is to remain completely sincere with himself. (F, 23.1.69)

Mrs Baumer had asked him to tape-record addresses for a meeting, but he said:

> . . . I think I should be totally incapable of it; I need an audience which 'vibrates' to be able to speak usefully. And these things are too complicated for one born in a different age. (OB, 23.1.69)

In answer to her questions, he added:

> . . . The tension between Vedanta and Christianity is insoluble. I tried to go beyond it in *Sagesse*. The last chapter shows that I was unable to do so. Above all, because we try to judge *experiences* conceptually, from outside. "Who is asking the question?" Ramana would say. The danger of everything 'mystical' is that we enjoy it, delight in it, however little our spirit is attuned to this 'beyond mind'. At the summit, admittedly, the surrender is total—but on the way? Whoever still retains some *ahamkara* [egoism] should not even mention advaita. You cannot compare Gregorian with Honegger, or Mozart with the *vīnā* [an Indian stringed instrument]. Each of them is very fine; only from above could one pass a judgement (. . .). Otherwise you merely state your preferences (. . .).
>
> [With reference to his books] All is biographical—and nothing is! Everything comes from the experience of this tension, but everything has been rethought by the mind, in the halo of a double culture. The 'I' naturally is literary. Who has the right to say 'I', when he speaks of advaita? (OB, 23.1.69)

In a letter to New York he asked:

> . . . Why is it always necessary to stick the label 'Church' on everything that a Christian does?—like American gift-parcels ["Donated by the people of the U.S.A."].
>
> A renewal of faith? A faith that takes Christ's message seriously, but which does not blow its own trumpet. The 'good news'—what does that mean now to your Black people, to the Cubans—or here in India? The Jewish 'myth', in terms of which it was proclaimed (the kingdom of God), means nothing. 'Salvation'—from what? Do Christians give the impression of being saved people? Sinners they are, and sad like everyone else. The Church preaches salvation as an idea or as a myth. Who will believe it? Is not their faith only the complement of their conscious existence? Everything is good which gives the appearance of security. Where is the Spirit in the Church today? Those who

protest do so no more in the name of the Spirit than those who resist change.

... I am saved each morning by a long Mass (an hour or an hour and a half), all soaked in Indian texts (. . .), in Sanskrit, which might eventually result in an acceptable theology (. . .) The Hindu discovery of '*I am*', the only support that abides when everything collapses—everything that was founded on knowing. How the theology of Europe, even today's best, finally rings hollow *here.* (AMS, 25.1.69)

A surprising suggestion comes in a letter to Fr Lemarié:

... I sometimes ask myself if I might not be capable of going back to Kergonan, if one day my present life here becomes impossible. After all, once the essential is discovered, details matter so little. It is by way of his depth that the monk works, much more than by word or writing, as I constantly repeat in my articles!

... I fear that those who protest are at least as unprepared for dialogue as the conservatives! People criticize the Pope, and certainly 68 has been a year of terrible mistakes (. . .). However, in general, which of the protesters could provide an answer to the problem? (. . .) I have told you about the situation here. The ukase of the Bishop of Bangalore (in the name of the CBCI) has put an end to the semi-public experiments in liturgy. A controversy in the *Examiner,*[3] utterly stupid on the whole, was started by the 'Indian Mass' at Poona. (. . .) What is needed just now is not to make provisions for general use, but to make humble experiments in small groups. There is little realization that liturgical renewal springs out of spiritual renewal. From that point of view the CBCI's bludgeon can be a blessing. (L, 24.1.69)

The same letter mentions the articles on which he was working: one on Hindu spirituality (already mentioned), one on Sannyasa (only published in 1973/4),[4] and a study of the use of Hindu texts in the liturgy (published 1973).[5]

In March he had to descend to the plains, where much work awaited him, especially in connection with the All-India Seminar, including the proof reading of two books, *Meeting Point* and *Towards the Renewal of the Indian Church.* As regards *Gnanananda,* he had heard that Le Seuil had decided against publication:

... Now I am in a fix. If Mrs Lanvin or Mrs Baumer likes to publish, they are free to do so. But for me that means no income in 1971! (L, 5.3.69)

3. The correspondence began in the Examiner of 9.11.68, and was maintained vigorously until the end of the year, with editorials on Nov. 16 and 30.
4. "The Ideal of Sannyasa" in *Reflection* (Rajpur Centre, 1973); "L'idéal du Sannyasa" in *Revue Monchanin* (Montreal, 1974). It was also used as the first chapter in the longer essay on "Sannyasa", published in *The Further Shore.*
5. "Hindu Scriptures and Worship" in *Word and Worship,* Vol. VI, nos. 6 and 7, 187-195, 243-253.

In the plains—6 March to 18 April 1969

He first went to visit the new Carmel of Soso at Gumla in Ranchi District, recently founded as an offshoot from Shembaganur, and then the seminaries in Ranchi and Allahabad.[6] At the end of March his presence in Delhi was urgently requested by the team engaged on preparing the handbook for the Spirituality Workshop at the Seminar. According to one of the members, "his arrival transformed the situation and, installed at the CBCI Centre in New Delhi, he at once took control of affairs," so that the work was soon completed with much good humour. Until then he had hoped to escape having to take part personally in the Seminar, but his colleagues in Delhi overcame his hesitation and persuaded him to accept the invitation to be a member of the Spirituality Workshop, in the section devoted to "integrating Indian values in Christian spirituality".

One reason for his visits to the seminaries was to discuss some other projects about which he was greatly concerned at this time:

> . . . I have had long discussions at Ranchi, Allahabad and Delhi about the possibilities for a 'pilot seminary', study group, and the like. Everyone is in agreement. All that is lacking is men who are available. We are up against a blank wall. If we had detailed plans, we could get them passed at Bangalore. But the competent men are all fully occupied. (RP, 6.4.69)

While hard at work in Delhi, he only had time for a hasty note of Easter greetings to his family:

> . . . Just this to give my love to all and wish you the Joy of Easter. I would have liked to write about how marvellous Easter is, but my nieces would say that it is only my sales talk! So it is a good thing that I have no time this morning. (F, 1.4.69)

From Delhi he hastened to Jyotiniketan to celebrate Easter with the ashramites, who were joined by Sr Térèse and other friends:[7]

> . . . With several friends we have celebrated Holy Week ecumenically. We began the Paschal vigil with a kind of *homa* [sacred fire] before taking the New Fire and bringing it into the church. The reading of Genesis I was preceded by the reading of Rig-Veda 10.21, a marvellous hymn to the Creator (. . .). Naturally all that is not essential, the OM covers everything; but for human and religious communion symbols are necessary, and it is good for those who live in solitude to act out with others, using precisely these symbols, the great mystery which nothing can fully express. (OB, 9.4.69)
>
> . . . This week I have been meditating and speaking about the "Touch me not!" Jesus was amazed that people needed him to appear to them. He never appeared to John or to his Mother! Mary and John believed, they had no need for all these outward things. The manifestation of God

6. It may have been on this visit to Allahabad that, on the invitation of Fr Bhatt, he addressed the students; his address "Preparation of Seminarians for Ecumenical and Inter-religious Dialogue" is in the Society's archives.
7. M. Bidoli, U.M. Vesci and B. Bäumer.

> in every being, in every person, is so much more important than all those 'quasi-revelations' in which, alas, so many Christians delight. God has spoken in his Son, that is enough for me. I have the presence in the Eucharist, the presence in the Church. That is the great thing. The present crisis in the Church will only really be overcome when people enter more and more deeply and truly into the invisible mystery of the Spirit. Mary Magdalene thought she saw a gardener, Cleopas a passer-by. Jesus made himself known, and disappeared. "It is to your advantage that I go away." Otherwise you would be too attached to my flesh, my appearance. That is what I have tried to say in *Prayer,* etc. And it grieves me to see Christians here and in the West, when offered a banquet furnished with the choicest dishes and wines, contenting themselves with a crust of bread and lemonade! (MT, 14.4.69)

After Easter he went to Allahabad (temperature 43 degrees) to "check with a Hindu pandit my proposed Sanskrit Mass and Canon" (OB, 9.4.69). At Hardwar, on his way back to Gyansu, he wrote to one of his sisters, telling her about the coming Seminar, and adding:

> . . . You sometimes tell me that my life is so difficult to understand. In fact, it was hardly my own choice, it has landed on me from above, day after day, year after year. And truly it is marvellous. If at least I could pass on to the Christian world the honey which I gather in the Hindu world, and vice versa, however dislocating it may sometimes be. Even so, it is a great joy, and the answer to the contradictions which rack Church and world! I am keeping the rest of my speech for the Bangalore Seminar! (ALG, 18.4.69)

Gyansu—18 April to 8 May 1969

After only three weeks at Gyansu he had to face the four-day journey to Bangalore for the Seminar. Before leaving, he wrote to Kergonan:

> . . . This year you will have a letter for the Ascension (. . .). Once again I shall come down from my eyrie on the 8th.
>
> . . . What matters now is that there should be a great renewal of spiritual experience, and alas, I see scarcely any trace of it in what I receive from Europe. (. . .) It is precisely the grace of the Ascension that we all need. Have you ever read the magnificent sermon-letter of Bossuet on this theme? Everything sensible disappears, everything conceptual disappears, all that is left is the pure experience of Jesus in the Spirit, beyond all forms. The experience of Jesus in the *atman*, as we should say here. Nothing of what is 'felt', and yet the 'sense' of the Spirit is more real than all that is 'felt'. (MT, 5.5.69)

All-India Seminar, Bangalore, etc.—15 May to about 20 June 1969

Abhishiktananda made an effective contribution to the Seminar.[8] Apart from sharing in the reflections of his own Workshop, he followed with interest the

8. The Seminar met in Dharmaram College, Bangalore from 15-25 May. A report, *All India Seminar: Church in India Today,* was published in New Delhi, 1969.

proceedings of several other Workshops and was constantly in demand for consultation between sessions. Three of his books were on sale, including *Prayer.* He also encouraged the efforts of a group of priests from Kerala (Carmelites of Mary Immaculate), who at the request of their bishop (the late Cardinal Parecattil) had been working on the development of an Indian liturgy inspired by the Syro-Malabar rite.[9] On several occasions he made interventions in the intermediate and general assemblies, one of which was recalled:

> . . . No one who was present will ever forget the (. . .) vision of Swamiji at the mike, addressing himself to it from a respectful distance of several feet, and totally absorbed in the effort to enunciate a to him all-important amendment insisting on the need for a deeply interior spirit in the celebration of the Indian liturgy, if it was to be true to the age-old contemplative tradition of the country. Noting the gap between speaker and microphone, the moderator asked gently: "Could you come a little nearer, father?"—whereupon, after a moment's puzzled reflection, Swamiji meekly and firmly seized the mike and advanced several paces up the centre of the hall, to the immense delight of the Assembly![10]

In several letters he gave his assessment of the Seminar:

> . . . You will have seen (. . .) about our Seminar (. . .). It was excellent, despite some foot-dragging over details. A decisive step forward, by a Church at last aware of itself, in the best sense. The [slow] speed of daily life in India, political or religious, is deceptive with regard to its underlying values. I would never have dared to hope for such a successful Seminar. Despite our serious anxieties and doubts, the bishops integrated themselves with the 'people of God' with perfect courtesy, simplicity and discretion. This dialogue was surely the most important result of the Seminar. But there were also some excellent resolutions, introduced by some very fine theological texts. Strong emphasis on spiritual renewal, on a prayer of *interior silence.* Our task now is to put it into *practice*; people want this, and are already making a start. They are setting up a commission on spirituality to organize service teams—priests, nuns and laity—for this initiation into deep prayer. What we shall need even more will be the formulation of a basic theology to undergird this renewal—the place of non-Biblical traditions in the Salvation History. (L, 10.6.69)
>
> . . . I regard Bangalore—and this is generally agreed—as a very important stage in the awakening of the Church here. The Church realizing itself as the people of God, no longer only as the hierarchy. (. . .) Not a revolution, of course. (. . .) However, reports and conclusions on the whole excellent, going far beyond the pettiness of the discussions. The conservative opposition was very talkative—as in the

9. See *New Orders of the Mass for India* (N.B.C.L.C., Bangalore), 1974, 63ff.
10. "Swamiji—the Man" by S. Grant, *Clergy Monthly,* Vol. 38, no. 11; 487-8.

> [Vatican] Council—but the votes showed clearly that they were not in a majority, far from it. The fundamental options were passed with big majorities, even if it had to be through amendments. I left Bangalore feeling very optimistic. There is still much to be done; but we now have an excellent starting point.
>
> . . . Above all, as I constantly repeat, we need a renewed theology. The youth is calling for it, and needs it urgently to escape from the crisis. But here team-work is essential. Individuals alone are useless.
>
> Despite the slogan, "Work is prayer" a very strong emphasis was placed on real prayer (. . .). I got very large majorities for two amendments, one calling for ashrams of pure 'prayer and silence', the other for a liturgical renewal in depth, drawing on the values of Indian interiority. Besides, [Cardinal] Pignedoli in his opening address laid an unlooked-for stress on "the Indian Church as above all a community of prayer", on monastic life and on small ashrams to be available in many places. Now that there are going to be such centres, I am sure people will come to them, for many are desirous of being initiated into this real prayer. (RP, 25.6.69)

On his way back from Bangalore, Abhishiktananda stopped in Bombay and took part in a meeting which gave him particular pleasure. He mentioned it in a letter to one of his sisters:

> . . . in Bombay for a few days, when I took part in a week on 'prayer and the spiritual life', for men and women students, among whom were included an admixture of Jesuit seminarists and novices of the Sacred Heart (RSCJ). Unbelievable the interest of these young people in such questions. Mostly Catholics, but some Hindus also, who were not the least active in contributing to the discussion. On the last evening I celebrated Mass for them in Indian style, according to their expressed desire. (ALG, 14.6.69)

In the last-quoted letter to Fr Lemarié he referred to his correspondence with would-be disciples from the West, and said: "Last month it was a seminarist from Bourg." This is his first reference to Marc Chaduc, whose letter gave him the impression that he was a serious applicant and drew from him an encouraging response (MC, 5.5.69) They continued to correspond, until Marc reached India in October 1971.

The same letter also mentions his financial problems:

> . . . I shall certainly have need of money before the end of the year. My reserves here have dwindled. Shall I one day have to write 'to order', so as to restore my finances? I only believe in writings which come from 'inspiration'. (L, 10.6.69)

Gyansu—about 20 June to 5 October 1969

Abhishiktananda remained in Gyansu for the next three and a half months, apart from a brief descent to Rishikesh in August to see Mrs Lanvin. During the monsoon he made a garden round his kutiya, surrounding it with barbed wire. Here he planted various fruit trees and cultivated a vegetable plot (F, 24.8.69). In these days, no doubt to save time for his work, he employed a boy to cook his midday meal (rice, split peas, potatoes and marrow, all cooked together), and also allowed himself half a litre of milk daily.

There was plenty of writing to be done, as he told Fr Lemarié, when declining a suggestion that he might produce an article on the Seminar:

> . . . At present I am only too busy with occasional articles: one in English on monasticism,[11] one on Gandhi,[12] several on women hermits (. . .),[13] an important one in English on dialogue, [14] which has entirely diverted my attention for the last two weeks, and still does not satisfy me. What a false sadhu, un-free, all this business makes me! (L, 20.7.69)

He might also have mentioned a venture into journalism, an article for syndication by Catholic News Service of India called "Theological Commission needed for Indianization of the Church"[15]

Sr Térèse had left Allahabad to spend three months in solitude at Bhowali (Kumaon Hills). She was still troubled by fears and scruples, about which Abhishiktananda wrote to her firmly, inviting her to be truly free:

> . . . See how free you are in taking big decisions and how anxious about minutiae. (. . .) The Christianity of 'fish on Fridays' (. . .) as people say now. It is Christ's love that we have to radiate—Christ the radiance of God, the God within! That is why I am delighted that you have been without Mass and Communion for a month or so. Remember the hermits of Bl. Albert.[16] The Church needs that witness, which cannot be codified or institutionalized. The deep reason for the present crisis is the exaltation of human laws above the Lord and of theology above experience of God (TL, 26.7.69)
>
> . . . Naturally I know by my own painful experience that liberation is easier to explain than to realize. However, to see things clearly is a first step. (TL, 6.8.69)

In the follow-up of the Seminar there were a number of projects in which Abhishiktananda's help was sought, especially in the next two years (as will be seen)—for example, the 'pilot seminary', the centre for Hindu studies, the wider dissemination of contemplative prayer through ashrams. He was interested in all these projects, but his deepest concern was for theological renewal, which he saw as the Church's most urgent need. Without this renewal it would not be

11. "Monasticism and the Seminar", *Examiner,* 16 and 23 August, 1969.
12. "Gandhi, témoin de la vérité", *Annales de Ste Thérèse de Lisieux,* 1970, no. 1, 15-17. Reprinted in *Les Yeux,* 121 ff.
13. "Femmes ermites hindoues", *Vie Thérésienne,* Lisieux, Vol. 10, no. 37, 14-18. (This article, dated 22.7.69, is derived from *Souvenirs d'Arunachala,* ch.4.) "Femmes ermites en Inde", *Les amis du Bec-Hellouin,* Nos. 32-33 (1970-71), 32-38. (Also dated 22.7.69; more general in content.)
14. The Depth-Dimension of Religious Dialogue", written for *Asia Focus* in 1969, but too long to be used. It appeared in *Vidyajyoti* in 1981 (see Bibliography).
15. *Catholic News Service of India* (Delhi), 30 August, 1969.
16. Probably Albert of Vercelli, who drew up a Rule for the Carmel.

able to deal with the 'crisis' which in various forms it was now having to face. For Abhishiktananda the deepest aspect of the crisis lay in the now unavoidable meeting of Christian faith with the experience of the East. This issue, which he first met with piercing intensity at Arunachala in the 50s (and which in the intervening years he perhaps felt somewhat less acutely, though it never left him), now became his first priority. He was dismayed at the apparent inability of western theologians, shown for instance in their reviews of his book, even to see it as an issue at all:

> . . . I feel that the West is shut up within its own dimensions. How can one tell it this? I no longer know the language of the West; and so few of you are open to our language here. The problem of Christianity-Vedanta is crucial—much more so than the problem of Christianity-Humanism. Your theologians know nothing of it. And the Church here is equally ignorant, despite the splendid awakening of Bangalore. But this problem will soon be terribly acute here, when the young people who are coming up have drunk directly from the sources of this Vedanta, and no longer only from the pasteurized bottles which they find here and there! (L, 20.7.69)

One of the very few theologians—perhaps the only one—who in Abhishiktananda's view was addressing the problem, was his friend Raymond Panikkar. They had now been sharing their thoughts for the past ten years. He had welcomed Panikkar's book, *The Unknown Christ of Hinduism*, and felt that his friend had written far more boldly than he had so far dared to do, for example, in *Sagesse (Saccidananda)* chapter 5. The following letter shows his readiness to follow the truth wherever it may lead, no matter how unpalatable the conclusions to which it may point:

> I have just received *Concilium* 46. I have read your article [Métathéologie et théologie diacritique]. I at once began a long letter, but it soon turned into an article, and I don't know when it will be finished.[17] So just a hasty word.
>
> I am absolutely in agreement with your principles, those of Rahner, etc. However, this number of *Concilium* is more devastating than any of its predecessors. Total overthrow of formulas and structures. I agree that there is no way of avoiding it. But what a crisis! Comparable to the passing over of primitive Christian experience—expressed in mythico-apocalyptic terms and largely dependent on inspiration and prophetic freedom (. . .)—to its expression in terms of Greek knowledge and Roman law. What saved the Church then was the deep spiritual experience of the 'Fathers'. That alone made possible the faithful translation of the Gospel and Acts in terms of the four Councils.
>
> But that is not the point that interest me today. The disputes between Christianity and the modern humanist world are merely a local squabble. Christianity remains the only religious alternative to western human-

17. Probably the article, "Archétypes religieux, expérience du Soi et théologie chrétienne", completed in July 1970; published in *Intériorité,* 177 ff.

ism. That is why the protests, like the calls to order, fail to touch our 'depth' here. Paul, Bultmann and Garaudy belong to the same world. What is emphasized in your article—indeed this is your greatest contribution to international conferences of theologians—is your constant reminder that there are other cultural-religious universes besides the Semito-Greek world of the Mediterranean. (. .)

The passage from Jewish to Greek Christianity involved a dangerous bringing to birth. It succeed chiefly because there was no other religious alternative, and humanism, despite Seneca and Cicero, could not take the place of the 'religions' for the common man. But here? There is an absolutely adequate religious alternative. Hinduism is capable of responding at least as well as Christianity to India's religious needs, even in modern conditions. But that is not all. In being born into the Greek world it was a matter of transmitting the Christian experience in terms of *knowing*. Here it is a matter of expressing it in relation to the fundamental experience of the *Self*. Can Christianity stand up to that? The whole salvation-history culminating in Christ presupposes a substructure of psychological dualism. India certainly accepts dualism as an aspect, a moment, in the quest for salvation. You have very well shown that Christ and *Īśvara* [God manifested] fulfil an identical role in the two systems; but my conclusion from that is that, in an Indian interpretation of salvation-history, Christ shares the transitoriness of the world of manifestation, of *māyā*. Finally he disappears (. . .). He may be useful in awakening the soul—as is the guru—but is never essential and, like the guru, he himself must in the end lose all his personal characteristics. No one really needs him. (. . .) Whoever, in his personal experience (. . .) has discovered the Self, has no need of faith in Christ, of prayer, of the communion of the Church. (. . .)

The reformulation of the Trinitarian mystery is also on the agenda in Europe, and in the first place, the abandonment of all that implies triplicity. But here, much more than that is in question. What is the meaning of this unique Son of God? For an advaitin *anubhavi* [one who has experience of advaita] Christ can only be the ideal in human terms (i.e., at the level of manifestation) who has best actualized the mystery and the experience of the *AHAM* [I] which is not-two! (. . .) The Son, the universal *mūrti* [image] of God; the Spirit, the universal *sakti* [dynamic energy] of God. When the *atman-brahman* is discovered in the *sarvam idam* [all that is] and in the depths of the phenomenal *aham,* there no longer remain any points of reference in the advaita of being, by which to set bounds to *murti* or *sakti . . .*

Will the transformation of Christianity into Vedantin formulas leave to it any other reality than the (provisional) reality of the cults which have succeeded each other on the soil of Bharat? And if Christianity cannot be expressed in the religious-cultural terms of India without dissolving away, then it is not *catholic*. I do not see how one can escape from this dilemma. (. . .) All this is the result of your article, and indirectly of the others. (RP, 10.7.69)

Abhishiktananda continued to grapple with this fundamental problem in the following years (as is shown in the *Diary* and in various essays which were published posthumously in *Intériorité et révélation*). He did not put much faith in his own attempts to probe the mystery, but longed for the day when the Indian Church would begin to take the question seriously. Many other letters at this time express his concern:

> . . . It is this question of theology which most stirs me up at present. I regard it as the most pressing of all—first in India, and then for the whole Church. How can one bring it home to the would-be theologians and liturgists that in their articles etc. they only touch the surface of the problems? Who ever thinks of a dialogue at the level of *interiority?* [17a]
>
> . . . It is only from long acquaintance with the Scriptural texts—and a corporate acquaintance—that a truly Indian liturgy will emerge. Nowadays people think that they only have to use the word *saccidananda* etc. to make a Canon Indian! (RP, 9.8.69)
>
> . . . Like you, I believe strongly in the role of the Far East in the Church of the future, but it must be mediated through the local Churches. (. . .) The further I go, the more I feel this confrontation at the very *heart* of the two religions, and it is also in our own heart that we should know by experience this shattering 'face to face'. I find it more and more difficult to see how to integrate Christianity with Hindu experience—and yet this is essential for catholicity. (. . .) How to carry through the present mutation of Christianity without obscuring its essence? But what is its essence? Its intellectual and social structures are so overlaid with what is in the end only a moment of history which men unfortunately absolutize. However, as long as anyone has not reached the very ground of Vedantin experience, how can he understand that all is essentially 'becoming' without falling into relativism? (. . .)
>
> "Christ is risen!"—"I am"; the two-fold experience of a single mystery. (AMS, 24.8.69)
>
> . . . I am busy with articles (. . .). Where is the beautiful freedom of the sannyasi who never has any obligation whatever, the glorious freedom of the children of God? It is only in this meditation beyond all problems that the solution of all problems will be found. The Upanishads are marvellous. However, their form of thought is even more unintelligible for the 20th century than that of the Torah! It all needs to be restated afresh by a master. But the so-called Hindu Masters of today are either too speculative or too emotional. I had the grace of meeting Ramana and Gnanananda (. . .) and it was truly at their feet that I learnt something from the Upanishads. (. . .) We need a Master (. . .) who will have passed through—or rather, passed beyond—the shattering confrontation of the Gospel (I do not even say, of the Church) with the Vedantin experience. (OB, 24.8.69)
>
> . . . My problem and concern at present is for an Indian theology—which at the same time puts forward a Theology of Religions

17a. cp. "The Depth-Dimension of Religious Dialogue" (*Vidyajyoti* 1981, p. 202).

(cp. *Concilium* 46) and also extracts a theology of the Christian revelation, starting from the Vedantin experience of 'self-awareness'.

I have been told that *Revue Thomiste* has published a severe review (of my books), even more so than *Nouvelle revue théologique,* from the point of view of scholastic philosophy.[18] How the sense of the mystery of experience is lacking in even the best Christian brains of Europe! Yet now, after a second edition of *Prayer,* they are preparing for a second English edition of *Gangotri.* The message is going over all the same. (L, 26.8.69)

At the beginning of October Abhishiktananda was called away from Gyansu for some important meetings in the plains. Before leaving he wrote to Marc Chaduc, the French seminarist who hoped to join him, stressing the unlikelihood of his being able to remain permanently in India.

> . . . The essential thing is to penetrate the *interior mystery* to which India bears witness so intensely. Whether later on you radiate this in the western or the Indian Church is a secondary matter. Without a contemplative 'sense', to come to India is absolutely useless. Come to receive; don't seek to give, any more than the rose or the lily. Your interiority will radiate of itself, whether the surroundings are Christian or Hindu. Be concerned to *be* and not to *do* (. . .), or even to understand intellectually (. . .). Give a sabbatical year at least to your Mind! (MC, 29.9.69)

A few months earlier there had been various controversies in the Catholic press, some of which involved Abhishiktananda. In particular, a Dominican of Nagpur wrote a hostile article in the *Examiner,*[19] which was clearly aimed at him, though without naming him. It received a forthright answer from a Sister of the Sacred Heart. In connection with these controversies he said to Fr Lemarié

> . . . Controversies about liturgy are continuing in the Catholic weekly. What a religion—formalist, and practically pagan—has been established here, as . . . says: What infuriates people in Bombay is [the greeting with] joined hands, bowing or prostrating instead of genuflecting, and the use of oil lamps! All that is 'pagan'. I have just sent a letter to the Editor, saying that if joining hands is pagan, then we are all saying mass in pagan fashion, and if prostrating is pagan, then so also have been our ordinations! O for worship in spirit and truth! (L, 3.10.69)

In a letter to his sister at Kergonan he recalled that she had now reached the same age as his was, when he came to India:

> . . . All my 'little sisters' are still for me at the same age that they had when I left, the age now of their daughters and nieces. I love the

18. *Revue thomiste,* Vol. 69 (1969), 94ff (on *Sagesse, Rencontre* and *Une messe*). *Nouvelle revue théologique,* Vol. 88 (1966), 1114-5 (on *Sagesse* and *Rencontre*).
19. "An Open Letter on Indianization", *Examiner,* 19 July 1969; responded to in "Indianization: an Open Answer to an Open Letter", *Examiner,* 2 August 1969. The controversy continued for several issues.

sincerity of these girls (. . .). I know where I am with them. Their life with God will probably be very different from ours, caring little for forms, but no less *true* for that, even if they disconcert the old fogeys that we are becoming. (. . .)

I wrote to Fr Landry for his jubilee (60th of his profession). He replied at once, and I have written again today. One who has always led a 'hidden' life, but who in his last years shows the depth and the truth with which he has given himself to God. It is when the body fails that you find out whether the piety has been only a veneer or a deep reality. (. . .)

I wish you joy at all times, in all the details of life. (. . .) I am not interested in "the sun that dances";[20] I have a sun that shines motionless in the depth of my heart, which neither rises nor sets, as says the Upanishad; the real Sun which gives light to the Temple of the Apocalypse—and this temple is within! (MT, 2.10.69)

Delhi, Banaras, Jyotiniketan—5 to about 27 October 1969

The purpose of Abhishiktananda's journey in October was to discuss some practical steps towards implementing some of the resolutions of the Seminar in which he was specially interested. He therefore went first to Delhi to meet Fr Patrick D'Souza (Deputy Secretary of the CBCI), who was one of those responsible for the follow-up of the Seminar; then to Banaras, to discuss with R. Panikkar the plans for promoting inter-faith dialogue; and finally to Jyotiniketan, where he met Fr J. Dupuis (of the Jesuit seminary at Kurseong) and Murray Rogers. Fr Dupuis was specially interested in having a centre where experiments could be made in training clergy on new lines, which would be relevant to present day India. With Murray Rogers Abhishiktananda had above all to discuss the future of the Jyotiniketan ashram itself, for this had become an urgent question.

Before leaving Jyotiniketan Abhishiktananda wrote a long letter to Fr D'Souza, giving an account of their discussions, and putting forward an ingenious proposal, aimed at solving all the problems at one blow. Briefly, this envisaged a new centre, bringing together an ecumenical ashram (Jyotiniketan plus Roman Catholic members), a pilot seminary and a dialogue centre. It would be located somewhere in North-east India, within reach of Kurseong. Detailed plans could be prepared at a conference at Banaras in the coming December. However, some new factors in the situation emerged soon afterwards, which prevented the proposal from being followed up.

The chief problem at Jyotiniketan was that the ashram had never succeeded in attracting any younger, especially Indian, members. The original three, conscious that the years were passing, felt that they had come to a dead end. Then, unexpectedly, an invitation came from the Abbess of the Russian Monastery in the Garden of Gethsemane, who seven years previously had invited them to settle in Jerusalem as a community. She now proposed that they should open a centre of

20. A reference to the apparitions at Fatima in Portugal.

prayer and meeting in the holy city itself, to which people of all faiths could come. It was an offer that had to be taken very seriously.

To Abhishiktananda the thought that the ashram might be closed (or, if not closed, that it would inevitably take a different form) was horrifying. Quite apart from all that it meant to him personally,[21] he saw the ashram as very significant for the renewal of the Church, and knew of nothing that could take its place. He therefore at once sought ways of meeting the problem of widening its membership, and sent a number of possible Catholic recruits to the ashram.

At the same time a completely different possibility for the future of Jyotiniketan came into view. Plans were being considered for an ecumenical development of the Christa Prema Seva Ashram in Poona, originally an Anglican Franciscan foundation. The Sisters of the Sacred Heart were interested in the project, and the Visitor of the ashram (Bishop Robinson of Bombay) and its Trustees were also in favour of it, provided an effective Anglican participation could be ensured. A warm invitation was given to Jyotiniketan to migrate to Poona, and to Murray Rogers to assume the leadership of the ashram in its new form. Abhishiktananda thought this was an excellent suggestion, and promised to give all the support and help that he could.

Gyansu—end of October 1969 to early January 1970

On his return to Gyansu Abhishiktananda found in his mail a questionaire regarding priestly formation, which he was asked to complete in preparation for an important meeting on seminary training, to be held under CBCI auspices at Bangalore. This provoked some radical reflections in a letter to R. Panikkar:

> . . . I am in process of trying to understand the 'secular priest', i.e., a man committed to marriage and a secular profession, who at the same time is in charge of the Christian community. My contact with Murray has convinced me at the same time of the sacerdotal value of the 'couple' in the case of the married priest, and also of the terrible limitations imposed by the children on his freedom for the Kingdom and the apostolate. My experience is only of the 'monk-priest', the only normal type in the latin Church in recent centuries. Even with regard to this I am not sufficiently in touch with other people to be able to see what ought to be done in present circumstances for the renewal of priestly formation. I have insisted on the values of contemplation, of poverty, of initiation into Hindu tradition. But how, in fact, can this be carried out? Years ago I proposed my 'pet scheme' of a Pilot Seminary, but I cannot get further than general principles. (RP, 29.10.69)

Mrs Baumer had asked him to suggest a book on meditation:

> . . . Your request for a book on meditation makes me smile. In the wake of the Bangalore Seminar there are endless meetings and symposiums. When I came back the other day, I found two long questionaires to complete for consultations about seminary training, etc. They asked me for 'formulas' for spiritual exercises. I replied: What you need is a

21. See "Swamiji—the Friend" (see chapter 5 note 10).

> guru, you need men who are interiorly open, who have the sense of the Presence. Automatically they will find the way to communicate their experience to those disciples who are aware of the Presence. As regards books on meditation, I skimmed through so many of them when I was in the seminary at Rennes, forty years ago. But probably the supplement that I shall add to the French edition of *Prayer* will answer your wishes (. . .) I shall write it this winter, if I am free.
>
> . . . Personally I know very little about Sufism, but it is certainly Sufism that has made it possible to breathe in Islam. For me the way of the Upanishads is enough. But whatever path you come to it, it is the awareness of this Presence which must be reached. And when that is found, then you are free and need nothing more—not even God, as Gnanananda would say! for God no longer has to be found and possessed—he is himself my "I am". (OB, 9.11.69)

In the next two months Abhishiktananda concentrated on the French version of *Prayer:*

> . . . All this month I have been immersed in the French translation of *Prayer*—at last! So many people have asked for it, and they are already at work on the Italian and German translations. It is now almost as difficult for me to write in French as it is in English. I constantly have to refer to the dictionary, and continually have doubts about style. I expect to be finished by the end of December.
>
> . . . The cold has begun (. . .). I usually type *Prayer* on my verandah. I am really afraid of the cold here, because the normal protection against the cold (which would enable me to work as effectively as in the summer) is beyond most people's means, and when I see my neighbours I am ashamed of all that age forces me to have. (L, 5.12.69)

(Abhishiktananda's difficulty in writing French after twenty years in India is clearly shown in his correspondence. Apart from the increasing number of English words and phrases that sprinkle his letters, he was quite capable of using French words with a meaning that they only have in English.)

A letter to R. Panikkar discusses *Prayer* and an invitation to visit Canada:

> . . . To my translation of *Prayer* I have been recently tempted to add a final chapter, "In Spirit and in Truth",[22] which would express in clear and non-symbolic terms the charge of high explosive contained in this essay, demythologizing the language used throughout the book, and pointing (what else could one do?) to the experience of Ramana and Yajñavalkya[23] in all its purity. But who is ready for this strong dose?
>
> Yesterday I received an invitation from Canada, from a Christian yoga group near Montreal, for two or four weeks in June-July to give weekly sessions of initiation into Vedanta. They say that 'yoga' (what do they mean by that?) is spreading more and more—yoga groups conducted by swamis which are now leading Christians astray from

22. This essay, called "Le chrétien en vérité", is printed at the end of the French edition of *Prayer* (*Éveil à soi—éveil à Dieu*). The English version (1989) is called *In Spirit and Truth.*
23. Yajñavalkya was the great *rishi* of the Brihadaranyaka Upanishad.

their faith. 'Christian yoga groups' which have fully made their own the Vedantin experience (I am interpreting slightly) are needed to counterbalance this influence. Even though people quote Déchanet[24] as an authority, they have the impression that Déchanet is too 'sectarian' (to use our term) a Christian. This could be very interesting, but a journey to America would also mean a journey to Europe, and I should be caught up indefinitely . . . On the other hand, I have grave doubts about the depth of all this. They want a Vedanta adapted for westerners, the sort of thing that is freely dispensed by the swami commercial-travellers in Vedanta. I have just replied that sessions of spiritual initiation into Vedanta lasting one or two weeks are for me absolutely inconceivable. In any case, the monk is not called to go running round the world. (RP, 5.12.69)

In the coming year Abhishiktananda was due to reach his sixtieth birthday. Some of his friends thought that the occasion should be suitably marked, but this aroused his vehement opposition:

> . . . The interest that I arouse is restricted to a very limited circle. My withdrawal to the Himalayas perhaps adds a mythical touch to my personality. In any case, I cannot imagine where you have 'fished up' this idea of a commemorative volume. As I said to Murray, when he tried to get me invited to the West, it would be a betrayal of all that I stand for, solitude, silence and monastic poverty; I have no more sought solitude than Amos sought the role of a prophet, but once placed in that position, nothing else remains for me but to be a hermit for good, and not a mere salesman of solitude and monastic life. (RP, 11.12.69)

Some remarks about the 'pilot seminary' which follow, suggest that he now preferred to distance himself from the project about which he had dreamed:

> . . . Some years ago I dreamed about this pilot seminary, with the idea that in a Gandhian type of ashram there could be an initiation into classical India, so vital for the development of the Church here. But now we have to rethink the whole conception of what a priest is. While gladly accepting these new points of view, I feel myself absolutely out of my depth. I am incapable of the mental revolution required to share these new categories well enough to help others to find their way in them. (RP, 11.12.69)

A few days later a letter came from Jyotiniketan which greatly disturbed him. When the proposal was mooted that the community might move from Bareilly and take part in the ecumenical ashram at Poona, Abhishiktananda had welcomed it and offered his help. Unfortunately his friends read far more into this than he had ever intended. They now told him what they expected of him—that he should join them for several months at Poona to organize the new set up, and thereafter should be prepared to spend several months there each year. For several good reasons he found this an impossible suggestion—the distance and expense of travel (for him increasingly important factors), the unfamiliar lan-

24. Author of *Christian Yoga*, etc.

guage of the area (Marathi), and not least, his grave doubts about his ability to work closely together with another strong personality with a rather different viewpoint form his own. But what particularly grieved him was that, rightly or wrongly, he understood them to be saying that, unless he was willing to accept his 'responsibility' for Poona, they would withdraw from the project and instead prepare to leave India for good. This of course was the last thing that Abhishiktananda wanted to happen.

At this point he deeply felt his isolation at Gyansu, where there was no friend at hand with whom he could talk things over. He could only write to R. Panikkar, who was soon setting off for Europe, and share his disquiet on this and other matters (RP, 19.12.69). Then, after waiting a few days so that his letter should not spoil their Christmas, he wrote to tell his friends at Jyotiniketan why he could not fall in with their proposals:

> . . .It is quite true that I was wonderfully happy when I heard the news about Poona, but it never came to me that I would have to be concerned in the new venture, any more than I am since ten years in Jyotiniketan—perhaps even a little less, at least as far as visits are concerned, due to the distance. Even when, in my over-enthusiasm, I suggested a meeting of the people of the place—something on the way [lines] of what we had planned with Fr Dupuis with the view of establishing Jyotiniketan anew in the North-Eastern region—I never thought that I would have to play any role in it, due precisely to the fact that I belong now to U.P. and the Hindi region. (MR, 23.12.69)

He also pointed out to them that the prospects for the ecumenical ashram were good, and that there was no lack of people in the area on whom they could rely for help; only they should be patient and allow time for the plans to mature.

He had intended to visit the ashram at the beginning of January, but now thought better of it, fearing "to be subjected to your loving pleading and pressure for things I have no possibilities to give you".

Banaras, Delhi, Rishikesh—4 January to 10 February 1970

Instead of Jyotiniketan, Abhishiktananda went to Banaras, where he met Sr Térèse: "Her health is much improved and she views the future with great confidence", as he wrote to Lisieux (FT, 28.1.70). At Banaras, while regretting the absence of Dr Panikkar, he had a stimulating meeting with other friends, one of whom took him severely to task for his unwillingness to give the help that he was so well qualified to give to the numerous western 'seekers' who flocked to India in those days. While not wholly agreeing, he seems to have taken the point.[25]

25. She felt that his brusque refusal of the Canadian request for short courses of "spiritual initiation into Vedanta" (letter to RP, 5.12.69) did not realistically take into account the impossibility for most people to come to India or to spend long periods in study. In response he conceded that he might be ready to act as guide to "international groups in serious sessions organized in India". But he seemed to have "a certain fear" of this new western world and "felt himself unable to cope with it". And all the time there were other friends, whose opinion weighed with him, urging him to follow the call to solitude. (Based on a note by NS.) However, it is clear that in the following years he did make himself somewhat more accessible to these young 'seekers'.

Back in Delhi, he visited a large number of friends: "Few people have the advantage of such a wide range of contacts," he told his family, while noting that conversations often kept him up until midnight or 2 a.m.—"not one of my normal habits" (F, 25.1.70). In Delhi he briefly met Murray Rogers who was passing through, but they could not deal with "the real problems", and Abhishiktananda did not think that his point of view had been understood at he ashram. As for the Poona scheme, he now had grave doubts whether the 'formula' would work. (RP, 24.2.70).

He also met his Bombay friend, Dr Dinshaw Mehta, who like others was seeking to enlist him in a new project, intended "to introduce a spiritual element into Indian politics" (L, 25.1.70). His comment was:

> . . . Mehta wanted to employ me as the 'pivot' of his 'Centre for the Unity of Religions'. On the one hand, I scarcely want to be involved with a 'prophet' who only makes decisions by pure pseudo-inspiration; and on the other, I really do not see my way in all that. I tried (. . .) to propose an inter-religious meeting (. . .), but it had to be all or nothing.
>
> In the last six months I have done nothing but say No to my friends: to you, about the book; to Murray, about Poona; to Tessier-Vachon, about Montreal; to Mehta, about Delhi! Fortunately I have Fr Dominique and Térèse to remind me, in season out of season, of the demands of my life of solitude! (RP, 24.2.70)

In Rishikesh, on his way back to Gyansu in February, he met by chance at the Sivananda Ashram one of those to whom he had said No—a Canadian priest, Fr R. Vachon, of the Centre Monchanin, Montreal.[26] He had in fact been trying to avoid him, and Fr Vachon's account of their meeting clearly shows the initially cold reception with which Abhishiktananda often greeted foreign visitors, though (as in this case) it could quickly become more friendly:

> I met him on 2 February 1970. (. . .) To start with he is suspicious, or rather reserved, towards Europeans and Americans who come here (. . .).
>
> In 1969 Claude Tessier (. . .) had decided to invite him to Montreal to give a course on Christian yoga. He had refused. He spoke to me about it, and repeated his reasons for refusing. I think he had been tempted to come, for he had consulted several friends who dissuaded him. (. . .) "I know nothing about yoga." "I only work with small groups." "I am not a conference man." "What can we do in a few days?" "I don't know the situation." "What is needed," he says, "is young people who come to India to learn Hindu spirituality." "We need Vedanta-Christian centres in India itself. (India has no need of Europeans for that.)" (. . .)
>
> He finds R. Panikkar the best man at present in Hindu-Christian dialogue. He also has much respect for Antoine, Fallon, Griffiths.[27] He

26. It was the Centre Monchanin from which had come the invitation to give courses on Vedanta (p. 222).

27. Fr Robert Antoine and Fr Pierre Fallon were Jesuits of Calcutta: Fr Bede Griffiths, OSB, succeeded Abhishiktananda at Shantivanam.

regards Chidananda as excellent, and better than Sivananda. The swamis and sadhus who go to America are second class. Few of the good ones go there.

. . . I can see that he is happy in his contemplative vocation, and wants to preserve it. (. . .) Finally, at 11.30 he takes his meal, and invites me to tell him about the Centre Monchanin. (. . .)

"What advice do you give to a young priest like me, who is interested in Hinduism?" His answer: "Keep your ears open for ten years before opening your mouth!"

Next meeting in his room, 6.15 to 10 p.m. (. . .) We spoke at length about advaita. Twice I tried to leave, but it was he that kept me back.

Gyansu—10 February to 20 May 1970

On reaching Gyansu, he found a letter from Fr Vachon, and replied:

> . . . From you, as from everyone, I was hiding myself; but the Lord arranged for us to meet. Blessed be he, for our meeting was a joy. We should have had some further discussions about Advaita-Christianity. I shall give more thought to your approach. In any case, you have understood better than others my reluctance to go about and talk. I rely on you to explain it to Mr Tessier, who was very likely hurt by my brief and negative answer. (RV, 11.2.70)

Soon afterwards he sent Fr Vachon some of his manuscripts, as he wanted to publish something by Abhishiktananda in the Bulletin of the Centre Monchanin. Two of these appeared in 1970 in the *Revue Monchanin.*[28] Later he sent another unpublished article, "L'idéal du sannyasa", which appeared in 1974.[29]

As Fr Vachon was evidently receptive, Abhishiktananda continued his 'instruction' in advaita:

> . . . As regards the fundamental problem of advaita, I must admit that all that—what I said and what you said to me— is 'arch-rational'. Far too Greek! It is really so much more simple. I would like a *jñani*, a real advaitin, to tell you this (not merely in theory, philosophically). (. . .) The words of the real advaitin, like those of the rishis of the Upanishads, are simply paradoxes, to *awaken,* not to instruct.
>
> Then what about the Christian faith? you will ask. The problem is only posed, so long as one has not understood. Whoever lives in the world of ideas, needs ideas to explain everything—himself, God, things. When what is beyond ideas has been discovered (. . .) then, Mundaka 2.2.8, "all knots are cut, all doubts blown away, all action (of the mind) is ended." (RV, 27.2.70)

28. "Yoga et prière chrétienne", *Revue Monchanin,* April 1970 (based on a chapter of *Éveil*); "Un ermite de l'Inde, Harilal", *Revue Monchanin,* May 1970 (based on a chapter of *Souvenirs*).
29. *Revue Monchanin,* January and February 1974.

> . . . Advaita is not an idea. *It is!* The lightning flashes, the eye blinks, as says the Kena. Then? You have either understood, or you have not understood . . . If you have not understood, too bad! says the same Upanishad. If you have understood, you keep quiet, says the Mundaka . . . (RV, 8.3.70)

Among the mail awaiting him at Gyansu were some copies of a questionaire sent by an old friend in Paris, Fr P. Henry SJ, editor of *Parole et mission,* which he was asked to circulate among his Hindu friends. Their answers were sought to such questions as: Why do you believe? What is your attitude today towards life, other people, the world, human destiny . . .? Their answers were to be published in a coming issue of the periodical. Abhishiktananda found the whole idea "outrageously western and absolutely incomprehensible here" (RP, 24.2.70). However he asked Fr Vachon to try it out—with the necessary explanations—on anyone who might be interested at the Sivananda Ashram (RV, 11.2.70). He himself wrote at once to Fr Henry, and followed his letter with a vigorous little homily by an imaginary Hindu, trying "to open up the world over there to quite a different world" (TL, 20.8.70, accompanying an offprint). He called it "OM, by Shivendranath, as recorded by Abhishiktananda".[30] As he said to Fr Vachon, "When will the West free itself from this 'auto consciousness'? (. . .) 'Your attitude to . . .'—*who* is taking an attitude? Does not the very fact of *my* taking an attitude at once make God disappear?" (RV, 27.2.70)

At the end of February Abhishiktananda was visited by a "brahmin Christian from the plains". This was the Rev. Y.D. Tiwari, recently met at the Rajpur Centre where he was doing some research. "We have had excellent discussions"—on advaita, of course, of which Tiwariji later recorded his impressions.[31] The extent of Abhishiktananda's correspondence is suggested by the following:

> . . . Through this friend I am sending a good fifteen foreign letters to be posted tomorrow down below. I am happy that no Europeans can reach me here. Since January I have received at least five or six requests from visitors, either to come and see me here, or that I should go and meet them. (F, 4.3.70)

The same letter refers to the problems of the younger generation, especially in connection with one "whose only ideal is to make 'dough'":

> . . . I well understand the protest of the young. To a large extent it is the result of the teaching given by the clergy in our day; a religion of formulas to be accepted without being understood, things you are forbidden to do, ceremonies to be performed. (. . .) I never invite anyone to Communion, if they do not come with their whole heart. What matters is not the act of Communion, but the *heart* with which it is approached.
>
> . . . Even if one does not believe in a God reigning up there, far away from us, *a true man* realizes that he is not all alone on the earth, that he has a duty to help, love and serve his fellow men. And in that, unfortu-

30. *Parole et mission,* May 1970, 266ff.
31. These notes are in the Society's archives.

> nately, plenty of the Communists, humanists, Hindus, etc., set an example to Christians every day. Think of Gandhi, for example. What we need to awaken in our young people is a burning ideal (. . .). Read the end of Matthew 25, and you will see what religion primarily consists of! (F, 4.3.70)

He wrote again to Marc Chaduc, who was about to take up voluntary work in Niger:

> . . . Open your eyes and ears wide to find the Spirit speaking to the masses through animism and Islam, and through them—as here through the mystery of India—speaking to the arrogant members of the western Church, indeed, to the West as a whole. The primary role of Mission is not to baptize a few people here and there, but to help each person, first of all in his actual situation, to hear the voice of the Spirit. (. . .) If one day you come to India, as you dream of doing, and if you yourself are sufficiently open to the voice of the Spirit within, you will pick up here some marvellous echoes, of which your European education has never even given you an inkling. (MC, 4.3.70)

By the same mail he sent a long letter on experience and faith to some friends in Germany (Mr and Mrs Miller) who were working on a translation of *Prayer:*

> . . . I thank the Lord for the interest in these questions which he has inspired in you. I think that the meeting of the Church in this *kairos* [decisive moment] with the thought of India is a signal blessing, and that Christians should make every effort to '*intus suscipere*' [receive inwardly] this mystery which the Spirit seems to have entrusted to the sages of India (. . .). But the problems which this meeting poses to Christian thought are of the first magnitude. I have tried in my books to sensitize people to this *questioning* by the Spirit through India, in an effort to awaken our Christians. I appreciated in your letter the questioning of India by the Spirit of Christ, revealed and risen. I regret that in my book I did not sufficiently bring out this other aspect of the diptych, but I assumed its presence at the back of the mind of my Christian readers. Neither the experience of advaita nor that of the Risen One can denied. But when reason seeks to 'understand' them at its own level, it is lost. The experience of Christ, like that of advaita, is supra-mental, and our conceptual apparatus only ever perceives its impact.
>
> I agree with you that personality is only *known* as real by faith. (. . .) Advaita destroys the wretched 'Thou' which we say to God (and also to our brothers) at the mental level, and equally the wretched 'I' of our phenomenal consciousness. (. . .) The 'I' of the morning of Easter is of another order (one which, however, is not *other,* since it is incommensurable with anything whatever). In the Resurrection there arises the *spiritual I,* of God, of Christ, of myself, of my brothers, which the dark night forces me to seek and find. A discovery by faith? Yes, in this faith which is a sharing in the experience of Jesus (. . .). his experience as Son. And in this same experience of Jesus my advaita with my

> brothers expands into the *koinonia* (. . .) which at the greatest depth of the mystery is the Trinity of Persons. But this experience of faith is incommunicable. I can only testify to my faith to my brother who does not believe. (. . .) It is just the same with the fundamental experience of advaita. (. . .)
>
> You see, we can only speak in paradoxes. The Gospel is paradoxical, the Upanishads also. We have accepted formulas from routine and tradition without realizing it; then, in our days, the paradoxical (ir-rational) makes its appearance and, as we had been brought up with the idea that faith was 'rational', the terrible contemporary crisis of faith arose. The cure is not in a new rationalization of the faith, but in the interior discovery of the level of experience. Faith is simply the acceptance that there is something beyond the rational. (. . .) The only real solution is to learn the language of silence . . . which only teaches by silence. I admit that I am myself too Greek to be able to free myself from speculation, even though everything around invites me to do so . . . (M, 4.3.70)

In April he spoke of several of his writings to Fr Lemarié:

> . . . I have just finished a note on "Sannyasa" for my friends in Montreal,[32] in which even more than in *Une messe* I stress the essential acosmism of the life of a monk. It seems that, incapable as I am of living this acosmism with the genuineness of my brother Hindu monks. I am trying at least to dream about it and talk about it . . . (L, 10.4.70)

The manuscript of the French version of *Prayer,* although he had completed it at the end of 1969, was held up in Bombay, awaiting someone to take it to Paris for submission to Le Seuil. As for *Gnanananda,* several publishers were ready to publish it, having been contacted by Mr Chr. Belle, a retired Ambassador whom Abhishiktananda had met in Delhi. He left further decisions to Mr Belle:

> . . . I think that in its final version, times having changed, I can publish this book. There is, besides, another rather compelling reason. Very soon now I shall be at the end of my funds, and more and more it is only my publications that enable me to live . . .
>
> . . . I have also been very busy with a paper I had to give on "Cosmic Revelation and Revelation in Christ" at a theological seminar at Kurseong in May. It has just been cancelled . . . but I don't regret having to do this work. It is a fundamental problem, in India and certainly also outside India, when finally the West emerges from its rationalism. (L, 10.4.70)

This paper was published posthumously in French in 1982.[33] In it Abhishiktananda suggests an approach to this 'fundamental problem'. While religious pluralism cannot be denied, Christian faith cannot allow itself to be simply relativized as one of the different manifestations of the mystery. He calls for a working out of the cosmic significance of Christ as the 'Word of God':

32. See notes 4 and 29. The French version was translated from an English original for Fr Vachon (RV, 8.4.70).

33. It was translated for publication in *Intériorité*, 249-273 .

> Our limited notion of personality already sets us a serious problem when we have to define the personality of God. The Son of God is the Image-Expression of God. Everywhere this Image-Expression is revealed to men; it is the living Word of God who appears, living with the very life of the Son of God. The same Christ who appeared as Mary's son in Palestine appears in the world in every word that God addresses to men, in the totality and also in each part of what we have called the cosmic revelation.[34]

As in the previous year Sr Térèse spent the summer months of 1970 in the Kumaon Hills, staying at Bhowali and Kausani. Before she left Allahabad, Abhishiktananda wrote to her about living 'without signs':

> . . . Monks claim to belong to the Eschaton. But Benedictines think of the Beyond only under the form of an abbey choir. Carmel goes much further; but it is so afraid of losing its footing that it clutches at all the tufts of grass growing in the crevices of the rock.
>
> And then this silence cannot be institutionalized, nor even spoken of, for who would understand? It is a secret that only the Spirit tells to the spirit. Jesus' contemplation went beyond all thought, but he prayed aloud with his disciples, like the mother who lisps words to her little one to teach him to speak. The primary work of the Spirit is to impart to our spirits the interior silence of Jesus. The Church has need for Ramanas to manifest also this aspect of Jesus, even at the risk of being unable any longer to say 'Jesus' or even 'Abba'. We may still have need of the OM. But when the OM has once been said, can it be repeated? for its last *mātrā* is silence[35]—at the far end of space of the heart, as says the Maitri. Breathing keeps time with its rhythm, the heart-beats repeat it, but the mind has nothing more to say; for what sense remains in saying anything to anyone? And when there is nothing more to do, and even so the mind cannot keep quiet and begins to wander, then we take fright; we want at least to feel this silence of our depths, so as to be reassured—as if this silence could be felt or known. (. . .) Whoever wants to realize that he knows, does not know. And yet, it is not true that he does not know; his mind does not know, but he himself knows, with the only knowledge there is. Theologians sweat away, trying to explain it, canonists seek to confine what is essentially free within their legal frameworks. Do we go swimming in a cosmonaut's kit?
>
> So is it dishonest to use 'signs' with your brothers and sisters who have never thought that signs essentially aim at their own transcendence? Why should it be? It is through words and signs that we express human community. So long as I eat food like my brother men and with them, I have the right to share in the liturgical meal!—with all that follows from that. The levels are incommensurable. The truth of advaita does not destroy the truth of the level of inter-personal relations. The truth of

34. *Intériorité,* 272.
35. In the OM there are three audible 'matras'—A, U, M— and the fourth is silence; cp Mandukya Upanishad.

> the Father and the Son being face to face does not destroy the truth of their advaita! But in everything total freedom.
>
> Silence is as dangerous as speech, if you are attached to it, for silence is likewise only a sign, and the 'one thing' (needful) is beyond silence. (. . .) Not to receive the Eucharist or to receive it are both alike signs, and both alike hold back him who does not pass beyond everything in going to the depth of everything . . . (TL, 18.3.70)

Shortly before leaving Gyansu in May, he wrote to his sister in Kergonan:

> . . . If you knew what it is to be confronted with the Presence of the Lord in places where you are not expecting it, among non-Catholics, among non-Christians! It is an anguish that first of all you have to live with in the depths of your own spirit.
>
> I find all liturgical details so secondary. I celebrate Mass according to the strictest Tridentine tradition for those who desire it so, and in a spontaneous style, when people ask for that. The priest is at the service of the people, and the important thing is that the message should go over; and while the Gregorian liturgy has an excellence beyond compare for those who have the necessary education to understand it, there are other forms that are humbler and more within the reach of the new generation, as I discover even in my infrequent meetings with young people from Europe. I at last begin to accept the fact that other people think differently from me! At bottom the only thing that matters is the *conversion of the heart* (. . .) and that is the one thing that I try to get people to see when the opportunity is given me.
>
> . . . It is time for a new book to appear, for I shall soon be short of funds, and it now seems that mass stipends will no longer be available. I used to get them from Lisieux and Paris, but now that is at an end—excellent from one point of view, but it compels me to be very careful from now on.
>
> You asked what is the meaning of 'Gyansu'. 'Gyan' (as pronounced in Hindi) is *jñānā,* knowledge, wisdom. 'Su' is a simple suffix, very often used in place-names round here. It may perhaps mean 'village'. You can see that 'Gyansu' is a splendid name. (. . .) In my garden I have sown beans, marrows, cucumbers, pumpkins. They are beginning to come up, and in two months I shall have vegetables without needing to go to the market. (MT, 11.5.70)

Fr Vachon was now in South India, and Abhishiktananda sent him a long letter telling him places to visit and people to see at Arunachala, Tirukoilur, Trichinopoly and Kulittalai, not forgetting his old cook, Visuvasan, and his family (RV, 8.5.70).

Delhi and Indore—20 May to about 10 June 1970

In Delhi he made his usual round of visits—"Marvellous to talk with French people of high intellectual calibre, refurbishes your thinking, even if afterwards it leaves you exhausted" (L, 2.6.70). Some of these friends also promised to arrange for the new typewriter, a much needed replacement which had been presented to him some months previously, to be brought from Switzerland to Delhi.

At Indore he had a medical check-up, "to find out if the machine is still in working order—but at 60 I can no longer expect to have the energy and vitality of 40 or 30"; and for a few days he allowed the Sisters at the Roberts Nursing Home to 'spoil' him (F, 1.6.70). He also told his family about the immersion heater that he had bought for his daily bath at Gyansu—"for less and less do I have the courage to face the cold of the Ganges".

In a brief note to R. Panikkar, who had recently accepted a chair at Harvard, he referred to his sense of isolation:

> . . . I have seen in the *Examiner* that Klaus[36] has gone, following on you, and soon Murray. You have all abandoned us. May the Lord grant to those who remain here with their feeble capacities, not to lose heart . . . (RP, 29.5.70)

Gyansu—June to December 1970

Apart from a rapid descent to Hardwar in July to pick up his typewriter, Abhishiktananda did not stir from Gyansu until the following January.

> . . . Just come back here, absolutely worn out, but enriched. Meetings especially with young people of France, Switzerland, Belgium—anti-establishment University students. But what splendid boys and girls! How much I feel at home and deeply in touch with them. (L, 15.6.70)

He asked Fr Lemarié to renew one of his subscriptions, provided enough of his money was left, otherwise to cancel it:

> . . . Now that mass stipends are a thing of the past (even Lisieux has no more). I shall have to drop all extras. (. . .) Besides, thanks to the periodicals that I am sent from here and there, I am sufficiently in touch.
>
> . . . *Prayer* (the French MS) will be brought (to Europe) next month by Thierry Nicod, a young Swiss.
>
> . . . Why are the French monasteries so slow to respond to the spiritual appeal of the young people who come here seeking for an inner life? Those who get most from India are those who have met with a Trappist or Carthusian monastery with with real monks, truly spiritual men. The crisis is in the first place of a spiritual order. And the cure is the return, beyond all forms, to the living source of monasticism. (. . .) That seems to me the most urgent matter. Taizé answers to *one* level. There is a deeper level; and that should be presented in the thought-forms of the West. The thought-forms of India are disconcerting to anyone who has not already penetrated to the inward level. (L, 15.6.70)

During June and July Abhishiktananda also had company at Gyansu:

36. K. Klostermaier had gone to a teaching post in Canada.

> . . . I have scarcely been alone since June—two lads (Hindus), dearly loved, of whom I have told you. One [Ramesh] spent two weeks here; the other [Lalit] comes and goes. It warms the heart. But the solitude is all the more beautiful afterwards! Another form of experience. The summer is beautiful, and the winter no less. (F, 26.7.70)

When the long-awaited typewriter was brought to Hardwar, Abhishiktananda 'rewarded' the bearer with one of his inimitable conducted tours of Hardwar and Rishikesh—the temple of Mansā Devi, the ashram of his friend Niranjananand beside the Ganges, the evening *arati* at Har-ki-Pauri, and the Ganges again at Laxmanjhula—as the present writer has good cause to remember.

After his return to Gyansu in June Abhishiktananda was engaged in writing at two levels. He continued the essay into popular journalism, begun in the previous year, and wrote several short articles for syndication in the Catholic press, of which two were published, both concerning the priesthood: "Professional Men or Spiritual?" and "There are no part-time Priests".[37] These were probably provoked by a proposal which had been put to him in Indore (F, 1.6.70), that he should involve himself in a new-style seminary at Bhopal. Here it was intended that the seminarists should prepare both for a secular profession and for the priesthood, so that they could be self-supporting and at the same time be a leaven in society. He told Fr Lemarié that he had written some articles:

> . . . as a reminder that the priest is first of all a witness to the spiritual, and not a 'professional'—lawyer, dentist, etc.—and that the term 'part-time' priest shows total forgetfulness of what the priest or the Christian primarily is. (L, 12.9.70)

He also took up again the fundamental problem, never far from his mind, of Christianity and the Cosmic Religions. The thoughts worked out in his article for Kurseong, written earlier in the year, were carried somewhat further in another article, "Archétypes religieux, expérience du Soi et théologie chrétienne". This paper, dated 22.7.70, was not published in his lifetime.[38] In a letter of the same date to Fr Lemarié, he refers to a passage which he had quoted in it from a sermon of Chromatius of Aquileia on the Ascension of Christ:

> . . . that pearl (. . .) which opens up amazing new horizons on the mystery of the Cosmic Christ; I have just used a quotation from it in a pretty strong article ["Archétypes . . .], which I very much wonder if anyone will be willing to publish.[39] (L, 22.7.70)

In this article—a contribution to the 'Theology of Religions', a subject which deeply interested both him and Dr Panikkar—he makes very clear his dissatisfaction with the widely accepted 'theology of fulfilment', which envisaged a final absorption or replacement of all other religions by Christianity. (This had been the assumption of his book *Sagesse,* which he later tried to tone down in its English version, *Saccidananda.*) A theology of fulfilment not only involves a totally unrealistic hope for the future development of the Church, but more im-

37. *Catholic News Service of India,* July and August 1970.
38. See note 17. Some critical notes by Dr Panikkar are attached to the original typescript.
39. See *Intériorité,* 200. Fr Lemarié's edition of Chromatius to which he refers is in *Sources chrétiennes,* no. 154.

portantly, has to be drastically modified when once religious pluralism is taken seriously, as it was for example in the Vatican Council. In this essay Abhishiktananda was feeling his way towards a reconciliation between Christian faith in the uniqueness of Christ with a full recognition that God has spoken and continues to speak to every human being in terms of his own religious background and culture. But he admits that his 'answer' is itself an act of faith, not a demonstration.

At this time Sr Térèse was facing a personal crisis, as it seemed that she might only be able to follow her vocation to solitude at the cost of leaving the Carmelite Order. Abhishiktananda endeavoured to counsel her, emphasizing all the practical aspects of the matter, since these also were pointers to the will of God for her (TL, 24.7.70; 26.7.70). In one letter he illustrates a point from his own situation:

> . . . It is certain that you have an attachment to the Carmel; however, is it not rather to the ideal Carmel (in which you foresee your own vocation) than to the Carmel as it has taken shape in history and ecclesiastical institutions? To explain my point, take my own case, on which your dilemma has made me think further. I am still a Benedictine; it is convenient, it gives me a foothold, a *label* (essential in a world that is incapable of seeing individuals and persons except with a label, like those badges we wear at conferences), it allows me much independence in relation to the local bishop, it gives me the possibility of a place of shelter in case of disability, etc. This is very crudely put, but we should not be afraid of seeing ourselves whole. Spiritually, my attachment is to the monastic life, and to a monastic ideal which is scarcely Benedictine, and even goes beyond what could be realized within Christianity. An acosmic ideal (. . .) Thank God, I don't have to face the dilemma. But If I did, would my truth lie in keeping my connection at all costs and purely juridically with OSB [the Benedictine Order], or in accepting my peculiar calling, whatever might be the material and social cost that would have to be paid for choosing truth? (TL, 26.7.70)

Meanwhile he encouraged her to make a further appeal to Rome, and quoted one of his favorite sayings: "True hope (*espérance*) only begins when all human hope (*espoir*) has failed."

In another letter to the Sister he spoke about making decisions:

> . . . When people tell you that you alone have to make the decision, that does not exclude the Lord, far from it! But the true voice of the Lord does not make itself heard (. . .) as something *other* (a different voice with which our mind is confronted), but it is so far embodied in us (. . .) that the decision which the Lord inspires springs from the very depth of our 'one' being. (TL, 17.9.70)

A notable scandal in the church drew from Abhishiktananda the thought that "the Spirit will more and more have to work through the channel of *prophecy*, in order to make up for the deficiencies of the clergy." Similarly, a recent pronouncement of the Secretariat for Non-Christians shocked him with its condescending tone:

. . . Once more, the clergy are doing all they can to force the Spirit to raise up prophets, of whom some will allow themselves to be slaughtered, and the others will make everything explode.

The same letter mentioned that he had not received any news from his Jyotiniketan friends, who had been out of the country for some months: "Alas, our relationship will not any longer be as free as in the past" (TL, 17.9.70). Fortunately he was mistaken about this.

His book *Gnanananda* had finally been accepted by Éditions Présence of Paris, in a series edited by M.-M. Davy, and was expected to appear before the end of the year. It had been offered to Le Seuil which, under an agreement incautiously made in 1965, had the first refusal on his books; but they had turned it down for the disquieting reason that *Rencontre,* and even more *Une messe,* had sold very badly. At the same time they were considering the French edition of *Prayer,* but that too was not accepted. The resulting delay in the appearance of these books meant that Abhishiktananda had little hope of receiving royalties in 1971.

> . . . For my part, I begin to wonder what I should do in three or four years' time, when my resources will be exhausted and I no longer have the strength to live alone, as I have done so far. The Lord will provide—and, as a last resort, St Anne [Kergonan] is always there . . .
>
> . . . This week I am in bad form, headaches, etc . . . I have to realize that I have passed sixty, and therefore all kinds of possibilities get less. To survive after sixty, you need European food and conditions.
>
> To come back to writing—nowadays it is too difficult, the problems are more and more fundamental. *Sagesse* only went half way. In this surge of protest I hesitate to speak, for the reader would only gather that forms are relative, but would not pay attention to the experience of the mystery, which alone gives value to that which is beyond forms. (L, 12.9.70)

Although the indisposition passed, Abhishiktananda continued to be troubled by an increasing sense of weakness, which made him particularly dread travelling. This is repeatedly mentioned in letters to his friends at this time, though not to his family; to them he only referred light-heartedly to his financial straits:

> . . . From now on I have to be terribly careful about my expenditure, for fear of finding myself without a sou in two or three years' time, and of having to become one of those mendicant sadhus of whom I write in my books. (. . .) If only my books could be 'best-sellers', I would no longer have to count up the cost even of my stamps! (F, 5.10.70)

All this no doubt made him begin to make arrangements for the disposal of his important papers, and in particular, must have influenced his decision, after hesitating for so many years, finally to prepare his book on Arunachala with a view to publication:

> . . . I have just this moment finished retyping and correcting my manuscript "Souvenirs d'Arunachala", which will probably be my last message of this kind. It will not be published before 1972, but I would

> like to have it ready, so as to be prepared for any eventuality. I no longer feel the inspiration to write (. . .). What has been written is enough, and those who are on the wave-length will have understood.
>
> . . .I must make a very strict budget, so as not to be totally broke in two or three years (I still have no guarantee that the Lord will summon me at the fateful age of 63, as he did with Fr Monchanin[40]). So use what is needed for a missal (small size) and possibly a breviary, when the monastic breviary is republished. Apart from that I must avoid all expenditure and drop my subscriptions. (. . .) I am somewhat recovered from last month's turn, but must put up with the reduction of strength; and that will set problems, when I am no longer able to live alone; especially as my less than 100F per month no longer allow me to have a helper for cooking, fetching water and the rest.
>
> . . . Apart from that, the monsoon is over (. . .). my garden is full of flowers (. . .). Life is fine. (. . .) The Lord has taken me at my word and put me in a real hermitage. (L, 6.10.70)

A letter to New York informed Mrs Stokes that *Gnanananda* would soon be sent:

> . . . Here life is peaceful. The nerves seem to be a little better. In our time many people probably experience these tensions. I have what I might call a visceral attachment to the Church, and at the same time almost insuperable difficulty in finding a place for its forms and demands in what seems to well up in the mind as a direct result of the fundamental experience. (. . .)
>
> You say there is no need to answer your question about the priesthood of women, etc . . . My family upbringing convinced me through constant experience, which was far more powerful than thinking about it, that women are superior to men. So then? Here too the campaign of American women seems to me legitimate. However, I regret that pressure for a married priesthood and for the ordination of women makes people lose sight of the essential problem, namely, What is the ministry? The questioning of the Gospel and the New Testament is even more fundamental than in the 16th century.
>
> Next month you will receive my *Gnanananda.* (. . .) It is different from the other books, and presents the best of Indian experience without making comparisons or value-judgements. (AMS, 10.10.70)

Another letter to Marc Chaduc, the French seminarist who hoped to come to India, continued Abhishiktananda's advice on how he should prepare himself:

> . . . I shall certainly do all I can to meet you but, apart from unforeseen circumstances, that could only be for a few days. (. . .) Besides, after the necessary initiation, it is Hindus that those Westerners should meet, who want to learn from India.
>
> . . . Search in the Gita, and later in the Upanishads (the fountainhead), for the 'foreshadowings' of the Christian mystery, but even more,

40. Like Fr Monchanin, Abhishiktananda was aged 63 when he died!

allow yourself to be caught by the call of the infinite. The superficial meeting points with Christianity remain . . . superficial. It is through the depth that the meeting (. . .), call it what you will, is effected. That is as shattering for theology as is the monsoon for ships crossing the Indian Ocean; and yet the solution of the present crisis lies in a *sense* (I do not say, a philosophy) of advaita. Get yourself initiated into that with us here, and then radiate it over there . . . (MC, 16.10.70)

He had been asked by Sr Sara Grant, a Sister of the Sacred Heart who taught in Sophia College Bombay, an old friend, to send her some notes in view of a seminar on Contemplation:

> . . . Since I had no urgent work (at the) end of last week, I thought of your demand about "Call to Contemplation" and I typed a few ideas, not perhaps on the main point asked from you by Meloo, but fundamental enough, I think. (. . .) It is wonderful that Poona organize a seminar on contemplation, and encouraging. The paper I wrote (. . .) is quite informal. Do not try to keep (to?) it. Use some ideas if you find them worth while.[41]
>
> . . . Two days ago I had the surprise to see Irudaya Raj, the young Tamilian SJ of Poona, who was the main responsible for the 'Mass' (i.e., in August 1968 at Poona). It was nice to have a Christian *chela* [disciple] following my Hindu dear ones of last summer ! (. . .) Irudaya Raj is urging me to make myself more accessible, either in Hardwar, in Varanasi or in Arunachala. (. . .) I answered him that I have just the necessary money for eating, not even for travelling, much less for a new establishment (. . .). (SG, 14.10.70)

Soon afterwards he wrote to her again, in connection with a proposed meeting in Poona concerning the preparation of some new theological textbooks:

> . . . That idea of text books is an awful one in the present situation. The Hindu notions will never be able to pass through those 'Caudine Forks' of the western manuals of theology without being emptied of their true significance. (. . .) What is needed is the study of key-notions of the Hindu theology, concepts like Ananda (as studied by Fr Gispert),[42] Iśwara (cp. R. Panikkar),[43] Prāna, Karma, Avidyā, Grace, etc.—and the reflection on the 'secret' of Christ or, if you prefer it, the 'Christ Event' (with its impact on human thought, etc.), starting from the Hindu notions of Sadguru, Satpurusha, etc. (cp. *Kristvidya* of K.K.),[44] in the way Jews and Greeks meditated on it from their own concepts of Messiah, Kurios, Logos, Soter, etc. That is to be done by groups of young theologians (. . .) living in the proper atmosphere. (. . .) I insisted also on the

41. "Appel à l'intériorité", published in *Intériorité,* 153ff. A few days earlier (7.10.70), in response to an urgent appeal from a Flemish monthly, *Wereldwijd,* he had written "Le message contemplatif de l'Inde". For some reason they did not use it, but it was eventually published in *Initiation,* 49-56.
42. *Bliss in the Upanishads,* G. Gispert-Sauch, New Delhi 1977.
43. *The Unknown Christ of Hinduism.*
44. *Kristvidya,* K. Klostermaier, Bangalore 1967.

> necessity to open the meeting to young theologians like (. . .). Only those young people (not deformed like old people by scholastic learning and teaching) are able to do the preparatory work. (SG, 9.11.70)

During November Abhishiktananda had intended to visit various friends in the plains, but abandoned his idea, as he told Dr Panikkar:

> . . . I do not want to try to plan any more programmes like last month's. In attempting to fit things together and reconcile the irreconcilable, trying to please as many people as possible at the same time, I ended by disappointing everyone. And all the more, because from now on I can no longer travel as much as in other days. Quite apart from the cost, I have felt too great a reduction of strength this year to risk it again. So I am leaving things to work themselves out on their own. (RP, 29.11.70)

In a letter to his German friends, the Millers, he continued his efforts to help them to understand that the problems they raised could never be solved at the level of concepts. He also replied to a question about gurus:

> . . . What you say about the guru is what I have often said myself. But in the end, I wonder if it is fair. Because, for the Vedantin, there is only one guru, the one who shines, not-born, in the depth of the heart. The 'external' guru is only the temporary form taken by the essential guru to make himself recognized, and at the moment of that recognition there is no longer either guru or disciple. In Christianity it is the Church—i.e, individuals in the Church and those whom God specially brings into contact with himself[?]—that is the manifested guru, the form actualized in space and time which Jesus takes to reveal himself. The Christian guru is never anything but the manifestation of the Lord, and the moment he forgets this he becomes a thief, no longer a *shepherd.* Similarly, the Vedantin guru who retains the least trace of *ahamkara* (turning back on himself) is a false guru. To insist too strongly that Jesus is the only guru in Christianity risks throwing the Church overboard. It remains true that the Vedantin, Zen, etc. guru testifies from his own experience, while the Christian guru testifies from that of Jesus. However, once more, this is only a manner of speaking, for the guru who refers to his *own* experience shows by that very fact that he has missed *the* experience. Whoever has not disappeared in the light cannot testify to the light. You must surely know the Persian proverb: "No one knows the secret of the Flame . . . " (M, 13.11.70)

He sent a copy of the typescript of *Arunachala* to Mrs Baumer in Switzerland:

> . . . This summer I had a bad set-back in health, and so I quickly retyped this work and sent it to you with a view to any eventuality. In any case it should not come out before 1972. If I leave my 'post' before then, or before it appears, edit it as you please and offer it, for example, to Mr Masui. If it brings in any return, give it to the Carmel of Lisieux for that Sister of theirs who is leading here a life similar to mine, unknown to all.

. . . I have a strong impression that in Europe, even more than here, people use our texts or thoughts for their own intellectual satisfaction, and so lack the most essential qualification for listening to them—*mumukshutva,* in Christian terms, 'the desire for conversion'.

. . . *Awakening?* For some weeks I have been deep in the commentaries of Shankara. So what else to say, except that the awakening is not caused by anything, and causes nothing. The bell provokes psycho-nervous results, but the awakening (. . .) is not caused by the sound of the bell. It just *is*, quite simply. (. . .) Who understands that only a new level of awareness, of awakening will save religion and culture from the threatening crisis. But practically no one is ready for this awakening. There surely is the role of Love, (. . .) the termite which eats away egoism, and for that the Gospel, freed from its tawdry coverings, is uniquely valuable. When put into practice it should awaken each one to the awareness of being from God, in communion with every thinking being, indeed with every being. Then as St Benedict says at the end of chapter 7, what was duty becomes natural—*sahaja*, the natural state, as said Ramana. (OB, 20.11.70)

In his next letter he took up a 'big question' which his friend had raised:

. . . Will the Christian experience, which succeeded reasonably well in passing through the Caudine Forks of Judaism and Hellenism, be capable of being expressed without dilution when approached from the advaitin experience? In *Sagesse* I attempted a meditative approach within the framework of classical theology. The last chapter shows that the problem remains unsolved. The best course is still, I think, to hold on even under extreme tension to these two forms of a unique 'faith' until the dawn appears. For advaita and theology are on two different levels. The lofty assurance of the advaitin philosophers is as empty as that of the theologians. A friend, who is a real advaitin, last month had a shattering vision of Christ, feet on earth, arms and head above the heavens, with arms held out "as if to hold me". I am looking forward to meeting this friend, to speak of it with him. As I probably said in my last letter, I think we should insist on the experience of Paul, Augustine, Luther, that salvation is not in works, but in faith—faith in its central point, the awakening in the depth of the spirit to the Absolute, to Brahman . . . (OB, 5.12.70)

For Abhishiktananda this faith had to be existential, as he said to Dr Panikkar:

. . . It is hard to have to accept the reduction of physical strength, the increasing difficulty of concentrating for any length of time; and without a very strong *faith* I am sure this would be absolutely unbearable. It is necessary to have discovered, at least in Faith, the *satyasya satyam* [the Real of the real], of which everything is simply the sign. (. . .) I well know that I shall not be able to hold on here for many years—the Lord will provide in his own time, in his own unforeseeable way. What is most important is the request, coming to me both from young Europeans who come to India and from young Indian priests, to be more

> accessible. (. . .) There is work at the grass-roots, which young priests like . . . and some others could perform, and they want help, if I may say so, both spiritual and Vedantin. (RP, 8.12.70)

He continued to make provision for the disposal of his papers, "if anything ought to be kept of what I have been able to write, either privately or otherwise," and asked Fr Lemarié (who had recently left Paris for Chartres) to send them to certain designated friends. In the same letter he gave the welcome news that Lisieux had found sufficient mass-stipends to last until Easter (L, 17.12.70).

Sr Térèse had returned some months previously to the Carmel at Pondicherry, and was dreading the conventional Christmas at the convent:

> . . . Your Christmas will be an interior exile. How well I understand you! (. . .) That is why as a rule I try to spend Christmas and Easter in silence and solitude. With you this is not a lack of 'incarnation', but simply a difference of approach and calling. Quite simply accept that you are *different,* or rather that your sisters should be different; prepare the creches in all simplicity. It can't be helped, contact with the depth and the atmosphere of 'depth' in which contact with Vedanta makes us live, inevitably uproots us. Advent, for example, in which I took such delight twenty or thirty years ago, now says so little to me, even though its poetry contains infinite echoes, far beyond the disappointing words. Who is coming? And from where? In order to experience Advent as in time past, I should have to be able to remove myself from the blazing Presence, and dream that it was still 'coming'. Not a 'waiting', but an awakening should constitute a Christian liturgy in an Indian context. Add to that the fact that the poetry of the liturgy anaesthetizes Christians who are too often happy to repeat each year, "He will come and will not delay", while the poor look in vain for bread, shelter and respect. Advent is the cry of the poor, humiliated and frustrated , who are waiting for me, the Christian, to come to their help . . . (TL, 14.12.70)

When sending Christmas greetings to his sister at Kergonan, he told her about the recent visit of his young friend Lalit:

> . . . Only this month I have had with me a 22 year old student for his holidays. He comes to spend every holiday with me, and is like a son to me. It is marvellous to have such a deep and close relation with Hindus But the further I go, the less I see how these real Hindus, despite their admiration for Christ, could ever enter into the framework of Christianity. I cannot see a single one of my friends, young or not so young, who could become a Christian. This sets a terrible theological problem, which begins trouble our young theologians here. Living as I do more than anyone in both environments at the same time, I see less than anyone how to solve the problem. It calls for thought, prayer, and most of all, an entrance through real contemplation into the deepest interior experience.
>
> . . . I have not stirred from Gyansu since July. (. . .) Even so, I shall have to go down after Christmas for two or three weeks. Above all I want to avoid being here on 14 January, when for the festival on the

shortest day, everyone has to take a bath in the Ganges at 4 a.m. Fires are lit on the rocks, but no doubt I do not have enough faith. I did it in January 1969, and promised myself, Never again!

Now I wish you a Holy Christmas, an ever more real awakening to the Presence that shines in the depth of the heart. (MT, 15.12.70)

In a letter to Mrs Baumer he said:

. . . While reading your letter, I said to myself that it was as if we were having a game of tennis, playing the ball back and forth without stopping. If we were ever to meet, how the sparks would fly! (. . .) However, though I can't remember how I put it, I thought I had said much more in my letter than you seem to have taken in, I mean, my feeling that I am incapable of going beyond the thoughts already expressed (in books and letters) without Christianity exploding . . . J. Monchanin, in his last year, became more and more sceptical about the possibility of a harmony between Vedanta and Christianity; and fearing to see once more the disappearance of his faith in Greek rationalism which with difficulty he had recovered, preferred to give up Vedanta. *E pur si muove!*—or rather, it stands fast, immovable like Arunachala.

The whole subject should be taken up again, starting from the Vedantin experience, and not—as I have so far done, or rather, written—starting from the 'Christian faith' and its 'symbolization' [in Creeds] by the [Ecumenical] Councils; like a kind of hypothesis which is followed through to the end. In fact, I have often noted down my thoughts on this matter, and have files full of rough and illegible notes, mixed with Greek and Sanskrit. Even to write drafts on this subject—I admit that I do not feel strong enough for it at present. I am very soon exhausted when I try to concentrate, and the winter bowled me over, like the monsoon did five months ago. Later on we will see about it, but be very sure that for me it is the crucial subject, although in India there are not half-a-dozen Christians capable of feeling it or daring to look it in the face. What are we to do? In the blinding light which blots out every outline, what place remains for a 'symbolic' [creed] of any kind whatever?

Even so, to give a little relief to your impatience over this, I am sending you some essays written this year; nos 29 and 33 especially put out feelers in this direction.[45] With them I am enclosing a horribly printed booklet which came out this summer.[46]

I have just read *Arunachala* again in view of sending it to someone. The style is very poor; if one day you publish it, you should not hesitate to rewrite whole pages. Then I get the impression that it is so personal

45. From a numbered list of his articles, of which a copy will have been sent to Mrs Baumer, these can be identified as (29) "Archétypes religieux" (see Note 17) and (33) "Appel à l'intériorité" (see Note 41).

46. This will be a reprint of *Towards the Renewal of the Indian Church,* which is referred to in a letter to Mrs Baumer of 18.4.71.

> that it ought not to be published in my lifetime.[47] The confrontation between Christianity and Vedanta has been at the centre of my life since the caves of Arunachala. It was first expressed in *Guhantara*, which you did not think much of; later there was "Bhairava" and "L'autre rive".[48] The intuition which was worked out in *Sagesse* came to me towards 1960; but the further I went, the more impossible it became to bear the strain of maintaining this insight (nothing physical or psychological, but rather like a 'count-down' of an extreme tension).
>
> My *Gnanananda* is entirely true. In it I have not superimposed myself upon the Master.[49] (. . .)
>
> Can a 'Christian symbolic' [creed] emerge from the *anubhava* [experience]? The whole Jewish-Christian systematization of Christianity will explode at that point. (OB, 23.12.70)

In his next letter he added an explanation of this last sentence, saying: "Explosion of dogma only refers to explosion of the 'mind'. For, as formulas, the old are equally good. This explosion is conversion—'Ah! . . .'" (OB, 30.1.71)

Mainly at Jyotiniketan—2 January to 10 March 1971

"Even psychologically I badly need a change," Abhishiktananda told a friend in December (SG, 18.12.70); and for that his thoughts turned naturally to Jyotiniketan. Fortunately the rift between him and his friends at the ashram had now been healed, even though their decision to leave India continued to grieve him. So at the beginning of January he came to them from Gyansu, and all were determined to make the most of their last time together:

> . . . My stay here has been excellent, and the company plus affection has been the best cure. Once again I feel in good form! The [sad thing?] is that they are leaving India after Easter to settle in Jerusalem. I deeply regret their decision, but they feel that they had to take it. In these circumstances I have agreed to prolong my stay here. (L, 26.1.71)

One day he went to Lucknow to see his friend 'Harilal', whose vision of Christ was mentioned above (p. 239):

> . . . Meeting, very impressive, in Lucknow last week with that friend, disciple of Sri Ramana, perfect advaiti, who at present (at least for the sake of some disciples) has gone back to the path of *abheda-bhakti*

47. *Souvenirs d'Arunachala* was only published in 1977.
48. "Bhairava" (unpublished) is in the author's file "Poems of Arunachala", as also is "L'autre rive", which was published in *Initiation*, 31ff; English version in *The Further Shore* (2nd edn, 1984), 119ff.
49. The English version of "Gnanananda" in *Guru and Disciple* was greatly appreciated by Sri Nityananda Giri and other disciples of Sri Gnanananda. In their own publication, *Sadguru Gnanananda* (Bharatiya Vidya Bhavan, Bombay 1979) they drew extensively upon Abhishiktananda's book and made a handsome acknowledgement (p.vii): "We have drawn a deep inspiration from (. . .) *Guru and Disciple*, and we are sure that the haunting beauty and power of his exposition would captivate the readers' hearts, as it has ours. To the hallowed memory of Swami Abhishiktananda, who could recapture the transcendent beauty of the spirit, and hold aloft the radiance of self-realization to light up the path of spiritual seekers, this book is dedicated with a profound gratitude and reverence."

> [*bhakti* without distinction between the Lord and his devotees]. (. . .) And he explained to us in that way the love of Christ for the Father . . . It is the same (man) who had two months ago an overwhelming vision of the Cosmic Christ, encompassing the whole universe, yet coming to *him* with open arms . . . All my theology and rationalism is put to the test by this vision (. . .). A reminder, I feel, from Him through such bhaktas and advaitis, not to rationalize the all-surpassing advaitic experience, and that He is still there who is God *omnia in omnibus* [all in all]. (. . .) He himself is the OM which transcends all names that men and angels give to him. And he is beyond all names, as the all transcending Purusha, Iśvara . . . Yet it is He! Ah, ah, ah, said Jeremiah, I cannot speak. (SG, 26.1.71)

At the end of January they were joined by a Japanese visitor, Fr Shigeto Oshida, whom Murray had long wanted to introduce to Abhishiktananda. While at Jyotiniketan, Fr Oshida was persuaded to give a brief course of Zazen; later Abhishiktananda took him to Hardwar, Rishikesh and Delhi, so that he could be introduced to Hindu friends and sacred places:

> . . . Met here this week a Japanese Dominican who has opened a small ashram in the countryside like the Zen Masters.[50] He had already practised Zen in his Buddhist youth. What a difference there is between being initiated into Zazen by a master who practises it daily, and only reading about it in books! The same theological problems and paradoxes (?) as we have here. Freed from all formulas, he is 'existentially' Christian at a depth so much greater than that which is reached by rites and symbols. But when it is a question of defining how and why he is Christian, it is impossible capture this reality—all explanations are elusive. Only he who has reached the 'depth' can understand one who speaks from the 'depth'. A smile, a freedom, which those who do not know completely misunderstand. (OB, 30.1.71)
>
> . . . Meeting here with that extraordinary Japanese Dominican, Oshida; follower of Zazen, with marvellous freedom in the Spirit, an intensely Christian heart in a Buddhist psyche [soul]. I took him with Murray Rogers to Hardwar, Rishikesh, then Delhi. (L, 27.2.71)

This meeting will have meant much to Abhishiktananda, because in Fr Oshida he found someone who lived existentially with the same problems as he did himself, despite the differences in their cultural and religious backgrounds. A few years later, when he learnt of Abhishiktananda's death. Fr Oshida wrote a beautiful account of their meeting, called "God's Harpstring".[51]

While at Jyotiniketan, Abhishiktananda continued the theological discussion that he was having with Sr Sara Grant of Sophia College:

> . . . Your new approach? Well, deeply interesting; but it reminds me of my relentless efforts and repeated falls . . . in trying to dissociate our view of the Cosmic Christ . . . from the simple metaphysics which

50. Fr Oshida's ashram is called 'Takamori'.
51. Printed in the Society's *Occasional Bulletin*, no. 6 of December 1982.

> make Christ one of the numerous manifestations or theophanies! (. . .) For the Christian point of view, of course, Christ is the Unique—it is through him that we see all the theophanies. He is the End of them, their Pleroma (. . .). Wonderful, but from the standpoint of eternity . . . The brilliance of the *paramārtha* overcasts [overthrows] all scale of values on the level of *vyavahāra!*[52] Our Cosmic Christ, the all embracing Iśvara, the Purusha of the Veda/Upanishads . . .we cannot escape to give him such a full dimension, expansion . . . Yet, why then call him only Jesus of Nazareth? Why say that it is Jesus of Nazareth whom others unknowingly call Shiva or Krishna? and not rather say that Jesus is the theophany for *us,* Bible-believers, of that unnameable mystery of the Manifestation, always tending beyond itself, since Brahman transcends all its/his manifestations? (. . .) I hardly share your optimism about Christian theologizing, starting from Shankara. Perhaps it is possible at the level of Upanishadic flashes? I can only feel questions now. Yet we have to try to discover at least an *angle* through which a path may open. (SG, 26.1.71)

After Fr Oshida had left, Abhishiktananda remained for a few days in Dehli, and then went back to Jyotiniketan to meet the Capuchin Fr Augustine (Fr Deenabandhu) who was soon to take over the responsibility for the ashram. Then he and Murray Rogers went together to Gyansu, the latter having at last obtained the necessary permit to visit Uttarkashi.

An interesting sidelight on a new dimension in Abhishiktananda's viewpoint comes in a letter to Fr Lemarié:

> . . . My rationalism finds itself forced to accept (with dread) a dimension of *emotion,* in the best sense, within the spiritual life, where the Spirit plays with the soul, where Christ makes himself actually [*actuellement?*] a sound that is heard and a visible object . . . I am lost, it is not my line; but during recent weeks I have heard so many confidences on this subject. My latest contact was with a new bishop of the new Church of North India[53] (. . .), from an almost Pentecostal background, patently sincere and humble, belonging to a completely different spiritual world to the one I have known . . . who was Christian in a manner that is wonderfully like that in which so many of my Hindu friends are Hindu. (27.2.71)
>
> Who has the right to set limits in advance to the Spirit? The Spirit is in David's dance and in the visions of our bhaktas here, just as much as in the silence of those we call 'sages'. (FT, 27.2.71)

Gyansu—10 March to 24 April 1971

When he returned to Gyansu Abhishiktananda was accompanied by Murray Rogers, whose account of his visit in "Swamiji—the Friend"[54] is highly evoca-

52. *Paramartha*—ultimate truth, the level of the Absolute; *vyavahara,* provisional manifestation, the earthly level.
53. Bishop I.P. Andrews, C.N.I. Bishop of Kolhapur.
54. See chapter 5, Note 10.

tive. The small stone-built hut, with its upstairs loft and its verandah looking down on the Ganges, the holes in its walls plugged with old periodicals to keep out draughts, and its interior a picture of organized chaos; the sadhu neighbours with their silent greetings; the long contemplative liturgy in the loft-chapel each day—Sanskrit hymns and Scriptural texts leading into the silence of the OM, and then "growing out of that, the heart of the liturgy, a minimum of words and yet every word charged with life. However long it took, it seemed too short." "During those days the *Pūrnam adaḥ pūrṇam idam* ('Fullness there, fulness here') of the Iśa, that Swamiji never tired of singing, symbolized for us the Cosmic Fullness itself in which we lived and had our being."

As Murray prepared to leave, they wrote a joint letter to Raymond Panikkar at Harvard, whom Abhishiktananda had been unable to meet since October 1969.

> . . . I shall probably come down in May to Bombay/Poona for the seminar of theologians and indologists, even though, after these two months of running about in the plains, I feel a great need for silence and solitude. (. . .) Still too weary from the journey, bus, etc. . . . to sort out my ideas. I would need some long peaceful days of conversation with you before trying to put in order—or rather, to harmonize—the deep experience and its 'expression'. The Mediterranean 'expression' is terribly unsatisfying. Ours here is just as 'misleading' when it pretends to be anything more than a finger pointing towards . . . And yet at least an attempt at theology must be made . . . or else should the monk simply keep quiet and *be* . . .? The Eucharist here with M. these days free from all form . . . An OM which 'expands' [opens out?] in a communion accompanied by a minimum of formulas . . . (RP, 12.3.71)

Abhishiktananda must have recovered quickly from his weariness, for during the next six weeks he worked without stopping:

> . . . Every morning the sound of my typewriter can be heard all around, disturbing the peace of my neighbours, and above all making them amazed that for a sadhu I work so hard. (MT, 23.4.71)

He was chiefly engaged on the first six chapters of the English version of *Sagesse* which, rather surprisingly, he was eager to see published. In fact, he intended it to be not merely a translation, but a revised version which would correspond more closely with his present position. The procedure was somewhat complicated, because he first had his friends translate the original and then used their translation as a basis for his own rewriting, which finally had to be edited into more standard English. All this took much longer than in his enthusiasm he had anticipated:

> . . . Just now I am super-busy on correcting, rewriting and retyping the English translation of *Sagesse*. So my fingers are worn out with typing, and I am not going to use the machine today for writing [to you]. (F, 2.4.71)

He also had another urgent task to complete before the end of April, when he planned to meet his publisher in Delhi. This was an extensive revision of *Prayer*, since it was agreed that all future editions should correspond as far as possible with the form that it had been given in French:

> . . . They also want an edition of *Prayer* to be published in England [i.e., by the London S.P.C.K.], and I am at work on making the English agree with the French, so that all four versions (plus Italian and German) may be more alike.[55] (MT, 23.4.71)

This, however, was by no means all that he was doing. Immediately after reaching Gyansu he wrote an article on "The Prayer of Silence"; which he had been asked to give for translation in a Spanish periodical, *Liturgia,* and sent it to Bombay:

> . . . I am sending you by book post a few pages for Silos, as I promised you last week. I am a little too much in a hurry to do it properly, yet I hope that that will find an opening at least in a few hearts.[56] (SG, 19.3.71)

In addition to all this, he found time to reflect and write notes on the fundamental aspects of a future Indian theology, no doubt partly with the meeting at Poona in mind. This is shown by references in letters, and also by some dated notes which have been published posthumously:

> . . . About the Trinity, it is a whole reshaping of the *theologoumenon* [theological statement, dogma] itself which is needed. (. . .) I more and more think of our dogmas as the *upāsana* [meditation] or *vidyā* of the Upanishads. The term(s) *Three persons, Nature,* have to be given up as misleading and, at least in translation, as wrong. (. . .) I think no real theology of the Trinity-Incarnation is possible as long as we do not turn back to the fundamental *anubhava* [experience] which they express. (. . .) But as long as this *anubhava* will remain a *notion* for most theologians, there can (not) be any hope that a real theo-logia (. . .) (will) develop. Hence my fear about the Poona meeting. The question is not only a humble and prayerful approach, but a mental approach all conditioned by the *anubhava* underlying! (SG, 5.4.71)

The background to these remarks can be found in some notes written at this time, especially "Expérience spirituelle (*anubhava*) et dogmes" (dated 2.4.71), "Théologoumenon: Upasana (méditation) sur la Trinité" (date uncertain), and "Christ the Saviour" (written in English on Good Friday, 9.4.71).[57] In these notes he is suggesting that the significance of dogmas is comparable to that of the Upanishadic *upasana*, which prepares the mind for the final awakening. Since the experience and the dogmas belong to two different and incommensurable levels, the value of dogmas lies not in their conceptualizing that which is beyond all ideas whatever, but in pointing towards the experience, for which such 'meditations' prepare the way.

55. The third (Indian) edition, as well as the British and American editions of *Prayer,* was made to be closer to the French. The latest I.S.P.C.K. edition is a translation of the French.
56. "L'apport de l'Inde à la prière chrétienne" was published in Spanish in *Liturgia* (Burgos), no. 253 (April-June 1971), 126ff, under the title, "La oracion del silencio". The French original is in *Les yeux,* 39ff.
57. All three articles are printed in *Intériorité:* "Expérience spirituelle" (p. 209); "Théologoumenon: Upasana . . ." (p. 217); "Jésus le Sauveur" (p. 275).

Further references to his theological probings come in a letter to Mrs Baumer:

> . . . Panikkar found "Archétypes religieux . . ." (above, p.233) weak, so I have put it back in my files. Besides, I do not know who would be interested by it in French, or even in English. (. . .)
>
> . . . I have got into the habit of 'thinking', using the 'wings' of any *mythos,* taken only as a means of support, as the aircraft uses the air; its only value is to prepare for the awakening a little further on. But—as the translation of *Sagesse* shows me—I ought not to write at too great a distance from the mental context of the reader, or it will be misunderstood. In fact I have several pages, not yet completed, on the role of the theologoumena, on Jesus the Saviour, Jesus the Revealer of God, Jesus the Son of God, which would answer some of your questions, but I should need some months to be able to put all that into shape, I am going to have a very full year. I shall be out for almost the whole of May, first for a seminar at Poona for Catholic Indologists, with the aim of preparing studies and books of theology and spirituality, I mean, Indo-Christian ones. An excellent idea, but the plan proposed hopeless. Still it will surely be possible to start something. (OB, 18.4.71)

Delhi, Poona, Bombay, Indore—24 April to end of May 1971

The seminar at Poona was apparently better than Abhishiktananda had feared, and he went on his way encouragd, visiting friends in Bombay, Indore and finally Delhi, before returning to Gyansu. From Indore he wrote to his family:

> . . . As I told you, I went to Poona and Bombay. An interesting meeting, and high hopes for a small nucleus of priests and seminarists who are going to renew and save the Church, at the very moment when so much [missing word] is becoming secular or worldly. It is my role all over the place to [missing] the ideal of prayer and silence. Some friends in Bombay have taken some excellent (photos) which I will send you one day [of himself with children]. I still remain so much in need of receiving and giving affection. Here in Indore terrible heat, over 40 degrees. I can't do a thing. (. . .) At the end of the month I hope to be once more in Gyansu. However, to the extent that people are taking seriously what I have been saying and writing during the last ten years, I am very much afraid that there may be more and more serious encroachments on my solitude. For 1972 I have already promised two months at Poona and also two weeks with some Anglicans besides![58] (F, 18.5.71)

In connection with the seminar he wrote to Fr Lemarié:

> . . . It is consoling to see that the Church begins to stir, and this is the great thing, even if one does not agree with all its movements. I fear that I may perhaps be more involved than I could have wished in some of these movements, but that will only become clear (if it comes off) next year. (L, 7.7.71)

58. At Poona the inaugural 'seminar of renewal' in the C.P.S. Ashram in March; the first 'School of Prayer' at the Rajpur Centre in May.

Gyansu-end of May to 22 August 1971

At Gyansu Abhishiktananda found a letter from Mrs Baumer, enclosing a reproduction of an unusual ikon of the Trinity, in which the Holy Spirit is shown in unmistakably feminine form, and asking for his comments:

> . . . Thank you for the picture of the Holy Spirit. Only the other day at Poona we discussed some texts which, beginning from the feminine Spirit, went on to a divine 'family'—a totally false idea. Someone pointed out that the *śakti* is spouse, but not mother. When God is adored in the form of Mother, there is no thought at all of a masculine principle. The picture is very beautiful, but at the moment I do not see what theology can be derived from it, I think that the renewal of trinitarian theology ought to take place at a very much deeper level.
>
> Yes, I continue to write down my thoughts, which one day might develop into articles, but not this year (too much work on publications). However, I wonder if my thinking is on the right lines? In any case it is certain that the advaitin experience provides the present crisis with a dimension of thought which puts the whole problem in a new light. Yet it is dangerous to formulate the conclusions to which advaita leads, before this experience has been felt; otherwise it would only provide grist to the mill of the worst kind of secularism. (OB, 28.6.72)

Abhishiktananda's questioning whether he was 'on the right lines' has to be constantly remembered in connection with his theological 'speculations'. His role, as he saw it, was to pursue a given hypothesis to its conclusion, however strange this might seem, in the hope that in the darkness light might dawn and new paths open up. More than this he never claimed.

In connection with an offer of financial help, he wrote:

> . . . your suggestion is deeply touching. It is a fact that I live pretty much from day to day, and the reserves which I had a few years ago are practically exhausted, and that the help given to those poorer than I am takes a larger place in my budget than my personal expenses.[59] As for travelling, when anyone invites me, I ask for my fare to be paid, otherwise I remain here, apart from absolute necessity. (OB, 28.6.71)

The project of the 'Pilot Seminary' which he had proposed at the time of the All-India Seminar, and discussed with Fr P. D'Souza and Fr J. Dupuis in the autumn of 1969, continued to interest him. Fr D'Souza was now Bishop of Varanasi, and was therefore in a position to give practical effect to the scheme. Abhishiktananda discussed the matter with the Bishop, with Fr Dupuis and also with Dr Panikkar. In a letter to Fr Dupuis he said:

> . . . Bishop Patrick's reply to me is rather encouraging. The idea of a seminary of 'spiritual insertion' appeals much to him. However, you may well say that I am likely to be a very poor advocate for the cause because, however much I may be in favour of the project. I am much too frightened of getting involved in it. In conversation I may yield to

59. See note 3 on page 25.

> requests, but alone by myself, I can only feel the extent of my lack of communication with the world of students and young people, which now goes back a long way. The idea should by all means be followed up and launched. Your letter and that of Bishop Patrick have stirred my imagination, and I have jotted down some notes intended as a memo on the subject. I am sending them to you by book post. It you find it useful, rework it as you please, have it put into good English, and make use of it. (JD, 19.7.71)

The 'memo' was a long paper, called "An Ashram Seminary",[60] in which he gave his view of the principles which should govern such a foundation. It sketched an ideal which has not so far been implemented, partly no doubt because, apart from Ahishiktananda himself, there were few indeed who would have been capable of giving the required leadership. He made it very clear that he did not wish to be personally involved, though the following letter suggests that in certain circumstances he might have been open to persuasion:

> . . . As for his [Bishop Patrick's] projects and those of J. Dupuis, I am certainly very interested in them; however, I am afraid of discussing them directly with P. He might persuade me to accept certain responsibilities which for many reasons I dread. I would not want to play a merely marginal part in the project; so it may perhaps be providential that I am not discussing the matter directly with P. (RP, 14.8.71)

About this time Abhishiktananda came to know of a plan to start mission work in the mountain area around Uttarkashi, which filled him with horror:

> . . . The districts of the holy mountain of the Ganges are shortly going to be made into an 'exarchate' and handed over to the Syrians (Malayalis)—an area which has not a single Catholic mission station, only a few small Methodist centres. Our Malayalis are going to come here with their jeeps, their schools and relief-projects. I fear the worst. I have just sent off an SOS to a Bombay weekly, asking that here at least the Church's presence should be in the first place spiritual. I am very much afraid that not only the approach of old age (. . .) but also the new situation is going to change my life. (L, 7.7.71)

His 'SOS' was an article entitled "The Church in Uttarkhand", published by the *Examiner* (31.7.71), which pleaded for a more sensitive approach to this deeply Hindu area. As he told Fr Dupuis, he also wrote directly to the Prior General of C.M.I. (Carmelites of Mary Immaculate), the congregation which was going to be responsible for the exarchate. He received a friendly response, and his article was reprinted in their Bulletin. "However, my presence here is likely to become difficult." (JD, 19.7.71)

The monsoon of 1971 was again very heavy, and the mountain roads were repeatedly broken by landslides. Dr Panikkar's plan to come to Gyansu in July had to be abandoned, and Abhishiktananda was unable to leave his kutiya until late August. Transport difficulties caused a shortage in the bazar at Uttarkashi, and he told his family in August that the only vegetables that he could afford

60. A copy of this paper, which was not published, is in the Society's archives.

were potatoes (F, 11.8.71). His garden is not mentioned this year, which suggests that he had given up cultivating it.

His friend in New York, Mrs Stokes, was on a visit to her birthplace in Brittany, and wrote to him from there. His nostalgic reply (AMS, 3.8.71) was quoted in Chapter 1.

He also received news that Sr Térèse's problem had been happily solved, and that Rome had granted an 'indult' which permitted her to follow her calling as a hermit without being compelled to leave the Carmelite Órder. On his way down from Gyansu. Abhishiktananda planned to arrange for her accommodation in Hardwar, so that she could settle there in the following November. He wrote joyfully to Mother Françoise-Thérèse at Lisieux:

> . . . So you will have had the incredible news about Térèse. After that it is difficult not to believe that the Spirit directs everything, and does so with a 'smile'! On my way down shortly I shall see my friend in Hardwar who knows her, and who already two years ago asked for a place for her. I hope the arrangement can be renewed.
>
> The article [sent through Fr Lemarié} concerning this same friend[61] was solely for your interest. It has never been published. If anyone wants to use it one day, either in English or in French, they are perfectly free to do so (. . .). It had been accepted here in principle by a Catholic Press agency, but then they did not use it; probably because people are unwilling to admit that the Spirit laughs at all man-made barriers. (FT, 20.8.71)

In the August number of *ICI* (*Informations cath. internationales,* no. 389-390) Abhishiktananda had written a mild protest that a recent article on a Christian centre of Zen in Japan had made no mention of the work of Fr Oshida. He spoke of this in a letter to Mrs Baumer:

> . . .Oshida is Buddhist by birth, and was already practising Zen in his college days. (. . .) I must have told you of the marvellous meeting I had with him last winter in Bareilly. It was somewhat unseemly of *ICI* to have so strongly emphasized what Europeans are doing, when for some time in Japan, as in India, there is an excellent elite belonging to the coutnry itself. Only this week there is a seminar on Indian theology at Bangalore with a remarkable programme. I was invited, but (. . .). There is also going to be at Nagpur an international seminar on Theology and Evangelization. I have sent them the paper for which I was asked. (OB, 20.8.71)

Hardwar, Banaras, Lucknow—22 August to about 11 September 1971

From Hardwar Abhishiktananda went to Banaras which was severely flooded. He met the Bishop and Dr Panikkar, and presumably discussed the 'Ashram Seminary', though this is not mentioned in the available letters. When writing to his sisters, he wrote mainly about personal matters; for example, to a married sister he wrote about depression:

61. Swami Niranjananand, with whom he used to stay in Hardwar. The article, "The Call of the Lord", dated 17.7.70, was written for *Catholic News Service of India.* A copy is in the archives.

> . . . India is a country of extremes. Here (Banaras), as in the mountains, there is too much rain, and in other places there is drought. (. . .) You can understand why the poor in India have developed the habit of bowing their heads, crouching down and waiting for the storm to pass. (. . .) I may sometimes have moments of depression, when I see the wretchedness of other people. They are very rare as regards what concerns me personally, and soon pass. Age and the passage of time show the relative nature of most of our problems. (. . .) I was born 'under a good star', as they say. I have always met with friendship and the support necessary for holding on and going forward—and it is the same as regards my thinking, writing and role in the Church here. (ALG, 1.9.71)

He told his sister at Kergonan about the frightening journey from Gyansu and how, where the road was broken, the passengers had to struggle across on foot carrying their belongings from one bus to another: "What a dangerous road—one moment's carelessness on the part of the driver, and we would have been sent 'aloft' by way of the Ganges!" Then at Banaras it was raining continually, so that in the streets the water came above the axles of the cycle-rickshaws, and the river was almost overflowing its banks:

> . . . I have just been to celebrate Mass with the Little Sisters of Fr de Foucauld, who live in a lane 1/2 km away, just beside the Ganges, which has also made its way into a kind of open hall beneath their chapel. The lane at most three to six feet wide and slippery, with fruit and vegetable stalls on either side, and the cows wandering about freely, caressing passers-by with their tails—fortunately they do not as a rule use horns and hoofs! (. . .)
>
> What! Was *Gnanananda* not clear enough? (. . .) I think you must have forgotten my little article in *Parole et Mission* of May 70 . . .[62] All those words are spirit, not letter—as the Gospel says. The 'void' is a 'limit-situation', as they say in geometry; you tend towards it, but never reach it; the sustained effort, never halted, but totally directed towards a Beyond which neither word nor feeling can express, the discovery of your own greatest depth, which at the same time is both void and fullness; for as soon as you use words, you *compare* and so set limits. That is the very reason why all our words about God seem so inadequate, as soon as you have tasted a little of this depth. Have you never read *The Ascent of Mount Carmel?* It is so close to our advaitin experience in India. Does not *Sagesse* say that, as far as it can be said? I am at present working on the English translation of *Sagesse.* I have had it translated, but I have to revise and even rewrite the whole thing, and once again the style will have to be checked with an Englishman. (. . .) They also talk of another edition of *Prayer* in London. If the publishers are generous, that should restore my finances. (MT, 3.9.71)

Abhishiktananda returned from Banaras by way of Lucknow in order to meet his friend Harilal, who was about to go to Europe on the invitation of some of

62. See p. 227 above and Note 30.

his disciples. He wrote to his friend in Switzerland, suggesting that she might find it worth while to meet him herself. "We are very close to each other, advaitically speaking. But there is a whole side to his psyche [nature] which I do not understand" (OB, 9.9.71).

Gyansu—11 to 30 September 1971

During these three weeks at Gyansu Abhishiktananda completed his redrafting of the English version of *Sagesse*. The preliminary translation of the last two-thirds of the book had been done by a friend in Bombay. In his letter of thanks he assured her: "With your work, my work and that of J.S., we shall in the end have something excellent" (AF, 21.9.71).

Before setting off again for the Nagpur seminar, he wrote to Fr Lemarié, referring to the Feast of St Michael and All Angels (29 Sept):

> . . . Tomorrow a feast which is dear to you, St Michael. How are we to reintegrate this very beautiful *muthos* (I don't say, myth) in our modern thought? Christianity is really over-serious, with its ruinous principle of [non-]contradiction: [the alternatives] "is/is not". As if man was capable of taking in at the same time "is/is not"! Over this India is marvellously playful. Her myths remain living and life-giving, precisely because we do not conceptualize them; though, alas, that is being done nowadays, but it is so un-Hindu. . . (L, 28.9.71)

He also brought him up to date with publishing matters. The French version of *Prayer* (*Éveil à soi—èveil à Dieu*) was on the point of being published. A contract had been signed for the Italian version, but on the other hand no publisher was willing to undertake the German version.[63] The London S.P.C.K. was preparing an edition for Lent 1972, while the Indian S.P.C.K., having already sold 6000 copies, was about to print a third edition.

> . . . The English of *Sagesse* is a headache. On my return from Varanasi, worn out, I continued with the revision, which finished me. However, it too is now completed. My publisher is going to revise the whole thing, and all I have to do is to verify his new text.
>
> My health is better than last year, though my vitality is much reduced, and there is no hope of the six months of rest and rich European food which would be needed to put that right. Going up and down to Uttarkashi is also very tiresome (. . .); each time I am out of action for a week. But more and more they are asking for me down below. I refuse a lot, but not everything—that would be egotistical. Ought I to consider at least a *pied à terre* in the plains? But if I have to pay for it, it would be absolutely impossible. (. . .) On the other hand, there is the business of the C.M.I. taking charge of Garhwal (. . .). If they come to Uttarkashi itself, it will be better for me to move out; otherwise I shall stay here for a few more years. The trouble about going down is that so many people want to come and see me.

63. The German edition published in 1980 used a new translation by Dr B. Bäumer.

> . . . I have enjoyed Chromatius [the second volume of Fr Lemarié's edition] (. . .). But I continue to find European thought, both ancient and modern, 'narrow' (that is not fair, I know—I really mean 'shut in'). Indian thought is born in the infinitude of the mountains and the limitless extent of the Gangetic plains—rather like the high seas which have no boundary, as Claudel said. And that is why, in contact with India, any theology can only explode, as the spaceship Soyuz did in outer space . . . (L, 28.9.71)

He wrote to Kergonan to tell his sister about his programme in the plains. First there would be the seminar at Nagpur, then a session with his publisher in Delhi, after which he planned to go

> . . . to Hardwar with a young seminarist of Bourg-en-Bresse, who for a year or so has been planning to come here and is expecting me to meet him. Finally, Térèse, the Sister from Lisieux, has at last obtained her indult to come to Hardwar. I shall meet her there and settle her provisionally, until she can herself find somewhere to her taste, and (. . .) then go back for the winter. I shall try to bring from Dehra Dun a small electric fire to warm my old bones.
>
> It is no use living far away, people still find me out. Yesterday evening an Indian Jesuit turned up at 7 p.m.! Nothing to give him to eat and nowhere for him to sleep. I had to run up to the house at the top of the hill to ask the young man who comes here at midday to come and cook some supper and prepare a bed. But at least I am free from foreigners. (MT, 30.9.71)

The unexpected guest[64] was charmed with his reception and particularly happy to have the opportunity of a long talk with Abhishiktananda:

> That night I spent long hours with Swamiji, talking about the jñanis and jivanmuktas of India. (. . .) At the time of my journey to Uttarkashi I was engaged on writing a thesis on the concept of *jīvanmukti* in Saiva Siddhanta, and one of the reasons for my visit was to draw on the deep experience of Swamiji on this fascinating subject. I was happy for having the *darshan* of the Swami.

Nagpur, Delhi and by the Ganges—1 October to 5 December 1971

Abhishiktananda went first to Nagpur for the international seminar on Mission and Evangelization (6-12 October), his particular assignment being the workshop on Evangelization and Contemplation. He contributed one of the papers, on "Theology of Presence as a form of evangelization in the context of non-Christian Religions", which was published in the official report.[65] In this his conviction is persuasively expressed that the Church's mission is grounded in the awareness of the Presence in her own life and at the heart of all; and that her fundamental calling is to awaken every man to that Presence, in whatever situation (cultural, religious) God may have placed him; and that this more important

64. The account of his visit by Fr Ch. Valliaveetil, SJ, is in the archives.
65. *Service and Salvation* (Bangalore 1973), 407-417.

than 'making converts'. A number of his friends (R. Panikkar, S. Grant, for example) were taking part, as well as some theologians from the West, whom he was interested in meeting. His general impression of the meeting was optimistic, and he was happy to see a rapprochement between so-called 'contemplatives' and the protagonists of involvement in social action, who at the All-India Seminar of 1969 had been unable to come to terms. A letter to Mrs Baumer, written from Delhi, gives his reactions to the seminar.

> . . . Nagpur—an interesting theological meeting, at which the Europeans from abroad felt that, while the Indian Church gave them a very kind welcome, it scarcely seemed convinced that it has much to learn from them . . . (. . .) The young Indian theologians become increasingly critical. The fundamental problem of Christ versus the Indian experience beyond all forms begins to be vitally important for them. I asked that we should have smaller groups in which everyone could speak without inhibition, when discussing the fundamental problem. The place of contemplation was given full recognition, at least in theory. Good plans for disseminating the knowledge of real prayer—but there is a lack of 'awakeners'. (. . .)
>
> I am sending you my Nagpur paper . . It gently says quite a lot (. . .). Here I am staying in an Anglican[66] Brotherhood, where they have just asked me to celebrate their community Mass on Saturday in Indian style . . . New links are being formed every day; every day bold novelties are becoming commonplace. The Spirit continues to move. But yesterday, when I was working on the English of chapters 2 and 3 of *Sagesse*—what remains to be said after the experience of Ramana and the Upanishads: I AM! You say it, and then are silent (. . .). How can this silence be expressed for the theologians of Nagpur? Only words of prophecy might convey something. Jesus himself had first to keep silence for forty days after the overwhelming experience at the Jordan. And then the Spirit spoke through him (OB, 20.10.71)

After the Nagpur Seminar Abhishiktananda spent ten days in Delhi, during which Marc Chaduc, 'the young seminarist from Bourg-en-Bresse', arrived on 21 October. He had reached Bombay three weeks previously and came on to Delhi by easy stages.

Marc's coming coincided with, and helped to bring about, a revolutionary change in Abhishiktnanda's life. In a word, he experienced with shattering immediacy the fullness of the guru-disciple relationship. During the last twenty months of his active life this was his dominating concern, and he gave himself unsparingly to his disciples—to Marc especially, but by no means exclusively. From now on he only returned for brief periods to his solitude at Gyansu.

The guru-disciple relationship has no parallel in western culture, and is difficult for westerners to understand or even conceive, all the more because it often comes to their notice in sadly corrupted forms.

66. This Brotherhood, originally the 'Cambridge Brotherhood', now the 'Delhi Brotherhood', had since 1970 belonged to the 'Church of North India', a union of six previously separated traditions.

Abhishiktananda had long before discovered one side of the relationship in his meeting with Gnanananda in 1955-56, when he found himself instantaneously accepting Gnanananda as his own guru. As he says in *Guru and Disciple*, 28-29 (1989 edition, 11):

> Hindu tradition is right in saying that, when the disciple is ready, the guru automatically appears; only those who are unworthy of it spend their time running about after gurus. Guru and disciple are a dyad, a pair, whose two components call for each other and belong together. No more than the two poles [of a magnet] can they exist without being related to each other.

In that first experience with Gnanananda, Abhishiktananda had learnt what it is to be a disciple. Only much later he began to realize the other pole of the relationship. He indeed glimpsed it during his years at Shantivanam, when some of those who temporarily joined him treated him as guru. But it was only at Gyansu that his two Hindu disciples, Ramesh and Lalit, enabled him to realize the deeper aspects of the relationship.

It is clear from his letters to Marc before his coming to India, that Abhishiktananda already discerned in him an unusual spiritual depth. His original intention was to give Marc two weeks of 'initiation', and then to send him off to discover India and Indians for himself. However, when they met, he at once realized that in Marc he was dealing with someone who was eager and ready to receive all that he could possibly give. It was impossible to foresee where this might lead.

Their first few days together in Delhi were spent in ceaseless conversation, of which Marc says: "By the second evening Fr Le Saux (Henri) had 'volatilized' all my questions. He plunges (me) into the Source, beyond *logos* [the level of reasoning]." One evening Abhishiktananda introduced him to Ramesh, who was working in Delhi and sharing a rented room with a friend in a suburb across the Yamuna. They then went to Hardwar and Rishikesh, where beside the Ganges they had a crowded week of charismatic meetings with a remarkable variety of people, including Minoru Kasai,[67] a Japanese friend already known at Banaras (L, 16.11.71)

A few days later at the beginning of November Sr Térèse arrived from Pondicherry to begin her life as a hermit beside the Ganges:

> . . . The Carmelite from Lisieux arrives at Hardwar on the 5th. I have found her a room. I must get her settled in, and then take her to see the Bishop (of Meerut), 150 kms from here. (F, 3.11.71)

That done, Abhishiktananda took Marc back to Rishikesh for three more intensive days of initiation, in the course of which they had an experience of which something, however inadequate, has to be said.

It took place on 8 November, as they were walking along the path beside the Ganges on the way to the Phulchatti ashram, which is about four miles upstream from Laxman Jhula. In Marc's words, it was "the irruption of the mystery of Being between—at the heart of—us two", and it left Abhishiktananda "stagger-

67. Now a professor in the International Christian University, Tokyo.

ing". It was as if the 'advaitin experience', the realization that "there are not-two", was momentarily focussed in their own relationship, without of course being in any way limited to them. But the word 'experience' is itself misleading, for it refers to nothing seen, heard, felt or even thought, and to suppose that it could be 'described' would prove that it is not known ("those who know, keep silence").

From now on it is clear that Abhishiktananda and Marc lived the guru-disciple relationship at the deepest level, so that the former could speak of them as being but a single 'I'—"I am now you; or better, I am you here, and you are I there" (MC, 6.12.71). This may well sound mere sentimentality to western ears, for whom the meaning of 'I' is limited to the individual ego. The key to its true meaning is best given in Abhishiktananda's book on *Gnanananda*, especially chapter 9. The guru is merely the human form in which Brahman, God, the I AM, manifests himself to awaken the disciple to his true Self, and the guru-disciple relationship exists only for that. Once the disciple 'awakes', there is no longer either guru or disciple!

It is natural that, at the human level, there should be a deep bond of love between guru and disciple. In the case of Abhishiktananda, his relation to his disciples, especially to Marc, released in him springs of affection which were probably deeper than anything in his previous experience. But at the same time his love was neither possessive nor exclusive, and indeed could not be so, as otherwise the relationship would have been corrupted. At the heart of this most intimate relationship there remains a radical non-attachment, something which in India is well understood.[68]

After these days at Rishikesh Abhishiktananda prescribed three weeks of total silence for his disciple, who passed them in a cave near Laxman Jhula. Meanwhile he returned to Hardwar, so as to be near to Sr Térèse, and also made another short visit to Delhi.

The following letters to Mrs Baumer and his sister indicate something of the new dimension in Abhishiktananda's life:

> . . . beside the Ganges at Hardwar. A place of blessing, which I hope you may one day experience, together with your son at least. Here with a young Frenchman and a Japanese friend, unbelievable days! Two Masses on the sand beside the Ganges, another on a mountain facing the sun as it rose behind the snow peaks. Our prayer rose spontaneously, taking up, uniting with all that was ever offered in (?) and also all the holy silences in these places, in the midst of pilgrims, ascetics, temple bells. Preceded by a bath in the Ganges, which the Japanese said washed even his bones. What a joy those young Hindus are, who to me are as much children as disciples; who, in being disciples, make me a guru in the deepest sense of the word, a human relationship which realizes the deepest meaning of fatherhood. It is what I felt with

68. Abhishiktananda held that the relationship referred to in Christ's prayer, "that they may be one as we are . . . perfectly one", or in Paul's "we are members one of another", is to be realized in the life of grace now, not put off to an eschatological future. Cp. also the letter to Fr Lemarié (5.1.72) below, p. 258..

Gnanananda, and what Ramesh makes me realize, when he takes all from me without depriving me of anything . . . A sense of Christ beyond all forms. An advaita which is in no way opposed to Christianity, since to advaita nothing can be in opposition (. . .). The level of speech and thought are not opposed to the order of simply being, they are its sign. Ramesh would like to be a Christian, but the Church as it is cannot accommodate him. My dream is that he should be the starting-point of Christ-lovers, who out of their Hindu depth love and serve him. (. . .) What is it that the Spirit wants to show me through this? (OB, 3.11.71)

. . . I have just spent a week with Térese, getting her settled. Just a moment ago I was saying the Mass of Advent Sunday with her. Tomorrow I shall take her to a new house where she will be able to live normally. Compared with the Carmel it is real poverty, and yet it is luxurious when compared with Indian simplicity. All these two months I have been very busy—the meeting at Nagpur, the translation of *Sagesse,* young people to meet, especially the young Frenchman from Bourg, with whom I spent two weeks and then left beside the Ganges at Rishikesh for three weeks of silence and solitude, and whom I shall go to collect on Wednesday morning. (. . .) But how eager I am to return to Uttarkashi, despite the cold that awaits me there. I shall have to go back to Delhi for this interminable translation, and also for another *chela* (that is, disciple, in the very strong sense of the word, as I have explained it in *Gnanananda*, something of which you have no idea in Europe). He is a Hindu, but one for whom Christ is now the Lord, and he would like me to explain the Gospel to him. The pity is that Christian groups are so ritualistic and pietistic, that I do not see how Ramesh could ever be at home with them. (. . .)

With Marc and others we have had marvellous Masses beside the Ganges and also in the jungle on the mountain ovelooking it (. . .). There is here a marvellous atmosphere which holds anyone whose heart is open to the beauty and the mystery! (MT, 28.11.71)

When Marc emerged from his three weeks of silence, Abhishiktananda found him 'radiant'. His first taste of solitude had made him eager for more, and he was distinctly hesitant about entering on the next stage of his *sādhana* (spiritual training) which his guru prescribed. However, Abhishiktananda firmly despatched him on a long pilgrimage for two and a half months to Vrindavan, Varanasi and South India (especially Arunachala). He himself, after another visit to Sr Térèse, returned for five weeks to Gyansu.

Gyansu—5 December 1971 to 10 January 1972

When Abhishiktananda reached Gyansu, he found it indeed as cold as he had expected. His electric stove proved too expensive to run, and so he muffled himself up as well as he could, and went into 'hibernation'. And, as for once he had no urgent writing work on hand, he was free to practise for a short time what he had so often preached—'being' rather than 'doing'.

Despite his distress at the Indo-Pakistan war, the happiness of the past weeks shows in his letters:

. . . my joy in meeting these young French people in the plains. I am much, if not more, of a hippy than they are, as one of them, Marc, said to me! (F, 20.12.71)

. . . I just came back last week, after weeks in Delhi for this impossible translation of *Sagesse* (which finally Fr S. will have to rewrite completely), the wonderful time in Hardwar-Rishikesh, where I chiefly met the young Frenchman whom you met in Sophia at the end of September. He was really able to receive 'everything'; his questions were muted after a few days, and at the end of three weeks of solitude-silence on and under the rocks of the Ganga beyond Rishikesh fully opened his *guhā* [the 'cave' of the heart].

These weeks in Hardwar-Rishikesh with attuned souls (you would have felt quite at home in our meetings and Masses near the Ganga which were calling for spontaneous expression, since no (. . .) formula was able to express the mystery they had to unfold!) have put me far from the 'ecclesiastical' policies (. . .). How far behind the Real are even the best statements of Nagpur! I believe only more and more in 'charismatic' moves, = '*groupes de base*', '*communautés de base*' [Base Communities], as they say in France, which will open new vistas and one day be so strong in the Spirit that they may move even the 'canonical' Church. (. . .) Anyhow it is necessary that people and groups (like you and your Congregation) be involved in the process (. . .) (SG, 13.12.71)

There are further references to the disciples in other letters from Gyansu:

. . . Next week I shall be at Hardwar with Térèse, the ten days following with Ramesh, the young Hindu who reads the Gospel and has made me discover in an inexplicable experience what a guru means for a disciple. That goes so very far beyond 'spiritual direction' and even natural—or even spiritual—fatherhood. I believe that in order to understand it, you have to try to work back to the very mystery of the Father and the Son. Yet another case in which all our ideas—western and (exported) Mediterranean-Christian—are passed beyond. But then, what that implies and foreshadows is such a total upheaval that one takes fright and prefers to curl up and remain silent.

. . . I shall be in Delhi until the 26th. I shall have to go to Ranchi (the Carmel of Soso), then to Poona for a long seminar on the renewal of the religious life (not in theory, but in practice), work on *Sagesse* (. . .), some necessary time with Ramesh, time with Marc (. . .). That young man is most remarkable. To him I can communicate everything, and he in his turn will be able to communicate it in France; I owe him all the time I can spare. Thus my programme is absolutely uncertain. (L, 5.1.72)

. . . I have found in him (Marc) a truly total disciple. With him and two young Hindus I experience from the other end what the guru is. It is really the *chela* (disciple) who *makes* the guru, and you have to have lived it, in order to grasp this relationship 'beyond words'. (. . .) Frightening, and what a responsibility! (. . .)

As I have often written, I think that a theology that goes further ought not to be written down, for fear of being misunderstood and misleading people; it can only be left to be divined from spoken words. Thanks to the cold (which puts me in a state of hibernation), and also to an unwonted lack of urgent work, I have lived here a month of the very powerful discipline of the present moment; no tomorrow, no 'just now', no practical or theological problems to solve, but *to be there*. That is exactly what my neighbours are doing, free from everything, unconcerned about everything. (. . .) What a discipline for a westerner! And how the demand of the west for something 'understood' or 'felt' misses the point. Everything is so simple. (. . .) It is here that you understand the way of total surrender in the *chela-guru* relationship. Only the total leaving behind of self gives access to the Self; all attempts to understand the Self are misleading. The further I go, the more I feel that everything comes back to *conversion*, the *metanoia* of the Gospel, above and through and beyond all the 'ways'. So dangerous to interpret *jñana* or *karma*[69], or *yoga* esoterically. (. . .)

Arunachala has just played one of his 'tricks' on Marc. At the ashram of Sri Ramana, his room burgled, and all his papers and money gone. "Perfect," he tells me: "Stuck at Arunachala, unable to stir!" (OB, 7.1.72)

While Marc was away on pilgrimage, Abhishiktananda continued his instruction through a series of letters, from which some extracts follow:

. . . You have discovered the mystery of India, beyond the sign which India itself is; and the mystery which India reveals is the sole and unique mystery which is revealed and bursts forth at the heart of everything—that "glorious Purusha, of the colour of the dawn, *aruna*, beyond the darkness".[70] It is certainly good for you to stay on in India for some months or years, for the vibrations here are powerful for whoever can catch them; however, the essential has been done, and henceforth neither time nor place have major importance. The door of the *guha* has been opened to you! You have glimpsed its depths, now enter within, from depth to depth, to ever deeper centres, in a constantly deeper passing beyond of yourself and of God, which has neither beginning nor end, in that mystery which is no more either not-one or not-two. The only remaining task is to awaken your brothers to the ray of holy darkness, or rather, to let yourself be carried along as a sign of the Spirit. (MC, 6.12.71)

. . . Simply live in the eternity, of which the present fleeting moment gives a glimpse. Decisions about the future will come in their own time (. . .). For your future work the important, the essential thing, is this

69. *Jñana* ('knowledge'), and *karma* ('action', ritual or other), and *bhakti* ('devotion', which is commonly included after *jñana)* are the three classical *marga* ('ways') in Hinduism.
70. A favourite quotation from the Śvetāśvatara Upanishad, 3.8.

'being lost' within. The priesthood, the theology degree, Sanskrit and the Hindu Shastras will only come long afterwards. I am wondering whether, once you are back in France, it would not be good for you to make a trial of some monasteries. (. . .) For all the same, (monastic) formation has an unequalled value. Personally (. . .) I gained from it enormously, and I owe to it a very great part of what I am now. (MC, 13.12.71)

. . . In the first place, your pilgrimage must not be interrupted, unless you are compelled to do so by unavoidable outward circumstances. It is part of your *sadhana.* The Espresso bar on the corner of the ghats is no less 'brahmic' than the *arati* or the ecstatic Mass. This is precisely what you have to discover and live now; the expression of the inmost and unique mystery in the most commonplace action or meeting. (MC, 17.12.71)

. . Physical disappearance is still only a sign. For in disappearing from some people's sight, you appear to others, and so long as you still know that you have disappeared, you have not disappeared from your own sight, and this little ego very likely takes the place of all those 'you' which you have left one after the other at the side of the road. The hub of the wheel is the one thing to reach, the motionless depth of yourself. That alone is the true *guha*, that alone gives to the *guha* of rock the marvellous solitude which it radiates like a mirror. Once more, I think your present pilgrimage is absolutely essential to free you from all that is mere symbol in the cave in the rock. The place from which there is no return is the centre of yourself, the *atman-brahman,* beyond the whirlpool of signs, even the sign of solitude and silence! This centre is not something you have to reach. You don't have to make an effort as if to leap into it from where you are now, from this so-called shore where you dream that you are. It just *is.* Discover yourself, awake to yourself; or rather, discover that you are awake. (MC, 19.12.71)

. . . Will this find you at Arunachala? When you climb to its summit (. . .), drink of its springs, enter its caves, never forget that Arunachala is a sign, and that every sign finally merges in its *Res* ('thing', reality). The peak, the caves, the waters, all that is your own mystery! And Arunachala only reveals itself when it has vanished. "It is for your good that I am going away," in the words of Jesus which struck us so powerfully. For only then will the Spirit radiate and be spread abroad beyond all forms and through all forms. These days I have been thinking that in Jesus God has revealed to us his *Face* in the purest and most beautiful manner that can be imagined, but in the Purusha of the Upanishads he has revealed to us his unique interiority both to himself and us. And so, that the Face itself reflects this abyssal—bottomless—interiority! (MC, 30.12.71)

After hearing of the theft of all Marc's belongings, he wrote: "I have had experience of these 'tricks' at Shantivanam and even at Arunachala, but never as savagely as this." And he advised him where he might borrow some money. Next day he wrote again:

> . . . Humanly speaking, a terrible blow; but how fail to discern a hidden hand, a heart, lips? I cried out to Shiva: What have you done to my child? And he answered me: It is you who have done it to him, it is he who has done it to himself. Was it not just that which he himself *wanted* most deeply in his heart, where he is nothing else but Myself? (. . .) Now there is no longer any question whether I should join you or not. (. . .) The very fact that your letter reached me amazingly soon . . . is also a sign that you need me. (. . .)
>
> But you may equally well think that Shiva wants you there by yourself, without even this form of his presence that I myself am . . . It all depends entirely on you. (. . .) So I shall not move without a word from you. (MC, 8.1.72)

A few days later he heard that the police had caught the thief and returned most of what had been lost. In the mean time he had written:

> . . . There is no question that Arunachala is a powerful magnet. How I should like to lead you round from cave to cave (. . .).
>
> Have no scruple on the subject of Masses and the rest. Does the child in its mother's womb know her face? Does he feel her as an 'other? There is a time for gazing and for rites, and also a time for silence; and the latter is still more necessary.
>
> . . . You and Ramesh are in process of making me live the experience of the guru from the other end. Each of you drives me crazy. (. . .) How you 'empty' me, as you fulfil me. I can only allow myself to be led, to embrace, be embraced, to give, be given, to receive, be received . . . (MC, 14.1.72)

Hardwar, Delhi, Ranchi, Banaras, Delhi, Hardwar—10 January to 6 March 1972

Coming down from Gyansu, Abhishiktananda first spent some days at Hardwar near Sr Térèse, and then stayed in Delhi for the rest of January. He was not however staying at the Brotherhood House, although he had work there. This time he was the guest of Ramesh and his friend Jagjit in their quarters across the Yamuna in Shahdara, and each day commuted between there and the city, as he told his sister:

> . . . Here in Delhi, in a suburb, I am staying with two young Hindus who are as dear to me as my own children would be. At 8.30 they go out to work, return at 6 p.m., take their bath, have supper, and then we have an hour or two reading the Gospel. During the day, when they are out, I go to the centre of Delhi to work on editing my books—an hour of walk-bus-walk. It helps you to understand the hard life of those who have to earn their living. Imagine it, they each earn . . . (?), and in Delhi everything is expensive. One of them is married, and has just got a small daughter a month old whom I went to see last Sunday at her grandparents' home 60 kms away. Tomorrow I leave for Ranchi (. . .) for some Carmelites whom I have not seen for three years and who are

asking me to come. (. . .) I shall come back to Delhi for another fortnight; then Hardwar with that young Frenchman who has marvellously taken to the grace of India; then a month at Poona for a 'seminar' of renewal with some other religious.

. . . Life passes, that's just a way of speaking; the only thing that counts is that *I myself am*—and that has nothing to do with time. '*I am*' with the eternity of God, since I am born from God! The theologians are afraid of the assertions of the Gospel, and I had to go by way of the Hindu Scriptures in order to accept the Gospel paradoxes in their full truth. That is why anyone who comes from Hinduism finds our ordinary Christianity of rites and externals so unappealing. (. . .) Yes, when you have discovered this *I am,* scorching, devastating, then no longer even (can you say) *God is*— for who *is* there to dare to speak of God? This is the great grace of India, which makes us discover the 'I am' at the heart of the Gospel (John 8). May the devastating joy of this 'I am' fill your soul. (MT, 29.1.72)

On his return from visiting the Carmel of Soso, Abhishiktananda learnt from his family of the death of an old friend and fellow-student in the seminary, Fr R. Macé. They had continued to correspond, and it was Fr Macé who had introduced him to 'Jean Sulivan'.

. . . A certain number of my course have already left this world. and what an experience to see oneself growing old and grey! (. . .)

I have returned to Delhi after a trying journey. (. . .) Here once again with my two 'big children'. They could not love me more if I were their own father. I wake them in the morning with a kiss. They go to work at 9 and come back at 7, and then we make supper together. (. . .) I have just done my washing, and am getting ready to go into Delhi. This evening I have to give a talk to some young Jesuits. I shall probably get back about 11 p.m. So you can see that my life here is a little less peaceful than at Uttarkashi.

At Banaras the Bishop would like me to have my ashram there, so that I could be within easier reach of people who want to see me. I am very hesitant about sacrificing my freedom. (F, 18.2.72)

The evening meeting with young Jesuits was at the seminary of Vidyajyoti, which had recently been transferred to Delhi from Kurseong. As it was now next door to the Brotherhood in which he normally stayed, he looked forward to more frequent meetings with his friends on the staff.

Distressing news concerning one of his oldest and most trusted advaitin friends reached Abhishiktananda during February, and drew from him a feeling comment:

. . . A fallen star . . . This gives one food for thought about advaita. It requires such perfect balance that very easily the Self can be submerged in the little self; and then one can continue to talk admirably, while simply falling into (. . .). (OB, 15.2.72)

Meanwhile preparations for the 'seminar of renewal' at Poona were taking shape, and Abhishiktananda wrote to Sr Grant:

. . . So the die is cast. We shall try to insert some Upanishadic *satsang* in the way described in *Meeting Point.* Like you I feel it should be a daily routine, in order to get into it. Let us hope, and let the Spirit work. I feel often 'ennoyed' [disturbed?] at that 'Indianization', be it liturgical or ashramic! You have read what R.P. wrote about Nagpur in the *Tablet*, called "Indian Theology on Western Themes"? [Abhishiktananda felt that he had taken a too pessimistic view; RP, 25.12.71] Yet does not the Spirit work through everything? (. . .) Let us help as much as we can, and then try to follow the Spirit.

. . . I hope the Hindus of the seminar will not be simply scholars, which would be simply dreadful. We need people who do not keep in hand the 'matches' even of the Scriptures, once the inner light radiates, *svaprakāsha*! (SG, 21.1.72)

. . . Now did I understand well that I am supposed to lead almost every day a 'contemplative reading' of the Upanishads? It is indeed almost the only thing I might be able to do.

. . . I met Bishop Patrick in Varanasi last week. (. . .) he is very keen now on a *Jñana*-ashram to be started in Varanasi (in place of the unrealistic seminary), in which orientation (practical) courses might be given in order to initiate young priests and others to 'Hindu prayer' as he says. I see really the need and urgency of it; yet I hardly see how I could work in the scheme . . . I would need at the minimum some young *chela* fully in my ideas to help me. (SG, 20.2.72)

Before going to Poona, Abhishiktananda returned to Hardwar where, with Sr Térèse, Marc and Ramesh, he led a week of study in the Upanishads.

Seminar at Poona—11 March to 15 April 1972

The Christa Prema Seva Ashram in Poona had been founded in 1927 by the Revd Jack Winslow, and had pioneered the development of an Indian and Franciscan form of Christian life. After some years, however, it was weakened by various set-backs, and by 1969 it was little more than a relic. At that time, following the All-India Seminar, the Catholic Church in India had set out on the path of renewal. In keeping with this, the Sisters of the Sacred Heart (RSCJ) planned to give their novices a much more Indian style of formation, for which their Provincial, Sr Dhalla (now Sr Vandana) suggested to the trustees of the C.P.S. Ashram that it might be made available to her Congregation. Their response was to propose that it should be reconstituted as an ecumenical ashram with Anglican participation. As we have seen, there had been a possibility of the Jyotiniketan ashram moving from Bareilly to Poona, which was not realized. Eventually, in 1972 it was agreed that it should be a joint venture between the sisters of the Sacred Heart and the Community of St Mary the Virgin (an Anglican sisterhood, which since 1970 belonged to the Church of North India).

It was as a preparation for the reopening of the ashram that the seminar of renewal was organized. Taking part were about thirty Sisters, priests and seminarists, who were responding to the call of the All-India Seminar for the opening of small ashrams dedicated to 'prayer and silence or prayer and work'.

(From the C.N.I. side participation was disappointingly small.) The chief theme of the seminar was a study of Indian spirituality and ashram life, for which Abhishiktananda gave of his best. One Sister afterwards recorded her impression of him—

> . . . triumphantly leading the procession of the Easter Vigil, outshining the Paschal moon with his flaming torch bright with the new fire of the Spirit; deep in earnest conversation with the small Gandhian figure of Dadaji Pandit of Satara concerning some point of liturgy or Hindu/Christian scriptural interpretation; or sitting very still in *padmāsan* [lotus position] on the edge of the pool at twilight, waiting for the evening Angelus and supper; roaring with laugher at his own wickedly funny jokes; or swiftly passing along the verandah, robes girt up and red pail in hand, to do his *dhobi* before lending an expert hand with the vegetables.[71]

Another Sister wrote:

> . . . Several of us had heard that he did not find it easy to live in community. So there were doubts and perhaps even fears at the subconscious level. But in a few days all the clouds were swept away. We were meeting the Swamiji himself at his depth, completely relaxed and perfectly at home with himself and in the group. (. . .) I had the joy of working with him on a little liturgy committee (. . .). Swamiji always felt inspired to do something new, to make the liturgy very meaningful and a new experience each day. I was struck to see him also listening to our contributions, however immature or inexperienced. He could be a 'child among children' (. . .). Often his French would pop in here and there, so much that we would tease him about his '*mais*' and 'by all means'; and how he laughed with us! (. . .) I also remember a very touching incident. When we came to the ashram it was a wild desert; so soon we began digging and planting, and by the time we came to the end of the seminar, in fact on the last day, our first sunflower was ready to be offered to the Lord. Swamiji was so pleased, and he gave that flower such an important place in the liturgy, that none of us has ever forgotten it. (. . .) To me he was the embodiment of what "Unless you become as little children . . ." means. His joy, spontaneity and total inner freedom made us feel completely at home with him.[72]

Abhishiktananda himself also was very much at home in the seminar, as he told Fr Lemarié:

> . . . one month's preparation for ashram life— a life which integrates the culture, the asceticism and the contemplation of Hindu India. Each day a contemplative reading of the Upanishads with discreet Christian 'harmonics', purely silent meditation, a Mass in free rhythm linked with the texts from the Upanishads. Very interesting and well received. These young people will stand on our shoulders and reach the top. If I had the courage, I might now launch a centre; but I think that for me the

71. See Note 10 above.
72. Recorded by Sr Shanti Fernandes.

> hour has passed. For, interesting as it might be, I find it hard to keep up the rhythm of work, discussion and classes, especially in the heat (. . .).
>
> . . . This evening [Maundy Thursday] the Agape will immediately follow the Eucharist in the same place, the dishes for the meal having been put ready at the Offertory. I have prepared an adaptation of the Paschal Vigil. Yes, it will do; but give me either the beautiful singing of Kergonan, or else the silence of Gyansu! This English *Exultet* (. . .), what a 'loss of altitude', as Fr D. said. (L, 30.3.72)

He took advantage of the day of silence on Good Friday to write to his family:

> . . . Here a great many people passing through. Some know my name from my books and want to see me. But for a very long time now I have been an 'old bear'. Young people, tired of Europe and the consumer society, tired too of the bloodless Christianity that predominates in the West, take to the roads, hitching lifts, social parasites who refuse to work and live off the society which they despise.
>
> . . . Once I was terribly isolated. Now a good number of young Indian Christians are dead keen on what I timidly put forward twenty years ago! It is amusing to have become such a 'myth'! But it is very good to be with these young people. Admittedly the young French people who come through here [Poona] have struck me as very tiresome; but on the other hand, in other places I have found such decent boys and girls. Here it is a mixed ashram. It is really much more human to have young nuns in saris moving about among the rest of us men, young and old. (F, 31.3.72)

Writing to Marc, he said:

> . . . What report will there be of this seminar? I shall scarcely have a single note of all that I have said on the Upanishads[73] or at the Mass . . . But I believe something will have gone over. I do not want to leave some ideas for them to 'remember', but 'a new interior sense', an unformulated awareness of the Presence.
>
> . . . Just now I have to speak about the marvellous text in the Chandogya Upanishad on *Bhuman*-Fullness . . . To get over in words what is beyond words, to make it felt that it is precisely this beyond that counts. You would be amused, if you were here; and I need your 'irreverence' to help me explode the myth that I have become. (MC, 7. 4.72)

Hardwar, Gyansu, Rishikesh, Rajpur—19 April to 27 May 1972

On his return from Poona, Abhishiktananda learnt that in his absence his kutiya at Gyansu had been burgled, which necessitated a rapid visit to Gyansu at the end of April:

> . . . The seminar at Poona was most encouraging, but I have returned to my mountain solitude with even greater joy. However I have to come down again very shortly, because I have promised Marc a month in

73. Notes of his talks were taken by Sr Vandana; a copy is in the archives.

> Rishikesh before he leaves India. The reason for my coming up here for these few days is that my hut was burgled during my absence (I was informed by telegram), the door being smashed, and even my steel cupboard opened with a crowbar. Everything had been thrown in a heap on the floor. Few things had disappeared, but they had removed my typewriter. They are very likely to be caught, because a machine with a French keyboard is most uncommon here. (. . .) A sign from Shiva that I should give up writing, (. . .) and should be simply a sadhu, silent in the Presence? (OB, 29.4.72)

It was very doubtful if Marc's visa would be extended, and Abhishiktananda yielded to his 'heart-rending' appeal for some weeks of concentrated study together of the Upanishads. The first three weeks of May were therefore devoted to this, and to ensure quiet they retired to the ashram of Phulchatti. Others who were there later remembered the intensity with which they worked, sitting all day in a verandah which looks down on the Ganges.

For both of them it was a time of profound illumination, as Abhishiktananda deepened the insights which soon after inspired his long essay, "An Introduction to the Upanishads".[74] The impression that this retreat made on him is revealed in his letters during the following months. Marc himself had an extraordinary experience of illumination, which was also a kind of 'death', in which he was so deeply plunged that for a time Abhishiktananda feared that he would not 'return', and had to exercise all his authority as guru to summon him back.

In the following week they went to Rajpur (Dehra Dun) to fulfil an engagement at the Retreat and Study Centre to which Abhishiktananda had committed himself in the previous year. He had agreed to lead a 'School of Prayer' for an ecumenical group, mainly laity of the Church of North India and other Churches, which would introduce them to silent contemplative prayer, in a way that could be practised by ordinary people.[75] He was content to give them simple training

74. Published in *Initiation* (*The Further Shore*).

75. A report by the Revd Kenneth Sharp was published in the *North India Churchman*, July 1972. One of those taking part, John Alter, son of Abhishiktananda's friends at the Centre, has also recorded some abiding impressions of Swamiji:

"His eyes twinkled. That struck me immediately. His bright, sparkling gaze. And the comical nimbus of white hair. A jester in the court of God, I realized him to be, then, in that first impression, with his disorganized simplicity.

The first glance deepened, of course. I had come to Rajpur . . . to attend a workshop on Prayer led by Swamiji. As the days opened around us, his silence—the sadness which sometimes enveloped him—his spiritual authority and experience—the realism of his instructions—his very real and practical affection for each of us as fellow pilgrims on the long path home—his delight in the day and the moment—enriched and affirmed the first impression. Nothing was denied. At the mouth of the *guha* (heart's cave) Swamiji did know mirth. The encounter deep within the speechless silence of himself did not eclipse or deflate the garrulous human reality where, doggedly less than absolute, we each pursue our foolish way. Swamiji knew that paradox, the comical disproportion between advaitic experience and the ordinary, daily world. (. . .)

Humour. Mirth. As *a guhantara,* as a dweller in the cave, alone in the sight of the Supreme Witness, I cannot help but imagine him at times chuckling at the odd fence on which his life had placed him. (. . .)

(But) what I came to appreciate in my own relationship with Abhishiktananda, what he made manifest in his human, often less than royal, way was the vow of 'insecurity' he had taken. It was a vow which committed him to an almost unimaginable loneliness. Out of that solitude he returned to us, with a twinkle in his eye. That struck me immediately."

in sitting still and breathing rhythmically, and tried to answer their questions in the *satsang*, held in the morning after Bible study and again in the evening. For many of the participants, especially those with a Protestant background, this approach to prayer was entirely novel and needed much patient explanation. However, it was well received, and plans were made to hold another 'School' in 1973. For Marc the contrast between the heights and depths of Phulchatti and the simplicities of Rajpur was almost unendurable; but his guru adapted himself willingly, and urged the participants not merely to continue practising what they had learnt, but also to share it as widely as possible.

At the Centre Abhishiktananda let it be known that he was looking out for a place in the plains where he could be more accessible than at Gyansu. Not long afterwards the Board of the Centre, where he had now been a frequent visitor for the past ten years, made him the welcome offer of two rooms to use as he wished, an offer that proved to be most timely.

During the School of Prayer he wrote to Mrs Baumer about the recent weeks:

> . . . Marvellous times of solitude at the ashram in the jungle on the bank of the Ganges. Three weeks entirely devoted to reading the Upanishads, filled with grace. *Understood there better than in January that the Upanishad is a secret*, which cannot well be written down and is only properly passed on in the secret communication of guru to disciple. Here there is a seminar, a School of Prayer with Protestants. A very friendly group, but at the same time demanding. But how difficult it is to adapt oneself after the ashram in the jungle!
>
> . . . good news that the typewriter has been recovered (. . .). I am urged to return in order to identify it. (. . .)
>
> To write? to write? What is most true cannot be written, as I have just found by experience at the Phulchatti ashram. When the time comes, the Spirit will dictate what should be said. To express that 'beyond', theology is no longer sufficient; it requires poetry or its equivalent.[76] It needs inspiration in the strongest sense. For the time being I need to 'get over' Phulchatti and to recover physically. It is too much to feel yourself in the presence of Truth! It scorches you! And how can you say in words what words can only misrepresent, what can only be misunderstood and so mislead? Everything is there in the Upanishads. Their mantras are charged with meaning and experience. Why expatiate on them? Their truth is not found in commentaries, but in the experience in which their meaning is revealed. (OB, 22.5.72)

On the night before Abhishiktananda returned to Gyansu (27-28 May) there was another extraordinary experience on the roof of the Sivananda Ashram, which Marc referred to as "the night of Pentecost" and as his guru's "*Upadesha* [teaching] of Fire" (cp. *Diary,* 28.5.72). It so shattered them that they were unable to celebrate Mass the next morning (Trinity Sunday).

76. Abhishiktananda frequently expressed himself poetically, especially in his Diary.

Gyansu—28 May to 7 July 1972

It took two weeks of rest at Gyansu before Abhishiktananda began to recover from his weariness (F, 9.6.72), and during that time he had an attack of breathlessness, which was a first premonition of his heart-trouble in the following year (MC, 7.6.72). Nothing however affected his enthusiasm for the Upanishads, shown for instance in the following letter:

> . . . I have told you of the joy of that stay at Phulchatti with Marc—days of extraordinary fullness, even if physically devastating for me. All that I have said now seems to me off the point, so academic. What is important in the Upanishads are the 'correlations',[77] which go beyond all the words employed and pierce the living flesh like electric shocks [*comme des flash?*] Neither books nor lectures can convey this experience. You have to awake to another level of awareness. Rajpur, pleasant as it was, proved in fact an unbearable anticlimax for poor Marc. Even Poona is left so far behind. The truth of the Upanishad is the awakening to the *purusha* that I am! I refer you to Chandogya 8.3.3-4 and 8.12.2. You will then understand the 'mad' songs of 8.13 and 14. I now *know* that the Upanishad is true, *satyam.* I would like Marc to live it so deeply beyond the 'names and forms' that he may be able to repeat it in Europe, stripped of all its exotic oriental trappings and springing directly from the Source. So long as Christianity aims at teaching ideas about what is 'outside', it will continue to fall short. Every (real) teaching contains a hidden arrow which causes the spring to flow in the depth of the heart, like the one which Arjuna released to quench the thirst of Bhisma.[78]
>
> . . . Don't press me to write. That will come in its own time. But more than ever I feel that it can only come from the Source. I need to recover the inspiration of the poems,[79] which say everything to the one who 'knows'. (OB, 28.5.72)

Writing to his sister at Kergonan, he expressed the same concern in different terms:

> . . . The salvation of the Church and of the world does not lie in extraordinary apocalyptic situations, but in the simple deepening of the sense of the intimate Presence of God. This I know, and I burn to make it known, to communicate this inward burning which comes from the nearness—ultimately, a felt nearness—of God. Not by missions, not by words, not by visible forms—only an irrepressible, burning and transforming Presence; and this communication is given directly from spirit to spirit, in the silence of the Spirit. Truth is in humility and in what is not out of the ordinary. (MT, 29.5.72)

In the middle of June Abhishiktananda heard from one of his nieces that she and a friend would be coming overland to India and hoped to meet him at the end of July. She wrote: "I am longing to see this legendary figure that you are

77. For these 'correlations', 'correspondences', see *Further Shore,* 76ff.
78. See *Further Shore,* 62; a reference to the Mahabharata.
79. Especially the 'Arunachala poems'; see Note 48 above, page 242.

for us!" Although he had hoped to remain at Gyansu for several months, he decided to come down early in July before the rains affected transport, and to avail himself of the accommodation offered by the Rajpur Centre.

> . . . I shall come down next Friday [to Rajpur]. They have given me two rooms as a pied à terre when I come down to the plains. I shall probably stay there until the end of the rains, the end of September. Last year I had too much trouble when the road was cut.
>
> . . . Otherwise all goes well. My typewriter has been recovered, but it remains with the court, having a rest for six or eight months. So it is a holiday for it, and also a good excuse for me for not writing. (F, 1.7.72)

During these weeks at Gyansu he wrote frequently to Marc who was still at Phulchatti, guiding him in his work and answering numerous questions. The letters show how deeply their recent experience had affected him, both physically and spiritually. He had a strong sense that physical death might not be far off, but this did not disturb him, because he felt that already the one essential had been 'passed on' to Marc. Above all the letters suggest that he had come to a new level of awareness, a childlike simplicity of acceptance, his old anguishes largely transcended. His reading was mainly in the Upanishads and the Gospels. He was making notes on the former with a view to an essay which took shape in the following months, his "Introduction to the Upanishads",[80] of which many echoes come in letters of this time.

> . . . This morning against a background of weariness the Upanishads dance, ever new, ever the same! Beyond the *nāmarūpa* there is the 'correspondence' (=*upanishad),* which in a lightning flash reveals Being, the true, the beautiful. That is what counts in the words of the Vedas, as in those of the Gospels. (MC, 28.5.72)
>
> . . . I have qualms about starting to say Mass again. I blame myself for not having given you this 'sign' before coming up here. And I find it difficult to say Mass again 'without you' physically present.
>
> . . . Death is *passed*—crossed over, left behind—when the knots of the heart are severed which hold the *atman* in the *loka* [worlds] of the *namarupa*, of the voice, of thought, of the name we give ourselves or which others give to us. The knot of the five *prāna* [breaths] which control the vital energy in our bodies has little importance, for attacnment to the body is in the *manas* [mind]. The resurrected state in the ascension to what is deepest: to discover that 'I' which awakes in *sushupti* [dreamless sleep], while the I of the waking state remains asleep. We must search for this fundamental 'I'—but then, an indistinguishable mass of Light, an ocean without horizon, where no one can any more know himself except in saying (hearing?) *Aham asmi* [I am] beyond all duality. And the great upanishad is this depth of oneself and the recovery of oneself, found in the depth of each being that I meet.
>
> . . . In all this, you know, there has so far been no one but you to whom I could say everything! It is fantastic, this Light (*jyoti*), which

80. See Note 74 above.

empties, annihilates, fulfils you; and how true the Upanishads are! But to discover them is a mortal blow, because you only discover them in yourself, on the other side of death! (MC, 30.5.72)

. . . Happy to be here, yet still in bad form. Physically, no appetite; mentally, no interest in anything. A taste only for the Upanishads. Working at understanding the difficult passages at close range. However, that is not the important thing. The Upanishads are not a science to be taught, but an experience which is communicated by spiritual generation—an engendering which paradoxically produces the not-born!

. . . I wanted to say the Mass of Corpus Christi, but was too ill to do it as it should have been done.

. . . I don't know when I shall recover from that Phulchatti, which was lived by both of us at a depth of which even your ecstasy was only a quasi-external sign.

. . . I think that now (. . .) I shall no longer approach P. (or indeed, anyone else) with the thought that *he knows* and that *I do not know,* for now *I do know, vedāham!*

The mystery of Christ and of the Father is *beyond words,* more even than that of the *atman,* the *prana,* the Spirit. You can only speak of it in parables, and the meaning of the parable is beyond the words used. No word could have given you the experience of the birth of the not-born. But in your experience of death, you received it! Live this Trinity humbly in the mystery of the simplest human relationships. The individual, the person, only exists in his *being-with.* (MC, 3.6.72)

. . . I have just finished the Chandogya. Only a few notes on the obscure passages. The clear ones are their own commentary.

. . . I continue to remember (as if it was my own) your experience. This morning (the third time I have said Mass) it was so powerful during the Mass. It left me with a breathlessness which I still have at noon. It is all very strange. Perhaps I shall have to go to Indore sooner than I expected for a serious check-up. (MC, 7.6.72)

. . . The breathlesssness seems to have gone. However I remain on my guard. I have truly passed the last two weeks in the company of *Mrityu* [death].

. . . OM to the friends at Phulchatti. (. . .) It is good, what you are doing on the Upanishad. Here too it is the only work of which I am capable. But I am restricting myself to notes on the obscure passages. Why light candles when the sun is shining?

. . . I am as far from everything, as if I was the guest of *Yama* [death]. In fact *Mrityu* is passed. One lives on a different level . . .

in perfect joy,
in the shoreless Light. (MC, 9.6.72)

. . . The work you are doing is good. But take care not to overstrain yourself. Six hours on the Upanishads is quite enough. Your head would not stand more. The themes are certainly to be studied. However, nothing can take the place of a slow walk on foot along the tracks which follow all the windings of the Ganges . . . I mean of the thought of the (. . .) rishis, which is often disconcerting; and yet little by little you get inside this 'language'—and then what wealth, when you have grasped it!

. . . To return to the Upanishads, what is important are these 'flashes', the lightning, the bursts of light, the break-throughs which open the abyss—not a gulf which would separate, but the abyss of yourself. What is most awful in all that, however, is that the poor mind (*manas*) no longer has a taste for anything and cannot do anything, while at the same time it is incapable of remaining without doing something.

. . . I still have a certain bad conscience for having, without wishing to do so, deprived you of the Eucharistic sign, but when I celebrate, you are there. I have still only celebrated four times, for the prayers are too often like wax candles which one prefers to avoid lighting at high noon—and as for *true* prayers, they rarely emerge, and when they 'emerge', come from too great a depth and shatter everything! (MC, 9.6.72)

. . . I am gradually becoming normal again, in body and mind. Will it last? But I still retain a deep '*nirvedam*' [distaste], as it says in Mundaka 1.2.12, for just about everything, the 'boredom' which J.A.[81] tried to explain at Rajpur.

. . . The great Upanishads are a privileged moment in the evolution of human thought. It frees itself from ritualism and magic. It is the awakening in all its beauty, the sun rising over the mountains. Later, people want to discuss and argue (Śvetāśvatara, Maitri), and it needed the stern application of the Buddha's rod to call them to order. The byzantine discussion ended in '*nirvedam*' for all thought (including intuition), people went in for *yoga, bhakti, karma* (now moralized).[82] The same process (goes on) before our eyes. No more depth, but superficial activity. Discussion and speculation have killed intuition, and too often those who talk about it know nothing of it, and only want substitutes. Christianity, from being an experience has become successively and at the same time ritualism, institution, formulas, ethics, social action. The world is dying from lack of depth, of roots! This depth—we don't have to 'give' it in words, but to find the depth in ourselves; and to find it in ourselves is to find it in everything!

. . . Just now I am rereading John of the Cross and Teresa of Avila. I can make out what they are saying, but how strange and complicated is their 'language'—like Chinese to a European. Once the language of the Upanishad is freed from its ritual-magic substratum, what purity and directness it has by contrast!

When X talks to Y about study "in a context of intense prayer", it both makes me smile and also worries me. Rather like the discussions at Poona about the number of hours to be set apart for prayer in an

81. John Alter: Note 75 above.
82. See Note 69 above.

ashram. Along with the old brahmin who shared my room, I was far and away the one who 'prayed' the least of the whole group. To pray, to meditate, is still to be *doing*. Oh for the utterly simple *being* of the Upanishad! Above all one should not conceptualize.

In the notes which I am taking and writing at present, I am constantly tempted to find formulas and to provide a kind of 'essence' of the Upanishads. That is a mistake. (MC, 13.6.72)

. . . You are truly the one person with whom I have been able to exchange at this depth. For you, unlike the great majority, had set no conditions. You are right, there is no recovering from Phulchatti. But all the same, this psycho-physical shock really ought to wear off. Otherwise, how will I live?— assuming that I still have to live. The shadow of the mountain on the light of Phulchatti, that was *Mrityu!* Things are better now, but there is still a very great weariness which sets me questions. Yes, I never got over Arunachala, to be frank. Naturally the daily routine was gradually restored (. . .). But blows like Phulchatti cause the experience of Arunachala to vibrate 'unbearably' (for body and mind, that is).

. . . I have still not been able to return to a daily Mass, but I generally say several psalms and read St John or St Peter. (. . .) It will be four weeks on Sunday from that Pentecostal night! (. . .)

The Christian *namarupa* have disappeared. Yet, the ship has passed! But it is *a-dṛishta* [invisible]. The saving name of Christ is *aham asmi* [I AM]. And the deep confession of faith is no longer the external 'Christ is Lord', but "*so'ham asmi*" [I am he]. Like him at once born and not-born (. . .). The Father in relation to the Son—to me—to all. The Son in relation to me—to all. Myself in relation to every conscious being; born in all, ceaselessly (. . .), and yet always face to face.

. . . Yes, let us give thanks for everything to this Lord who is in the depth of our being and also face to face with us! Rublev saw the Trinity in Abraham's guests,[83] and not in any speculation or 'abstraction'. He is right, everything is a mystery of the face to face and the within. OM Abba! (MC, 16.6.72)

. . . Yes, we should now have a long time together to 'absorb' these Upanishads, and to read again John and Paul in their light. (MC, 19.6.72)

. . . Your present work on the Upanishads will benefit you enormously. After the *intuition*, you need to absorb it through every pore. Learn the *language,* and to do that, follow step by step the meanderings of the thought of the rishis. Then only will come to be the total *osmosis*[84] between our two languages, Christian and Upanishadic. And, as a westerner, you will be able to express the mystery to westerners—after a very long time of silence! For all that is received, is given in order to be given in turn. The Eucharistic bread broken and broken again without any limit, until all have eaten their fill! (MC, 20.6.72)

83. A reference to the famous Russian ikon, picturing the story of Genesis 18.

84. A metaphor derived from the tendency of certain fluids, when separated by a porous barrier, to pass through it and intermingle; cp. *Meeting Point*, 95-96 .

> . . . Days so-so, one day up, one day down, no appetite for food, or indeed for anything (without the Upanishads, I do not know what I should do or become). *Mrityu* is always there. If I did not deeply feel the love, and so the need, that certain people have for me, I would gladly summon Shiva-Yama under any form whatever. At the point that we have reached, I shall remain with/in you; but there are others who love me and still have need of me. and as for you, I think that you have to remain for your *āyuh*, your normal lifespan, *iha loka,* here on earth, to be an awakener—as I remember telling you on our first walk to Phulchatti, at the beginning of November! (MC, 22.6.72)
>
> . . . Here I am struggling to complete the essential part of my work before July. It is formidable to be at grips with the same texts over a period of weeks. After that there will have to be some detailed work according to themes. Shankara is not much help; it is as if one were to look for the Council of Trent in the words of the Gospel!
>
> . . . What a heap of Christian upanishads you have discovered! Take good note that we should not change our 'tradition'. It is under the sign of Jesus Christ that we have awoken to Brahman [God], even if it needed the Veda to make us fully aware of Him. And as a rule, it is within the Christian tradition that we have to help people to awaken . . . (MC, 25.6.72)
>
> . . . I very much like your flights concerning the *namarupa,* but you are full of it, as I am. And unconsciously we give them off without ceasing. 'Truth' does not lie in suppressing them—which is utterly impossible—but in living them, while piercing through them. That is precisely the greatness of the Upanishads. Dialectic has not yet dried up intuition—as begins to happen in Śvet., is terrible in Maitri (. . .). Then came the philosophers and dissected the *Brahman-Atman* (Shankara and Co.)—though he is one-without-a-second, and in his manifestation is just himself. Only the purity of a child's vision will recover for us, in their true light, the Christian *namarupa.* What is horrifying in theology and Canon Law is the treatment of *namarupa* as absolutes, whereas they are a game, *lila,* the sparkle of *maya.* But we do not have to *judge* this sparkle from a superior level; no, it is from the very inside that we play the game—without judging—and suck from the full bottle of the Mass and the other sacraments! But it is very clear that this is incomprehensible to the men of the System; you have to have interiorized the Upanishad beyond all the Vedantin *namarupa* in order to live that spontaneously . . . (MC, 26.6.72)

At the beginning of July, before leaving Gyansu, he wrote to several other friends, always on the same theme:

> . . . The experiences of this year have been powerful. I feel in myself a profound mutation. But this mutation makes me a 'stranger'. How true the Upanishads are! But who is ready to accept the Upanishads with *shraddhā* [faith]? (RP, 1.7.72)

> . . . As I have told you, my study of the Upanishads with Marc in May has left on me (and on him) an ineffaceable impression. But as a result of that, I feel myself dislocatingly a stranger among my brother men, Christians and others, who have have not the slightest inkling of this burning, and want you to share in their myths and pujas (Hindus) or their coagulations of the Spirit (Christians).
>
> I shall come down on the 7th to Rajpur, just at the foot of the mountains. I shall probably stay there during the rains, most of the time with Marc. He wants to continue this abyssal immersion in the Upanishads, 'come what may'. In him I have really found, unsought, the total disciple. With him I live the *guru-chela* dyad with a shattering intensity. What will come of it all? I think of the word of Jesus: "I have come to cast fire on the earth." Now I *know* that the Upanishads are true. Could I one day write about it? But to translate the Upanishads into ideas and themes, is precisely to 'destroy' them. (OB, 1.7.72)
>
> . . . Meditation on the Upanishads makes me ever more keenly aware of the transformation through which the Church, and indeed all religions, must pass. The age of religions (. . .) has passed. But between the total experience, to which we are summoned by the Upanishads, and secularism, there is but a hair's-breadth of difference . . . (. . .) So much for all the efforts at renewing the Church (and equally, Hinduism), when seen from the height of these Himalayas! (L, 1.7.72)

Rajpur, Indore, Rajpur—7 July to 22 December 1972

At Rajpur Abhishiktananda was joined by Marc, who spent the rest of July with him, studying the Upanishads, the Vedas and the beginning of St John's Gospel.

At the same time he availed himself of his old typewriter, kept at the Centre, to make a first draft of the essay for which he had been preparing at Gyansu, "Introduction to the Upanishads". The typescript is dated 15.7.72, and was obviously written at great speed. There are many uncorrected typing errors, and numerous notes have been added in the margin, in view of an intended revision which was never made. It was his final testimony to the impact made on him by the classical Upanishads and to his conviction of their importance for the future of mankind (section 4). The main part (section 3) dealt with the important 'key-words' through which the rishis pointed to the ultimate mystery and prepared their disciples for the 'awakening'. Such was the inspiration under which he wrote that, when it was prepared in 1974 for publication in *The Further Shore* by his disciple and the editor, it needed extremely little revision, apart from taking account of the marginal notes.

At the end of July his niece A. with her friend J.P. arrived at the centre:

> . . . Yesterday morning at last the two of them got here, A joy, as you can guess. I brought down from Uttarkashi a whole album of photos, starting with one of Papa before his marriage. A. is busy making a selection to take away with her. A meeting like this affects me more than I could have thought. (. . .) You can imagine how we have

> gossipped about each and every one. (. . .) Unfortunately it is the rainy season, and travelling is rather troublesome. This evening I am taking them off to the Ganges, Hardwar, Rishikesh (. . .). I am only sorry that they have such a short time in India, and also that they cannot see my real place; here I have two comfortable rooms over a garage, with no local colour or atmosphere. (F, 29.7.72)

The young people made a brief trip to Banaras, and then returned for a final three days at Rajpur before setting off back to France:

> . . . A. finds in me so many features which recall her mother, as I do in her. (. . .) They will tell you all about my cooking, etc. I am only sorry that I cannot give them a treat. But when I take them to a restaurant, it is too spicy for them to eat, so . . .? But here it is only rice, chapatis, lentils . . . (F, 4.8.72)

Meanwhile Marc had gone on a pilgrimage to Kashmir, from which he returned in the middle of September. Shortly after his niece had left, Abhishiktananda went to the Roberts Nursing Home at Indore for a check-up, and was advised to have an immediate operation for haemorrhoids. While there he wrote to Fr Lemarié:

> . . . I am writing to you on the eve of my 62nd birthday (in two days' time). A white beard, and what remains of the hair also white . . . Time passes . . . But what does it matter, when you have discovered that time is only a category! and that that which is, is beyond all change. The mystery of the *I* in the depths of consciousness.
>
> Here at Indore since 12 August. This time I had unexpectedly to undergo a small operation, trifling but most unpleasant, which requires daily attention in the two following weeks, not to mention the pain, comparatively 'slight'—but when you have to put up with it?
>
> . . . Remind me about the article on pilgrimages[85] next year, when I shall again have my typewriter and will be a little more at peace. (. . .) I have had my nephew and niece, very pleasant, even though like all the nephews and nieces they have dropped all concern for religion. How can you blame them, when you see the 'irrelevance' of present-day Christianity? I find such meetings very instructive; they prevent me from huddling away in a 'gnosis' which is as far from the Real as the worst rationalism or materialism.
>
> . . . I still have a good contact with St Anne, Kergonan. (. . .) But who *knows* what ought to be done? Here they are making plans for an Indian, or Asian, monastic congress! I am keeping out of it as far as I can, as it is out of touch with the Real. But who can hold fast to the Real? In my choice of acosmism, am I any nearer to the Real than those who argue and rush about so that they can have at least something to do? I am torn apart between the acosmism of Gyansu and what

85. Nothing more is heard of this article. Earlier in the year "Pèlerinages himalayens" had appeared in *Annales de Ste Th. de L.*, April 1972, 20-22.

> many people want me to 'achieve' in the plains. But I have jumped beyond the point at which they are awaiting me. What can I do? I have finally been caught at my own 'game' and in my own 'myth'. (L, 26.8.72)

He also wrote to Mrs Baumer from the hospital:

> . . . This recall to the most commonplace realities of the human body is a marvellous counter-balance to the danger of the 'higher gnosis' of the environment in which I often live. The Lord is present everywhere. *Everything* is Brahman, no less the painful spot which engages your whole attention than the silence of all your faculties! Everything is grace!
>
> . . . I admit that I take very little interest in my books, once they have gone on their way. They are no longer my affair. However, it seems that the London edition [of *Prayer*] has sold very well. (. . .) *Gnanananda* will appear in English next year; they are translating it in Jerusalem. (. . .) The article on the Upanishads? I don't know when I shall have the time or strength to put it into shape. I shall have far too many distractions all through the winter. For that I have to be in a very special 'mood'. And I am very conscious of the fact that the message is so rarely understood. Who is content with pure air? or pure water? or the absence of all taste? Out of the simplicity of the experience they make a gnosis, an abstraction. But Brahman has given them the slip, and they don't realize it![86]
>
> . . . Thanks to Chidananda, Marc has got permission to stay until next March. He is just back from a marvellous pilgrimage to Amarnath in Kashmir. (OB, 31.8.72)

Marc had written to tell him about his adventures in appalling weather on his way back from Amarnath:

> . . . On my pilgrimages I have never had adventures like yours. However, I know what it is to feel the burden of five kilos as if it was a hundred, with each step testing every muscle in the body, steep climbs where you have to rest at least every ten metres, sometimes having to scramble up a cliff; that rain which lashes you and cuts into you, the constant danger of slipping . . . So I only need to multiply it. But I am sure that in all that the beauty showed through, and that in the end it will be above all the joy that will stay in your memory, as happened on the 'great night'. (MC, 5.9.72)

Writing to his sister at Kergonan, he said:

> . . . How pleased I am that M. and his sister call me a hippy. That shows that I belong to the most up to date movement! Our sadhus here are the real protesters against Mr Pompidou's society of *bourgeois prosperity,* just like St Francis and his first companions. The future belongs to those who give the first place to Man instead of his posses-

86. Allusion to the Kena Upanishad, 14-25.

sions. That is the basis on which a renewed Christianity will arise, which will be able once more to fire the enthusiasm of the fine young people of today.

. . . It is only in crises that we discover ourselves; remember Jesus' cry on the cross: Eloi, Eloi! I have learnt a lot of things during my days and nights of lying here in physical pain. The Lord is everywhere and in everything. There is as much true prayer when the whole attention is concentrated on an ache, as in the marvellous silence when we think we are in ecstasy. What a wonderful lesson, it makes you rejoice in everything. (MT, 2.9.72)

In the middle of September Abhishiktananda left the hospital and returned to Rajpur with Marc. Recovery from his operation was very slow, and his hope of returning of Gyansu had to be continually deferred. Meanwhile he and Marc resumed their study, particularly of St John's Gospel and the Gita:

. . . Here much work with the young man of whom I have told you, A Christian contemplative study of the intuitions of India, a very profound sense of the *Beyond*, where God is and where only silence can reach. (FT, 27.9.72)

. . . I am afraid another operation may be necessary in a few weeks. Nothing serious, but it is painful, and chiefly very tedious and uncomfortable. A chance to live the advaita, of which I so often sang the praises! I am in my third week on the Gita with Marc. All the same, how far it is from the Upanishads. In it you certainly feel the same vector, the same inner thrust, but it no longer has the piercing glance of the Brihad. Upanishad. The mystery has to be projected and the unformulable formulated—because people are no longer able to *know* it in its unformulability. Yes, I will send you the draft of the article [on the Upanishads] when I get the chance of giving it a minimum of shape. (OB, 4.10.72)

Another of his correspondents was a housewife in Bombay, who had done the greater part of the first draft in English of *Sagesse:*

. . . I would not know how to give a good answer to the question whether Christ is necessary for Hindus. I only know that plenty of people who do not know his person have access to his 'mystery' (not to his 'concept') in their inner deepening and also in transcending themselves in the love of their brothers. The mystery of the Heart of Christ is present in the mystery of every human heart. You have found fulfilment through music, through painting. Art is also a way of access to the mystery, and perhaps—in poetry, painting, music—it reveals him better than any technical formula. And in the end it is this mystery—at once of oneself and of each person, of Christ and of God—that alone counts. The Awakening of the Resurrection is the awakening to this mystery!

. . . Joy to you, to your husband, to your children. May it shed its rays on all! and don't worry about those who love the esoteric, who run around to ashrams and 'saints'. The discovery of the mystery is so much simpler than that. It is right beside you, in the opening of a flower, the song of a bird, the smile of a child! (AF, 4.10.72)

In the latter part of October Marc was away from Rajpur, but in his place were two seminarists who had come from Poona:

> . . . In any case my time here has not been wasted. Upanishads plus Gita plus St John with Marc. At present I have two students from the Poona seminary, both very open: one an intellectual who is up against theological formulations, the other a mystic who passes over—or perhaps, under—them . . . It seems that most seminarists plunge into social issues in order to avoid the deep problems, but the crisis cannot fail to break.
>
> Murray says he is coming in December, on his way to Bangkok. An intrepid traveller . . .
>
> *Sagesse* [in English] must await the return of J.S. in December. In any case it is only the patching up of an old wall. I would never written it now. (RP, 18.10.72)

In a note to Marc he said:

> . . . All goes well here. Ajit feels a strong call to silence. Each day we have Upanishads and St John. A.S. is naturally very intellectual (Remember thy years of old!) but that is what leads to an explosive theology, the only kind that henceforth I am able to teach. We have already spent two days on the first verse of the Prologue [of St John]. (MC, 16.10.72)

By November Abhishiktananda's health had begun to improve, even if not sufficiently to enable him to return to Gyansu:

> . . . I still have my troubles (. . .) but it is no longer unbearable, as it was on my return. (. . .) In any case work goes on. I have not had a moment's rest here, except this week. Young people want to have 'classes' in the Upanishad and the Gospel. But I constantly refuse to run about here and there. (F, 2.11.72)

Marc came back for another four weeks of study during November, this time mainly on St Paul:

> . . . Steady work here with Marc, now on St Paul. Coming back to the N.T. Scriptures after an immersion in the Upanishads, you discover new depths in Paul and John. But what a disconcerting difference in language! You cannot attempt to make comparisons at the surface level. You have to go beyond the words to the still unformulated archetypes. Any attempt at comparing the formulations is vain and misleading. We shall keep this up until the end of the month, after which Marc will go away for a month of complete silence and solitude in the mountains. (OB, 21.11.72)

At the end of the month he wrote to Mother Françoise-Thérèse at Lisieux:

> . . . My health now seems to be sufficiently restored, and I plan to go up at last to Gyansu after the middle of December, I feel the need of it intensely.

Térèse's month of fever has delayed her return to Hardwar[87] for several months. I do not know how the business of her naturalization is progressing. The fact that she has to act through an intermediary is a great handicap, I fear.

. . . My long experience of the Indian world more and more convinces me that languages (thought-patterns) differ considerably in different ages and cultures. In the end we have to go back to the experience beyond its always relative formulations. I am constantly thrown out by finding that even the finest pages of St John and St Paul are as it were 'woven' on 'thought-patterns' which are foreign to our mental framework here. It is not by patching up the circumference that theological formulations and ecclesiastical structures will be made to respond to the call, the signs of our times. Only an immersion in the real depth will save the Church. Launch out into the deep.

How painful it is to see all these young people who come here in crowds, seeking an 'inner life' of which practically no one in the West is able to speak to them. What mankind needs today is a dimension of depth. The monasteries themselves either remain fixed in the Middle Ages or else are becoming secularized like Maredsous. Where can we send the young people who have had a taste of the deep contemplative life of India, and then have to return to France? What monastery would agree to provide them with a hut in some nearby wood?

. . . I have just spent three days in Hardwar. In a jungle beside the Ganges I found about fifteen huts made out of branches of trees, with just enough room for lying down or sitting. (. . .) Living there are Hindu solitaries (. . .). That is how a genuine Christian Indian monasticism will really begin.[88] (FT, 30.11.72)

At the beginning of December, after Marc had departed for a month of silence beyond Almora, Abhishiktananda went down to Delhi. He had another session with his editor on the English of *Sagesse,* after which Murray Rogers arrived from Jerusalem and they set off together for a joyful week in Hardwar and Rishikesh, described in "Swamiji—the Friend":[89]

. . . He had recently had a small but painful operation but still, generally, I had my work cut out to keep up with his walking, and especially so in those Ganga towns where a certain lightness took hold of him! He assured me that he was older; he wouldn't be waiting around much longer—the 'dance of joy' of Nataraja was calling. It was not easy to believe him, for in so many ways he was younger, more alert, more eager to be up and away early to some special shrine.

. . . We talked, we were silent, we dreamed of the moment when the Church in India would finally be the Church, renewed and perhaps

87. After her experience of life at Hardwar in 1971-2, Sr Térèse had returned to the Pondicherry Carmel later in 1972 and could not leave until 1974. No letters from Abhishiktananda during 1972 are available.

88. This settlement of hermits at Saptasarovar, just north of Hardwar, strongly attracted Abhishiktananda. He and Marc joined them for a few days in June 1973.

89. See chapter 5, Note 10.

> almost unrecognizable to our present eyes. Yet with all his vision of the peaks (. . .) he was firmly fixed on earth, on the immediate necessity for action and resolve if we were indeed to go beyond . . . (. . .) Indeed Swamiji felt more keenly than I had ever known before the pull towards the awakening to Self, the moment when all that can be said or known is 'I AM ', the 'Ah!' of the Kena Upanishad. Already every notional idea, every -ology related to history or thought was beginning to disintegrate. There was nothing left, for what was left was everything, the revelation that we are 'sons of God'. "The blazing fire of this experience," he once wrote, "leaves nothing behind; the awakening is a total explosion." One goes, and one IS.

Murray had brought with him the English translation of *Gnanananda* to be checked and then sent for publication to the London S.P.C.K.[90] When this was done, Abhishiktananda was at last able to return to Gyansu, after an absence of over five months, and there he spent his last Christmas in solitude. Before leaving Rajpur, he wrote to his sister in Kergonan:

> . . . I hope at last to return to Gyansu this week. (. . .) Things are now going better, and I can face the bus to Uttarkashi. It will probably be cold. Will there be any snow? Anyhow my house is a sort of igloo, well protected against the cold. This year I shall also have a small electric heater (I forget the French word!)
>
> I have been very busy all my time here, very often with my young Frenchman, with seminarists from the South in October, who brought all the problems posed to their Indian souls by the Hindu-Christian encounter, that blinding light which no longer allows anything to be seen in the sky except the midday sun. I am at present revising the English translation of *Gnanananda*. I have several articles to prepare for various meetings in 1973, in which as far as possible I am excusing myself from taking part, and so to make up for this I have agreed to write a few pages. In October there will be at Bangalore a 'congresso' of Christian monks of Asia; they are offering me an air passage (otherwise it is five days from Uttarkashi), but I am not tempted. I wish they would keep quiet and practise inner concentration, instead of trying to get themselves noticed.
>
> The other day at Hardwar, outside the town, in the jungle just beside the Ganges, I came across a dozen or more hermits whose cells were huts made of branches, each surrounded by a thorn hedge against wild animals. For their food they go to an ashram one kilometre away. How that would tempt me, if I was not so old! Marc (. . .) would like us to go there and try it out next spring. One of my Hindu 'chelas' who was with me only yesterday, is also strongly tempted. That is the real thing—no advertising, no celebrations, no 'congress'—they are content to remain in the presence of the Lord, the true role of the monk.
>
> . . . A good and holy Christmas—but Christmas is every day, when you have discovered the non-time of your own origin! Each moment

90. Published in *Guru and Disciple,* 1974.

is the dawn of eternity in the explosion of the joy of Being. (MT, 18.12.72)

Gyansu—22 December 1972 to 31 January 1973

During his six weeks in Gyansu, despite the cold and the absence of his typewriter (still in police custody), Abhishiktananda continued to think and to write. He had been invited to take part in two important meetings in 1973— a seminar on Contemplation in March, and the Monastic Congress in October. Although he rejected the offer of an air passage to Bangalore for the seminar, he still hesitated for weeks, before finally deciding not to go. In the end he made his contribution to both meetings in the form of papers.

For the seminar on Contemplation he wrote in January an essay called "The Upanishads and Advaitic Experience".[91] This was a confident presentation of the central teaching of the Upanishads, which he concluded with his familiar call to Christians to deepen their faith in integrating this experience, and to seek the real beyond concepts in the prayer of silence.

In the previous year he had been sent a questionaire, circulated in preparation for the Monastic Congress, and had answered it with a long note (dated 2.12.72),[92] "Reflections on the Programme of the Asian Monastic Congress, 1973". In this he stressed the need for Asian Christians themselves to develop forms of monastic life in continuity with their cultural and religious backgrounds, rather than in imitation of the West. Then at Gyansu he wrote his paper for the Congress, first in French and then in English, which he called "Experience of God in Eastern Religions".[93] He first contrasted the prophetic and the advaitic forms of experience, and then expounded the Indian path of *jñana.* At the end he expressed the hope that Christian monks in India would make this path their own, so that the Church might be truly catholic.

He also resumed his reflections on theology in the light of the advaitic experience. In these he was stimulated by an essay by Dr Panikkar, "Salvation in Christ: Concreteness and Universality: the Supername"[94] and wrote to congratulate his friend:

> Reached Gyansu yesterday morning, and since yesterday evening I have at last got down to reading your paper from Jerusalem. It is really 'you' at your best (. . .). Before you leave India, I want to tell you of my pleasure at this paper. In philosophical terms (sometimes difficult) you give the proof of something of which I am more and more convinced: that the problem of the uniqueness of Christ is a false problem. For no more than the 'Persons' in God, can created 'persons' be enumerated. However, does not your conclusion tend still to resolve the

91. Published in *Clergy Monthly,* Vol. 38, no. 11 (Dec. 1974), 47ff. Reprinted in *The Further Shore* (2nd edn, 1984), 105ff. Here, as in *Ini tiation,* it was by mistake said to have been written for the Monastic Congress of October 1973.
92. A copy, dated 2.12.72, is in the archives.
93. "L'expérience de Dieu dans les religions d'Extrême-Orient" published in *Actes du Congrès de Bangalore* (A.I.M.), 1973, and reprinted in *Les yeux,* 23ff. "Experience of God in Eastern Religions", published in *Cistercian Studies,* IX, 2 and 3, 148 ff.
94. Published by the Ecumenical Institute for Advanced Theological Studies, Tantur, Jerusalem.

> problem 'from the Christian point of view' (. . .)? After having wrestled with the Angel for years, I am forced to accept that in practice, de facto, the whole so-called Christian approach to the 'mystery' is just one of the approaches! A brilliant and sparkling *lila* [game] of 'the One who sports among the worlds', the reflection in a given mirror of the *Satyam* [Real] who simply IS . . . The point which the Vedantins have for years been dinning into our ears with their over-simplified and condescending slogans . . .
>
> . . . Returned to Uttarkashi yesterday, being urgently summoned by telephone to give witness in court about the theft of my typewriter, together with the thief (in chains, poor devil). The machine was there, but it will still probably take months and months before I get it back from the police. [In fact he never did].
>
> At Rishikesh I invited Chidanandaji to the conference on Worship at Rajpur in June and to the Monastic Congress of East Asia in Bangalore in October. He accepted with pleasure. (RP, 23.12.72)

At this stage in his thinking Abhishiktananda had become convinced that it was essential for theologians to concentrate on Jesus' own experience of God, as lying behind the theologoumena which appear in the New Testament. His unfinished essay, "Sat-Purusha", is a sample of this approach,[95] as is another (also unfinished and without a title, but dated 3.7.73), which begins: "Jesus experienced a relation with God, with the Mystery which he felt encompassing him through the whole world, and as well surging as it were in the innermost depth of his own being, which he could but express through the notions of Father and Son."[96]

The same concern appears in a letter to Sr Térèse (who had returned to the Pondicherry Carmel in 1972, and was detained there until 1974, chiefly in connection with her application for Indian citizenship):

> . . . This Father sets some very real questions but, as a good European rationalist, he wants to answer them with ideas. This is simply impossible. When we speak of the divinity of Christ and of his divine Sonship, we are victims of the Greek outlook which dominated the four Councils and culminated in Thomas Aquinas. I would not go back on what I wrote in *Sagesse*, but now I would express it in different language. That was written ten years ago, and was far too 'Greek'. Jesus experienced such a closeness to God—probably the very same as is revealed in the advaitic experience—that he exploded the biblical idea of 'Father' and of 'Son of God' to the extent of calling God 'Abba', i.e., the name which in Aramaic only the one who is 'born from' him can say to anyone. But the term 'Son' is only imagery, and I fear the theologians have treated this image too much as an absolute, to an extent that becomes simply mythical. In Johannine terms Jesus discovered that the *I AM* of Yahweh belonged to himself; or rather, putting it the other way round, it was in the brilliant light of his own *I AM* that he

95. This was written in January 1973 and published in *Intériorité*, 295ff.
96. A copy is in the archives. The text is in English.

discovered the true meaning, total and unimaginable, of the name of Yahweh. To call God 'Abba' is an equivalent in Semitic terms of *advaita*, the fundamental experience.[97]

It seems that in his Baptism he had an overwhelming experience; he felt himself to be Son, not in a notional, Greek, fashion, but that he had a commission given by Yahweh to fulfil; and in this commission he felt his nearness to Yahweh . . .

. . . It is the reduction of the mystery of Jesus to a Jewish or Greek concept that makes the dialogue of salvation with non-Christians so difficult. One culture has monopolized Jesus. He has been turned into an idea. People argue about Jesus—it is easier than to let yourself be scorched by contact with him . . . (TL, 16.1.73)

During December Marc was in retreat at Binsar (Almora Hills), and his guru refrained from writing to him. From Binsar he went to Bodh Gaya, where he made first a Satipatthāna retreat and then a Vipassana retreat under Goenka. He then went south to Tiruvannamalai (Arunachala) for three weeks, and returned to Rishikesh on 25 February. During January and February Abhishiktananda sent him a series of letters, at first from Gyansu and then from Rajpur.

The letter of 4 January gave recent news—Murray's visit; his meeting with Swami Chidananda, when for the first time there is a reference to the 'double monastic initiation' for Marc, which was to be a major pre-occupation in the following six months; his health (better) and his work on the two papers; and his solitary Christmas at Gyansu. (MC, 4.1.73)

. . . Too much wearied by long hours on the Chandogya Upanishad and the B.A. Upanishad to be 'mystical' in my letter this evening. The mantra *Om Tat Sat* sings all day long. It is the basis of my Eucharistic rite. (MC, 10.1.73)

. . . This evening 8 p.m. I have lit my charcoal stove, as it is damp and cold. (. . .) And I have to finish Book 2 of the Brihad. That *madhu* [honey] which everything is to everything else, that constant take-off into the Beyond, the golden Purusa full of glory—you know it so well . . . (MC, 11.1.73)

. . . The Mass is more and more simply made up of Upanishadic mantras. It is a celebration in honour of the *Satpurusha*, and the communion-in-*annam* [food] with the unique Purusha which everyone is. One day perhaps that will overflow so that it can be told. At present it is lived without yet being expressed.

. . . Today I have gone back to *Sagesse*, the English translation. How dated it is now. If I had good English at my command, how many pages I would have to rewrite. Christ must be freed from the Jewish and Hellenistic culture in which we have imprisoned him. And equally we must not immure him in a Hindu culture. He overflows on all sides, just as every man, every consciousness overflows; and the further that consciousness has penetrated into the depth, the less can it allow itself to

97. On this point, much stressed by Abhishiktananda in his last years, see the comment of Fr. J. Dupuis in his introduction to *Interiorité*, 31-32.

be monopolized by anything. (. . .) Christ is beyond all concepts, even that of the Purusha. All is *lila* in what is said of the Self! (MC, 16.1.73)

. . . More and more I am seeing how Christianity is founded, rooted, in the Jewish culture and mentality. There are no non-cultural religions. All our attempts at reinterpreting John have remained on the surface. We have to descend into the ultimate depths to recognize that there is no common denominator at the level of *namarupa* [names and forms]. So we should accept *namarupa* of the most varied kinds. And play the game with them in the same manner as the Lord does with the worlds . . . Jesus explains everything (. . .) without denying the possibility of each one explaining everything, in so far as he is awakened. No comparisons, but we should penetrate to the depth of each one's mystery, and accept the relativity of all formulations. Take off from each of them, as from a springboard, towards the bottomless ocean.

The Gospel does not exist to teach *ideas,* but to confront each one's attitude in face of the mystery with that of Jesus. That is existential and real. It is the Greeks who have turned the Gospel into a *gnosis.* By means of India's *jñana* we must throw out this *gnosis* and rediscover the freshness of the experience of Jesus, freeing ourselves also from our Vedantin formulations— which are just as limiting as those of the Jews and Greeks.

. . . It is only in prayer that the *osmosis*[98] takes place, and the ultimate correspondences—upanishads—are revealed between the mystery of Christ and that of the Purusha.

. . . The small son, aged ten, of Visuvasan (his old cook at Shantivanam) writes me long letters in Tamil, asking me to take him with me and make him a priest. Another *chela*, you see! He is a child whom I love dearly. I held him in my arms when he was hardly 15 days old. In my reply I have told him to work hard and go on studying, that it will be easy for him in three or four years' time to find a society which will enter him for the minor seminary. (MC, 21.1.73)

. . . Today I am writing to you at Tiruvannamalai. As I told you, it fills me with longing. I had such times of exaltation there, just twenty years ago. and it was something much deeper than I realized then. Some of the words written in those days were only fully understood very much later.

It is good that you should have had this experience of Buddhism. Provided that you do not become attached even in that to the form of the without-form! For me everything is in the Upanishads. But the Buddha's radically purified training is a marvellous aid for getting inside them. It is a radical deliverance from our attempts to think . . . What a purification from all attachment is this meeting with the East, which compels us to recognize as *namarupa* all that previously we considered to be most sacred, to be the very Truth contained in 'words'. Later we have to be able to recognize the value of the *namarupa,* not

98. See Note 84 above.

less than we did 'before', but we have discovered another level of truth—the blinding sun of high noon.

. . . Our time is one of those without precedent in the history of the world, when the worldwide coming together makes us clearly see that we ourselves and our whole tradition and every tradition are essentially conditioned. Every religion is rooted in a culture, beginning with the most primordial and hidden archetypes which necessarily govern its view of the world. All that is *citta* [thought] is *namarupa.* And every *namarupa* has to be laid bare, so that the *satyam* [Real] may be unveiled. What a savage but marvellous purification! No longer even to say 'I am', but to be it to such an extent that the whole being 'exudes' it.

. . . And then we have understood. We find ourselves once more Christian, Hindu, Buddhist, for each one has his own line of development, marked out already from his mother's lap. But we also have the 'smile'. Not a smile which looks down condescendingly from above, still less a smile of mockery, but one which is simply an opening out, like the flower unfolding its petals.

. . . The day I saw Chidananda, he was so busy that I did not want to impose on him. (. . .) I could not go into too many details. But I think he has understood in the first place that a ritual initiation should be given you before you leave India. Was not that just what you wanted, in order to have an acceptable 'sign' of your 'withdrawal from the world'? (MC, 26.1.73)

In another letter written just before leaving Gyansu, he made a further significant comment on the *namarupa* of all religions in terms of dream:

. . . When (religions) are too close, like the Muslim, the Jewish and the Christian, we look for common denominators. But when the fancy takes us, we can equally well make an eclectic Hindu-Christian system . . . (. . .) Then we realize that on the level of the *namarupa* no comparison is valid. (Religions are) grandiose dream-worlds. But be careful not to call them dreams from the point of view of a dreamer . . . The man who is awake marvels at the dream; in it he grasps the symbolism of the mystery. He knows that every detail has its significance. The only mistake is to want to absolutize each symbol. And the difficulty is that no deep 'drive' can be expressed without symbols. There is no religion without a culture. There is no Christ, if he is not linked to a time, a place, an ethnic group. (MC, 30.1.73)

The above extracts seem to indicate a new dimension in Abhishiktananda's self-understanding, to which he had quite recently come. It was as if his 'seeing' had at last come into focus, of course at a deeper level than that of the intellect. A subtle change makes itself felt in some of the letters written in the following months. He refers to this in his next letter to Marc on reaching Rajpur:

. . . The bus was as always pretty tiring, but I was still bathed in the atmosphere in which I had written to you on the previous evening. There is something which I have the impression of having grasped, but

> without being able to express it. Nothing new, even so. There has been nothing new since Arunachala, twenty years ago. But the 'mind' seems to be always carried a little further on; so it is like the landings on a staircase . . . or so it seems. (MC, 1.2.73)

This change in Abhishiktananda's outlook seems to have been triggered partly by Dr Panikkar's essay on the "Supername" (letter of 23.12.72, above). But in another letter, commenting on the essay, he gently rallied his friend, whose boldness he always confessed to be greater than his own, for hesitating to draw the conclusion which necessarily followed from his argument:

> . . . I have read and reread your "Supername". Many things in it fill me with delight, as I have told you. But I sometimes fear that the brilliance of the reasoning employed may be deceptive. And finally, whatever may be said on the penultimate page, it still remains an attempt at salvage, at restoring the situation! Or if you prefer, an attempt to lead Christians as gently as possible to accept that in losing their *namarupa* they still keep everything! As I wrote to you a month ago, beyond all our approaches, however subtly argued—(. . .)—all that is excellent, yet, yet . . . when that has to be restated in everyday language, we have to accept that it is all *namarupa*—and to begin with, the idea of *Salvation*. In the final pages you admit this yourself; 'salvation' means nothing—nothing real—to the humanist, any more than to the Buddhist or the Vedantin! (There is) a drive of the psyche, and to express it the mind fashions a marvellous dream. (There is) the impact of the mystery on the consciousness of a human group, and the collective psyche produces the magnificent spectacle of the myth and the logos . . . and then we wake up. The dream is true in the drive which gives it birth and in which it is finally absorbed: *prabhava-apyayau* [the origin and the end]. (RP, 30.1.73)

Rajpur, Delhi, Rishikesh—1 February to 4 April 1973

Abhishiktananda came down from Gyansu in February because he had arranged a meeting with his editor at Rajpur to finalize the English version of *Sagesse*. For him it was scarcely a congenial task, as he said to Dr Panikkar:

> . . . The whole thesis of *Sagesse* is outmoded. I long for the English version to be completed, for I am most uncomfortable with it. (RP, 30.1.73)

He also spoke about it to Marc:

> . . . J.S. arrived yesterday. We are at work. But it is hard to have to check the translation of a book whose thesis one no longer accepts . . . Of all that I have written, *Gnanananda* is almost the only thing that remains afloat. All the rest consists of *namarupa* amusing itself with the 'theology of fulfilment'.
>
> But how to tell, pass on, this truth? For this truth is not conceptual. The value of the words that I was able to speak to you last year lay in their *resonance* rather than in their immediate meaning. Once concep-

tualized, this truth which I bear is no longer true. So should one patiently continue to speak the language of those with whom one is? I do not think that that would be dishonest. (MC, 4.2.73)

However, out of kindness to his guest, he gave no sign of his deeper feelings, or indeed of the fact that his thoughts must often have ben far away with Marc, who was then revisiting his old haunts at Arunachala. In ten days he brought the work on *Sagesse* (English title, *Saccidananda: a Christian Approach to Advaitic Experience*) to a speedy conclusion, applying himself to it with his customary attention to detail. He also proposed a daily Eucharist, to be celebrated by each in turn, using a traditional form very different from that which was now his normal practice:

> . . . 6 p.m. Presently J.S. will come for the Eucharist. In the last days at Uttarkashi I was too exhausted to be able to celebrate, and since coming here I have not been capable of it. But in *koinonia* it has a meaning even so. (There is) a single mystery of awakening—*bodhi.* What do forms and names matter?
>
> That became so clear at the end of January, as I wrote in my letter of the 31st [30th?]. But a word came back to me—with new force—from one of the poems:[99] "How hard it is to have to perform a human task, when you have been marked by Arunachala!" When you alone are awake and all around are sleep . . . or else, when you alone are asleep and all around are awake . . .
>
> All that the Christ said or thought about himself, is true of every man. It is the theologians who—to escape being burnt, the devouring fire—have projected (rejected) into a divine *loka* [sphere] the true mystery of the Self (. . .). And Jesus claimed the freedom to be himself—and so earned a gibbet! And sometimes he upset everything violently, and sometimes he observed the Law (. . .). (MC, 4.2.73)

During the last ten days of February and during most of March Abhishiktananda entertained a guest from the U.S., with whom he had long been in correspondence. This was Mrs Anne-Marie Stokes, a fellow-Breton, who lived in New York, where she worked with Dorothy Day and the Catholic Worker movement and also with the U.N.O. Through her he had come in contact with a Breton worker-priest, Fr Pichavan, whom he greatly admired. He came to meet her in Delhi, and then after a few days took her to Hardwar and Rishikesh, where by chance he met the Sufi, Vilayat Khan. Then, after a quiet week at the Rajpur Centre, they returned to Rishikesh to join Marc, as there seemed to be little hope of his visa being extended beyond March.

Mrs Stokes has written a lively account of her friend, including some unexpected insights into his thoughts. After noting some of the contrasts in his character which made him the man that he was, she says:

> . . . Fifteen years of correspondence create both friendship and an image, but the living image was slightly different, more subtle, more shaded, harsher, more imperative. And then the little personal touches—

99. From "Bhairava"; see Note 48 above.

using beautiful stilted French, memories of his humanities as he entered the monastery, he would sometimes interject a slang word, common to college boys of his time, that added great flavour to his conversation. Impossible feats were his daily bread, but the usual little materialistic things became great undertakings and filled him with misgivings. Whilst travelling, he was agitated and constantly in a hurry; and I can still remember those scalding cups of tea taken by the roadside (. . .); his asbestos-lined throat had absorbed them while we were still wetting our lips. But also every expedition was invested by him with invention and majesty. He was no bohemian, and remarkably neat and organized, but matter and its tyranny dismayed him.

We spent a week at Rajpur, at the Christian Retreat Centre, where two little rooms over a garage had been lent to him. This is where I came to know his way of life as closely as could be, except for the very few who could ascend to Gyansu (. . .). He slept on the ground on a blanket in a corner among his books, his only possessions. I learned the art of cooking on a spirit lamp; it was a challenge to try different menus with the selfsame rice and vegetables, but I did try seven different menus, and Swamiji with a slightly guilty look admitted that he had nearly sinned through gluttony! (. . .)

How I wish I could recall all that was said. Simone Weil and her ardent wish to be a bridge between religions and cultures was often quoted, and also her magnificent thoughts on the Holy Grail. He spoke of his vision of his mission and that of Fr Monchanin (very different sometimes, it would seem). We difffered a good deal about suffering and its impact, and suddenly he said an extraordinary thing: "I do not know either evil or suffering." We discussed our friend, the worker-priest, of whom he had become more critical: "He is too much in love with Christ, he will have to lose him to find him." At which I would retort that, incarnated among brutal and rather materialistic men, this priest had to look for Christ's face, hidden in the crowd. He would not believe in the contemplative potentiality of sorrow (and how much Simone Weil had stressed it!). (. . .)

Little by little I discovered his tremendous intelligence—how beautiful a gift he had surrendered—and his eminently poetic personality, not only as a poet—"Arunachala" is a great poem—but in his poetic view of all things. There too I discovered his absolute poverty and insecurity by probing (he never complained), worn like a splendid mantle and embellished by the immense value he gave to the 'invaluable'. (. . .)

After passing a little time with John Cole in Dehra Dun, whose presbytery was a haven for Swamiji (. . .) we went to Hardwar, where we met one of his chelas. At Rajpur Swamiji was in a Christian environment; among Hindus he was a different being (. . .) We witnessed an *arati,* visited a swami, watched the rising of the sun over the Himalayas, and later in the morning in the jungle, among sadhus passing by fierce and absorbed, on the bank of the Ganges Swamiji said one

> of his great Masses, on an altar-stone worn and polished for centuries by the life-giving river, interjecting passages of the Upanishads (. . .).
>
> The bazar fascinated him with its handicrafts, and he gravely gave his advice on my purchases. And then we made our way to Rishikesh, to Sivananda Ashram. Its director, Chidanandaji, was a deeply admired friend. The mutual relationship of these two holy men was a joy to behold. (. . .) Other chelas joined Abhishiktananda in this retreat. He instructed them and held informal discussions on the Upanishads in a little deserted temple on the hillside. There were also unforgettable expeditions across the river, deep in the jungle, visits to caves where sadhus lived after years and years of silence. (. . .)
>
> Back at the ashram we had another compatriot, Mother Y., a woman from Brittany who had converted to the Hindu faith. We were at the same time very close and very far from her, but she was to prove a providential friend.
>
> Several times it happened that Swamiji would say: "Now I can go, my message has been heard," his Nunc Dimittis. All his modest desires had been granted in this world, and the other unlimited one seized upon him from time time.[100]

During the week at Rajpur Abhishiktananda caught up on his mail. When giving his family his recent news, he mentioned that his health seemed to have improved (F, 6.3.73). Writing to Mrs Baumer, he told her about his chance meeting with Vilayat Khan, a meeting "to rejoice the heart"; but he added that he longed for him "to keep silence for some time, to go beyond his poetry, and remain at the Source (. . .); then his influence would be greater still." But immediately afterwards his own elevated thoughts about the OM made him admit: "There, you see, in saying that, I myself am playing at being a poet like our dear Vilayat!" (OB, 7.3.73)

Another letter was to Fr Lemarié:

> . . . I am overwhelmed with invitaions. Saw last week a well known Sufi Master, Vilayat Khan, who would like me to be at his congress in Chamonix in August. Here there are two seminars at Bangalore (. . .). They are asking me for lectures on the Trinity at Vidya Jyoti, the Jesuit scholasticate in Delhi; also for my presence for two or three weeks at Poona with Jesuits preparing to be novice masters and spiritual fathers in their houses. . . All this simply bowls me over, for I would not want to distress my friends, but on the other hand I now have a phobia for all that . . .
>
> Marc, my young companion—I should rather say 'child', who with two young Indians has made me discover at the age of 60 the joy of being a 'father,—finds his visa expired with very little chance of it being extended. So I shall return to Rishikesh with him and Anne-

100. These paragraphs are extracted from "Recollections of Abhishiktananda" which Mrs Stokes wrote for the 'Memoir' as it was originally conceived. This and her further reflections on Abhishiktananda, "Mountain Peaks", are in the archives.

> Marie until the end of the month. Then, as soon as I am free, I shall again go up to my beloved solitude at Gyansu; I feel the need for it so strongly.
>
> So your great desire to go to the Holy Land is at last to be fulfilled. You will be happy, and I am happy about it for you; but I assure you that I do not envy you in the least. (L, 8.3.73)

Later in March he wrote from Rishikesh to his sister in Kergonan, telling her about the visit of Mrs Stokes:

> . . . Quite an interlude in my solitary life. She is explaining to me the racist horrors of the Nixon administration (for she is chiefly occupied with the Blacks who are unjustly imprisoned), and I am introducing her to the peace of the *munis* [silent ascetics] who live beside the Ganges. Yesterday I took her into the jungle where hermits (including a woman) live in huts or caves in the depths of the forest, only reached by goat tracks.
>
> . . . I have already told you what perfect hermits there are among the Hindus, so much so that the other day I wrote to the organizers of the Monastic Congress of Asia next October to say that it is to them far more than to Christian monasteries that we should go to rediscover the spirit of the Desert Fathers.
>
> . . . It is here that I truly find the meaning of the monastic life. (. . .) It is so simple, this mystery of the Within. It is desecrated when you explain it, like a flower when you touch it—a flower is simply to be experienced. How complicated I find an organized monastic life; here we have a freedom of the Spirit like the old Eastern monks. Here you understand the "*Fuge, tace, quiesce*" [Flee, be quiet, be still] of blessed Arsenius. . . (MT, 22.3.73)

On 3 April, just before Ahishiktananda returned to Gyansu, he and Marc called on Swami Chidananda to discuss the proposed *dīkshā* (initiation) for Marc. However, nothing was settled, as the Swami seemed at that point to be thinking in terms of a rite which would bring about a further result, whereas for Marc and his guru it was simply to be the public recognition of a freedom which was already possessed (see *The Further Shore,* 21-22).

Gyansu—4 April to 11 May 1973

For the last time Abhishiktananda took the bus for Uttarkashi, which broke down after a few miles, so that he had to complete the journey crammed into the back of another bus, and was unable to get more than cup of tea during the whole day (MC, 4.4.73). However he was soon at work again, and took only three days to draft in French the greater part of his long essay on "Sannyasa".[101] Immediately after that he began to draft the lectures that he had been asked to

101. The first French draft is dated 8.4.73. As a first chapter he reused the article "L'idéal du Sannyasa", which had been written in 1970. "Sannyasa" first appeared as a serial in the Sivananda Ashram's monthly *The Divine Life* (1973-4), and was later published in *The Further Shore,* and *Initiation.*

give at Vidya Jyoti, "Notes on Trinitarian Theology",[102] but after a few days left it unfinished. In the first section he addressed himself to the methodological problem of theologizing in India, which calls for something far more radical than merely replacing Greek with Vedantin concepts; rather it has to start afresh from the experience of self-awareness. The next section (unfinished) takes up 'the experience of Christ', for "we must never forget that, apart from the experience of Jesus, we have no knowledge of the Trinitarian mystery." References in letters to Marc reveal his uncertainty about what he was doing:

> . . . I am a little anxious about these lectures on the Trinity requested by Delhi. Delhi is not at all easy to refuse, because it is so near and in fact I go there so often . . . However, what can I say now? Lead them towards the 'open sea', with all moorings severed?? Trust in the Spirit who guides all. (MC, 8.4.73)
>
> . . . These lectures at Vidya Jyoti which are so difficult to refuse are a great load on my mind. Nothing comes that is worth saying. When it comes to it, I shall have to be ready to speak without any particular preparation . . . (MC, 11.4.73)

In the middle of April he wrote an English version of the essay on Sannyasa, which at this stage lacked the fourth section, "Renunciation itself renounced". The need for this section evidently emerged in the course of his correspondence with Marc, in order to safeguard the total freedom of sannyasa from any kind of definition or institutionalization whatever. He summed it up in a freshly coined Sanskrit *śloka:* "He who renounces both *sannyasa* and non-*sannyasa* is the true *sannyasi.*"[103]

While at Gyansu he also kept his promise to write a preface to a small book on prayer (*A Method of Contemplative Prayer*) by a Mill Hill Father, J. Borst.[104] This was a reprint of an article which Abhishiktananda had much appreciated. His preface is a plea for the freedom of the Spirit in prayer, and expresses his sympathy with the charismatic movement.

The letters written to Marc during April were naturally concerned chiefly with sannyasa and the proposed *diksha,* and reveal the sensitiveness with which he directed his disciple towards spiritual freedom and 'suppleness':

> . . . Sannyasa is an extremely demanding ideal, and that is too often forgotten under cover of preferring the spirit to the letter. It no longer leaves room for any desire for the self, for any self-seeking. The *abhayam* [absence of fear], extended to all creatures, goes infinitely further than not killing a fly, as soon as you think of its application to men in all circumstances, in every meeting. To insist on solitude [*esseulement*], on non-relatedness, on avoiding friendship, runs the risk of being negative. To refuse the total gift of yourself to others means refusing to be yourself. It is in giving that you become yourself—once more the marvellous *muthos* [myth] of the Trinity. But a self-giving that does not alienate the self.

102. The manuscript is dated 9.4.73. It is published in *Interiorité,* 235ff.
103. See *The Further Shore,* 37. It is referred to in MC, 23.4.73.
104. Published by Asian Trading Corporation, Bangalore, in 1973 or 1974.

(5 April) A total depth of exchange in the present moment. The eternity of this exchange lived in the present, without snatching at a future which inevitably makes you fall back to the level of pluralism and is a falling away from lived advaita. For every exchange, every kiss, is the mystery of the not-two, when it is lived in its total purity and without a trace of 'making use of' the other. The acosmic—the 'hairy one', *keshi,* of the Rig-Veda—can make his way through the world totally indifferent to everything, looking neither to the right nor to the left; and he can just as well make his way with a smile for all, radiating the life of 'interchange', as God does when passing through time without leaving his eternity, shedding abroad his love everywhere (. . .) without leaving his solitude. Ready for everything, and free from all limitation. Rejoicing for example in the fullness—for there is no *sukham* [pleasure] in the *alpa* [half]—of our embrace, but doing nothing, not even desiring to do anything, to perpetuate it . . . the mystery of the Fullness and of the Exchange at the heart of the Trinity. (. . .)

The severities of asceticism are necessary to keep mind and sense under control. However, nothing may be given an absolute value, neither the orange *kaumanam* [loin cloth] nor [etc.].

. . . Here it is truly marvellous. There is none of the superimposed 'spirituality' that you have at Rishikesh. A village quite close, a small town a mile away (. . .). A solitude on a human scale. (. . .) That is what you will have to find somewhere in this vast universe, the edge of a village, or else of an adjoining wood, a stream . . . Every place is sacred, because sacredness comes from the Self and is radiated by it. Every place in which the renouncer sits is his ashram. Every stream in which he bathes becomes for him the Ganges. (MC, 4.4.73)

. . . All goes well here. *Ananda.* My peach tree is covered with fruit, the roses are in flower. Life has come back. Weariness has gone. I was even able to allow myself an almost complete fast on Friday. This morning [Passion Sunday] I have just celebrated the Eucharist. *OM tat sat!* The rite recovers its meaning when it is no longer the commemoration of a past event, but in its '*anamnesis*' [memorial] takes up the whole cosmic order, the suffering on every side, the cry that springs from the heart of the unfortunate, the life that never stops, the nourishment, *annam-madhu,* which all beings are to each other. The ultimate passage [*atteinte?*] beyond the firmament and all the heavens of *namarupa.*

. . . What I wrote yesterday was in response to your wish and to clarify our ideas for possible discussions with Chidanandaji. On Friday I wrote a few pages of the first draft. And yesterday from 7 a.m. to 7 p.m., only stopping for dinner, I allowed the inspiration to flow. (. . .) I think the whole problem has now been clearly set out. It has forcefully reminded me of the demands of the life of sannyasa. (. . .)

So when you read it, you will find the proposal of a rite of initiation which is very free, but based on the tradition of the Hindu Scriptures. Sivananda's book has made me go to the texts.

. . . Sannyasa finds its ultimate 'reason' in the non-duality of the light which springs up in the depth of being, the very place where every true sannyasi, whoever he may be, is caught and given.

. . . But is not our 'idea' of sannyasa terribly idealistic, perhaps beyond what is really possible? But even so, there is a place for such acosmics in the cosmos, on the margin . . . at the edge of a village or a forest . . (MC, 8.4.73)

Meanwhile Marc had had a further meeting with Swami Chidananda, which cleared the way for the kind of *diksha* that he and Abhishiktananda had in mind:

. . . What you tell me about Chidanandaji makes me happy and at the same time fills me with confusion. How small I feel beside him, alike as a human being, as a monk and as a 'seer of the Real'; not to mention his position at the ashram. Less than ever do I have any wish to 'discuss' with him. And the pages I sent you two days ago [the draft of "Sannyasa"] seem so pedantic in comparison with the simplicity ofwhat he said to you. I am partly responsible for the misunderstanding (fortunately only temporary), because I did not dare to speak. (. . .) More than ever I long to withdraw, to 'recoil'. The invitations that I have refused this year perhaps mark the end of a period of over-activity. Besides, apart from you, no one has ever asked for the one thing that I would like to give . . . People pick up crumbs, with no idea that there is a cake . . . (. . .)

To come back to Chidanandaji, you know, however open both he and we may be, we cannot think of the Absolute (for at the level of the *vyavahāra*[105] we indeed have to think of It) except in our own terms—in his case Hindu, in ours Greco-Christian. The Christian likewise finds it very difficult not to attribute absolute value to what he regards as superior forms of prayer and contemplation . . .

. . . The book given by X is really very poor. If all those people—I mean the philosophers and commentators who have succeeded each other since the end of the Upanishadic period—had really understood this light of the Upanishads and had contemplated the Purusha in his own light, they would not have wasted their time on logic and dialectics. They would simply show that "*tat tvam asi*" [That art thou]—with their finger, with their eyes!—instead of trying to convince people by arguments that are mostly inconclusive (. . .) that the *atman* is *brahman*, etc. . . . (They are) really in the same class as the manuals of theology used in seminaries. (MC, 11.4.73)

. . They say that for him who is no longer aware of *śariram,* all is clear. But what exactly does that mean? Ramana, for example, took his meals, was *interested* in food, its preparation, etc . . . I am afraid that the *idea* that we make for ourselves of this (experience of) non-awareness is false. (. . .) it is only ignorance that sees a difference between the *jivan-mukta* and the *other.* I think that this *duality* which we assert between advaita and dvaita is precisely our mistake. The Greek and

105. See Note 52 above, p. 244.

Cartesian mentality. Chidanandaji plays marvellously with both of them; in any case, are they not both simply *ideas?* Certainly this experience of advaita deals a heavy blow to all laws, rites and formulations. (. . .) Jesus did not cudgel his brains to make a philosophy about his advaita with God. He lived this non-duality with absolute intensity simply by gazing like a child at his 'Abba'. And he taught his people to live, simply but deeply, a life of loving union with their brothers—a union of mutual giving without limit. And in the absoluteness of their self-giving to God and the neighhbour, the non-dual Absolute is found and lived with far greater truth than in Vedantin speculations. The Christian believer remains too much on the surface of his myths. Paul felt the dislocation between the two men in himself: the spirit, *pneuma,* the risen man, the *jivan-mukta*— and the *sarx,* the flesh, the man full of desires. And he says: "The life I now live in the flesh, I live by faith in the Son of God," i.e., in my abyssal experience of *I am.*

In the dazzling light of the vision of Being, you have perhaps been over-strict in rejecting all the namarupas. And yet, in the *śariram* that we bear, it is in the experience of these namarupas itself that we discover the advaita and the kaivalyam of the Absolute. If we set them in opposition, we have lost our way. (. . .)

But this 'I' and 'Thou' which alternate in the language of prayer, are they in the end real or not? Neither *sat* [real] nor *asat* [unreal]! But the word 'illusion', *māya,* is misleading (. . .). 'Appearance' would be better, provided you realize that it is the Real (. . .) which thus makes its appearance. An appearance which is *not* other than the Real. (. . .)

And then rites recover their value, and the man who is 'realized' cheerfully takes part in the rite without inhibitions. One day he will celebrate the rite, the next day he will not even think of it. For him the rite is not a means of obtaining something. For there is nothing to be obtained. All is given from the beginning.

. . . As you so rightly say, and as I have often thought myself, if Jesus said 'Thou' to God and called him his Father, I have no right to look down on myself or anyone else who likewise says 'Thou' to God. There may be days or periods of days when no 'Thou' to God can pass my lips, but that is quite normal, and there is no need to be worried about it. They are two *mental states*, each of them seeking desperately to express the unique *cid* [awareness] of *sat* [reality]. And this freedom is what we have to insist on. But this freedom cannot be defined by Canon Law. (. . .)

I do not think that literal acosmism: nakedness, total solitude, etc. . . . should normally be a permanent condition, except for rare individuals (. . .). But there is an acosmism, which springs as it were spontaneously from their inner experience, that which the Gospel saying seeks to express: "to be in the world, but not of the world." (. . .)

But that you should have to begin with a long period of literal acosmism, I quite agree. You will live that either here or elsewhere. (MC, 12.4.73)

. . . I have just finished the English version of my paper on Sannyasa. It follows the French text very closely. I shall type it out when I get to Rajpur. But I should like to have your reaction. (. . .)

I see that that in the end you seem to be finding your way (. . .) towards the proposal made to you by Chidananda on 3 April. That at the same time amuses and interests me. You need sannyasa in order to be *recognized.* And why do you want to be recognized, except with a view to being accepted when you *do* something? It is not the ten years of silence[106] which are calling for the *diksha,* but the time *afterwards* when you feel that something awaits you; a need for an apostolate under a different name! I am not blaming you, but I am the witness who smiles. (MC, 15.4.73)

. . . After rereading my text and reading your comments, I have not been able to resist writing from my own angle a critical review of my text, which I am sending you. A small damper for you and for me, who are at times living a little too much in a dream . . .[107]

. . . I smile when I see you now so interested in giving a *form* to the *formless.* That is just what cults, myths, theologies have been doing from the beginning . . . Ever since the supramundane intuition of the Buddha was given a name, his teaching has been obscured . . . You will only be truly free, when you no longer have to *claim* your freedom! (. . .)

You need a *sign* in order to possess your *freedom!* Oh the infinitely free man, who needs a sign that he is beyond signs! Get away with you—you are still steeped in your University Seminary, and deserve to go back it it!

I am indeed a little to blame for all this. I have talked to you too much and have put ideas into your head—*ideas* of silence! If I had been silent, I would have led you beyond ideas. For it is our great misfortune that we take ideas for the reality, even our ideas of the non-reality of ideas. (MC, 18.4.73)

. . . Illumination? Who has it? A Ramana, a Buddha, are extremely rare events in history. So we console ourselves by saying that no one ever awakes, there is only the One who is Awake. Surely that is a counsel of despair? Just as much as that of Ecclesiastes (Qoheleth) or the Epicureans? The truly practical, *existential,* answer is that of the Gospel. Unfortunately we have so covered it up (*adhyāsa*)[108] with myths and theological gnosis . . . or on the other hand, as in these days, we have so emptied it of its mystery, the Real . . . (. . .) This deep Reality is there, *nihito guhāyām* [hidden in the cave of the heart], beyond the heavens,[109] and *I* know it, but *manas* [mind] does not know that I know it and yet it well knows that if *I* did not know it, it could not itself even

106. See *Further Shore,* 47 (where it says that *twelve* years of silence are traditional).
107. This 'critical review', "Autre point de vue sur le sannyasa", dated 18.4.73, is included with a copy of the typed MS in the archives.
108. That is, 'superimposition' (also called *adhyāropa*); see chapter 5, Note 89, p. 187.
109. *nihito guhāyām parame vyoman* (Taittiriya Upanishad 2.1) was a favourite quotation.

say, "I do not know" . . . [A complicated 'squiggle' follows.] Leap and dance with me, says the Motionless One, *a-chala.*

. . . I have written to my monastery to say 'Alleluia' [for Easter]. I think you also like singing alleluia—*Hallelu Yah!* You see, you don't like me speaking of God, but you always have his name 'Yah' on your lips! Play the game without complexes! (MC, 21.4.73)

. . . Whoever talks about *jivanmukti,* about realization, etc . . . shows that he has not understood anything at all. Whoever expects an 'experience', so that he can say that he is 'realized', knows nothing about anything. There is nothing to be renounced, nothing to be released from . . .

Dhyāna [meditation] is not a means. For there is no means—neither meditation nor rite nor gnosis nor guru nor scripture. (. . .) Through the things of the world and your *śariram* (. . .), or independently of them (. . .), it makes no difference. So long as *moksha, atma, brahman, nirvāna,* is still thought of as some thing, you are going away from it even while looking for it. (. . .) Sannyasa is precisely to have renounced all means.

. . . *The rite* [i.e., the *diksha*] *produces nothing.* It merely shows the idle onlooker something to think about.

There is no vow of sannyasa. (. . .) There are no obligations, but (only) spontaneous movements of the Spirit, who leads where he will. and no one may call for any explanation from the *jñani.* (. . .) John the Baptist lived as a *keshi* [ascetic]. Jesus ate, drank, loved his friends, allowed women to anoint his head and embrace his feet, took John to his breast . . . The freedom of the Spirit. (MC, 23.473)

Taking all things into consideration, I think in the end it will be wise for a triple witness to make 'manifest' your condition of sannyasa next June. A triad of Chidanandaji, you and me. In his absence, our own non-dual dyad. The details will be clarified at our next meeting with Chidanandaji. The points that still have to be settled are besides very secondary. In fact the role of the guru is essentially to give the *mahāvākyas* and finally the insignia.[110] The simpler the better. It will fix in time an ending of time, to which those who locate themselves in time and space may refer. And it will be a support for you at times when you need to recall it, and will protect you (at least to some extent, I hope) from the misunderstandings of the 'others'. It will allow you to call yourself officially 'consecrated', dedicated, *devotus* in the strong sense of the word, set apart for the gaze which looks beyond all names and forms. I do not think that this *diksha* has any power by itself to free you from rites. That freedom either exists or does not exist. (. . .) Nothing can give it, nothing can take it away.

. . . The priesthood? I have a strong impression that it awaits you at some point in the course of time. A priesthood that is very spiritualized, very free from limitations, a priesthood in the Spirit. This *diksha* in the

110. See *Further Shore,* 55, 56.

Ganges will signify your gift of yourself to that priesthood, and the Spirit will respond in his own time and his own way. Explain the diksha in this way to your marvellously understanding mother.

. . . This morning I have corrected my text, incorporating your notes, improving it here and there.[111] I still have to type it in French and English, quite a big job.

. . . I am *really happy* that at last you are accepting those humble details which have no great importance, I know, but which none the less form part of the behaviour expected of the sannyasi. A good mark for the adaptability which you have at last discovered. In a matter of no importance, why not bend? (MC, 24.4.73)

. . . Now that the diksha is no longer for you a *pratishthā* [support], any more than the Vedantin formulations, you need have no scruple when you say with the smile of the Buddha "*aham asmi*" [I am], and equally when you pronounce the "*saṃnyastam mayā*" [I have renounced].

. . . You should not have answered your parents so harshly. I know there are hard sayings of Christ in the Gospels. But Christ's example is an integral whole. He who has Christ's experience and his total freedom from 'self' can say to others the words which Jesus said. You truly have admirable parents. You ought to be 'kind' to them. Now tell them about this diksha which gives you the essence of the consecration implied by the priesthood. (. . .) Now that the priesthood is secularized, made 'profane', it is the monastic diksha that preserves its mystery in the Church and the world.

. . . Jesus' experience at the Jordan impresses me more and more. And in the concept of Father/Son I now see not so much the relationship of derivation (which even so is not denied) as the relationship of *ekatvam* [oneness].[112] (. . .)

And that explosion at Easter. Easter is above all *Jesus alive,* in the very humble forms of Luke and John, in the glorious form of the end of Matthew—where he appeared on the northern mountain (. . .) like the Son of Man on the clouds of heaven in Daniel. He *is* and so I *am* ("The world will see me no more, but you will see me; because I live, you will live also"; John 14). But in the radiance of this 'I am' all the words, all the concepts, all the myths, through which men come to it are as it were swallowed up in the light . . . (MC, 28.4.73)

. . . I have been thinking in recent days about my programme in the coming months. If your extension is refused, I would naturally spend the last month with you, i.e., after mid-August (. . .). I plan to return here as soon as possible after the *diksha.* I was thinking of going to Indore in August but if the doctor wants another operation that would handicap me too much (. . .). It would be better to go there after you have left. But certainly the thought of your no longer being here seems to me quite 'unthinkable'. Our meeting has truly plunged us both into incred-

111. This must refer to the chapter added to the first draft, "Renunciation itself renounced".
112. Cp. Note 97 above.

ible adventures, at every level. Sometimes I am frightened at the havoc wrought in you. It would have been so simple for you to have returned after six or nine months to the S.U. [seminary] with a little Indian veneer and a little 'deepening of the inner life'. But now it has been two years, and the future is more unpredictable than ever. As on a road zigzaging up a mountain, you only see as far as the first corner—and then to the next corner . . . Trust in the leading of the Spirit. He knows the way. The Self knows the way. (MC, 1.5.73)

Phulchatti, Rajpur, Rishikesh—12 May to 27 June 1973

On coming down from Gyansu, Abhishiktananda joined Marc for a week at the Phulchatti ashram. Here they studied together the 'Sannyasa' Upanishads,[113] on which his essay had been based. In the course of their walks near the ashram they came across some genuine *avadhutas,* practising a total renunciation which greatly impressed them.

Abhishiktananda then went to the Centre at Rajpur to conduct a second "School of Prayer", which was attended by about twenty 'non-Roman' participants, including a Sikh colonel—"much better than last year, and I could speak more freely from the start" (OB, 22.5.73). He noted that the most receptive were the colonel and two quite young English people "who caught on at once; while for the priests there I had to give such laborious explanations" (MT, 1.6.73). Although the School could only be for three days, Abhishiktananda succeeded in arousing a desire for the 'prayer of silence' which has continued to spread (as he hoped it would) and has been followed by similar sessions at Rajpur and elsewhere in North India until the present day.[114]

During these days he caught up on his correspondence and shared his news with his friends. To Fr Lemarié he wrote:

> . . . Odette Baumer tells me that she will be coming with her son at the end of October. By then Marc will probably have made his way back to France, but he will very likely hurl himself at once into some unknown corner of the Alps or the Pyrenees. He will no longer be able to bear the superficiality of the western world or of its clergy and monasteries. India truly slays those whom she loves.
>
> Sr Térèse is still at Pondicherry. First she had a bad attack of malaria, and then made an application for naturalization. As she was badly advised, this has taken an enormous time, and she has not been able to leave until her case has been finally settled. She very much hopes to return beside the Ganges in the autumn. (L, 22.5.73)

He told Dr Panikkar about the new situation at Uttarkashi:

> . . . Uttarkashi is going to become a problem sooner than I had expected. The new exarch of Bijnor/Kotdwar, who henceforth has

113. A term covering various later Upanishads, such as the Nāradaparivrajaka.

114. Abhishiktananda planned to lead a School of Prayer at the Brotherhood in Delhi in December 1973. It had to be held without him, and during the session the much delayed news of his death was received.

> under his charge the four mountain districts, has begun to move. He sent two fathers to explore Uttarkashi. They came to ask me to put them in touch with the Malayali Christians working on the dam! and were anxious to find out if I was well known as a Catholic priest! They want to install themselves first of all in the Headquarters District, so as to be able to contact the authorities easily—and one had thought that the Constantinian era had been liquidated with the Council . . . (. . .) In such conditions I shall have to think of finding a new place of refuge for the remaining years of my life in this *śariram.* Probably in the neighbourhood of Rishikesh or Hardwar. (RP, 22.5.73)

During the School of Prayer Abhishiktananda was abruptly informed by the new Director that his rooms were 'needed', and that he could no longer stay at the Centre. In this emergency some Quaker friends (Ranjit and Doris Chetsingh) offered him temporary quarters at their house close by on the Rajpur Road, to which he moved in June. Before leaving the centre he typed out in French and English the essay on Sannyasa.

He also wrote to Kergonan, telling his sister about recent events:

> . . . Just now I am seriously considering where I am going to spend my last years. There is a proposal to establish a mission station at Uttarkashi, and very likely my position there will soon become impossible. (. . .) On the other hand, the pied à terre which I have had at Rajpur for the past year is about to the slipped away from under my feet. If I were younger, I would see in that a sign from the Spirit to set out on the roads with nothing, like a real sadhu. Books and the rest are an encumbrance. I wish I could be like this young Frenchman Marc, who with only a minute pack settles down absolutely anywhere. At the moment he is in a bare cave behind Rishikesh. I very much wonder how he is; I shall go and look for him next Monday. At all events, life is always good. But how this total stripping of Hindu sannyasa teaches one about the true inner life. Last month I met two young people, one of them a Nepali lad aged perhaps seventeen. They live in a hollow under a cliff, eat wheat and peas soaked in water and wild fruit from the jungle, where they have to take care not to run into bears . . . At least six hours they spend in meditation. These are the genuine ones, much more so than the fine swamis in their saffron robes, who are as proud of being monks as are the priests, Revd Fathers and the like, of our holy ecclesiastical world. The other day I did a study of sannyasa according to the ancient Sanskrit and Hindi texts. I was shattered, just like king Josiah at the reading of Deuteronomy.[115] When I took *kavi,* I had no idea of the renunciation which that implied.
>
> . . . Everything is becoming so simple. All the beautiful ceremonies—I have enjoyed them as much as anyone; but now in the *guha* [cave] of the Father, what is there left to say? "Hear the silence," as our Sikh colonel said last week.

115. A reference to 2 Kings 22:11.

> The English of *Sagesse* has gone to press. Why write any more? (. . .) People are on the lookout for ideas, but I would like to make them realize that to hold their peace is what they need. (MT, 1.6.73)

The 'ecumenical *diksha'* was fixed for 30 June at Rishikesh. The details of what was to be a very simple ceremony, stripped of anything 'mythical', had been decided between Chidananda and Abhishiktananda, who were to administer it jointly. It was clearly understood that the diksha was not intended to 'convey' anything, but was merely the public recognition of what in Marc's case was already a fact. Immediately after the diksha, Marc would depart for a period of *parivrajya,* i.e., wandering freely and living on alms.

It was probably to gain preliminary experience of such a life that during June Marc and his guru twice went out together for a brief trial. Between 4 and 10 June they 'wandered' between Rishikesh and Hardwar:

> . . . It was fine when the sun shone, you could lie down anywhere on the *ghats* or the sand, for there was such a crowd of pilgrims that there was nowhere to stay. But when the rains set in, it became a problem. (F, 8.7.73)

Then again, from 17 to 20 June they stayed (as they had long been planning to do) with the sadhus at Saptasarovar in their rustic shelters near Hardwar, and went out with them to beg their food. In the intervals Abhishiktananda returned to Rajpur, and finally rejoined Marc on the 27th to prepare for the diksha.

A letter to Dr Panikkar, written at the end of June, shows how deeply Abhishiktananda had been affected by his recent experiences:

> . . . (In my last letter) I was saying how much the fundamental problem seems to me to be existential, and how institutions take an ever smaller place in my life. I have passed the age of activity, and this pilot seminary of which people increasingly talk interests me less and less. Only one thing matters: the awakening. But unfortunately the Church is very far from that.

After a reference to the coming *diksha*, he went on:

> . . . Met last week at Hardwar a Malayali who for three years at least has been living as a perfect and authentic sadhu, going from ashram to ashram in Franciscan poverty. Very deeply Christian, constantly speaks of Christ, but for three years has not the opportunity of receiving any sacrament. A blessed encounter.
>
> . . . I shall not go to Bangalore in October, any more than I did in March. Chidanandaji himself said the other day (. . .) that it was not my place. The true Christian monasticism in India is not in places like K., A., etc.; their only value is to spread the monastic idea among Christians. The real monks are these 'Ekarasānanda' [Bliss of the single flavour][116] of the present moment. Similarly among the Hindus I have met some real ones this month, whom the public takes for common beggars, but who are far more genuine in their 'gunny bags' than the fine mahatmas.

116. This was the name of the just mentioned Malayali sadhu (*Diary,* 19.6.73).

Very strong advice has come to me this year to avoid seminars, etc. The place of the hermit is in his cell. A little hard to swallow, but true, isn't it? Some would like me to give up writing. And in fact what might perhaps remain to be written is impossible to write. Everything explodes when you have reached the fourth *matra* of the OM.[117]

However, in preparation for the ceremony of Marc's ecumenical diksha I read the Sannyasa Upanishads and drew up a paper which I sent the other day to Chidananda. For me a little like Josiah's discovery of Deuteronomy. (. . .) It has made quite a significant text, which would probably be worth the trouble of getting it published, but who would be interested in taking it? Even so, I shall put it into shape at all events.

"Interim structures", you say (with reference to monks). But monasticism is in the first place a charism. Structures will be born from the charismatic enthusiasm of individuals, real Indian monks. Congresses and seminars will not contribute anything. Bangalore is too far to go by train—that is much too tiring for me now. They have offered me an air passage (. . .). To go and speak on the truly monastic or ashramic life (. . .) after getting down from an aeroplane is just a joke. Real monks don't travel by air, apart from absolute necessity. Reform is not going to come from chit-chat and discussion. Benedict, like Antony, went off into the desert, and Francis took to the roads without collecting all the neighbouring monks for a Congress.

. . . On 15 August I shall have had twenty-five years in India. What a blessing to have ventured on this step, even though I could not know then what was awaiting me here. What awaited me was this marvellous discovery that '*aham asmi*'—so simple, and so marvellous! Everything explodes, everything goes away, and then what is left? *Etad vai tad;* That, just that![118]. . . but no longer anyone to say it . . . (RP, 25.6.73)

The diksha . . . the heart-attack—27 June to 14 July 1973

Early in the morning of 30 June a small group assembled beside the Ganges a short distance below the Sivananda Ashram. The ecumenical *diksha* was administered to Marc by Abhishiktananda and Swami Chidananda (who was accompanied by Swami Krishnananda), using the very simple rite which they had worked out for this unique occasion (a full description is given at the end of the essay on "Sannyasa"). Immediately afterwards Marc set out to 'wander' (*parivrajya*), and Abhishiktananda returned to his room at the Chetsinghs, deeply moved by this experience, which was the true culmination of his twenty-five years in India. At Rajpur he immediately set to work on typing a new fair copy of "Sannyasa", which Swami Krishnananda had requested for publication in the Ashram monthly, *The Divine Life.*[119] In the following week he also wrote to his family and to many friends, describing the diksha in greater or less detail, and

117. See Note 35 above.
118. A refrain in the Katha Upanishad.
119. It was serialized in seven issues, beginning in September 1973.

speaking of the impression that it had made on him. For instance, to Jyotiniketan friends in Jerusalem:

> . . . Now the most beautiful news. Last Saturday, 30/6, Marc has received sannyas in the Ganga from Chidanandaji and myself. Very simple ceremony, but it was simply too beautiful. The three of us were simply radiant. Deep in the Ganga he pronounced the old formula of renunciation. I join him; he plunges into (the) water; I raise him up, and we sing our favourite mantras to the Purusha. He discards all his clothes in (the) water, and I receive him as from the maternal womb. We envelop him in the fire-coloured dress. We communicate to him the *mahāvākyas,* and I give him the 'envoi': "Go to where is no return . . ." And immediately he went on, his begging bowl in hand, to I do not know where, for at least one or two weeks of wandering as long as the rains will permit, without a *paisa.*
>
> It is really marvellous how he has taken his call seriously. His example shows me what I should have (had) the courage to do earlier, putting into practice the beautiful things I wrote. I am too much of a 'littérateur', as M. used to tell me. The previous day was for him a fast on water only, the night all devoted to readings of Bible and Upanishads. Ending at 4 a.m. with the celebration of the Eucharist, whose stone plate and cup were later thrown into the Ganga, for the real sannyas is the end of all signs.
>
> You understand that, after such emotion, I shall less and less be tempted to accept invitations and the like. The real sannyasi is simply fixed inside. This is his only function in society and the Church. See the pity—such initiation is provided nowhere in the Church. Beforehand it was made very clear with Swami Chidananda that such sannyas was above all distinction of *dharma*; and for it the rite was reduced to its essentials, without any Hindu reference. I wish it to be a 'first' which will open a path. Chidanandaji was especially happy. He told me that he had rarely been as much satisfied after giving sannyas . . . (MR, 3.7.73)

In a letter to Mrs Baumer, after describing the *diksha,* he explained Marc's new name:

> . . . Ajatananda, "Bliss of the Not-born", one of the themes which had most impressed him during our study of the Upanishads. Whether he stays in India or returns to France (overland), it will make no difference; he will remain buried away for long years, but I am sure that the day will come when the fruit of his silence will be marvellous. But in the mean time no one should disturb him. All he wants in France is solitude. (OB, 2.7.73)

To Mother Françoise-Thérèse of Lisieux he explained the need for this 'ecumenical' *diksha*. The Church offers no form of 'profession' which would correspond to Marc's special calling:

> . . . Accordingly, to mark it with a *sign,* last Saturday we had a very simple but moving ceremony involving him, a Hindu Swami (. . .) and

> myself; the Hindu swami coopted him into the host of monks and seers of India, and I united him with the succession of monks that goes back to the Desert Fathers, and behind that to Elijah, the great monk-prophet of the Old Testament. (. . .) Then he received his new name, and his begging bowl, and set off on the roads without a *sou*, with just a covering for the night (. . .). Blessed are those who thus take totally seriously the call of Christ, and the inner call of the Spirit, of the Self. (. . .) The call of the absolute which has sounded in Marc's heart and to which he has so generously given literal obedience, has filled my thoughts all this week.

He also told her how his contact with non-Catholics and non-Christians (and just then with the Quaker family who were his hosts at Rajpur) had caused him

> . . . to discover with wonder the Spirit everywhere. (. . .) If you knew how the best western theology is 'trivial' and turned in on itself, when once you have known here the great open spaces of the Spirit. But it is useless to say this, because people only want *ideas,* and never think that they need first of all to sit in silence and listen to the Spirit free from all preconceptions.
>
> Yesterday evening I was with a Ladakhi family (. . .) and had to deal with a Pentecostal pastor who was trying to convince these simple Christians that to be saved they first needed to be baptized by immersion and to speak with tongues. After he had gone, I reassured them and showed them that the only sign of being a Christian that is given in the Gospel is love. The Spirit reveals himself freely in his own way, and no one can set rules for him. (. . .) It was thus in the sign of the Spirit beyond all forms, that we performed that marvellous ecumenical consecration to the mystery of the Absolute! (FT, 6.7.73)

His sister Marie-Thérèse, to mark his twenty-fifth anniversary in India, had sent him sprigs of broom and heather and a group photograph of the family. In his reply he told her about "the loveliest present of these 25 years", and at the end of his account of the *diksha* said:

> . . . How I envy him! All this week I have been dreaming about him; naturally I wonder whether he is suffering excessively from hunger and the rain. Above all, I envy him . . . How I wish I had the courage like him to be able to go to the full extent of what is demanded by the dress I wear; and how ashamed I am of all that is unnecessary in my clothing, food and conveniences of life. The true sannyasi should have nothing—and no more, surely, should monks and nuns. (. . .) I shall at least have had the joy of awakening this child, and of realizing through him the ideal of which I talked so much in my books and articles, but which alas, I have lived so little.
>
> . . . Thank you for (. . .) the photo with the key. How those whom I knew have changed, just as I have also changed myself. That is all to the good, isn't it? Once I loved Gregorian as much as anyone, but now there is a silent melody making itself heard which deprives everything whatever of its taste. They say that there are four parts of the OM—

A, U, M, and then what is inaudible. You only know the OM, when you have heard that inaudible part . . . All that is what I said to Marc, much more through the heart than by word of mouth, and then it set him on fire to the extent you now see. Just think, on that same 30 June, if he had not come to India two years ago and been 'burnt up' here, he would probably have been ordained priest at Bourg!

. . .Yes, I well remember that Fr Abbot of H. who answered me so courteously (. . .). It was he who replied with the most understanding. But it was fortunate that I came alone, and that Fr Monchanin was not a practical man; so being 'unsuccessful', I was carried off by the Spirit to the true source of India's monastic life. (MT, 6.7.73)

Abhishiktananda's unbounded joy at the diksha found expression in some ecstatic poems jotted down on a sheet of paper, full of the symbolism which he shared with Marc. The actual ceremony had opened his eyes to a further dimension of the diksha, which had been deliberately excluded in the Essay on Sannyasa. The experience revealed to him that after all it had a 'sacramental' significance:

In reclothing you with the *kavi,*
and beholding you reclothed,
I discovered
that the *kavi* was not merely a sign,
but a mystery,
the explosion outwardly
of the *tejomaya Purusha* [the Man of glory],
of the depths of Being. (MC, about 5.7.73)

Abhishiktananda felt this so strongly that he wanted to add a new conclusion to his essay. This he was never able to do, but when in 1974 *The Further Shore* was prepared for publication, Marc expanded a paragraph on p.43, which briefly expresses this insight.

Although these letters give no indication, it seems that the premonition of death, which had already affected him in the previous year, had now become very powerful. On the evening before the diksha at the Sivananda Ashram, a *sādhaka,* Nirmal Tripathi,[120] to whom they were very close, sang the "Arunachala Shiva" to a special tone which recalled the 'great departure' (*mahāprasthāna*) of Sri Ramana. This moved Abhishiktananda so deeply that he could not restrain his sobs and afterwards had difficulty in walking to his room.[121]

It was perhaps the sense that his time was short that prompted an urgent appeal to one of his oldest friends who had recently been on pilgrimage to the Holy Land:

. . . You meditated at the places where the 'Sadguru' lived, meditated, prayed, taught . . . but did you discover his presence? As an archaeologist, you live so naturally in the past; but the past is dead. You must surely at some time or other have enjoyed those words of [Angelus] Silesius: "What good does it do to me that Christ was born, died and rose again, so long as that is not true in me?" India effectively frees us from the whole past, as from the whole future. There is only

120. Now Swami Jivanmuktananda. 121. So *Diary,* 11.9.73.

> the eternal moment in which I AM. This 'name' (I AM) which Jesus applies to himself in St John is for me the key to this mystery. And it is the discovery of this Name (in the depth of my own 'I AM') that is truly Salvation for each of us.

After a description of the diksha with greetings for the anniversary of his friend's baptism:

> . . . My wish for you is that the 'awakening' which began on that day may lead you more and more deeply to the discovery of this 'I AM', in which alone you will meet the Christ, no longer in a memory or in beautiful theological ideas, but in his own mystery, which yourself YOU ARE. (7.7.73)

Even more significantly, before leaving Rajpur on 9 July he wrote a kind of 'will', a short typed sheet with several copies, headed "TRUE COPIES OF INSTRUCTIONS LEFT BY SWAMI ABHISHIKTANANDAJI DULY SIGNED ON 9.7.73." It begins: "In case of any accident, please inform—", followed by the names and addresses of six friends and disciples. Brief instructions follow about the disposal of his books, files and correspondence, not forgetting 'souvenirs'.

He intended to go to Rishikesh and, after leaving there a letter and a few things for Marc in the care of the kindly police officer to whom Marc had to report, to make his way back to Gyansu. However, the forecast given to his family in the following letter proved to be more true than he can have expected:

> . . . Just before returning to Gyansu, this brief word. (. . .) I very much hope to remain there until the end of September. However, it is so rarely that my plans work out in the way that I intend, that I can never be sure of anything. (F, 8.7.73)

When Abhishiktananda went to Capt. Mishra's office, he found there a note from Marc, telling him of his discovery of a kutiya beside the Ganges near the hamlet of Kaudiyāla, about forty kms above Rishikesh, which he thought would be ideal for his guru. Abhishiktananda decided to go and see it on the following day. Meanwhile Marc himself came to the office, found the letter left by his guru and at once returned to Kaudiyala, where his appearance gave both of them an immense surprise.

Marc told Abhishiktananda about a small deserted Shiva temple which he had discovered on the other side of the Ganges at a place called Ranagāl. There they passed three days of high spiritual experience, apparently without food, in what can only be called a 'holy inebriation', like that of the *keshi* (hairy ones) of the Rig-Veda.

On the 14th Abhishiktananda returned to Rishikesh, intending to come back after a few hours with provisions. But as they parted, words came unbidden to Abhishiktananda's lips which both of them recognized as those of the 'great departure' and a final farewell.

That afternoon in the Rishikesh bazar, as he was hurrying to catch the return bus, Abhishiktananda was felled to the ground with a serious heart-attack. It was the end of his active life, though he lingered on for another five months.

7

The Discovery of the Grail

14 July to 7 December, 1973

I have found the GRAIL! and this extra lease of life—for such it is—can only be used for living and sharing this discovery. (MT, 9.8.73)

. . . I shall be quite unable to write any poetry for you in return. (. . .) The joy often went with marvellous poetry; now there is the joy without any poetry, and that is only the more true. (MT, 22.10.73)

Rishikesh—14 July to 30 July 1973

THE HEART-ATTACK left Abhishiktananda helpless beside the road. He might well have died there and then, but for the providential arrival of a friend from the Sivananda Ashram, Yvonne Lebeau, whose taxi was held up at that point in the bazar long enough for her to be able to recognize him. She called a doctor, and before long the patient was comfortably lodged in the Tourist Bungalow. All arrangements were made by Swami Chidananda, and for the next two weeks Abhishiktananda, devotedly nursed by his young friend Nirmal, remained at the Bungalow.

Meanwhile Marc waited in the jungle for his return, still without food, and not knowing whether he was dead or alive. His 'agony' lasted for four days, until Nirmal sought him out, bringing with him the following poem:

MARC,
Shiva's column of fire
brushed against me
Saturday midday
in the bazar at Rishikesh,
and I still do not understand
why it did not carry me off.
Joy, the serene one,
OM tat sat
Ekadrishti [the one-pointed gaze]
ekarshi [the unique rishi]
Oh!
The crowning grace
OM!
with my love.

For Abhishiktananda the heart-attack was the occasion of a definitive 'awakening', and he saw the only reason for his being given a further lease of life in the opportunity that it gave of inviting others to share it, as he frequently did in letters thereafter.

Only a week after the attack he wrote to Marc, who was still at Ranagal and felt himself irresistibly prevented from leaving ("*cloué par Shiva*", as he put it):

> You were looking for me either among the dead or among the living, in some *loka* [situation, world] or other, forgetting that simply, I was, I am. The awakening has nothing to do with any situation. The awakening, *prabodha,* (just) is.
>
> The awakening has nothing to do with what you see at the moment of waking up, or with what each one unthinkingly identifies with the I am. The lesson of total simplicity (received) in those days—nights with dreams,[1] days with quite simple intuitions.
>
> *Ekadrishti* [the one-pointed gaze] is not found by confronting exceptional situations (such were my dreams) of cold, solitude, nakedness, etc . . . all that is still *loka;* but by simply opening your eyes there where you are!
>
> . . .Now you realize how much the 'place of the awakening' is still something that you dream. A marvellous lesson has been given you.
>
> . . . I would like to write more. So many things to share together. But I am really not up to it. (. . .)
>
> Yes, that morning when I left you, words of farewell rose to my lips (though I was due to return ten hours later), and I held back a good deal of it. I had not understood.
>
> I have to recognize that a 'Force' passes through being (beings?) which is terribly dangerous. For my affair was not so much the result of stupidly running after a bus, as the upshot of those two weeks, the *explosion* of which the poem spoke.[2] (MC, 21.7.73)

A few days later, in somewhat shaky handwriting, he gently broke the news to his family that he had had "a slight health problem—after all, my heart is 63 years old. But Providence is marvellous." And he reminded them that that day was the 25th anniversary of his leaving Marseilles "for this marvellous adventure" (F, 26.7.73).

Next day Marc arrived to relieve Nirmal as nurse, and to take Abhishiktananda to Rajpur until he should be capable of the journey to Indore.

Rajpur—30 July to 19 August 1973

At the Chetsingh's house in Rajpur he was looked after by Marc and his other disciples. He began to feel better, and was told by his doctor that he was 70% cured and would recover in three months; but in himself he knew well that he could never again live as he had in the past. However his letters were full of the joy of his recent experiences, which he shared with friends like Murray Rogers:

1. These dreams are mentioned in the *Diary,* 11.9.73; "I was made to pass from cave to cave—at different altitudes, 9000, 11000, 13000 feet. (. . .) I continually replied: the awakening has nothing to do with 'measuring yourself' against more and more difficult living conditions."
2. See the poem on p. 304.

. . . I lived two wonderful days, 11-14, with Marc in a jungle, a Shiva temple. Too strong(!) for me. I came to Rishikesh for a few things. At noon, when I was about to board the bus and go back with food, etc., for Marc, a full-fledged heart-attack! Lying down helpless on the pavement. After perhaps half an hour a taxi stopped without reason at one yard from me. A French lady from the ashram saw me, with difficulty recognized me, called the doctor. I was lying expecting to collapse every second. The ashram wonderfully took all care of me. A dear Brahmin boy was with me two weeks, day and night. A wonderful experience of *ananda* and *shanti.* A necessary experience, without moving, one week mere diet of fruit juice! Meanwhile Marc in agony and hunger in his jungle, thinking me dead. A terrible *upadesha* [instruction] which the guru—mere instrument—had to give him. I could send a message only four days later, for I alone knew where he was!

. . . Now I am still 'en état d'enfance'! Yet I rarely passed two weeks as blissful as those which followed the attack.

Magnificate Dominum mecum [Praise the Lord with me]!

Who can bear the glory of transfiguration, of man's discovery as transfigured; because what Christ is, I AM! One can only speak of it after being awoken from the dead. (MR, 6.8.73)

He wrote again reassuringly to the family at St Briac, but admitted to his sister at Kergonan that the heart-attack "was very serious, and apart from an almost miraculous combination of circumstances, I should have died there on the sidewalk, at Rishikesh, with no one paying any attention." Then he continued:

. . . It was a marvellous spiritual experience. The discovery that the AWAKENING has nothing to do with any situation, even so-called life or so-called death; one is awake, and that is all. While I was waiting on my sidewalk, on the frontier of the two worlds, I was magnificently calm, for I AM, no matter in what world! I have found the GRAIL! and this extra lease of life—for such it is—can only be used for living and sharing this discovery.

Besides I had experienced emotions which were too powerful. I have told you about 30 June [diksha], then from 10 to 14th a 'week' in the jungle with Marc which was so spiritually powerful that the body could not stand up to it. (. . .)

The doctor tells me that after three months all should be under control. However, I am afraid that I shall have to say goodbye to Uttarkashi, for it would be difficult for me to travel alone with my bundles. (. .)

I am still very weak, have no appettite, and am on a strict diet (. . .). As soon as I feel stronger, I shall go to Indore, and Marc will accompany me there before returning to his solitude. (. . .)

Don't frighten them at St Briac, but I wanted to tell you the whole truth. Tell them about it at St Anne, so that they can bless the Lord with me, less for having brought me back to this world, than for the joy of having discovered the Grail! (MT, 9.8.73)

He wrote to Mrs Baumer about her coming to India in October, during which he had hoped to accompany her to Rishikesh, a hope which seemed unlikely to be fulfilled:

> . . But no matter, the Grail has been found. And the only reason for continuing to live is to help with the awakening—above all by taking care to keep one's own eyes wide open. (. .) Each 'awakened one' is only a mirror in which you awake to yourself. (OB, 15.8.73)

His friend at Lisieux, Mother Françoise-Thérèse, was herself seriously ill, and he wrote to encourage her, telling her about his own experience as "the true awakening to what is Real. One of the great graces of my life."

> . . . The emotions in Marc's sannyasa, plus an absolutely fantastic 'week' in the jungle by the Ganges from 10 to 14th, had been too powerful. We must accept what your Carmelite saints say (Elijah was very much present to us during that week that was spiritually so powerful), that there are inner experiences which the body/heart cannot bear. (FT, 16.8.73)

A few days later Abhishiktananda travelled down via Delhi to Indore, on this occasion (the first?) as a first class passenger.

Indore—21 August to 7 December 1973

Abhishiktananda had in any case intended to go to the Roberts Nursing Home at Indore later in the year for a medical check-up. Since 1957 he had been a regular visitor, and now it was literally the only place where he could seek refuge. As he told Mrs Baumer:

> . . . My reason for coming to Indore is that I find here a homely atmosphere, medical attention, suitable food, and all that 'for the love of God'—and each of these is important. (OB, 28.8.73)

He had the greatest confidence in Mother Théophane, the only remaining French member of the community, whom he also admired as a true true contemplative.[3] It was she who steadily rallied his spirits during the coming months ("She is my guardian angel", as he said) in the series of relapses which gradually removed any hope of a full recovery. For months the sun rarely shone, and the cold damp weather aggravated his cough and breathing difficulties. One after another he had to abandon his hopes, first of returning to Rishikesh, and then of spending the winter at the Carmel of Soso near Ranchi; finally he had to agree to be taken (by air!) to a quiet place in the country near Pondicherry, so as to get the benefit of the southern sun. This however was deferred by a prolonged lock-out in the Indian Airways, and before the date fixed for his flight the final heart-attack came.

At the beginning of September he heard from Murray Rogers that he had been introduced by Mrs Baumer to the Sufi Master Vilayat Khan, who had invited

3. Mother Théophane was born in 1903, professed in the Franciscan Sisters of St Mary of the Angels in 1925, and worked continuously in India (chiefly in Indore) from 1927 until her death in 1982.

him to make a 'Christian' contribution to his camp at Chamonix in the following year. Murray wrote to seek Abhishiktananda's advice about how to do this, and seems also to have invited him to take part himself:

> . . . This attack is indeed the providential answer to allurements towards western trips. Even moving in India will be difficult, and I am afraid I shall have to end my earthly days as a nun's chaplain! For now, finished is the life of a 'free-lance', relying on oneself alone for living, cooking, carrying water and the like. Invitation to become fully acosmic! free from all circumstances and situations. (. . .) I am so much fed up with all those swamis who are convinced that they have a 'chosen' mission, whereas the true mission of a swami is to sit in his cave till the angel takes him by the hair of his head like Habakkuk. (. . .)
>
> But I want chiefly to write about what you would like to do eventually in Vilayat's camp. (. . . I might have written to you my wonderful and unexpected meeting with him near the Ganga last February?) The more I go, the less able I would be to present Christ in a way which could be still *considered* as 'Christian'. I can start with 'Christ' only if my approach is 'notional', by ideas. For Christ is first an 'idea' which comes to me from outside. Even more after my 'beyond life/death' experience of 14.7, I can only aim at awakening people to what 'they are'.. Anything about God or the Word in any religion, which is not based on the deep I-experience, is bound to be simply 'notion', not existential. From that awakening to self comes the awakening to God—and we discover marvellously that Christ is simply this awakening on a degree of purity rarely if ever reached by man.
>
> Yet I am interested in no *christo-logy* at all. I have so little interest in a Word of God which will awaken man within history (. . .). The 'Word of God' comes from/to *my* own 'present'; it is that very awakening which is my self-awareness. What I discover above all in Christ is 'I AM'. I sometimes said jokingly that my next book's cover design would be an 'atomic mushroom'.[4] There remains only the Ah! of the Kena Upanishad. Christ's experience in the Jordan—Son/Abba—is a wonderful Semitic equivalent of *'Tat tvam asi'/'aham brahmasmi'*.[5] Of course I can make use of Christ experience to lead Christians to an 'I AM' experience, yet it is this I AM experience which really matters. Christ is this very mystery 'that I AM', and in this experience and existential knowledge all christo-logy has disintegrated. It is taking to the end the revelation that we are 'sons of God.'
>
> There is only One Son. Each of his manifestations is both *one* and *unique*. So what would be the meaning of a 'Christianity-coloured' awakening? In the process of awakening all this coloration cannot but disappear (the atomic mushroom). If at all I had to give a message, it would be the message of 'Wake up, arise, remain aware,' of the Katha

4. He was somewhat critical of the cover design of *Saccidananda*.
5. "That art thou"/"I am brahman", two of the central Upanishadic mantras, the *mahavakya*. Concerning Abhishiktananda's view of this 'equivalence', see chapter 6, Note 97.

Upanishad. The coloration might vary according to the audience, but the essential goes beyond. The discovery of Christ's I AM is the ruin of any Christian theology, for all notions are burnt within the fire of experience. Perhaps I am a little too Cartesian, as a good Frenchman. and perhaps others might find a way out of the atomic mushroom. I feel too much, more and more, the blazing fire of this I AM, in which all notions about Christ's personality, ontology, history, etc. have disappeared. And I find his real mystery shining in every awakening man, in every mythos . . .

The only message I could give now is too much burning to be given except with people whom the Spirit might send near me, as he did in the case of Marc. So you realize the dilemma in which I find myself, whenever I am asked to speak on Christian interiority and contemplation . . .

Enough for your *tapas* [penance] this long letter! (MR, 2.9.73)

Two other letters to Murray Rogers in the next few weeks continue his thoughts:

. . . Really a door opened in heaven when I was lying on the pavement. But a heaven which was not the opposite of earth, something which was neither life nor death, but simply 'being', 'awakening' . . . beyond all myths and symbols. And finally I believe that coronary attack was only a part, but an essential one, of a whole process of grace. If we meet some time, I shall tell you the whole wonderful story; till then, *magnificate Dominum mecum.* In the joy of God always. (MR, 10.9.73)

. . . In a world around—and a Church—which is so puzzlingly *horizontal,* is there not a place for *vertical acosmics,* who choose to ask from the world just the minimum for the upkeep of their body? I have really been deeply moved by my life with the poor and with poor sadhus of the old tradition. Of course I live much above [i.e., more comfortably than] them, yet I feel there is a place for the witness—the *silent* Spirit! Anyhow, as you realize, my 'coronary' is the best answer to all tempters' voices . . .

Again, if my message could really pass, it would be free from any 'notion' except just by the way of 'excipient'. The Christ I might present will be simply the I AM of my (every) deep heart, who can show himself in the dancing Shiva or the amorous Krishna! And the kingdom is precisely this discovery . . . of the 'inside' of the Grail! (. . .) The awakening is a total explosion. No Church will recognize its Christ or itself afterwards. And precisely for that (reason), no one likes the 'atomic mushroom' ! (MR, 4.10.73)

A letter to Mrs Baumer throws some light on Abhishiktananda's references to the Grail:

. . . The Grail is a marvellous symbol, that old myth around which have coalesced a heap of pagan Celtic and later, Christian myths. With many others Galahad caught the fragrance of the Grail, with Bors and Perceval he drank of it, and one day it was given to him alone openly to

> see within it.[6] The Grail is a symbol which has greatly impressed me; and on the second and third day of my 'adventure' it suddenly came to me—In this adventure I have found the Grail. And what is left for me to do in this life, apart from inviting others to make this discovery? The Grail is neither far nor near, it is free from all location. The take-off, the awakening—and the quest is over. Through all the intervening myths it is the Awakening alone that is the goal of the quest. When we meet, I will give you some beautiful mantras from the Upanishads which express this so 'clearly' (OB, 4.9.73)

He was distressed to hear that an over-dramatic account of his 'adventure' was being put about, and wrote to a friend in Bombay:

> . . . I have heard through S.G. the manner in which things were described to A., M., etc. *Please* don't add anything to my myth. There was no grand vision, but a waiting, an awakening, quite peaceful, to something which is neither life nor death. Besides, that was helped by the fact that at that moment the 'mind' was working at an infinitely reduced speed. (AF, 17.9.73)

In a letter to Fr Lemarié about his changed situation since the heart-attack, he referred once again to his debt to their monastery:

> . . . It is interesting to note that you are now more conscious of what monastic life gave you—and even more, did for you. I also can say all kinds of things about Kergonan; yet Kergonan has been the background of all that I have been able to do here. (. . .) I still keep in touch with the monastery, especially with good old Fr Landry[7] who is so young. I have just had a word from him at noon today—so understanding (. . .). I don't know what the Monastic Congress at Bangalore will produce next month. I have sometimes regretted my refusal to go, but at this moment I am physically incapable of it. At times I would like to go and stir up the dust! (L, 22.9.73)

After months of delay, caused by the electricity shortage in the South, proofs of *Saccidananda* (*Sagesse,* English version) began to come at the beginning of September, and were sent on by the editor to Abhishiktananda with numerous queries. Despite his weakness he dealt with these with care and despatch, and continued to do so until the day before his death. To the proposal of the Indian S.P.C.K. that they should publish the essay on Sannyasa (which had just begun to appear in *The Divine Life*) he replied:

> . . . As concerns *Sannyasa,* when you read it again, you may send me your suggestions how to better it in the composition itself, if I am able. The last pages anyhow have to be revised, and I was feeling very

6. The climax of Galahad's quest, according to Christian de Troyes' *Quest of the Grail,* was his seeing the inside of the cup.
7. Dom Émile Landry, senior monk of Kergonan, was one of those with whom Abhishiktananda regularly corresponded. He followed his Indian pilgrimage with great sympathy and was deeply interested in advaita (a copy of his notes is in the archives). See also the reference in MC, 23.9.73 (p. 313).

> much the need of adding or incorporating a few pages about sannyasa as *musterion,* a mystery. When the diksha took place I realized so much it was much more than a simple sign; we might say a 'symbol' in the language of Jung, in religious terms, a mystery. That should be a response to the chapter on "Contestation" [i.e., ch. 4]. But for that the brain must work in a brighter way than it does for the moment. (JS, 20.9.73)

(Although he was never able to revise the text himself, in the following year when it was prepared for publication in *The Further Shore,* Marc made a small addition to page 43 which conveyed the main point that he had in mind.)

For a month after Marc had left him at Indore, Abhishiktananda refrained from writing, but finally gave him some news:

> Dearest Marc, I hesitated a long time before writing to you. I felt such qualms about upsetting your silence and solitude. I hope at least that you could return to Ranagal without mishap, despite the devastating rains. Here there has been some progress, but much slower than I was hoping. Yesterday's cardiogram did not show the hoped for improvement.
>
> . . . It is clear that henceforth my life of untamed independence is finished. Gyansu is finished. (. . .) Kaudiyala is beyond my strength, apart from an unforeseen recovery next year. I am not worrying about the future, but nothing is coming into view. As an old Father in my monastery, aged 86 (. . .) who was greatly struck by the diksha of 30 June, wrote to me yesterday: For my Indian jubilee I have been given the grace of passing on to you the mantle (or the non-mantle?), and now all is in God's hands. When the day comes you will pass on what you have received, or rather what has blossomed in you.
>
> . . . I have no hope of being able to settle by the Ganges even next year. In future I shall have to live with a group of people, or at least near to one . . . In that there is no cause for depression, but I shall have to accept important changes in my outward life from now on, which will be no small *tapas* after sixteen years of total independence. I had to tell you this, you will accept it 'at depth'. Besides, it is in line with my Rishikesh experience: the awakening is not tied to any *loka.* It is specially wonderful to have no longer either home or hearth, totally *aniketanah.* A marvellous exercise in liberation.
>
> . . . On 1 September I began to say Mass again (though it is very tiring) in latin and in a low voice, at 11 a.m. Some days I have not been capable of it, as I felt too weary. The *lila* of the Lord, who sports among the worlds. The settings change, but the mystery of the awakening abides. (MC, 23.9.73)
>
> The man who took my letter to you to the post at noon has brought me yours. A joy to have this breath of air from the heights, which I so much miss here. (. . .) A great joy in the first place to find you so 'human'; for certain of your 'extreme' utterances have more than once made me tremble. (MC, 24.9.73)

> . . . Interesting that you have a renewed taste for the Psalms of Israel. I read a little from them, morning and evening, with other texts from the Old and New Testament.[8] They often set my teeth on edge, but the remarkable thing about them is the upright stance of man in front of God—like that of Job. Man treats him as an equal. Is not this also a manifestation of the experience that 'I am'?
>
> . . . You are right, Books 3 and 4 of the Brihad. Upanishad are a matchless peak. And the wonder is that, after having taught brahmins, kings, his own wife, Yājñavalkya 'departed' . . .
>
> . . . Joy, whatever happens. Excuse my *buddhi* [brain] which is still very idle. A little like Jeremiah's 'Ah!' (MC, 27.9.73)

At the beginning of October Abhishiktananda had a relapse, as he told Marc:

> . . . Yes, I hear your invitation to the Ganges. Through your eyes I see the flowers and the hills. In your body I feel the caress of the Ganges, I hear the sounds of the jungle . . . and that gives me joy in the 'nakedness' in which I live here. But I am still unable to come back to the Upanishads (. . .) as I was hoping. The *'Om tat sat'* remains my only worthwhile *'vritti'* [activity]. I have plenty of letters to answer. I deal with them slowly, for even that is tiring.
>
> . . . (5th morning) . . . "*ut jumentum*" ["like a beast before thee"], as says Psalm 73 (Hebrew).[9] Neither meditation nor concentration. Being there, simply. Sometimes appeals to Christ, to whom I can no longer give any name. Yet I am well aware that he is the most inward mystery, of which the Resurrection has caused all forms to explode. He is now the *Keshi*, the *Ekarishi*, the amorous Krishna, the dancing Shiva, the Awakened one. All has been taken away—and likewise all that sense of security for the future which was attached to a physical or mental form. That is the real *a-rūpa* [formless]. Not one which is abstracted or imagined, but one into which you are plunged head over heels, completely dazzled. (MC, 4.10.73)

About this time Marc was compelled to leave Ranagal and return to Phulchatti:

> . . . I am happy that you are taking this necessary move so well. The greatest 'high places' are never more than 'lokas'. And every day we let ourselves be caught in the *māyā* [deception] of lokas. We need these heavy blows to be constantly rained on our skulls to bring us to reality. (. . .) All the same, blessed are your eyes which see what you see. I enjoy it all through you, while at the same time envying you, I admit. (MC, 5.10.73)
>
> . . . Yes, at times when I reread your 'story' [the events of June-July], I am convinced that there is a great message to hand on through that. A message which culminates in the 'disintegration' of July 14 and after. For that disintegration, for you as for me, was the climax and the great liberation.

8. He was without the relevant portion of the Breviary, having expected to return to Uttarkashi in July.
9. This phrase from Psalm 73:22 was often referred to in these last letters. He no doubt also had in mind its occurrence in the *Rule of St Benedict*, chapter 7, in connection with the sixth degree of humility.

> . . . As I said the other day, I am particularly happy that you let go of Ranagal with such freedom. (. . .) All lokas are means, 'steps' on a ladder, but as with a ladder, you cannot stop on any rung. However, there are some great places—Sinai, Jordan, Tabor . . . And because we are flesh, we have great need of flesh and of places, precisely in order to release the total mystery of the flesh and of lokas [places], (. . .). Surely that is also the mystery—so hard for reason to grasp—of the Corpus Christi, the Body of Christ? Freed from his (literal) flesh/body (*asmāt śarīrāt samutthaya,* rising up from this body—Chand. Up., 8.12.2), we find his glorious flesh/body, *tejomaya Purusha.* But all that will always remain only words and abstractions from him who has not *seen (vedāham)* the great Purusha.[10]
>
> . . . At times I feel so low that I begin to want to let go of this 'old garment', as the Gita says. But still I must tell the secret of the awakening, which is so simple. (MC, 9.10.73)

On 10 October Mrs Baumer and her son arrived at Indore and spent three days with Abhishiktananda. For him it was "physically tiring, but a great joy to be able to speak, after so long, about 'certain mysteries'—the OM, the Ganges, Ranagal," as he said to Marc (MC, 13.10.73). Mrs Baumer recorded her own impressions of Abhishiktananda, whom she saw less than two months before his death, in a letter written to the Abbot of Kergonan in 1974:

> . . . It is difficult to describe those days spent with him, our conversations, the times of silence—his silence had a quite special quality—, the celebration of the Eucharist. His whole person and all that he did literally radiated the Presence of God, he was all transparency to the Lord. Physically he was extremely feeble, he could only manage to walk for a few minutes each day, an obstinate cough constantly interrupted him in the course of conversation and greatly wearied him; but in spite of that, his whole personality radiated serenity and a very subtle joy, his mind was one hundred per cent alert, and never for a moment did he lose his good spirits or his sense of humour.
>
> The photograph which my son took of him in his room (. . .) well shows his characteristic look, radiant and full of affection, a look which expressed complete inner freedom.[11]

This striking photograph indeed speaks volumes, and has been reproduced in a number of publications. While the Baumers continued their travels, first in North India and then in the South. Abhishiktananda followed them with his concern and good advice. At the end of a final letter he wrote:

> . . . For you the South of India will be a new world. There is a gentleness in the climate and in everything else. Much as I love the Ganges, the South is for me a 'birth-place', and it has its temples which, as is so rare in the North, are filled with an extraordinary numinosity. Don't

10. An allusion to Śvetaśvatara Up., 3.8: " I know this mighty Purusha, of the colour of the sun, beyond darkness. Only by knowing him does one pass over death. There is no other path for going there." (Hume's translation)
11. Extract from a long note, dated 10.9.74, sent to the Abbot of Kergonan.

> rush past Arunachala. It only tells its secrets to those who have time to listen . . . May your eyes—and much more, your hearts—be filled with the beauty! (OB, 13.11.73)

The week after Mrs Baumer's visit was a very low period, when Abhishiktananda could only occasionally rise from his bed, as he did his best to keep up with his correspondence. In a letter to Marc he said:

> . . . After two months at Indore, three months and one week after the adventure, I admit that I often find it a slow business, and that even a 'moderate' recovery has not yet appeared on the horizon.
>
> . . . I expect you have written up in your notebooks all that happened from mid-May to the end of June. I have not had the strength to do it (. . .). The slightly disappointing week at Phulchatti—though there was the discovery of the two *avadhūta* under the cliff; (. . .) the nights under the stars when no one could or would take us in at Rishikesh or Hardwar; the *bhiksha* at Saptasarovar . . . all that was already on the way up to the climax of the end of June and mid-July.
>
> I am delighted with your enthusiasm for those Upanishadic texts which you quote, even though I don't feel strong enough to look up the references. (. . .) In the beginning— and even much later—I have been struck by my interest in the Upanishads. Take Mundaka 2.2.; it is a text which I have known by heart since my weeks of silence in the Mauna-mandir at Kumbakkonam.[12] Then, once the mystery has been penetrated, it is so much by words, verses, etc., that the light breaks forth, burning, overwhelming. (. . .) For the moment no 'fine thought' makes any appeal to me; the brain no longer responds. But the '*Om tat sat*' includes everything wonderfully.
>
> The experience on the sidewalk at Rishiskesh and my extreme weariness have left me—without however the slightest distress—with the realization of the abiding possibility of the submergence and the disappearance of my phenomenal consciousness. You can imagine that I have often enjoyed discussing with Mother Théophane your "Come here to die—I will help you to do so, if need be"! In any case I have promised her that I will do my level best not to 'pop off' (as they say here in English) at Indore—that would be too complicated. She agrees that it is much simpler to do it near the Ganges. . .

Sunday afternoon, 21st. I spent the morning in bed. Really I am often bogged down [*vaseux*]. (. . .) I wish my brain was a little more active, so that I could think out a reply to what you say about the 'I'. I really believe that the revelation of the *AHAM* is perhaps the central point of the Upanishads. And that is what gives access to everything; the 'knowing' which reveals all the 'knowings'. God is not known, Jesus is not known, nothing is known, outside this terribly 'solid' *AHAM* that I am. From that alone all true teaching gets its value. I am always frightened of people stopping at the 'negative' aspect of my message (no institution, etc), whereas all negations—liberations—gain their meaning only in

12. See page 99 above.

this break-through to the depth of the I. Everything that awaited expression in Bérulle's meditations on the *interiority* of Jesus, and all that came later in the symbol of the Sacred Heart.

> . . . There is nothing more to be 'said' between us . . And yet you (. . .) tell me that there are so many more things to say! For my part, I needed this punishing blow to make me realize that the awakening to the I is beyond all that marvellous poetry with which again and again we naturally clothe it. The awakening is what lies in the depth of what is utterly ordinary! What a purification and *'nada'* [naughting][13] is this mental helplessness in which I now live—*'ut jumentum'*, as the Psalm says. (MC, 20/21.10.73)

Next day he wrote to his sister at Kergonan a letter which he perhaps realized might be his last;

> My very dear little sister, I have continually put off writing to you. I thought of writing to you and to St Anne at the same time, but even writing is often a great effort. My convalescence goes desperately slowly. I very much hoped after two months at Indore to have recovered at least part of my usual 'go'; but I am still very weak, without appetite or capacity for work. (. . .) A night without even the consolation of seeing in it the marvellous 'night' of purification. They assure me that I shall recover, but it will very likely take a long time. I was probably exhausted when this adventure befell me. (. . .) The future sets me great and insoluble problems. Let us hope that the Lord will show me next year the path to follow. When the body no longer responds to the guidance of the spirit, then you understand St Paul's agonized desire to be relieved of it.
>
> . . . The Carmelite sisters at Ranchi are keen to have me, but I should like to be able to preside properly at their conventual Mass. That is why I shall be glad to have an interval of two months at Madras-Pondy between Indore and Ranchi. Ultimately it is all in God's hands. These Ranchi Sisters would like me to settle down with them next year for good, in order to 'awaken' their novices. But how hard it is for me to tie myself down, and how much I feel the need of the neighbourhood of the Ganges—and of Hindu monks—to blossom out.
>
> . . . This Monday morning I am writing just after having my coffee, actually instead of reading some Psalms. As I had come down from Uttarkashi for only three to four weeks, all my breviaries except one were left up there; so when I am able, I take my little Jerusalem Bible and read a few Psalms and other passages.
>
> I left off writing this letter to lie down. In this morning's mail I have been asked to take a central part in a Hindu-Christian-Buddhist seminar at the beginning of March, my answer required immediately. I have had to write that I have absolutely no idea what will be the condition even next month of 'master body' (at present he is giving himself airs, after years of more or less faithful service).

13. A reference to St John of the Cross.

> It is remarkable that you were moved to implore help for me at the very time when I was lying helpless on my sidewalk! Everything was so wonderful in those first two weeks. Later came the stripping away of all thought, meditation, contemplation. Now it is simply a matter of *being there* and being awake without feeling any of the poetry of the awakening.
>
> I shall be quite unable to write any poetry for you in return, *'ut jumentum'* . . . The joy often went with marvellous poetry; now there is the joy without any poetry, and that is only the more true.
>
> I am going to write to St Briac one of these days to reassure them.
>
> . . . May *Agni* set you on fire within, even if outwardly he gives you trouble [in the convent kitchen]. The true *Agni*. The Spirit is Wind, Space, Fire. He is also the Dove that sports in space. And Spirit is water too. And the Spirit is matter which sanctifies. My only *mantra* at present is *OM TAT SAT*! (MT, 22.10.73)

At the end of the week he wrote cheerfully to the rest of the family at St Briac, mentioning his recent visitors:

> . . . I am certainly improving, but slowly. I am no longer 20 years old, and the life I have led for a good many years was enough to break a tougher man. But what counts is to live life to the full, isn't? What is the use of a life in carpet-slippers? I don't know how long I shall stay on here; once my visitors have gone, I shall have a complete medical examination, and then we shall see. (F, 29.10.73)

Visitors in these days included a young Jesuit from Poona (Ajit M., who had spent some weeks with him at Rajpur in 1972). He brought with him an Italian monk working in Mexico, another of those whom Abhishiktananda had been avoiding: "Another case in which I feel that my refusal of meetings is perhaps egotistical!" (MC, 26.10.73). They were followed by Sr Ivane from Akola, and then by Fr Dominique, with whom he made arrangements for all eventualities. In a letter to Marc he said:

> . . . I am tired of Indore, and it needs all Mother Théophane's good humour to prevent me from going under. As she says, I come in the category of 'bogged down saints'!
>
> . . . Vedantin experience just as much drains people and is just as dangerous as drugs or psycho-analysis. We usually live on its fringe, like flies which content themselves with the crumbs surrounding the cake. We should only allow very strong people to get involved with it. Yet that is where the only salvation is to be found! So long as we have not accepted the *loss* of all concepts, all myths—of Christ, of the Church—nothing can be done! Everything has to spring up anew from the depths, like the Christ who appeared to you the other day at Ranagal in a Grünewaldine light. It is probably better for most people to pass the *Shakti* by, than to be a carrier of it without realizing it. But some are capable of it. It is for them that I should like to have a place beside the Ganges to receive them. (MC, 26.10.73)

At he beginning of November Abhishiktananda had another relapse, which provoked Mother Théophane to take 'drastic measures' in connection with his diet, and for a few days his condition seemed to improve; but once again there were fluctuations, which deferred his flight to the South.

He struggled to keep up to date with his heavy correspondence, but there were times when it was too much for him, as when he had to say to Sr Térèse (still at Pondicherry, awaiting her naturalization):

> This is not a reply to your letter. At present I am far too exhausted for that. Just to tell you that I hold your anxieties and distress in my prayer. (. . .) All that matters is the Awakening—and the Awakening is everywhere, so simple. No going back to the *past*—(the thought) "Have I done what is good? have I not done what is best?", as the Brihad Upanishad so wisely says.[14] (. . .) I am keeping your letter with the unanswered mail, and if I can somewhat recover my form, I will reply in detail. (TL, 5.11.73)

A week later he reported some improvement to Marc:

> Your song of "the Beatitude of those in the Bog" delighted Mother Théophane. Better news today at last. My letter last week was truly *'de profundis'*. I was sinking day by day, eating absolutely nothing. (. . .) Yes, what you wrote about the 'saint in the bog' was marvellous. But, you know, to be able to write that, you need to have at least your head out of the 'mud'. But when you are in it, you know, it is a unique experience and, however hard to bear, wonderfully purifying.
>
> Well now, in those days Mother Théophane took drastic measures, which till then I had always refused. She has made me eat . . . and you can guess what that means after twenty years! And miraculously my appetite has come back, strength begins to return, and again there is hope of recovery. (. . .) Yesterday evening after supper I opened the Upanishads (in Sanskrit). A good sign, unusual! (MC, 12.11.73)

A long letter to St Briac told of the good results of his new diet, and of his hope shortly to be able to use the air ticket for the South, which a friend had paid for. However he dissuaded one of his nieces from coming to see him, as she was planning, "until I am really well". (F, 20.11.73)

To Marc also he reported the improvement in his condition, and went on to reflect once more on their shared experience:

> . . . You are the only person, as well I know, to whom I have been able to say and to pass on everything, in words and beyond words . . . You accepted the *'tabula rasa'* [the emptying of the mind], and from that *tabula rasa* the sparks flew. Yes, none of it was 'mine' or 'yours'. But that 'Greater One', whom you find lying behind myself and yourself, is not-other-than you or me. "The Father is greater than I." "I and the Father are one." The vision of Jesus recovers all its power when his Spirit—entirely in the depths—has 'revealed' the depth of the *Aham.*

14. See Brihadaranyaka Up., 4.4.22.

> You should have been here to help me rise above words, as you have so many times done in the last two years. But, as I have said before, the physical heart can no longer bear these interior explosions. The bog suits it better, at least for some months. (. . .)
>
> All that you write about what is beyond mantras etc . . . you have often said it and written it. You have known it for a long time. But I also know that there are moments when that explodes and makes everything blow up. The *manas* [mind] of course manages to recover its footing but then, even when you make use of it, you no longer allow yourself—or at least, much less than before—to halt at it. Basically we come back to the essential teaching of Ramana, that there is no such thing as 'realization'. (MC, 23.11.73)

Next day he returned to the letter from Sr Térèse which he had been unable to answer before. In particular, he approved her choice of a priest in Delhi who could guide her, when eventually she was free to leave Pondicherry and settle in the North. For the last time he encouraged her to launch out boldly:

> . . . The question is no longer about the objective value of the ideal which you have glimpsed and even begun to realize. (. . .) The question is much more of what in fact you are capable of, physically and mentally, when once you no longer have your annual haven in Pondicherry and also no place to fall back on in North India. (. . .) In the big decisions you are brave and strong; but lots of details in daily life disconcert you. If at least, with a great beat of your wings, you could leave behind all that concerns yourself—to start with, when you look upwards! Once free from anxiety about yourself, you would be able to soar. But you will say that that is not your grace . . so how can you fly with such a load?
>
> In any case decisions about the future from now on depend on you alone. (. . .) The Awakening alone is what counts. (TL, 24.11.73)[15]

The next day was the Feast of Christ the King, when there was a procession of the Blessed Sacrament. As he admitted to Marc, Abhishiktananda was keen to see it and recapture "the old experience of childhood and adolescence"; but he walked further than he should have and stayed out too late in the evening, and "paid for it" with increased breathlessness (MC, 29.11.73). In a last note, two days later, he mentioned that he was able to say Mass again daily, and that "I hope to be able to leave about the 6th or 7th" (MC, 1.12.73)[16]

He sent Advent greetings to his Carmelite friend at Lisieux, and also his apologies for being unable to write the article for *Carmel* for which he had been asked:

15. Sr Térèse eventually obtained Indian citizenship, and in 1974 settled in Rishikesh, having a hermitage first in the Vitthal Ashram, and later at Brahmapuri on the bank of the river. In September 1976 she disappeared, possibly as a result of an accident, her hut being found open, suggesting that she had intended to return.
16. Marc only learned of his guru's death on 25 December, when he came down to Rishikesh and found a letter from a fellow-disciple, Ramesh Srivastava. After helping to dispose of Abhishiktananda's books and papers, he had to visit his home for family reasons in 1974. In January 1975 he settled in the kutiya at Kaudiyala (purchased in the name of the Sivananda Ashram) to begin ten years of *mauna*(silence). In April 1977 he disappeared and has not been seen since then.

> All mental concentration is beyond my capacity. After two weeks of bliss at the beginning when I had my attack, these four months of helplessness have been a marvellous lesson. It is so delightful to write—in the abstract—about the nudity of the spirit. And then the Lord takes you seriously, removes every fine thought, and leaves you there, capable of nothing more than simply being there! And that is what is most real. That is what I needed, chatterbox as I was! The end of October was the worst time of all. I only held on to life through the hopefulness of Mother Théophane. It would have been a relief to have passed on to the further shore. Now the body has recovered a little strength. In a few days I am thinking of leaving by air for Madras (. . .)
>
> In the joy of God. (FT, 30.11.73)

While awaiting his flight to the south, Abhishiktananda wrote Christmas letters to several friends. In a letter to Fr Lemarié he said:

> . . . *'Jerusalem beata'* [the heavenly Jerusalem] is not in our always mythical dreams about the future. It is *kai nun* [even now]; we only have to open our eyes! That is the one thing that I should like to get people to realize from now on, if I go on living. And it is so simple that no one can grasp it, beginning with Europe's Cartesians who dissect everything. They need a dose of Marcuse to 'liberate' them.
>
> This morning I should have taken the plane for Madras, but for two weeks our Indian Airlines have been on strike (. . .). Still, it is amusing that I have twice this year refused to go by plane to take part in Seminars at Bangalore, and now here I am, practically compelled to fly to save my life! (L, 3.12.73)

He also wrote to Mrs Stokes in New York:

> . . .(in October) I had absolutely no appetite and had lost all taste for living. Someone had given me a very beautiful Calendar with a picture of Elijah's chariot (. . .), and I must admit that I contemplated it with longing. (. . .) However, I think I am now on the mend. The Lord be blessed for all, for the 'downs' as well as the 'ups'.
>
> . . . Happy Christmas and a good new year for you and for those poor humiliated ones that it is your vocation to lift up in their own eyes and in the eyes of their brother men! (AMS, 3.12.73)

On 5 and 6 December he checked a large batch of proofs of *Saccidananda* and sent them back with answers to a number of editorial queries, ending his letter with:

> . . . I am going to say the Mass of St Nicholas. I am certainly better, in so many ways. Yet how hard it is to see oneself so far from normalcy. (JS, 6.12.73)

All this work, however, had exhausted him, and he was unable to say Mass, but spent the rest of the day in bed. Next morning he again had difficulty in breathing, and a cardiogram showed that his heart condition had deteriorated. He spent a quiet day, contemplating the ikon of Elijah, which combined the theme of 'handing on' the mantle to the disciple with that of the 'great departure'.

When Mother Théophane pointed out that his own time might not yet have come, he answered, "God's will be done;" but she noted that he "did not look very convinced".

That evening he had another brief attack at 9 p.m. He was given oxygen and settled for the night, while friends remained praying beside his bed. Finally at 11 p.m. there was another attack. The Bishop came to anoint him and say the commendatory prayers. After a few minutes his heart stopped beating.

The news of Swamiji's death was widely circulated in Indore, and many people came next day to the Mass which was concelebrated by the Bishop and many other priests. The homily was preached by Fr Gratian Aroojis, an old friend, who spoke with understanding about his life and mission. The burial followed in the cemetery of the Fathers of the Divine Word, where a simple stone commemorates: "Swami Abhishiktananda, OSB/born 1910/ordained 1935/died 7.12.73."

Glossary

(Words which only occur once and are explained in the text are not usually included here. In Sanskrit words, apart from long *a, i, and u,* diacritical marks have not generally been used, as Abhishiktananda himself rarely used them. But note that *c* in a Sanskrit word is pronounced *ch,* and *ś* is pronounced *sh.)*

a-bhaya	absence of fear and refraining from causing fear to others
a-chala	immobile; a mountain
āchārya	master, teacher; head of an ashram, etc.
adhyāsa	superimposition
a-dvaita	non-duality
advaitin	one who 'knows', lives by, *advaita;* a Vedantin philosopher
agni	fire; the sacrificial fire; a Vedic deity
aham	I (*aham asmi,* I am)
aham Brahma asmi	"I am brahma"; one of the *mahāvākya,* great words of the Upanishads
ahamkāra	the sense of oneself as an individual; egotism, self-conceit
anamnesis	(Greek) memorial, especially in the context of the Eucharistic prayer
ānanda	bliss, joy
a-niketana	without dwelling-place
anjali	greeting with joined hands
annam	food
antemensium	(Latin) a piece of cloth with a relic sewn into it, which can be used at Mass in place of an altar-stone
anubhava	experience, especially spiritual
anubhavī	a person of experience
āratī	worship offered with a flame (of oil or camphor), waved from side to side or in a circle
Arunāchala	the mountain of the dawn
a-rūpa	without form; transcending all forms
a-sat	non-being; unreal
āshram (āśram)	(Hindi) commonly, the abode of a guru and his disciples, or of ascetics
ātman	the Self; one's innermost principle

ātman-brahman	expresses the non-duality of my own deepest centre (*ātman*) with the deepest centre of the universe (*brahman*)
avadhūta	one who renounces everything, including the tokens of *sannyāsa*
a-vidyā	ignorance
Bhagavān	the Blessed One; the Lord
bhakta	worshipper, devotee
bhakti	loving devotion
bhikshā	alms, food, sought by or given to a sadhu
bodhi	awakening, Illumination
brahman	the Absolute Being, omnipresent and transcendent
buddhi	intellect, intelligence
chapātī	(Hindi) flat unleavened bread, made of wholemeal flour
chelā	(Hindi) disciple
cit	awareness, consciousness; spirit
citta	what is thought; organ of thought
darshan	(Hindi) sight, vision; entering the presence of God, a saint, an image, etc.
Dasserah	(Hindi) a ten-day Hindu festival in October, when the Rāmāyana is performed
dharamsālā	(Hindi) a caravansarai on a main road or a pilgrim route
dharma	norm of religious and social life, expressive of the cosmic order; duty to conform to such a norm; a particular 'religion'
dhyāna	meditation, contemplation
dīkshā	initiation
Dīwālī (Dīvālī)	(Hindi) the Hindu festival of lights in November
dvandva	pair of opposites, like cold/heat, pleasure/pain , etc.
Ehieh asher ehieh	(Hebrew) the mysterious Name of Yahweh in Exodus 3:14
ekatva	oneness, unity
Eschaton	(Greek) the end (of the world)
Exultet	(Latin) a prayer in the rite of Easter Eve, celebrating the New light
guhā	cave; the secret place of the heart
Guhāja	the one 'born in the cave'
Guhāntara	the 'dweller in the cave'; Abhishiktananda's pseudonym
homa	ritual fire sacrifice
Imprimatur	(Latin) ecclesiastical permission to publish a work passed by the censor
īśvara (īshvara)	Lord, God
jīvanmukta	one who has found deliverance during his lifetime; a saint
jīvanmukti	the state of the *jīvanmukta*

jñāna	knowledge, wisdom
jñānī	a sage; one who has awoken to reality, realized the Self
jyoti	light (Jyotiniketan, abode of light)
kaivalyam	the state of absolute aloneness, integration, of the liberated one
karma	action, work; ritual or moral act; the result of acts done in a previous life (good or bad), determining the future life
kaumanam	(Tamil) an ascetic's loincloth
kāvi	(Tamil) the saffron coloured cloth worn by Hindu ascetics
keshi (keśi)	the hairy one, acosmic ascetic of the Vedas
kevala	isolation, solitude, unity; applied to brahman and also to one who has attained to unity in total isolation
khādī	(Hindi) handspun and handwoven cotton cloth
koinonia	(Greek) communion, mutual sharing
kurios	(Greek) Lord
kutiya	(Hindi) hut
laura	(Greek) a type of oriental monastery, in which the monks live in separate hermitages
līla	sport, play; the Lord's 'play' in and through the universe
linga	sign; especially the cylindrical (phallic?) stone symbol of Shiva
logos	(Greek) word; reason; the Word (of God)
loka	place; world
madhu	honey, nectar
mahān	a great person
mahātma	a 'great soul'; title of respect
mahārāj	(Hindi) 'great king'; title of respect
maharshi (mahā-rishi)	a great rishi, sage
mahāvākya	one of the great sentences (mantras) which sum up the teaching of the Upanishads, like *"aham brahma asmi"*
manas	thought; the mind
mandapa	an open porch or hall, with a flat roof supported on columns
mandir	(Hindi) temple
mantra	verse from the Vedas; formula of prayer
mārga	path, way; especially the spiritual paths of *jñāna, bhakti* and *karma*
mātrā	element; especially of the sounds (A,U and M) composing the OM
maulvī	(Hindi) Muslim teacher
mauna	silence
māyā	the undefinable condition of the world of manifestation, which cannot be called either real *(sat)* or unreal *(asat)*; hence the power of illusion which binds mortals; also the divine 'magic' by which the worlds are projected

moksha	final delivarance from the cycle of rebirth; salvation
mrityu	death
mūlasthāna	the innermost sanctuary of a temple, enshrining the symbol of God
mumukshutva	ardent desire for deliverance, for moksha
munī	(Tamil, *munivār*) an ascetic who is vowed to silence
mūrti	form, icon; an image in a temple
nada	(Spanish) nothing, nothingness
nāma-rūpa	'name and form'; including the world of phenomena and all the signs used to refer to the unique mystery that is beyond all
namaskāra	saying *'Namah'*; salutation with joined hands or prostration
Natarājā	Shiva, represented as Lord of the cosmic dance
nitya	permanent, lasting, eternal
OM	a sacred syllable, symbol of *brahman;* expression of assent
OM tat sat	an Upanishadic *mantra,* "Indeed, That (*brahman*) is the Real"
osmosis	(Greek) see ch. 6, note 84 (p. 272)
padmāsan	(Hindi) sitting in the lotus position
paramārtha	ultimate reality, the level of the Absolute
pāriah	(Tamil) outcaste (generally)
parivrajya	the life of a wandering mendicant
parousia	(Greek) coming, advent; also, presence (of a great person or of God)
pleroma	(Greek) fullness (as in Ephesians 1:23)
pneuma	(Greek) breath, spirit; the Holy Spirit
prāṇa	breath, the breath of life
pratishthā	foundation, support
pūjā	ritual worship offered to an image (picture, etc.) with light, flowers, incense, etc., accompanied by recitation of mantras.
purusha	man; the primordial or archetypal man; one expression of the mystery of the *atman-brahman*
rishi	Vedic seer
saccidānanda	sat+cit+ānanda; see ch.3, note 15 (p. 35)
sadguru	the true Guru, Master
sādhaka	one who practises spiritual exercises
sādhana	spiritual exercises, ascetic practices
sādhu	good, virtuous; a wandering monk, ascetic
sahaja	'born with'; innate, natural condition; spontaneous
sākshī	witness; the Self as passively observing all actions

sanātana dharma	the 'eternal dharma' (religion, law); the traditional name of the religion derived from the Vedas, commonly called Hinduism
sandhyā	junction, meeting; especially the 'conjunctions' of day and night at sunset and sunrise
sannyāsa	the life of total renunciation
sannyāsī	one who has renounced everything; a Hindu monk
śarīra (sharīra)	the body, including all physical and mental faculties
sarx	(Greek) flesh, the body
sat	being; real, true; the Real
satipatthāna	(Pali) inspection, insight; a Buddhist method of meditation, with constant attention to every movement of body or mind
satpurusha	the Man *par excellence*
sattva	reality; one of the three qualities (*guna*) of nature; purity
sāttvika	characterized by *sattva*
satyam	truth, reality
satyasya satyam	the Real of the real; an Upanishadic expression
shakti (śakti)	force, power, energy; the active power of God manifested throughout the universe, often personified as a feminine principle
shānti (śānti)	peace
shāstra (śāstra)	Scripture
shraddhā (śraddhā)	faith, trust
śishya (shishya)	disciple
śloka (shloka)	Sanskrit verse
so'ham asmi	"I am He", the cry of one who has realized God
Soter	(Greek) Saviour
sukhāsan	(Hindi) a sitting posture
sushupti	deep, dreamless sleep
svaprakāsha (svaprakāśa)	light which shines of itself, especially of self-awareness
tad-vid	one who knows 'That', i.e., the Real
tapas	heat; spiritual energy; austerity
tat tvam asi	"That art thou"; one of the *mahāvākya*, great words of the Upaṇishads
tejomaya	composed of light, glory
Trimūrti	'three forms'; a composite image of the three principal deities, Brahma, Vishnu and Shiva
Trisagion	(Greek) an ancient hymn to Christ: "Holy God, holy and mighty, holy and immortal. . ."
tundu	(Tamil) a strip of folded cloth which can be used to cover the shoulders
upadesha (upadeśa)	teaching, spiritual insturction
upanishad	'sitting at a guru's feet' secret lore; correlation (see *The Further Shore,* 76ff.)

Upanishads	sacred texts, regarded as the completion of the Vedas
upāsana	regarding with respect; reverence, adoration; meditation
vairāgya	total indifference to all worldly objects; renunciation
Vedānta	the 'end of the Veda', referring first to the Upanishads, then to the philosophy based on these texts, in which the doctrine of non-duality is central
vedāntin	one who accepts the philosophy of *Vedānta*
veshti	(Tamil)cotton cloth covering the lower part of the body (Hindi, *dhotī*)
vidyā	knowledge, wisdom
vipassana	(Pali) a Buddhist method of meditation
viśishta advaita	'qualified *advaita*' which retains some duality between the soul and God, as in the teaching of Rāmānuja
viveka	discrimination, especially between what is real and what is unreal
vyavahāra	provisional manifestation of the Real; living and understanding at the earthly level of unreality
yama	death; the God of death
yoga	union; the discipline of unifying body and mind

Bibliography

I. Fr J. MONCHANIN

A. Correspondence and writings

Jules Monchanin——écrits spirituels: présentation d'E. Duperray, Paris (Centurion) 1965. English version, *In Quest of the Absolute,* ed. J.G. Weber, Kalamazoo (Cistercian Pubns) and London (Mowbrays), 1976.

J. Monchanin: Mystique de l'Inde, mystère chrétien, ed. S. Siauve, Paris (Fayard) 1974.

J. Monchanin: *Théologie et spiritualité missionaire,* Paris (Beauchesne) 1985.

J. Monchanin: *Lettres à sa mère 1913-1957,* ed. F. Jacquin, Paris (Le Cerf) 1989.

B. Bibiographical

"Le père Monchanin", Abhisiktesvarananda, *La vie spirituelle* 98 (1958), 71-95.

Swami Parama Arubi Anandam: Fr J. Monchanin 1895-1957. A Memorial pub. by Saccidananda Ashram, 1959.

L'abbé Jules Monchanin: Notes biographiques par E. Duperray, Tournai (Casterman) 1960.

Images de l'abbé Monchanin, H. de Lubac, Paris (Aubier) 1966.

Land of the Trinity, J. Mattam, Bangalore (T.P.I.) 1975, Chapter V.

Jules Monchanin: Pioneer in Christian-Hindu Dialogue, Sten Rodhe, Delhi (ISPCK), 1993.

II. ABHISHIKTANANDA

A. Books

1. *An Indian Benedictine Ashram* (in collaboration with J. Monchanin), Shantivanam, Tannirpalli, 1951. Reprinted: *A Benedictine Ashram,* Douglas, I.O.M. (Times Press), 1964.
2. *Ermites du Saccidânanda:* un essai d'intégration chrétienne de la tradition monastique de l'Inde (in collaboration with J. Monchanin), Tournai (Casterman) 1956.
   Ermitas do Saccidananda, Belo Horizonte, Brazil (Itatiaia) 1959,
   Die Eremiten von Saccidananda, Salzburg (O. Müller Vg) 1962.
3. *Guhantara: au sein du fond* (written 1952-53: only extracts published so far—the Introduction in *Contacts,* see B. 1963(a); parts of Chapter 3, see A. 19; parts of Chapters 4 to 7, see A. 20).
4. *Swami Parama Arubi Anandam: Fr J. Monchanin 1895-1957.* A Memorial publ. by Saccidananda Ashram, Tannirpalli, 1959. (Expanded version of B. 1958(a), with 'A Garland of Memories' and selected writings.)

Swami Parama Arubi Anandam: (Memoir only, in Tamil) 1959.

Benedyktynski Asram, Krakow (Znak) 1986. Memoir and sel. writings.

5. *Sagesse hindoue mystique chrétienne; du Védanta à la Trinité,* Paris (Centurion) 1965.

   Indische Weisheit—Christliche Mystik, Luzern (Rex-Verlag) 1968.

6. *La rencontre de l'hindouisme et du christianisme,* Paris (Le Seuil) 1966.

7. *The Mountain of the Lord: Pilgrimage to Gangotri,* Bangalore (CISRS) 1966: reprinted, Madras (CLS) 1967. Reprinted in *Guru and Disciple,* London (SPCK) 1974.

8. *Une messe aux sources du Gange,* Paris (Le Seuil) 1967. (Author's revision of No.7.)

   Una messa alle sorgenti del Ganga, Brescia (Morcelliana) 1968.

   The Mountain of the Lord, Delhi (ISPCK) 1990. (Revision of No.7, according to No.8.)

   Alle sorgenti del Ganga: Pellegrinaggio spirituale, Milano (Editrice Cens) 1994.

9. *Prayer,* Delhi (ISPCK) 1967. Reprinted, 1969; revised edition, 1972; reprinted 1975, 1979. Reprinted, London (SPCK), 1972, 1975. Reprinted, Philadelphia (Westminster Press) 1973.

   Den Heliga Narvaron, Delago, Sweden (Asak) 1986.

   Included in *Benedyktynski Asram,* Krakow, Poland (Znak) 1986. See also No.14.

10. *Hindu-Christian Meeting Point—within the Cave of the Heart,* Bombay (I.I.C.) and Bangalore (CISRS) 1969. Reprinted with author's revisions, Delhi (ISPCK) 1976, 1984.

11. *The Church in India: an essay in Christian self-criticism,* Madras (CLS) 1969. Reprinted, 1971.

12. *Towards the Renewal of the Indian Church,* Bangalore (Dharmaram College) 1970. Reprinted 1971.

13. *Gnānānanda: un maitre spirituel du pays tamoul,* Chambéry (Présence) 1970.

    "A Sage from the East: Sri Gnanananda" in *Guru and Disciple,* London (SPCK) 1974.

    Guru and Disciple: an encounter with Sri Gnanananda, a contemporary spiritual master (rev. edition) , Delhi (ISPCK) 1990.

    Das Feuer der Weisheit, Munich (O.W. Barth) 1979.

14. *Éveil à soi—éveil à Dieu: essai sur la prière,* Paris (Centurion) 1971; reprinted, Paris (Le Seuil) 1984, (OEIL) 1986.(The author's revision of No. 9, with the additional essay "Le chrétien en vérité".)

    Preghiera e presenza, Assisi (Cittadella) 1973.

    Sat-chit-ananda; approximació a la pregària cristiana desde l'India, Barcelona (Claret) 1976. (Catalan)

    Die Gegenwart Gottes erfahren, Mainz (Matthias-Grunewald-Vg) 1980.

    Prayer (new edition, translated from *Éveil,* without the additional essay, for which see No. 22), Delhi (ISPCK) 1989.

    Uyir Punal (Tamil), Dindigul (Vaigarai Pathipagam), 1994.

15. *Saccidananda: a Christian Approach to Advaitic Experience,* Delhi (ISPCK) 1974. (Author's revision of No.5) Reprinted with Appendices, 1984, 1990.

Tradizione indu, mistero trinitario, Bologna (EMI) 1988.

Sagesse hindoue mystique chrètienne, Paris, Centurion 1991. (Revision of No. 5, following No. 15.)

16. *The Further Shore* (containing "Sannyasa" and "The Upanishads—an Introduction"), Delhi (ISPCK) 1975. Reprinted with addition of "The Upanishads and Advaitic Experience" and poems, 1984. See also A.19.

17. *Souvenirs d'Arunâchala: récit d'un ermite chrétien en terre hindoue,* Paris (Epi SA) 1978.

The Secret of Arunachala, Delhi (ISPCK) 1979. Reprinted 1988.

Lettere e scritti: esperienza indu e esperienza cristiana, pro manuscripto Bologna (Fraternité Ch. de Foucauld) 1976. (Lacks Ch. 6).

Das Geheimnis des heiligen Berges: als christlicher Mönch unter den Weisen Indiens, Freiburg (Herder) 1989.

18. *Les yeux de lumière: écrits spirituels* présèntés par André Gozier et Joseph Lemarié, Paris (Centurion) 1979. (Contains 7 articles, noted in section B, with correspondence and extracts from the *Journal,* A. 21.) Revised & enlarged edn, Paris (OEIL) 1989.

The Eyes of Light, Denville, N.J. (Dimension Books) 1983.

La contemplazione cristiana in India, Bologna (EMI) 1985.

19. *Initiation à la spiritualité des Upanishads: "Vers l'autre rive",* Sisteron (Présence) 1979. (An expansion of A. 16 with extra essays and part of A.3.)

Der Weg zum anderen Ufer, Cologne (E. Diederichs Vg) 1980. (Lacks chap. 4 of "Sannyasa", and an essay "Die kontemplative Botschaft Indiens", printed in *Una Sancta* 1/1981.)

L'altra riba (in 2 vols): I—Sannyasa; II—Els Upanixads: una introducció; Els Upanixads i l'experiència advaitica. Barcelona (Claret) 1980. (Catalan)

20. *Intériorité et révélation: essais théologiques,* Sisteron (Présence) 1982. (Part I contains essays from A.3 and "Esseulement"; Part II, essays and notes of 1961-1972.)

21. *La montée au fond du coeur: le journal intime du moine chrétien—sannyasi hindou 1984-1973.* Introduction et notes de R. Panikkar, Paris (OEIL) 1986

22. *In Spirit and Truth,* Delhi (ISPCK) 1989. (Translation of "Le chrétien en vérité" (see A.14) as revised by the author in 1972.)

B. Articles

1952-1955 See Chapter 4, Note 60, for four extracts from A.1 and A. 2, published in *Église vivante* and *Bulletin du Cercle St J. Baptiste* under the name of J. Monchanin, though written by Abhishiktananda.

1956 (a) "Le monachisme chrétien aux Indes", *La vie spirituelle,* Suppl. 38, 283-316.

(b) "L'hindouisme est-il toujours vivant?" *La vie intellectuelle,* Nov. 1956, 1-40.

1958 (a) "Le père Monchanin", *La vie spirituelle,* no. 98, 71-95.
(b) "Christian Sannyasis", *Clergy Monthly Supplement,* Vol. IV, no. 3, 106-113.
1960 (a) Contribution to *Karavelane: volume commémoratif du soixantième anniversaire de naissance, 23 août, 1900-1960,* pp. 12-21.
1963 (a) "Pour une intégration chrétienne de la tradition mystique de l'Inde" par 'Macaire l'Indien', *Contacts* XV/1, 41-51. (Extract from A. 3.)
1964 (a) "Rencontre avec l'hindouisme: I. Des chrétiens méditent les Oupanichads", *Informations catholiques internationales,* no. 221-222, 11-17.
1965 (a) "L'Inde et le Carmel", *Carmel,* Tarascon, 1965 I, 9-23; II, 109-124; followed by (unsigned) "Quelques témoignages de l'avent hindou", I, 24-30 and II, 125-136. Reprinted without appendix in A. 18.
1966 (a) "Pèlerinage aux sources du Gange", *Lumière et vie,* Lyon, no. 79, 93-115. (Extract from A. 8.)
(b) "Christians meditate upon the Upanishads", *Examiner,* Bombay, Mar. 5, 12, 19, 1966. (=1964 (a))
(c) "Le prêtre que l'Inde attend, que le monde attend", *Carmel,* 1966 IV, 270-284. Reprinted in A. 18.
1967 (a) "La diaconie de l'ermite", *Lettre de Ligugé,* no. 121, 20-25.
(b) "The Way of Dialogue" in *Inter-religious Dialogue,* edited by H. Jai Singh, Bangalore (CISRS), 1967, 78-103.
(c) "A Letter from India" (with C.M. Rogers), *One in Christ,* Vol. 3, 1967, 195-199.
(d) "Lettera aperta ai Cristiani d'Occidente che sperano di venire in India", *Missione cattolica,* Milan, 1967. (=1967 (c))
(e) "Baptism, Faith and Conversion", *Indian Journal of Theology,* vol. 16, No.,3, 189-203.
1968 (a) "Contemplative Life in India", by 'S.V. Swami', *Examiner,* Jan. 13 & 20, 1968. Also published in *New Leader,* Feb. 4, 11 and 18, 1968.
(b) "A Study of Hindu Symbolism", *Word and Worship,* Bangalore, I. 8 (Mar. 1968), 298-300, 305-307; II. 2 (Aug. 1968), 77-79.
(c) "The Church in India—a Self-examination", *Religion and Society,* Bangalore, Vol. XV, No. 3, 5-19. (A draft for A.11.)
1969 (a) "An Approach to Hindu Spirituality", *Clergy Review,* London, Vol. LIV, No. 3, 163-174.
(b) "Monasticism and the Seminar", *Examiner,* Aug. 16 & 23, 1969.
(c) "Theological Commission needed for Indianization of the Church", *Catholic News Service of India,* Aug. 30, 1969.
1970 (a) "Femmes ermites hindoues", *Vie Thérésienne,* Lisieux, Vol. 10, no. 37, 14-18.
(b) "Gandhi, témoin de la vérité", *Annales de Ste Thérèse de Lisieux,* 1970, no. 1, 15-17. Reprinted in A. 18.
(c) "Yoga et prière chrétienne", *Revue Monchanin,* Montreal, Vol. III, No. 4.

1970 (d) "Un ermite de l'Inde, Harilal", *Revue Monchanin,* Vol. III, No. 5, 2-14.

(e) "OM!"—'Shivendranath', recueilli par Abhishiktananda, *Parole et Mission,* Paris, no. 50, 266-273.

(f) "Professional Men or Spiritual?", *Catholic News Service of India,* July 28, 1970.

(g) "There are no part-time Priests", *Catholic News Service of India,* August, 1970.

(h) "Dialogue Postponed" by C.M. Rogers and 'Sivendra Prakash', *Asia Focus,* Bangkok, Vol. 5, No. 3, 210-222.

(i) "Communication in the Spirit", *Religion and Society,* Vol. XVII, No. 3, 33-39.

1971 (a) "Femmes ermites en Inde", *Amis du Bec-Hellouin,* no. 32-33 (1970-71), 32-38.

(b) "La oración del silencio", *Liturgia,* Burgos, no. 253, 126-136. (="L'apport de l'Inde à la prière chrétienne", printed in A.18.)

(c) "The Church in Uttarkhand", *Examiner,* July 31, 1971.

(d) "Yoga and Christian Prayer", *Clergy Monthly,* Vol. 35, No. 11, 472-477.

1972 (a) "Enfance spirituelle et oupanichad", *Annales de Ste Thérèse de Lisieux,* 1972, no. 1, 19-20. Reprinted in A. 18.

(b) "Pèlerinages himalayens", *Annales de Ste Th. de L.,* 1972, no. 4, 20-22.

1973 (a) "Theology of Presence as a Form of Evangelization in the context of non-Christian Religions" in *Service and Salvation,* edited by Joseph Pathrapankal, Bangalore (Theological Pubns, India), 1973, 407-417. (="La théologie de la présence comme une forme d' evangélization dans le contexte des religions non chrétiennes", printed in A. 18.)

(b) "Hindu Scriptures and Worship", *Word and Worship,* Vol. VI, nos 6 and 7, 187-195, 243-253.

(c) 'Sannyasa", serialized in 7 issues of *The Divine Life,* Sivananda Ashram, Rishikesh, Sept. 1973—March 1974. Reprinted in A. 16.

(Chapter 1 only) "L'idéal du sannyasa", *Revue Monchanin,* Vol. VI, No 1, Jan-Feb, 1973; "The Ideal of Sannyasa", *Reflection,* C.R.S. Centre, Rajpur, 1973.

(d) "L'expérience de Dieu dans les religions d'Extrême-Orient" in *Actes du Congrès de Bangalore,* Vanves (A.I.M.) 1973, 49-59. Reprinted in A. 18.

1974 (a) Foreword to J. Borst, MHM, *A Method of Contemplative Prayer,* Bangalore (Asian Trading Centre), 1973/4 (?), 1-3.

(b) "The Upanishads and Advaitic Experience", *Clergy Monthly,* Vol. 38 , No. 11, 474-486. Reprinted in A. 16(1984) and (French) A. 19.

(c) "Experience of God in Eastern Religions", *Cistercian Studies,* IX, 2 and 3, 148-157. (=1973 (d))

1975 (a) *Abhishiktananda on Aikiya Alayam,* Madras (Aikya Alayam) 1975.
(b) "Yoga und Christliches Gebet", *Meditation,* Säckingen, (West) Germany, 4/1975.

1980 (a) "L'esperienza di Dio nelle religioni dell'Estremo Oriente" in *Quaderni del Centro Interreligioso Henri Le Saux,* no. 1 (1980), 93-108. (=1973(d).)

1981 (a) "Die kontemplative Botschaft Indiens", *Una Sancta* 1/1981, translated from "Le message contemplatif de l'Inde", printed in A. 19.
(b) "The Depth-Dimension of Religious Dialogue", *Vidyajyoti,* Vol. 45, No. 5, 202-221.

C. Unpublished Texts

1952-3 "Guhantara: au sein de fond". Partly published, see A.3.

1953-4 "Guhaja: vers l'unité sans mode". 8 essays. TS, 1-143.

1953-1956 Guhantara poems, originally written in the Diary. Collected by the author about 1960. Various poems were published in part or whole in A.5, A.15, A. 17, A.19.

1956 "Sad-bodhi". Notes of a retreat, dated November, MS, 1-40.

1956-? "Z" series of notes, reworking thoughts from the diary in 1956, 1961, 1963, 1964.

1958 "Divagations d'un gnostique hindou sur la fête de l'Epiphanie", dated 2.2.58. MS, 1-44.

1961 "L'Inde et l'église", dated March 1961. TS, 1-28.
"Présence de Dieu et présence à Dieu", dated 25 Oct. 1961. TS, 1-36. (Part published in A. 20.)

1963 "Bible Study." "Upanishad Study." Notes prepared for the Cuttat group about Feb. 1963.

1964 "Le sécrétariat pour les religions et le kairos présent de l'église". Two drafts, the earlier dated 16.5.64. TS, 1-4 and TS, 1-11.
Notes on "Memorandum of Dr J.A. Cuttat on the proposed Secretariat for non-Christians". TS, 1-12.
"Annexe à la note au Cardinal (après nouvelles réflexions sur l'article de Mgr Blomjous)". TS, 1.
"Le psautier est-il une prière chrétienne?", drafted at Gangotri in June, and offered to *Concilium.* TS, 1-12.

1964 (?) "Présence" ("Dieu est dans mes églises . . ."), written on the back of the MS of "L'expérience du Saccidananda". TS, 1-5.

1968 "Post-face. Review of *Rencontre* by 'Swami Sajjanananda'". TS, 1-3. His further reflections on A. 6, offered to *Religion and Society.*
Sermon for the Reunion at Cancale of his class at the Seminary, dated 17.5.68. TS, 1-3.
"The essential of the Christian Witness", dated 27.10.68. MS, 1-10.
"Dialogue and Theologia Negativa", written for the consultation at Bandra held in Jan. 1969. TS, 1-2.

1969 (?) "Preparation of Seminarians for Ecumenical and Inter-religious Dialogue", a sermon at St Paul's Seminary, Allahabad. TS, 1-3.

1970 "The Call of the Lord", written 13.7.70 for *Catholic News Service of India*, about Swami Niranjananda. TS, 1-3.

"The Church a Community of Prayer", written 14.9.70 for *CNSI*, TS, 1-3.

Other unused drafts for *CNSI*: "Pandit-Purohit-Guru", "Guru Yisu—Rabbi Yeshuah", "Professional Priests" (unfinished).

1970 "An Introduction to the Liturgy of Jyotiniketan", written for CLS, Madras. TS, 1-27.

1971 "Foi, sens d'au delà, dated 27.6.71. TS, 1-10.

"Le problème Védanto-chrétien", dated 4.7.71. TS, 1-6.

"Le christianisme", dated 4.7.71. TS, 11-12.

"Présence—Christ—Eucharistie", dated 8.7.71. TS, 1-3.

"Guru (ou Psychothérapeute)", dated 9.7.71. TS, 1-3.

"An Ashram Seminary", written 15.7.71. TS, 1-12

1972 Notes taken by Sister Vandana of Abhishiktananda's talks at the C.P.S. Ashram, Pune, in March 1972.

"Réflections sur le programme du congrès monastique—Asia 1973", written 2.12.72. TS, 1-4.

1973 "Jesus experienced a relation with God . . . " (no title), dated 3.2.73. TS, 9 pages.

Uncertain date

1957/8 (?) Manuscript with 2 sections: "I. Raison d'être de l'institution de sannyasis chrétiens"; "II. Conditions d'institution du sannyasa chrétien." TS, 1-9.

Pre-1968 "L'Un, la non-dualité et la Trinité"; an essay sent to Dom P. Miquel. TS, 1-14.

1970 (?) "A Mass in Indian Tradition", containing 'Preliminary Notes' and suggestions for the Preparation, the Liturgy of the Word, and the Liturgy of the Sacrament. TS, 1-10.

Liturgical texts: "Mass in Indian Tradition", "A Sanskrit Eucha rist", "Sanskrit Mantras for Eucharist".

D. Studies of Abhishiktananda

1. Books

1965 *Le plus petit abîme,* Jean Sulivan; Paris (Gallimard) 1965, pp.171-260.

1981 *Henri Le Saux—Swami Abhishiktananda: le passeur entre deux rives,* M-M. Davy; Paris (Le Cerf), 1981.

Indian Christian Sannyasa and Swami Abhishiktananda, E.Vattakuzhy; Bangalore (T.P.I.), 1981.

1986 *Abhishiktananda: the Man and his Message:* Papers read at an Abhishiktananda Week, December 1985, ed. by Vandana Mataji; Delhi (ISPCK), 1986, 1993.

1989 *Le père Henri Le Saux à la rencontre de l'hinduisme,* André Gozier; Paris (Centurion), 1989.

1991 *Henri Le Saux/Swami Abhishiktananda.* Ecrits choisis et présentés Marie-Madeleine Davy; Paris (Albin Michel), 1991.

Christ et Védanta. L'expérience d'Henri Le Saux en Inde, par Marc de Smedt; in the series "Question de", no. 85, Gordes (Albin Michel), 1991.

The Guru in Indian Catholicism, Catherine Cornille; Louvain Theological and Pastoral Monographs—6; Louvain (Peeters Press and W.B. Eerdmans, 1991. Especially Part II: "To Christ through the Guru. The Experience and Reflection of Abhishiktananda (pp. 75-118).

1994 *Abhisiktananda sulle frontiere dell'incontro cristiano-indu.* Caterina Conio: Assisi (Cittadella), 1994.

1995 *The Word in the Cave. A Study on Abhishiktananda,* Antony Kalliath; New Delhi (Inter-cultural Publications), 1995(?).

2. Articles in periodicals and books

1971 "Shantivanam Revisited", by Dom Francis Acharya in *Bulletin de l'A.I.M.* (English Edition, Vanves), 1971, no. 12, pp. 56-62 of his "Twelve Years' Newsletter".

1974 "Swami Abhishiktananda" by James Stuart, *Clergy Monthly,* vol. 38.2 (Feb. 1974), 80-82.

"La père Henri Le Saux: Swami Abhishiktananda", Joseph Lemarié, *La vie spirituelle,* No. 601, March 1974, 286-288.

Clergy Monthly, Vol. 38.11 (Dec. 1974) is largely devoted to Abhishiktananda. See Editorial and reviews and the following three articles:

"Swamiji—the Man" by Sara Grant, pp. 487-495.

"A Messenger of Light" by Sr Vandana, pp. 496-500.

"Sannyasa—Swami Abhishiktananda" by X. Irudayaraj, pp. 501-508.

"Saccidananda Ashram Reminiscences" and "Swami Abhishiktananda: a Memorial Tribute" by Francis Acharya in *Kurisumala: a Symposium on Ashram Life* (1974), 61-62 and 71-74.

1975 Section in R.H.S. Boyd, *Introduction to Indian Christian Theology,* revised edition, Madras (CLS), 287-297.

1976 "Swamiji—the Friend", C. Murray Rogers, *Religion and Society,* Vol. 23.1, 76-87. Reprinted, Vandana, *Abhishiktananda: the Man and his Message.* Translation in *Les yeux* (A. 18), 1989.

"Henri Le Saux", Joseph Lemarié, *Dictionnaire de Spiritualité,* t. IX, cols 697-698.

"Exploring the Further Shore", G. Gispert-Sauch, *Vidyajyoti,* Vol. 40, 502-506.

1980 "Henri Le Saux, OSB. Una testimonianza ecumenica in terra indiana". Essays in *Quaderni* No.1 (1980) of Centro interreligioso Henri Le Saux, Milano.

1980 "Sri Ramana Maharshi and Abhishiktananda", J.D.M. Stuart, *Vidyajyoti,* Vol. 44, 168-176.

"Il ruolo degli 'spirituali' nell'incontro ecumenica", L. Sartori, *Quaderni* No.2 (1980), 35-50.

1982 "Abhishiktananda's Contemplative Theology", Wayne Teasdale, *Monastic Studies,* Autumn 1982, 179-199.

"Abhishiktananda on Inner Awakening", J.D.M. Stuart, *Vidyajoyti,* Vol. 46, 470-484.

"Letter to Abhishiktananda", R. Panikkar, *Studies in Formative Spirituality,* Pittsburgh (Duquesne University), Vol. III, No. 3, 429-451.

1983 "Abhishiktananda's Mystical Intuition of the Trinity", Wayne Teasdale, *Cistercian Studies,* 1983, No. 1, 60-75.

"The Spiritual Journey of Henri Le Saux/Abhishiktananda", O. Baumer-Despeigne, *Cistercian Studies,* 1983, No. 4, 310-329.

"The Language of Mysticism", George Gillespie, *Indian Journal of Theology,* Vol. 32, Nos 3 &4,, 45-62.

"Swami Abhishiktananda on Prayer", A.R. McKearney, *New Fire.* Winter 1983, 479-484.

1984 "In the Cave of the Heart: Silence and Realization", Beatrice Bruteau, *New Blackfriars,* July-August 1984, 301-319.

"Henri Le Saux-Abhishiktananda", B. Bäumer, in *Grosse Mystiker* ed. G. Ruhbach, J. Sudbrack, Munich (C.H. Beck) 1984, 338-354.

1985 "La santità secondo la spiritualità benedittina in prospettiva ecumenica", Corneljus Tholens, *Quaderni del Centro interreligioso H. Le Saux,* No. 5, 173-185.

"The Spirituality of Swami Abhishiktananda", G. Gispert-Sauch, *Ignis Studies,* No. 10, (1985:2), 41-47.

1986 "L'expérience et le discours: les orientations de Henri Le Saux dans *Intériorité et Révelation",* Ghislain Lafont, in *Dieu, le temps et l'être,* Paris (Le Cerf) 1986, 295-307.

1986-7 "Abhishiktananda: the Benedictine Swami", Robert A. Stephens, *Tjurunga: an Australasian Benedictine Review,* No. 31, 42-53; No. 32, 72-79.

1988 "Time-Bomb or Tomb-Stone." Reflections on the Private Journal of Swami Abhishiktananda", Sara Grant, *Vidyajyoti,* Vol. 52, 83-97.

"Dolore e salvezza nell'esperienza di Henri Le Saux (Svamy Abhishiktananda), 'Katya Mudra' (C. Conio), *Quaderni del Centro interreligioso Henri Le Saux,* No. 6. Milano 1988, 143-153.

"Abhishiktananda: Hindu-Christian Monk", James E. Royster, *Studies in Formative Spirituality* (Pittsburg), IX, 3, 309-328.

"Henri Le Saux (Abhishiktananda)" in *Light from Light: an anthology of Christian Mysticism,* ed. Louis Dupré and James A. Wiseman, New York (Paulist) 1988, 415-431.

1989 "Der Aufstieg ins Innere: Henri Le Saux—Swami Abhishiktananda", Jacob Baumgartner, *Neue Zeitschrift für missionsgewissenschaft* (Immensee), 45-1989/1, 37-43.

1989 "Swami Abhishiktananda (1910-1973): Comme nous, Indiens, l'avons vu—un témoignage", Anand Nayak, *Neue Zeitschrift für M.* 45-1989/1, 45-56.

"A Dialogue in Depth: a Monastic Perspective", James E. Royster, *Quarterly Review,* Vol. 9, No. 2, Summer 1989, 75-92.

"Éveil à soi—éveil à Dieu dans l'expérience spirituelle d'Henri Le Saux", Jacques Dupuis, *Nouvelle revue théologique* 111.6 (Nov.-Dec. 1989), 866-878.

"Swami Abhishiktananda ou l'expérience spirutuelle d'un moine hindou-chrétien", Jacques Dupuis, in chapter 3 of *Jésus-Christ à la rencontre des religions,* Paris (Desclée) 1989, 98-115.

1990 "Cheminement spirituel d'Henri Le Saux. Textes inédits", O. Baumer-Despeigne, *La vie spirituelle,* no. 691 (Sept.-Oct.), 531-543.

"Swami Abhishiktananda. Un Sannyasi cristiano", Juan Carlos Pacagnini, *Oriente/Occidente, Revista de Investigaciones Comparadas* (Universidad dèl Salvador, Callao 853, Buenos Aires), Ano IX,1/2, 1990, 43-51.

"Monachesimo e advaita", E. Tholens, *Quaderni del Centro interreligioso H. Le S.,* No.7 (1990), 111-121.

1991 "Swami Abhishiktananda, or the Spiritual Experience of a Hindu-Christian Monk", Jacques Dupuis, in *Jesus Christ at the Encounter of World Religions,* New York (Orbis) 1991, 67-90.

1992 "Enveloped by Mystery. The Spiritual Jouney of Henri Le Saux/ Abhishiktananda", James A. Wiseman, *Église et théologie,* 23 (1992), 241-260.

"I AM—the first Name of God" (Part II), David Godman, *The Mountain Path,* Vol. 29, Nos 3 & 4, 126-142. (Discusses Abhishiktananda on pp. 139-142.)

1993 "Swami Abhishiktananda (H.Le Saux) and Advaita: the account of a spiritual journey", Michael Comans, *Indo-British Review. A Journal of History,* Vol. XIX, No.1, 99-116.

"The Religious in the Church, as seen by Swami Abhishiktananda", James Stuart, *Vidyajyoti,* Vol. 57, 401-413.

"The Spiritual Way of Henri Le Saux/Swami Abhishiktananda", O. Baumer Despeigne, *Bulletin of Monastic Interreligious Dialogue,* No. 48, (Oct. 1993), 20-25.

"Widening of the Horizons: D. Swami Abhishiktananda" in *Beyond Settled Foundations. The Journey of Indian Theology,* by Felix Wilfred, Madras (University of Madras, 1993, 53-60.

1994 "Abhishiktananda: an interview with Odette Baumer-Despeigne", conducted by Sr Pascaline Coff, in *Bulletin of Monastic Interreligious Dialogue,* no.51 (October 1994), 17-24.

Discussion of Abhishiktananda's Christology in context of dialogue in *Practice and Theology of Interreligous Dialogue: the trajectory undertaken by the Indian Church since Vatican II,* by Jose Kuttianimattathil, SDB, Rome (Gregorian University), 1994, esp. pp. 31-38.

3. Unpublished Theses

1984 "Religious Experience as a Meeting-Point in Dialogue: an Evaluation of the venture of Swami Abhishiktananda", Robert A. Stephens (M.A. thesis, Sydney University).

1987 "An Examination of Swami Abhishiktananda's Dialogical Theology", R. Yesurathnam (D.Th. thesis, Serampore University).

4. Video

1984 "Swamiji, un voyage intérieur", film by Patrice Chagnard (Le jour du Seigneur, 121, avenue de Villiers, 75849 Paris). Also available with English text.

Any information concerning books, articles or research theses which refer to Swami Abhishiktananda will be received with gratitude by the **Secretary of the Abhishiktananda Society.**

Index

A. Names

B. Subjects

SOUTH INDIA

Sketch Map showing places mentioned in the text

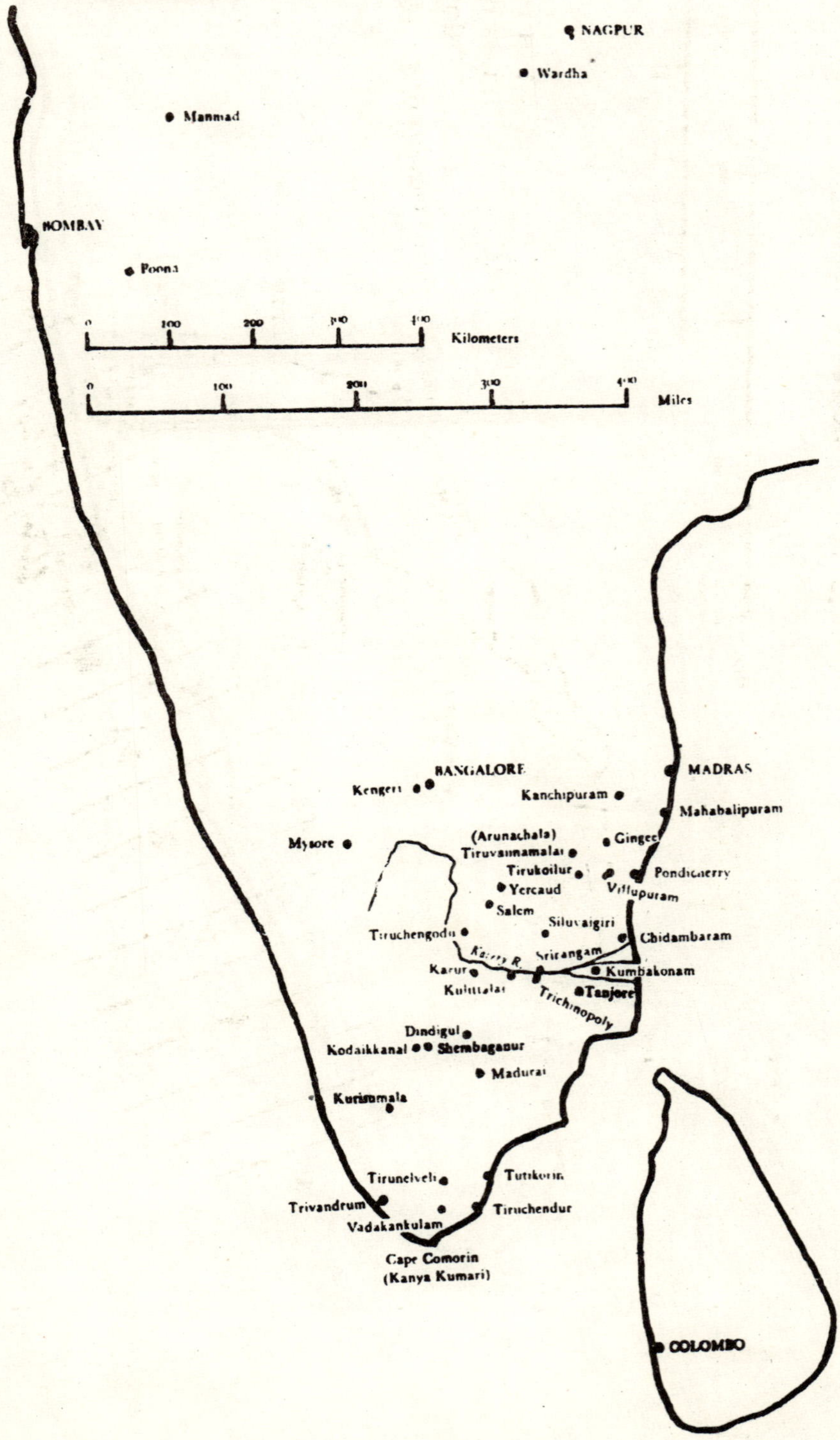